D1104865

FINANCIAL
ACCOUNTING
FOR
MANAGEMENT

FINANCIAL ACCOUNTING FOR MANAGEMENT

Almand R. Coleman

*Distinguished Lecturer in Accounting,
Washington and Lee University
Charles C. Abbott Professor of
Business Administration, Emeritus*

E. Richard Brownlee, II

*Associate Professor of
Business Administration*

C. Ray Smith

*Professor of
Business Administration*

*The Colgate Darden Graduate School of
Business Administration
University of Virginia*

*Robert F. Dame, Inc.
1905 Huguenot Road
Richmond, Virginia 23235*

ISBN 936328-03-7
Library of Congress Catalog No. 81-65306

PRINTED IN THE UNITED STATES OF AMERICA

Designed and typeset by Publications Development Co.
of Crockett, Texas, Developmental Editor: Nancy Marcus
Land, Production Editor: Bessie Graham

To Louise,
Diane, and
Phyllis

Contents

Preface

This book was written primarily for graduate business students and managers attending financial management programs. As the title suggests, the emphasis throughout the book is on the management perspective of accounting. The book is intended more for the user of financial accounting information than for the preparer, as it focuses on developing an understanding of figure relationships and accounting concepts instead of the mastery of accounting techniques.

The role of financial accounting and reporting has increased substantially during the decades of the 1960s and the 1970s, and we have written this book in a manner that emphasizes both how and why this has occurred. This book stresses the importance of accounting data to management, and at the same time provides an understanding of how accounting data are used by investors, creditors, and various government agencies.

As accounting has changed during the past two decades, so has the image of accountants and the accounting profession. No longer is an accountant perceived as the ink-stained wretch with green eyeshades and a three-legged stool. Accounting has become increasingly popular among students at both the undergraduate and graduate levels. Students expect the study of accounting to be interesting, challenging, and relevant to contemporary business and economic environments. We have written this book with the objective of meeting these well-founded expectations.

Our approach is somewhat unusual in a number of respects. The presentation of accounting "mechanics" is limited to those aspects we feel are essential to understanding the accounting process and the uses and limitations of financial statements prepared in accordance with generally accepted accounting principles. We generally avoid the use of "debit" and "credit" and speak, instead, in terms of account increases and decreases. We avoid the need for periodic closing entries by recording revenues and expenses directly in the retained earnings account.

We also place considerable emphasis throughout the book on cash-flow analysis and the relationship between income and cash-flow. Consequently, we introduce the statement of changes in financial position much earlier in the text than is found in more traditional financial accounting books. The increased importance that has been placed on the concepts of cash-flow and liquidity by management, the FASB, and the SEC in recent years lends considerable support to the emphasis we have given them.

This book also contains comprehensive coverage of two important, yet difficult, contemporary issues—accounting for business combinations and accounting for inflation. These topics are discussed both from the perspective of complying with generally accepted accounting principles and from the perspective of the management considerations associated with them. Included in the management considerations are some fundamental income tax issues.

We have found that many of the problems encountered by students in financial accounting courses result from general unfamiliarity with the "language," therefore, we have prepared a rather extensive Glossary to the text.

This book was written for students with diverse backgrounds who are interested in careers that require reasonable expertise in the use of financial accounting data. Because the emphasis is on the user rather than the preparer, this book can be used effectively in classes where wide variances exist in student familiarity with business in general and with accounting in particular. The instructor's guide that accompanies this book contains several different course configurations along with some additional material and suggestions for designing a course that meets the needs of students of the 1980s.

Acknowledgments

The authors are indebted to our colleagues on The Darden School Faculty—Brandt Allen, Bill Harper, Cathy Kahn, and Bill Rotch—for their suggestions in improving the earlier drafts of the material in this book.

Wilson Goh, a student research assistant, was particularly helpful in the final preparation of the manuscript and the Questions and Problems. We also benefited from the many contributions made by our students in the past several years.

The two former Deans of The Darden School, Charles Abbott and Stewart Sheppard, and the current Dean, Robert Haigh, have been most generous in their support and encouragement. Dean Edward Atwood at Washington and Lee University, where Mr. Coleman is currently Distinguished Lecturer in Accounting, has also provided strong encouragement. Our friend for many years, Robert Dame, has been the driving force in motivating us to prepare the book for publication. His associate, Nancy Marcus Land, has been most helpful in editing and producing the final product.

Our secretaries have typed from drafts that even we had difficulty reading. We are particularly grateful to Karen Dickinson, Zelma Watson, and Dorothea Govoruhk.

And, finally, we gratefully acknowledge the sincere interest and faithful support of our families.

Almand R. Coleman

E. Richard Brownlee, II

C. Ray Smith

Accounting: Entering A New Decade

In this chapter, the role of accounting in the contemporary United States business environment is discussed. The nature and purpose of accounting are presented, along with the different types of United States organizations. Emphasis is placed on financial accounting principles and practices as they pertain to corporations.

The dynamic nature of America's business and economic environment was never more evident than during the 1970s. The combination of double-digit inflation, rising unemployment, drastic increases in the price of oil, energy shortages, and high interest rates produced an environment that was considerably different at the end of the decade than it had been at the beginning. During the latter part of the 1970s, many businesses reported record earnings, yet claimed that these earnings were more fictitious than real. The blame for this alleged misrepresentation of corporate profitability was placed largely on the accounting profession for not responding in a timely fashion to the need for some type of inflation accounting. Serious questions were raised by investors, creditors, and other external users of corporate financial information as to the usefulness of financial data reported in accordance with the traditional accounting concepts of "historical cost" and "constant dollars." These users argued that prolonged inflation resulted in a business and economic environment that could no longer be meaningfully represented by financial statements based on existing accounting concepts and principles.

Because reported corporate financial information plays such an important role in determining how and where business and economic resources are allocated, financial representation of economic reality during the inflationary period of the 1970s was a major concern, not just of the accounting profession and its critics, but of businesses, not-for-profit organizations, government, and society in general. What people wanted was a relevant, unbiased, and understandable financial reporting system capable of providing an accurate accounting of business and economic activity during a period of rapidly rising prices. Accountants were called upon to develop such a reporting system but were unable to agree on how it should be done.

The widespread interest in and confusion over the extent to which reported corporate profits were "real" eventually resulted in congressional concern that perhaps the establishment of generally accepted accounting principles, upon which financial reporting is based, is too important a task to be left to the accountants. After considerable investigation and deliberation, Congress decided to allow the establishment of accounting principles to remain in the private sector but recommended more active participation in the entire standard-setting process by those outside the accounting profession. The end result of all the attention directed toward accountants, accounting principles, and corporate financial reporting was both a better informed public regarding the role of accountants in society and a more dynamic and responsive accounting profession.

NATURE AND PURPOSE OF ACCOUNTING

The extensive publicity of the 1970s helped to dispel at least some of the misunderstandings people had about accounting and accountants. Before commencing with a discussion of the nature and purpose of contemporary accounting, it is important to mention a few of the common misconceptions about accounting. Contrary to popular belief, accounting is *not*

- Unchanging and unimaginative.
- Difficult or impossible to understand.
- Concerned only with taxes.
- Mathematically complex.
- Among the most effective known cures for insomnia.
- Best suited to men who are short, thin, slightly bald, wear green eyeshades, and live alone.

Although this list of common accounting misconceptions is far from complete, it does illustrate the type of thinking that has served to inhibit an understanding of accounting and the profession. Let's avoid any such mistake by setting aside all preconceived notions as we begin to look at what accounting really is.

Accounting may be defined as "... the process of identifying, measuring, and communicating economic information to permit informed judgments and decisions by users of the information."[1] Not too many years ago, accountants were generally thought of primarily as clerks rather than as interpreters of financial data. As businesses and their environments increased in complexity, however, the nature and scope of accounting changed considerably. Accounting in the 1980s is an interesting, challenging, and rewarding profession that requires considerable analytical ability.

In a broad sense, accounting may be thought of as a service activity that provides financial information about an economic entity that is useful in making rational investment, credit, and similar decisions. Relevance and reliability are the two primary qualities that make accounting information useful for decision making.[2] Accounting serves as the financial measurement and communication system for both profit and nonprofit organizations. Because of its vital communicative aspects, accounting is often referred to as the "language of business."

---

[1] *A Statement of Basic Accounting Theory* (Evanston, Illinois: American Accounting Association, 1966), p.1.

[2] A discussion of other qualities of accounting information can be found in Statement of Financial Accounting Concepts No. 2, *Qualitative Characteristics of Accounting Information* (Stamford, Connecticut: Financial Accounting Standards Board, 1980).

FINANCIAL AND MANAGEMENT ACCOUNTING

Accounting may be subdivided into two classifications based on the intended purpose of the data presented. *Financial accounting* provides users "external" to an organization with quantitative information regarding its economic resources, obligations, and financial performance. External users include investors, creditors, various government agencies, and the general public. *Management accounting* provides essentially the same information to "internal" users such as management and the Board of Directors.

Even though the information needs of internal and external users are similar, there are several important reasons for distinguishing between financial and management accounting. First, management needs financial data more frequently and in greater detail than do external users. Second, the form and content of the accounting reports for management are of unlimited flexibility. By contrast, reports prepared for external users often must conform to standards defined by the accounting profession or various regulatory agencies. Third, external users' decisions are principally financial, whereas those of management are both financial and operational.

TYPES OF ACCOUNTING REPORTS

Three general types of accounting reports are prepared by business organizations. These are external financial statements, internal financial reports for management, and income tax reports.

External financial statements are those contained in annual reports to stockholders and filings with various governmental organizations. Also included are the financial statements submitted to banks and other financial institutions.

The external financial statements of one organization may also be used by another organization to appraise the issuer's desirability as a customer or as a possible investment opportunity. For organizations in similar businesses, external reports provide information useful in evaluating the competition. The distinguishing characteristic of external financial statements is that they are prepared in accordance with certain established standards called "generally accepted accounting principles."

In order for management to make ongoing decisions regarding past, present, and future business operations, *internal financial reports* are usually prepared more frequently and in considerably more detail than is customary for external financial reporting. Although internal reporting includes the same types of information contained in the financial statements prepared for external users, management needs additional data about such things as cost allocation, cost control, and performance measurement and evaluation. Because internal reports do not have to conform to generally accepted accounting principles, their form and content depend on factors such as the decisions to be made, the availability of data, and the cost associated with preparing the reports.

Income tax reports are prepared periodically by profit-oriented organizations. Specific tax reporting formats have been developed by federal, state, and local tax authorities to be used by businesses in determining their taxes. As will be discussed later in this chapter, a business may take one of several legal forms, and the income tax returns required depend on the business' form of organization. Although the income tax laws generally require that taxable income be calculated in accordance with generally accepted accounting principles, a number of major differences do exist between the contents of a company's external financial statements and its tax return. As will be discussed in subsequent chapters, these differences are due primarily to the fact that the two types of reports have different objectives.

Notwithstanding the emphasis in this text on financial accounting, we will deal to some extent with all three types of accounting reports. Unlike more traditional financial accounting texts, the perspective taken herein is principally that of how management uses financial statements prepared in accordance with existing generally accepted accounting principles. Because taxes play an important role in management's decision-making process, however, due consideration will be given to income taxes and related reports. In addition, the management perspective will necessitate consideration of the usefulness of published financial information to investors, creditors, and other external users. Accounting is a means to an end and is so presented throughout this book.

TYPES OF ORGANIZATIONS IN THE UNITED STATES

There are a variety of ways in which U.S. organizations may be classified. One way is in accordance with profit objectives: profit-oriented or not-for-profit. Most businesses are profit-oriented, whereas charitable, governmental, and many educational organizations are of a nonprofit nature.

Another classification is in accordance with their form of organization: proprietorship, partnership, or corporation. Proprietorships and partnerships are quite similar in form, except that a proprietorship is owned by one person and a partnership has two or more owners, called partners. The corporate form of organization, however, is considerably different from both proprietorships and partnerships.

Many small businesses are organized as proprietorships or partnerships, as both types are relatively simple and inexpensive to form. About the only legal requirement for establishing a proprietorship is obtaining any required government-related permits to do business. The same is true for a partnership, except that the partners should execute a written contract among themselves that contains the terms under which the partnership is established. The desirability of having a written agreement, known as the "articles of copartnership," is as great for partnerships having only a few partners as for partnerships comprised of hundreds of partners. Some of the items usually included in the partnership agreement are the amount of each partner's investment, the rights of partners to withdraw funds, the manner in which profits and losses are to be divided, and the procedure to be followed in connection with admitting a new partner or changing the original terms of the partnership.

A *partnership* is defined by the Uniform Partnership Act as "an association of two or more persons to carry on, as co-owners, a business for profit." It has the following major characteristics:

- *Limited ownership:* As a practical matter, most partnerships have relatively few partners.
- *Owners are managers:* The partners frequently manage the business.
- *Mutual agency:* Each partner, acting within the scope of reasonable partnership activities, acts as an agent for the partnership.

- *Unlimited liability:* Each partner is ordinarily personally liable for all of the debts of the partnership.
- *Division of profit and loss:* Partnership profits and losses may be divided in whatever manner the individual partners agree.
- *Withdrawal of resources:* Unless the partners agree otherwise, they may withdraw resources from the business in an amount equal to their total investment in the partnership at any time they wish to do so.
- *Limited life:* Unless the partners agree otherwise, the death or withdrawal of a partner automatically dissolves the partnership.

In contrast to partnerships, *corporations* have the following major characteristics:

- *Diverse ownership:* The owners of a corporation are called stockholders, and ownership in a corporation is evidenced by shares of capital stock. Private, or close, corporations are owned by relatively few stockholders. Public, or open, corporations may be owned by a very large number of stockholders. Because most of the larger U.S. corporations are public, diversification of ownership is usually associated with the corporate form of organization.
- *Separation of ownership and management:* Managements of public corporations generally own only a small percentage of the outstanding capital stock.
- *Limited liability:* As a separate legal entity, a corporation is responsible for its own debts. Stockholders are not personally liable for the debts of a corporation, and the maximum financial loss that a stockholder can incur is equal to the amount of his investment in the corporation.
- *Withdrawal of resources:* Stockholders are entitled to withdraw resources from a corporation only in the form of dividends and only after the Board of Directors has authorized their payment. Dividends may only be paid to the extent that the corporation has accumulated earnings, i.e., stockholders are not entitled to receive any dividends that represent a return of stockholders' original investment in the corporation.
- *Transferability of ownership:* Stockholders may buy and sell shares of capital stock in a corporation without interfering with

the activities or the life of the corporation. Most of the millions of shares that are traded daily on the stock exchanges represent private transactions between independent buyers and sellers, so that the resources or the financial obligations of the corporations are unaffected. Changes in ownership do not affect the life of a corporation.

- *Government regulation:* Even though corporate charters are granted by the individual states and not by the federal government, they are subject to both federal and state regulations. One of the complaints frequently expressed by corporate managements has been the existence of too much government regulation, particularly at the federal level.
- *Taxes:* As separate legal entities, corporations pay federal and state income taxes on their earnings. When all or part of these earnings are subsequently distributed to stockholders in the form of cash dividends, the stockholders also pay income taxes on the amount of dividends received, a phenomenon referred to as *double taxation*.

Under certain conditions specified by the Internal Revenue Code, corporations with no more than fifteen stockholders may elect to be treated as a "Subchapter S" corporation and thus pay no corporate income tax. Instead, like partnerships, the owners of Subchapter S corporations pay personal income taxes on their respective shares of business earnings regardless of whether the earnings are actually withdrawn from the business.

MORE ABOUT CORPORATIONS

Because of the dominance of the corporate form of organization in terms of the aggregate dollar volume of U.S. business activity, the emphasis throughout this text will be on accounting for profit-oriented corporations. There are, however, relatively few differences between corporate accounting and accounting for proprietorships and partnerships.

Probably the most commonly used definition of a corporation is the one given in 1819 by Chief Justice Marshall in the Dartmouth College case. He stated: "A corporation is an artificial being, invisible, intangible, and existing only in contemplation of the law." It is created when a corporate charter is issued by one of the states subsequent to the submission of required legal documents and the payment of the incorporation fee to the state's Corporation Commission. Once established, a corporation may issue stock certificates to its owners, take title to property, enter into contractual agreements, incur debts, sue and be sued, and conduct such business as stated in its charter. Corporations whose stock is widely held are known as public corporations, whereas those whose stock is held by relatively few owners are called private or close corporations.

One of the first responsibilities of the stockholders is to elect a Board of Directors who become responsible for the overall management of the corporation. The directors, in turn, elect the corporate officers whose duties involve the day-to-day management of the corporation. The officers usually include a president, vice-president, secretary, and treasurer. They report periodically to the Board of Directors, whose management role is largely advisory and supervisory in nature. During the 1970s, many large corporations increased the number of "outside" directors in an attempt to give their Boards greater independence from the corporate officers. Outside directors are those who are associated with the corporation only in their role as directors. By 1980, the average number of directors of large U.S. corporations was fifteen, of which ten were outside directors.

Corporations hold an annual meeting of stockholders subsequent to the end of each fiscal year. A *fiscal year* is the twelve-month period a corporation has selected as its accounting year, and it may or may not be the calendar year. The annual meeting is held for such purposes as reviewing the year's financial performance, discussing business, economic, and political issues of importance to the corporation, selecting the accounting firm to perform the following year's independent audit of the corporation's financial records, electing directors whenever vacancies on the Board exist, and transacting any other business that requires ratification by the stockholders.

The stock of many public corporations is bought and sold daily on the various stock exchanges. Even though such changes in corporate ownership represent private transactions among investors, corporations must keep an up-to-date record of their stockholders. When shares of stock are sold, the seller assigns the stock certificate representing the number of shares sold to the buyer and sends the certificate to the corporation. The corporation cancels the certificate received and issues a new one in the name of the purchaser. As long as the stock is purchased from an existing stockholder and not from the corporation, the only effect on the corporation is a change in its *stockholders of record*. Many corporations engage the services of a transfer agent and registrar to cancel old stock certificates, issue new ones, and maintain a current record of stockholder names and addresses and the number of shares owned by each stockholder. Transfer agents and registrars are usually banks and trust companies.

Public corporations also issue annual reports to stockholders and other interested parties. These reports generally include letters to stockholders from both the chairman of the Board and the president, a description of the company, audited financial statements, the report of the independent accountants, and management's discussion of past performance and future goals and objectives. The accountant's report states whether, in the opinion of the independent accounting firm, the financial statements presented in the annual report were prepared in accordance with *generally accepted accounting principles* applied on a basis consistent with the previous year.

GENERALLY ACCEPTED ACCOUNTING PRINCIPLES

Financial accounting is based on a set of standards that have evolved over time through the efforts of numerous individuals and organizations. These standards, known as generally accepted accounting principles, provide the basis upon which corporate financial reporting is based. Although the term "principles" creates the impression of immutability, this is not the case. Changing business and economic conditions require a continual monitoring of generally accepted accounting principles (GAAP) to ensure their relevance to contemporary environments. The name also suggests the existence of a complete and comprehensive list of such principles. This, however, is not the case. Let's briefly look at why.

Generally accepted accounting principles can be thought of as the ground rules that govern the preparation of corporate external financial statements. In the United States, these principles have developed in the same way as English Common Law; they are manmade, accumulate case-by-case, and are subject to continual revision. Accounting principles can become generally accepted only after they have obtained substantial authoritative support from the business community and related organizations.

Historically, three organizations have been particularly influential in establishing accounting principles: the American Institute of Certified Public Accountants (AICPA), the American Accounting Association (AAA), and the Securities and Exchange Commission (SEC). Two significant events in the early 1930s laid the foundation for the development of GAAP. In 1934, a special committee was formed by the AICPA and the New York Stock Exchange (NYSE) to develop an approach and a philosophy toward establishing accounting principles. The committee's concluding report contained the following passage:

> The more practical alternative would be to leave every corporation free to choose its own methods of accounting within the very broad limits to which reference has been made, but require disclosure of the methods employed and consistency in their application from year to year. . . .
>
> Within quite wide limits, it is relatively unimportant to the investor which precise rules or conventions are adopted by a corporation in reporting its earnings if he knows what method is being followed and is assured that it is followed consistently from year to year. . . .[3]

In essence, the committee rejected the idea of compelling all companies to use identical accounting principles regardless of circumstances and accepted, instead, the idea of establishing broad standards upon which individual organizations could base their accounting principles and procedures. In short, the concept of uniformity in accounting principles was discarded in favor of reasonable flexibility coupled with full disclosure and consistency. Once adopted by a company, however, the selected principles had to be followed consistently from year to year. Thirty years after this committee published its recommendations, a member of the accounting profession underscored the significance of the committee's approach as follows:

> In spite of the fact that the committee was the first to use the term "accepted principles of accounting" and the first to attempt a formal statement of accounting principles, its most important contribution was more basic. The fundamental framework of accounting

---

[3] *Audits of Corporate Accounts* (New York: American Institute of Certified Public Accountants, 1934), p. 9.

which the committee established has guided the development of accounting for thirty years. The recommendations were not fully im-
plemented, but the basic concept which permitted each corporation
to choose those methods and procedures which were most appropriate for its own financial statements within the basic framework of
"accepted accounting principles" became the focal point of the development of principles in the United States.[4]

The second major event was the establishment of the Securities
and Exchange Commission (SEC). Through the Securities Act of
1933 and the Securities Exchange Act of 1934, Congress created the
SEC and charged it with the responsibility of protecting the public
from false and misleading information. Publicly-owned corporations
were required to disclose financial and other data in a manner that
fairly represented the underlying economic events. Congress gave the
SEC broad authority to establish accounting principles and reporting
standards. Rather than exert its authority directly, the SEC chose
instead to allow these principles and standards to be set by the
private sector. This decision has remained unchanged. A close working relationship continues to exist between the SEC and the AICPA,
the organization in the private sector that for many years was recognized by the SEC as having the responsibility for establishing accounting principles. As will be discussed shortly, this responsibility now
rests primarily with the Financial Accounting Standards Board
(FASB).

During the more than forty years since the SEC decided to allow
the private sector to develop accounting principles, several different
groups of accounting and financial experts have participated in the
process. In 1938, the AICPA organized its *Committee on Accounting
Procedure* specifically for this purpose. During its twenty-year existence, the Committee issued 51 Accounting Research Bulletins. Its
approach was primarily practical: the Committee developed "principles" as the need arose in actual problem situations. During this
same period, the American Accounting Association (AAA) was also
actively involved in establishing accounting principles. The approach
taken by the AAA was more theoretical; the AAA attempted to establish a broad set of interrelated, consistent, and comprehensive
standards. The AAA believed that "real world" problems could then
be solved by accounting procedures developed in conformity with

[4] Reed K. Storey, *The Search for Accounting Principles* (New York: American Institute
of Certified Public Accountants, 1964), p. 12.

these standards. Of the two organizations, the AICPA had the greater impact on the practice of accounting.

By the mid-1950s, the need for more research and for a "theoretical accounting framework" became evident. In 1959, the AICPA formed the Accounting Principles Board (APB) to supersede the Committee on Accounting Procedure. The AICPA intended that the Accounting Principles Board would emphasize accounting research and would articulate a theoretical framework. The Accounting Principles Board never quite achieved its goals, however, primarily because the accounting issues it faced were too urgent, complex, and time consuming to permit much theoretical work. During its fourteen-year existence, the APB issued 31 "Opinions" and 4 "Statements." The former were pronouncements that the Board considered authoritative. The latter were merely informative reports without official status.

In 1973, the Accounting Principles Board was superseded by the Financial Accounting Standards Board (FASB). Unlike the Committee on Accounting Procedure and the APB, the FASB is not part of the AICPA. It is an independent organization comprised of seven members who report to a nonprofit corporation known as the Financial Accounting Foundation (FAF). Financial support for the FASB is received from six sponsoring organizations: the American Institute of Certified Public Accountants, the National Association of Accountants, the American Accounting Association, the Financial Executives Institute, the Financial Analysts Federation, and the Securities Industry Association. By the end of 1980, the FASB had issued over 40 "Statements of Financial Accounting Standards." Subsequent to the formation of the FASB, the term *standards* has largely replaced the term *principles* in the accounting profession. We use these two terms interchangeably in this text.

FUNDAMENTAL ACCOUNTING CONCEPTS

The development of accounting principles in the United States has been greatly enhanced by the identification and acceptance of certain broad fundamental accounting concepts. In this section, those concepts that have had the greatest effect on financial accounting and reporting practices are briefly discussed.

Business Entity. A business entity is an organization that sells products and/or services at a profit. When external financial reports are presented, the business entity should be clearly identified. If a single owner conducts several separate proprietorships—for example, a laundry, a dairy, and a drugstore—each of these entities should be clearly identified and reported upon separately. When the business entity is a corporation, it should be made clear that the financial statements are those of the business which is separate and distinct from its owners. When one corporation owns more than fifty percent of the capital stock of other corporations, the external financial statements of the entire group are usually presented on a "consolidated" basis. When this occurs, the business entity is identified as the consolidated group of corporations.

Going Concern. External financial reports are prepared based upon the assumption that the business entity will continue to operate indefinitely and will not be liquidated in the foreseeable future. No attempt is made to disclose the financial effects of sudded liquidation.

Accounting Period. For purposes of measuring financial performance and financial position, the life of a business is divided into discrete time periods. The most common accounting period is twelve months in length and is known as a fiscal year.

Objectivity. Business transactions are recorded only when they can be supported by reasonable and verifiable evidence.

Historical Dollar Accounting. Transactions of a business entity are recorded in its accounting records in terms of dollars at the time each transaction occurs. Because these accounting records contain dollars recorded at different times, summarization adds together dollars of different vintages without recognizing their differences in purchasing power. The double-digit inflation of the 1970s caused the usefulness of this concept to be seriously questioned by external users of corporate financial statements.

Realization. This concept refers to the time when a business should recognize sales revenue. Ordinarily, revenue is realized at the time title to goods passes to the buyer or the service is performed. Realization usually does not depend on the timing of the cash receipts.

Matching. This concept pertains to the timing of the recognition of associated revenues and expenses. Generally, expenses should be recognized during the same accounting period as are the revenues to which the expenses relate.

Use of Estimates and Exercise of Judgment. Financial statements are not as precise as they usually appear. Financial reports are prepared for designated periods and points of time, but because time is a continuum, business transactions do not always fit neatly into designated accounting periods. This results in the need for estimates and judgments.

Consistency Between Periods. So that external users may compare financial reports for the same entity over several years, it is essential that they be prepared on a consistent basis from year to year. If changes occur in reporting methods or accounting principles, the reports should disclose the reason for and the effects of such changes.

Diversity in Accounting. Users of external financial reports should expect to find some diversity in accounting and reporting among business entities. Accounting authorities disagree as to the degree of diversity that should be tolerated. Most authorities believe, however, that accountants should try to narrow the range of divergence in "generally accepted accounting principles" to the end that there may be more comparability of reporting among companies.

Conservatism. When several acceptable alternatives exist for the preparation of external financial reports, the choice should be made in favor of "conservative" reporting. Accordingly, the report must provide for all known losses and liabilities regardless of whether they are definitely quantifiable, but must not anticipate income until it is definitely realized. In short, provide for all losses but do not anticipate income.

Materiality. External financial reports should disclose all essential information, yet be uncluttered with the trivial. Materiality of information is determined by whether its disclosure would alter the judgment or conduct of the intended users.

SUMMARY

As the language of business, accounting is expected to provide both internal and external users with relevant and reliable financial information about an organization that is useful in making rational investment, credit, and similar decisions. Financial accounting pertains specifically to providing external users with data about an organization's resources, obligations, and financial performance. Financial accounting is governed by generally accepted accounting principles that must be adhered to in the preparation of external financial statements. These principles are based on certain broad fundamental accounting concepts. Neither the concepts nor the principles are immutable, however, and both are continually evaluated to ensure their relevance to a changing environment. As became particularly evident during the 1970s, accounting plays a vital role in the allocation and use of business and economic resources. As the United States enters a new decade, the accounting profession will be expected to make whatever changes are necessary in external financial reporting to provide users with relevant data upon which to base their decisions.

QUESTIONS AND PROBLEMS

1. How would you describe accounting to an undergraduate history major who was considering applying to an MBA Program?

2. Why was so much attention directed at accounting and the accounting profession throughout much of the 1970s?

3. What is the relationship between accounting and economics?

4. Do nonprofit organizations need accounting information? If so, why?

5. What are the objectives of: (a) financial accounting, (b) management accounting, and (c) tax accounting?

6. Who are the principal users of accounting information? For what types of decisions are accounting data used?

7. What are generally accepted accounting principles and how are they established?

8. What is the relationship between the Securities and Exchange Commission and the Financial Accounting Standards Board?

9. What do the accounting concepts of *historical cost* and *constant dollars* mean to you?

10. Relevance and reliability are considered to be two primary qualities that make accounting information useful for decision making. How do these two qualities relate to each of the twelve fundamental accounting concepts discussed in this chapter?

11. Assume that you and two of your friends are about to form a business. Ignoring income taxes, what factors should you consider in deciding between establishing a partnership or forming a corporation? How would consideration of income taxes affect your decision?

12. What are the tax advantages and disadvantages of a Subchapter S corporation?

13. Why are most large businesses organized as corporations?

14. What are the duties and responsibilities of a corporation's Board of Directors? Does it matter whether most of the Board members are insiders or outsiders?

15. Do publicly owned corporations care who their shareholders are? If so, why?

16. What is your estimate of the number of shares of capital stock that are bought and sold on the New York Stock Exchange each day? How do such purchases and sales affect the corporation whose stock was involved?

2

Traditional Financial Statements

In this chapter, the balance sheet, income statement, and statement of retained earnings are illustrated and discussed. Also presented is the importance of the fundamental accounting equation to the preparation and understanding of these three financial statements.

Traditionally, businesses have periodically prepared three basic financial statements as a means of assessing the financial consequences of their activities. These are the *balance sheet* (also known as the *statement of financial position*), the *income statement*, and the *statement of retained earnings*. The income statement and the statement of retained earnings are often combined into a single statement. In 1971, the Accounting Principles Board added a fourth basic financial statement, the *statement of changes in financial position*.

For external purposes, corporations normally publish their financial statements annually. Annual financial reporting is often supplemented by the issuance of quarterly financial statements. For internal purposes, financial statements may be prepared on a monthly, weekly, or any other basis. Regardless of the frequency of their preparation, internal financial statements generally include substantially greater detail than those prepared for external use.

ASSETS, LIABILITIES, AND OWNERS' EQUITY

To describe the contents and purposes of all the basic financial statements, we will trace the business activities of a small, closely-held corporation, Corner Drugstore, Inc., from the date of incorporation through the first several years of its existence. We will begin by looking at its financial status immediately following the approval of its charter by the State Corporation Commission and the issuance of capital stock to the owners on April 3, 1978.

Specific requirements for incorporation are established by state law and are reasonably uniform among the states. Incorporation may be accomplished by one or more individuals, and there frequently exists a minimum legal requirement as to the amount of the owners' initial investment. In exchange for their investment, the owners receive shares of capital stock issued by the newly formed corporation. These shares provide written evidence of ownership in the corporation and are distributed to the owners in proportion to their share of the total amount invested in the corporation.

In the case of Corner Drugstore, two incorporators each invested $5,000 cash in exchange for an equal number of shares of capital stock. Immediately thereafter, the new corporation owned by the two stockholders consisted of only one financial resource, cash, in the amount of $10,000. This initial financial position would have been reflected on the drugstore's balance sheet prepared as of the date of incorporation.

The purpose of a balance sheet is to present an enterprise's resources, obligations, and the amount of the owners' investment, all as of a specified point in time. The resources are known as *assets*, the obligations as *liabilities*, and the owners' investment as *owners' equity*. To elaborate, assets are all items of value, tangible or intangible, that a business owns. Liabilities are debts or obligations. Owners' equity refers to the total investment of the owners at the balance sheet date. For corporations, owners' equity is referred to as stockholders' equity. Subsequent to incorporation, Corner Drugstore had one asset, $10,000 in cash, no liabilities, and owners' equity of $10,000.

The relationship between assets (A), liabilities (L), and owners' equity (OE) is the foundation of accounting. This fundamental relationship is expressed as follows:

$$A = L + OE$$

At any time, a company's assets always equal the sum of its liabilities and owners' equity. Keeping in mind that assets are things of value owned by a business, that liabilities are debts or obligations, and that owners' equity represents the owners' total investment, we can see that the equation makes good common sense. It simply states that the assets of a business must always equal the sources of those assets. These sources are the *owners* and the *creditors*, the latter being individuals or organizations providing assets in exchange for the corporation's promise of payment or repayment at a later date.

As its name suggests, the equality of an enterprise's assets and its liabilities and owners' equity is always reflected on the *balance sheet*. In recent years, the balance sheet has increasingly been referred to as the *statement of financial position*.

Balance Sheet Illustrated

Let us suppose that at the end of its first year of existence Corner Drugstore had the following assets, liabilities, and owners' equity:

Assets:
Cash on hand and in bank	$ 2,500
Due from customers	4,200
Merchandise inventory	12,700
Store equipment (cost $10,000)	9,000

Liabilities:
Owed to suppliers	$ 3,800
Owed to employees	700
Owed to utilities	200
Federal and state taxes owed	2,300
Owed to bank	7,500

Owners' equity:
Capital stock issued	$10,000
Retained earnings	3,900

Before elaborating upon any of these items, let's see how they would appear on Corner Drugstore's balance sheet. Although a balance sheet may be prepared in several different forms, the "account form" is illustrated here as it is the one most commonly used.

The first thing to notice about the balance sheet is its heading. A proper heading for any type of financial statement should answer these questions:

1. WHO?   That is, the name of the business whose financial data are being reported.

2. WHAT?   That is, the name of the statement itself—balance sheet, income statement, etc.

3. WHEN?   That is, the *point in time* or the *period of time* to which the statement relates.

In Illustration 2-1, the heading answers these three questions as follows:

1. WHO?   Corner Drugstore, Inc.

2. WHAT?   Balance Sheet

3. WHEN?   March 31, 1979

Notice two things about the date of this balance sheet. First, like all balance sheets, this one applies only to a specific point in time. The

---

Illustration 2-1

Corner Drugstore, Inc.
Balance Sheet
March 31, 1979

Assets		Liabilities	
Cash	$ 2,500	Accounts payable	$ 3,800
Accounts receivable	4,200	Wages payable	700
Merchandise inventory	12,700	Utilities payable	200
Store equipment		Taxes payable	2,300
(cost $10,000)	9,000	Bank loan payable	7,500
		Total liabilities	14,500
		Owners' Equity	
		Capital stock $10,000	
		Retained earnings 3,900	13,900
		Total liabilities &	
Total assets	$28,400	owners' equity	$28,400

---

balance sheet can be thought of as a snapshot of the business entity's financial position. Second, Corner Drugstore has chosen to end its fiscal year on March 31. As mentioned in Chapter 1, a fiscal year is the accounting year over which a business reports its activities and at the end of which it prepares financial statements for external use. A fiscal year is usually selected so that it ends at a time when business activity is comparatively slow and the amount of merchandise on hand is relatively low. Businesses may choose any fiscal year period that they wish, and it is possible to change fiscal years. Companies frequently select the calendar year as their fiscal year because it ends immediately following a period of heavy sales.

Assets Explained

The assets of Corner Drugstore are representative of those of most retail establishments. Cash is the first asset listed on most balance sheets. The amount shown in Illustration 2-1 represents the store's total cash balance on March 31, 1979, whether it was physically located at the store or held in deposit by a bank. The term "accounts receivable" (or trade receivable) represents the amount owed to the drugstore by customers who purchased merchandise but as of March 31 had not yet paid for those purchases. From the drugstore's perspective, such customer purchases represented "credit sales" or "sales on account." Instead of receiving cash at the time of sale, Corner Drugstore received customers' promises to pay cash at some future time, often within 30 days.

The merchandise inventory figure of $12,700 represents the total *cost* of all salable merchandise that the drugstore owned at fiscal year-end, such as toiletries, drugs, toys, and small appliances. It is not uncommon for retail stores to display merchandise that they do not own. Such merchandise is "on consignment" to the retailer. For example, magazines are often placed in drugstores on consignment. If the Corner Drugstore had any merchandise on consignment in its store on March 31, 1979, this merchandise would not have been included in the balance sheet figure of $12,700 because such merchandise was not owned by the drugstore.

The $9,000 amount for store equipment is a little more difficult to explain. During the fiscal year, Corner Drugstore purchased display counters, shelves, cash registers, and various other types of store equipment. The total cost of all such purchases was $10,000, and all were paid for in cash. At the time these purchases occurred, the drug-store simply traded one asset for another; specifically, cash was given in exchange for store equipment. Total assets remained unchanged, and liabilities and owners' equity were unaffected. The $9,000 figure shown for store equipment in Illustration 2-1 represents the *unallo-cated cost* of the equipment at fiscal year-end. The $1,000 difference represents the *allocated cost*.

"Allocated to what?" is a question that will be answered more ful-ly later in this chapter. For the moment, let's view cost allocation as follows: The store equipment was estimated by the owners of Corner Drugstore to have a useful life of 10 years. At the end of that period, the owners expected that the equipment would have no value to the drugstore. Because assets represent items having value to a business, at the end of the 10-year period the store equipment could no longer appear as an asset on the balance sheet. The allocation process permits the $10,000 initial cost of the store equipment to be reduced to $0 over the 10-year period. In this case, $1,000 of the cost would be "allocated" or "written off" the balance sheet each year for 10 years. Recalling the accounting equation, $A = L + OE$, we realize that if the allocation process reduces assets, then either liabilities or owners' equity must also be reduced. In fact, owners' equity is reduced, the reasons for which will be explained further on in this chapter.

Liabilities and Equity

Liabilities are represented on the balance sheet according to the type of creditor. A *creditor* is an individual or organization provid-ing a business with an asset or assets in exchange for its promise to pay cash at some later date. Accounts Payable represents the amount owed by a business for merchandise that it purchased; Wages Payable are wages earned by employees but not yet paid; Utilities Payable represents the amount owed for utilities at the balance sheet date; Taxes Payable reflects the amount owed to federal and state govern-ments for taxes imposed on the profits earned by the drugstore dur-ing the fiscal year. The Bank Loan Payable was incurred because Corner Drugstore did not have enough cash to acquire all of the assets that it needed to do business. Shortly after incorporating, the drug-store borrowed $9,000 from a local bank. The loan was to be repaid in equal installments on March 31 each year for 6 years. The first installment was paid to the bank in 1979. Although interest rates had begun to rise, the previous relationships that the two owners had with the bank allowed Corner Drugstore to negotiate a 5 percent interest rate. Interest on the unpaid balance was also due annually on March 31.

The owners' equity in Corner Drugstore at the end of its first fiscal year consisted of the owners' original investment of $10,000 (the amount shown for capital stock on the balance sheet) and $3,900 retained earnings. This $3,900 figure means that as a result of all of the business transacted at the drugstore during its first year of existence, the excess of assets over liabilities (a relationship known as *net assets*) increased by $3,900. The drugstore's net assets on the date of incorporation had been $10,000 ($10,000 in assets less $0 in liabilities). As the owners did not invest anything beyond their $10,000 original amount (capital stock at fiscal year-end was still $10,000), the increase in net assets of $3,900 had to be attributed to profitable operations. Understanding the concepts of "profits" and "operations" requires a discussion of the second basic financial statement—the income statement.

Income Statement Illustrated

The income statement that Corner Drugstore prepared at the end of its first fiscal year is shown in Illustration 2-2. As we did with the balance sheet, let's begin by looking at the questions answered by the statement's heading.

1. WHO? Corner Drugstore, Inc.
2. WHAT? Income Statement
3. WHEN? Fiscal Year Ended March 31, 1979

Notice that, unlike the balance sheet, the income statement covers a *period of time*. It presents the results of the operations of a business entity over a specified period of time, usually a fiscal year for statements prepared for external use.

Revenues

The purpose of the income statement is to show the change in owners' equity during an accounting period arising from the sale of

Illustration 2-2

Corner Drugstore, Inc.
Income Statement
For the Fiscal Year Ended March 31, 1979

Gross sales		$75,800
Less: Sales returns		1,300
Net sales		74,500
Deduct: Cost of merchandise sold		44,700
Gross margin on sales		29,800
Less Operating expenses:		
Employees' wages	$15,300	
Rent	3,600	
Utilities	650	
Allocated cost of store equipment	1,000	
Other	500	
Total operating expenses		21,050
Income from operations		8,750
Less: Interest on bank loan		450
Income before income taxes		8,300
Less: Federal and state income taxes		2,900
Net income		$ 5,400

products and/or services to customers, less the cost of the products and/or services sold, and less any other expenses incurred during the period. The income statement consists of two major components—revenues and expenses. *Revenue* is the increase in an organization's net assets (assets less liabilities) resulting from the sale of a product or service. *Expense* is the decrease in an organization's net assets that occurs in connection with the revenue generation process; that is, the sale of products and/or services.

At Corner Drugstore, revenue arose from the sale of merchandise. In generating this revenue, the store incurred various expenses. The difference between the total amount of revenues and the total amount of expenses is known as *net earnings, net profit,* or *net income.* These three terms are used interchangeably to refer to the net change in owners' equity arising from day-to-day business operations. The specific revenues and expenses for Corner Drugstore that resulted from its first year of operations are shown in Illustration 2-2. These are typical for any type of merchandising business.

The total sales price of all merchandise sold by Corner Drugstore is reflected in the *gross sales* amount of $75,800. Merchandise is considered to be sold at the time that the title to the merchandise (ownership of the merchandise) passes from the seller to the buyer. In the case of the drugstore, a sale occurred when a customer received merchandise and, in return, provided the drugstore with cash or a promise to pay cash at a future date. Pay particular attention to what has just been said. A sale occurs when ownership of merchandise transfers from seller to buyer, *not* when the seller receives cash from the buyer. In the case of cash sales, the transfer of ownership to the buyer and the receipt of cash by the seller occur simultaneously. Such is not the case, however, for sales that are made to customers "on credit." For credit sales, the seller records a sale at the time ownership transfers, but because no cash is received from the buyer at that time, the seller records an account receivable. We know from Illustration 2-1 that Corner Drugstore made credit sales because the March 31 balance sheet contains $4,200 in accounts receivable. A fundamentally important concept is to be learned from this discussion: revenue is recognized when earned, regardless of whether cash has been exchanged. Additionally, the receipt of cash by a business does not necessarily mean that revenue has simultaneously been earned.

Like most merchandising organizations, Corner Drugstore had some of its sales returned by customers during the year. The amount of such returns is shown in the income statement as sales returns. In the case of Corner Drugstore, sales returns amounted to $1,300. Gross sales less sales returns is known as *net sales*. Net sales represent the actual sales for the period.

Expenses

The *cost of goods sold* figure of $44,700 represents the actual cost to the drugstore of the merchandise that was sold at a total sales price of $74,500. The $29,800 difference between net sales and cost of goods sold is referred to as *gross margin* or *gross profit*. The relationship between net sales and gross margin is important, and businesses watch it quite carefully to make sure it does not get "out of line" because of changes in either selling prices or the cost of merchandise sold.

The *operating expenses* shown in the income statement represent items that decreased net assets but were necessary in order for the drugstore to maintain its day-to-day operations. As might be expected, the largest operating expense was compensating employees for their services. We can also see that the drugstore incurred rent expense for use of the building in which it was located, and utilities expense for light, heat, power, etc. As no "building" asset appeared on the balance sheet in Illustration 2-1, we could have concluded at the time we discussed the drugstore's assets that it didn't own a building and, therefore, must have been renting the facility in which it was located.

The $1,000 expense called *allocated cost of the store equipment* reflects the gradual allocation to expense of the $10,000 cost of the store equipment purchased during the fiscal year. The "process of cost allocation" was described earlier in the chapter when we discussed the $9,000 figure for store equipment listed as an asset on the March 31, 1979 balance sheet. At that time, we stated that the effect of such a cost allocation was to reduce the dollar amount shown for store equipment from its original cost of $10,000 to the unallocated cost of $9,000.

We also said that in addition to reducing the asset amount by $1,000, the allocation also reduced owners' equity by a like amount. The allocation diminished owners' equity because it represented an operating expense (commonly known as *depreciation*), was listed as an expense on the income statement, and reduced the amount of the net income. We can conclude from this example that all expenses reduce owners' equity and that all revenues increase owners' equity. We shall see shortly why these relationships exist.

The "other expenses" of $500 represent the total amount of the miscellaneous expenses incurred during the year. These would include expenses for postage, advertising, and various supplies (payroll taxes have been ignored). If we subtract the total operating expenses from the amount of the gross margin, we get $8,750 *income from operations*. This figure represents the income that was earned by the drugstore during the year from its day-to-day operations. Two additional expenses of considerable importance must then be deducted to determine the amount of the increase in owners' equity during the year that was attributable to the overall business activities. These two expenses are *interest* and *income taxes*.

We know from our discussion of Illustration 2-1 that Corner Drugstore borrowed $9,000 from a local bank shortly after incorporating. We also know that on March 31, 1979, Corner Drugstore paid the bank one-sixth of the amount borrowed or *principal* of the loan plus an amount for interest. Interest is the fee that a bank charges a borrower for the use of the money borrowed, the amount of which is determined by three factors: the amount borrowed, the length of the loan, and the rate of interest. In this case, the bank charged Corner Drugstore a 5 percent interest rate.

The amount of interest to be charged is calculated in accordance with the following formula:

Interest =   Principal × Annual Interest Rate × Time (expressed as a fraction of a year)

Thus,
$$I = P \times R \times T$$

Applying this formula to the bank loan granted to Corner Drugstore, we get:

$$I = (\$9,000) \times (.05) \times (1); \text{ so } I = \$450$$

By subtracting the interest expense from the income from operations, we get "income before income taxes." The $2,900 amount for federal and state income taxes represents that portion of the *pretax income* of $8,300 to which the federal and stage governments have a legal claim. The remaining $5,400 represents *net income*. The drugstore's owners' equity was increased by this amount during the year as the result of the store's business operations.

It is important to understand that at no time during our discussion of the expenses shown in the income statement did we make any reference to cash. Expenses are shown in the income statement during the period in which they are incurred; that is, during the period in which they cause the net assets of a business to be reduced. Whether or not actual cash disbursements were made during the period in connection with the expense item does not affect their recognition as expenses. In those cases where cash disbursements were made for an expense, net assets decreased because the asset, cash, decreased. In those cases where cash disbursements were *not* made for an expense, net assets decreased because a liability increased or some asset other than cash decreased. We can see these liabilities on the balance sheet in Illustration 2-1. As of March 31, 1979, Corner Drugstore owed $700 in wages to employees, $200 for utilities, and $2,300 in federal and state taxes. These are liabilities because the drugstore incurred wage, utility, and tax expenses during the fiscal year but, as of the fiscal year-end, had not yet paid for them in cash.

To summarize several important points about the income statement:

1. All revenues should eventually result in cash inflows to a business, and all expenses should at some point result in cash outflows. However, the recognition of revenues and expenses in the income statement has practically *nothing whatsoever* to do with the *timing* of the cash receipts or the cash disbursements.
2. Revenues that have been earned for which no cash has been received will cause accounts receivable to appear on the balance sheet. Expenses that have been incurred for which no cash has been disbursed will cause liabilities to appear on the balance sheet or an asset other than cash to decrease.
3. Every revenue and expense contained in a company's income statement will also affect the assets or liabilities of that company. The net income for the period will cause a like increase in the company's owners' equity. A net loss (wherein revenues are less than expenses) will cause a like decrease in owners' equity.

The method of income determination just described is known as the *accrual method* of accounting. It states that: all revenues are recognized when earned; all expenses are recognized when incurred. The accrual method is required for preparing external financial statements in accordance with generally accepted accounting principles. Because it is not possible to tell anything about a company's actual cash flow from its income statement, one *cannot* assume that if a company reports a substantial net income, it must also have substantially increased its cash balance. As we will discuss in subsequent chapters, it is not unusual for profitable companies, especially those whose sales volumes are growing, to be "short on cash."

Statement of Retained Earnings Illustrated

The final concept to be addressed in this chapter is that of *retained earnings*. In Illustration 2-1, we see that Corner Drugstore's retained earnings as of its first fiscal year-end were $3,900. We know from Illustration 2-2, however, that the drugstore's net income (earnings) was $5,400. We have stated that a company's owners' equity increases by the amount of its earnings for a given period. This increase is reflected on the balance sheet through a component of owners' equity called *retained earnings*. It would seem to make sense, then, for the amount of Corner Drugstore's retained earnings at March 31, 1979 to be identical to the amount of net income reflected in its income statement for the fiscal year ending on that date. This indeed would be true if the company had chosen to retain all of its earnings for the year rather than to distribute some of its earnings to the owners in the form of *dividends*. We can conclude that during its first fiscal year, Corner Drugstore paid dividends to its stockholders in an amount equal to the difference between its net income for the year of $5,400 and its increase in retained earnings during the year of $3,900; a difference of $1,500.

The $5,400 net income represents an increase in net assets (total assets less total liabilities) during the year. It cannot be assumed that *cash* increased by $5,400, but only that total assets increased by that amount in relation to total liabilities. The increase in net assets due to earnings can be reflected not only through an increase in cash, but through increases in accounts receivable, inventory, equipment, and other assets as well. There is no such thing as a "retained earnings vault" wherein a company keeps cash equivalent to the amount of retained earnings shown on its balance sheet. Those who have searched for the key to such a vault have been the victims of accounting mythology.

On the other hand, dividends to stockholders are usually paid in cash. The purpose of dividend payments is to distribute some of a corporation's cash generated from profitable operations (earnings) to the owners, thus providing them with a return on their investment in the corporation. In order to pay dividends, a company must have: (1) cash, and (2) retained earnings, both of which are equal to or greater in amount than the dividend payments.

The decision by a corporation to pay a dividend is the responsibility of its Board of Directors. If the Board decides to authorize a dividend payment, three chronological dates associated with the dividend take on particular significance. These are:

1. *Date of Declaration*   This is the date of the Board's assertion that the company will pay a dividend. At this point the company incurs a liability for the dividend payment.
2. *Date of Record*   This is the date used to determine the specific stockholders to receive the dividend. Whoever owns capital

stock on this date is entitled to receive a dividend equal to the number of shares of stock owned times the amount of the per share dividend.

3. *Date of Payment* This is the date on which the cash dividend is paid to those stockholders who owned capital stock on the date of record.

Even though dividends represent cash disbursements, they are *not* an expense. They merely represent distribution to the owners of cash arising from corporate profits. Notice that dividends were not shown as an expense in the income statement and did not enter into the calculation of net income. Once the amount of net income has been determined, then the Board of Directors must decide how much should be "retained" and how much should be distributed to the owners in the form of cash dividends. Dividends can even be paid during years when a company reports a loss so long as the cash is available and the retained earnings balance exceeds the amount of the dividend.

To reconcile a corporation's retained earnings balance at the beginning of its fiscal year with its retained earnings balance at fiscal year-end, accountants prepare a third basic financial statement, the statement of retained earnings. Illustration 2-3 contains such a statement for the first fiscal year of Corner Drugstore.

Illustration 2-3

Corner Drugstore, Inc.
Statement of Retained Earnings
For the Fiscal Year Ended March 31, 1979

Retained earnings, March 31, 1978	$ 0
Add: Net income for the year	5,400
Total	5,400
Less: Cash dividends	1,500
Retained earnings, March 31, 1979	$3,900

Once again, let's consider the information provided by the heading of the statement.

1. WHO?   Corner Drugstore, Inc.
2. WHAT?   Statement of Retained Earnings
3. WHEN?   Fiscal Year Ended March 31, 1979

Like the income statement, the statement of retained earnings covers a *period of time*, usually a fiscal year. As mentioned earlier, corporations often combine the income statement and the statement of retained earnings into a single statement. A *statement of income and retained earnings* is illustrated in Chapter 3.

SUMMARY

For external reporting purposes, businesses have traditionally prepared three financial statements: the balance sheet, the income statement, and the statement of retained earnings. All three statements are based on the fundamental accounting equation:

$$\text{Assets (A)} = \text{Liabilities (L)} + \text{Owners' Equity (OE)}$$

The balance sheet presents the dollar amount of business assets, liabilities, and owners' equity at a specific point in time. The income statement presents business revenues and expenses during a specific period of time. The statement of retained earnings presents a summary of the changes in business retained earnings during a specified period of time.

The fourth basic financial statement, the statement of changes in financial position, will be discussed in detail in Chapter 4.

QUESTIONS AND PROBLEMS

1. How do a company's balance sheet, income statement, and statement of retained earnings interrelate with one another?
2. How are the amounts shown on a company's balance sheet determined with respect to: (a) assets, (b) liabilities, and (c) owners' equity?
3. Distinguish between *cost* and *value* and explain the use of these two types of measurements in the preparation of financial statements.

4. Explain why all companies do not use the calendar year as their fiscal year.

5. Explain the conceptual basis for the fundamental accounting equation, assets = liabilities + owners' equity.

6. Define the term "net assets." What is the relationship between net assets and owners' equity?

7. Inventory represents a significant component of total assets for most merchandising companies. How do companies determine the specific dollar amount shown on their balance sheets for inventory? What difficulties might a company encounter in determining its balance sheet figure for inventory?

8. How does the accrual basis of accounting affect the preparation of the income statement?

9. What is the major purpose of the income statement? What are its major components? How exact is the net income figure shown in the income statement?

10. Why isn't interest expense shown as an operating expense in the income statement?

11. If a company reported a substantial income for its fiscal year ended December 31, 1980, would you expect its cash balance on December 31, 1980 to be larger or smaller than its cash balance on January 1, 1980? Explain.

12. What is the major purpose of the statement of retained earnings? What are its principal components?

13. Depreciation is referred to as a non-cash expense. What is depreciation? Why is it treated as an expense? Why isn't depreciation a cash expense like most other expenses?

14. Explain how each of the twelve fundamental accounting concepts discussed in Chapter 1 affects the preparation of (a) the balance sheet and (b) the income statement.

15. Identify each of the following accounts as either assets, liabilities, or owners' equity:

a. Accounts Payable	h. Advance Deposit by Customer
b. Prepaid Insurance	i. Loan Payable
c. Cash	j. Accounts Receivable
d. Capital Stock	k. Retained Earnings
e. Supplies Inventory	l. Warranty Liability
f. Rent Payable	m. Marketable Securities
g. Land and Building	n. Receivables from Employees

16. Using the information presented below, prepare an income statement, a balance sheet, and a statement of retained earnings for the Wishbone Corporation as of December 31, 1980.

Accounts Payable: $22,200	Accounts Receivable: $25,300
Advertising: $3,500	Capital Stock: $50,000
Cash: $1,100	Cost of Goods Sold: $228,000
Dividends Paid: $7,500	Gross Sales: $300,000
Income Tax Expense: $10,000	Income Tax Payable: $4,000

Interest Expense: $1,200
Building (net): $25,000
Depreciation Expense: $800
Notes Payable: $4,000
Office Salaries: $25,000
Office Supplies Used: $1,500
Salaries Payable: $800

Land: $32,600
Merchandise Inventory: $32,000
Long-Term Debt: $15,000
Notes Receivable: $4,800
Office Supplies Inventory: $700
Retained Earnings: 1/1/80: $18,000
Sales Returns & Allowances: $15,000

17. On December 31, 1980, Craig Company's balance sheet listed assets totaling $170,000 and liabilities totaling $80,000. The company's year-end balance sheet listed assets of $195,000 and liabilities of $85,000. What additional information do you need in order to determine the company's income for the year?

18. At the end of its first year of operations, the Helms Company prepared a balance sheet that showed total assets of $250,000, total liabilities of $180,000, and capital stock of $45,000. What were the company's major sources of assets, and how much was obtained from each source?

19. You are the sole owner of a company whose books reflect net assets in the amount of $275,000. Why might a prospective buyer of your business offer to pay you an amount greater than $275,000? If you decide to accept an offer in excess of $275,000, how will the net assets purchased be shown on the balance sheet of the buyer? If you decline an offer in excess of $275,000, should you revalue the net assets of your business to reflect the amount a prospective buyer was willing to pay?

20. The Hunter Corporation recently completed construction of a manufacturing plant that was located on a parcel of land donated to the company by the local community as an incentive for the company to build its plant there. Should the land be shown on Hunter Corporation's balance sheet? If so, at what amount? If an amount for land is shown on the balance sheet, won't the balance sheet be out of balance?

21. Indicate the effect of each of the following occurences on a company's assets, liabilities, and owners' equity:

    a. Sale of capital stock.
    b. Signing a three-year lease on a building.
    c. Payment of three-months rent in advance.
    d. Purchase of supplies for cash.
    e. Purchase of equipment on account.
    f. Purchase of merchandise on account.
    g. Obtaining a six-month bank loan.
    h. Selling merchandise for cash in excess of its cost.
    i. Selling merchandise on account in excess of its cost.
    j. Payment of an account payable.
    k. Payment of property taxes.

22. Using the following information, prepare an income statement, balance sheet, and statement of retained earnings for the Jackson Corporation for its

fiscal year ended June 30, 1980:

Accounts Payable: $5,600	Accounts Receivable: $7,200
Advertising Expense: $2,500	Building (net): $42,000
Depreciation Expense: $2,500	Equipment (net): $16,000
Insurance Expense: $700	Land: $27,300
Miscellaneous Expense: $1,500	Prepaid Insurance: $1,400
Net Sales: $97,000	Salaries Payable: $500
Salary Expense: $22,500	Supplies: $1,200
Supplies Expense: $1,400	Taxes Payable: $7,000
Tax Expense: $25,000	Utilities Expense: $4,400
Capital Stock: $40,000	Beg. Retained Earnings: $17,500
	Dividends Paid: $12,000

3

The Accounting Process

In this chapter, business events and transactions are defined, and the manner in which they are treated in a company's financial records is discussed. The double-entry system of accounting is described, and the procedures that comprise the accounting process, beginning with the initial recording of business transactions and ending with the preparation of financial statements, are illustrated.

In Chapter 2, we described the nature and purpose of the balance sheet and the statements of income and retained earnings. In this chapter, we will explain how these financial statements were derived. To do so, it will be necessary to consider everything that occurred between April 3, 1978 and March 31, 1979 that affected either the resources or obligations of Corner Drugstore. We will also describe the accounting procedures used by Corner Drugstore in recording, summarizing, and presenting the results of its first year's activities.

BUSINESS EVENTS

Business events can be divided into two classes: those that cause a company's financial position to change, and those that do not. Only those events that affect a company's financial position are given accounting recognition. We will refer to events of this type as *transactions*. Thus, business transactions affect the financial position of a company and must be recorded on a company's books and reflected in its financial statements.

Examples of common business transactions are the sale of capital stock, the purchase or sale of merchandise, and the purchase of equipment. Business events that do not affect a company's financial position (and therefore are not transactions) often take the form of *executory contracts*. These are agreements a company makes with one or more other companies or individuals, the terms which have not yet been fulfilled. No accounting recognition is given to executory contracts at the time they are made. As these contracts are fulfilled, appropriate accounting recognition occurs. Executory contracts include (1) employment agreements, (2) rental agreements, and (3) agreements to purchase or sell merchandise at a future time.

ACCOUNTS AND THE DOUBLE-ENTRY SYSTEM OF ACCOUNTING

As business transactions occur, their effects upon a company's assets, liabilities, and owners' equity are recorded on the books through the use of *accounts*. In its simplest form, an account resembles the letter "T" and is referred to as a *T-account*. Its purpose is to provide an easy means for recording the dollar amount of an increase or decrease in each individual asset, liability, or component of owners' equity. In a manual system, all of a company's accounts are bound together into a type of book called a *ledger*. Each page of the ledger contains a separate account, and each account represents a different balance sheet component, such as merchandise inventory or wages payable. Each T-account is divided in half by a vertical line drawn down the middle of the page. One side records the dollar amount of increases in the account; the other side records the dollar amount of account decreases. The *balance* of each account is determined by subtracting the total of the decrease side from the total of the increase side. The name of each account is placed at the top.

The double-entry system of accounting provides the basis for recording changes in account balances. The financial consequences of every transaction recorded by the double-entry system must result in equal amounts placed on the left side of some accounts and on the right side of other accounts. As a result, the sum of all accounts with left-side balances must always equal the sum of all the accounts with right-side balances. A ledger is said to be *in balance* when such a state of account balance equality exists. Illustration 3-1 contains the balances for each of Corner Drugstore's accounts as of the end of its first fiscal year.

As a practical matter, companies assign a number to each of their ledger accounts. Both the quantity of accounts and the numbering system will vary among businesses due to differences in such factors as the nature of the business, the size of the business, and the extent to which management desires detailed records to be kept. Accounts are numbered in ascending order and are usually arranged in the ledger in the order in which they appear in the financial statements. Balance sheet accounts are generally shown first, then income statement accounts. Small companies may need only two-digit numbers, whereas large companies may need four or more digits. The account numbering system is frequently designed so that the nature of each account (i.e., asset, liability, etc.) can be identified from the account number. Companies maintain a *chart of accounts* that consists of a complete listing of all their account titles and corresponding account numbers.

Rules for Entering Amounts in the Ledger Accounts

The increases in some accounts are recorded on the left side, whereas the increases in other accounts are recorded on the right side. The following conventions are prescribed under double-entry accounting:

Type of Account	How Recorded
Asset	Increases on the left; decreases on the right
Liability	Increases on the right; decreases on the left
Owners' Equity	Increases on the right; decreases on the left

Notice that asset increases are recorded on the left side of the account but that the opposite is true for liabilities and owners' equity. The logic of this inverse relationship can be explained through the accounting equation, $A = L + OE$. In any mathematical equation,

Illustration 3-1

Corner Drugstore, Inc.
Ledger Account Balances
March 31, 1979

Cash (A)

3-31-79 Balance	2,500	

Accounts Receivable (A)

3-31-79 Balance	4,200	

Merchandise Inventory (A)

3-31-79 Balance	12,700	

Store Equipment (A)

(Original Cost $10,000) 3-31-79 Balance	9,000	

Accounts Payable (L)

		Balance 3-31-79	3,800

Wages Payable (L)

		Balance 3-31-79	700

Utilities Payable (L)

		Balance 3-31-79	200

Taxes Payable (L)

		Balance 3-31-79	2,300

Bank Loan Payable (L)

		Balance 3-31-79	7,500

Capital Stock (OE)

		Balance 3-31-79	10,000

Retained Earnings (OE)

		Balance 3-31-79	3,900

moving from one side of the equation to the other requires that the sign (+ or −) of the number be changed. Similarly, moving from one side of the accounting equation to the other requires that the manner of recording increases and decreases in accounts be reversed. Thus, the rules for recording changes in assets are just the opposite of those for recording changes in liabilities and owners' equity.

In summary, the rules of entering business transactions are as follows:

$$A = L + OE$$

Asset Accounts	
Increases	Decreases

Liability Accounts	
Decreases	Increases

Owners' Equity Accounts	
Decreases	Increases

ANALYSIS OF BUSINESS TRANSACTIONS

The analysis of any business transaction can be accomplished by answering the following four questions:

1. What accounts in the ledger are affected by the transaction?
2. What kind of accounts are these (A, L, or OE)?
3. Are the affected accounts increased or decreased by the transaction and by how much?
4. What are the "left-hand" and "right-hand" effects of the transaction according to the rules of double-entry accounting for entering transactions in the ledger accounts?

Let us illustrate the process by applying it to a transaction involving the purchase of $300 of merchandise on account by Corner Drugstore.

1.	Accounts affected:	Merchandise Inventory Accounts Payable
2.	Kinds of accounts:	Merchandise Inventory (A) Accounts Payable (L)

3.	Accounts increased or decreased and by how much:	Merchandise Inventory (A)
		    increased $300
		Accounts Payable (L)
		    increased $300

4.	Left-hand and right-hand effects:	Enter $300 on left side of Merchandise Inventory account Enter $300 on right side of Accounts Payable account

Illustration 3-2 shows the manner in which Corner Drugstore would

Illustration 3-2

Analysis of Transactions

Accounts Affected	Amount of Increase or Decrease			
(1)	Left		Right	
Merchandise Inventory (A)	Incr	300		
Accounts Payable (L)			Incr	300
(2)				
Accounts Receivable (A)	Incr	100		
Retained Earnings (OE)-(Sales)			Incr	100
(3)				
Accounts Payable (L)	Decr	300		
Cash (A)			Decr	300
(4)				
Cash (A)	Incr	100		
Accounts Receivable (A)			Decr	100

record the $300 merchandise purchase, as well as the three addition-al transactions described below. A *journal* is used by businesses to record business transactions chronologically as they occur. The form for making entries in a journal is somewhat similar to that used in Illustration 3-2. In this text, we shall refer to the process of recording transactions on a company's books as the *analysis of transactions*.

The other transactions appearing in Illustration 3-2 are:

Transaction 2:   The drugstore sold for $100 merchandise cost-ing $60. The sale was "on account." (Notice that at the time of sale, the sale but not the cost of the goods sold is recorded. The cost of the merchandise sold is recorded at year-end, as we will discuss later in this chapter.)

Transaction 3:   The drugstore paid for the merchandise previ-ously purchased.

Transaction 4:   The drugstore collected its account receivable of $100.

The generally accepted form associated with the analysis of trans-actions requires that:

1. The left-hand portion of each entry is shown first.
2. The right-hand portion is indented to the right of the left-hand portion.
3. Each account is given the exact title it has in the ledger.
4. An entry affecting the Retained Earnings account includes a brief parenthetical explanation so that when the entry is made in the Retained Earnings account in the ledger, the explanation can also be shown there.

CORNER DRUGSTORE'S TRANSACTIONS FOR ONE YEAR

Let us now go behind the financial statements presented in Chapter 2, and at the same time further illustrate the analysis of transactions by recording Corner Drugstore's transactions for its first fiscal year. These are actually *summary transactions* because we have grouped all similar transactions that occurred throughout the year and will record only the yearly totals. For example, Transaction C of Illustration 3-3 reflects the total merchandise purchased by the drugstore on account throughout the entire fiscal year. Keep in mind that on the company's books, each purchase of merchandise would be recorded separately and chronologically in its journal. In Illustration 3-3, each summary transaction described is immediately followed by an analysis of the transaction. For ease of illustration, all payroll taxes have been omitted from the Corner Drugstore example.

It is now possible for us to derive the individual account balances for Corner Drugstore as of March 31, 1979 that were presented in Illustration 3-1. All that we need to do is establish a separate account for each specific asset, liability, and component of owners' equity; enter the balance in each account as of the beginning of the 1979 fiscal year (which was $0 in every case since 1979 was the first year of operations); record each transaction in the appropriate accounts; and determine each account's fiscal year-end balance. The results are shown in Illustration 3-4. Before continuing, *trace all of the transactions in Illustration 3-3 to the accounts listed in Illustration 3-4.*

The following important characteristics of a company's ledger accounts are illustrated by those of Corner Drugstore in Illustration 3-4:

1. Balance sheet accounts carry forward from year to year, with the dollar amount of the fiscal year-end balance becoming the

Illustration 3-3

Corner Drugstore, Inc.
Analysis of Summary Transactions
Fiscal Year Ended March 31, 1979

Transaction A: Issued capital stock to the two incorporators in exchange for $10,000 cash.

Cash (A)	Incr	10,000	
Capital Stock (OE)		Incr	10,000

Event B: Signed a three-year lease on the building in which the drugstore was to be located. The lease called for a monthly rental of $300 and was cancellable by either the lessor or the lessee (Corner Drugstore) upon at least sixty days advance notice.

No entry for Event B

This business event does not affect the financial resources or obligations of Corner Drugstore. Even though the drugstore signed the lease, the agreement is an executory contract that has yet to be performed. Corner Drugstore does not incur a liability to the lessor until the lease period occurs and the drugstore uses the building. At the time the lease is signed, no assets or liabilities are affected and no amounts are recorded in any of the drugstore's account. Thus, no "transaction analysis" is needed.

Transaction C: Purchased merchandise in the amount of $57,400 all on credit. (Payment was usually due within 30 days of the purchase date.)

Merchandise Inventory (A)	Incr	57,400	
Accounts Payable (L)		Incr	57,400

Transaction D: Borrowed $9,000 from a local bank on April 4, 1978. Repayment was to be made in six annual amounts, beginning on March 31, 1979. Interest of 5 percent per year on the unpaid balance was also due on that same date each year.

Cash (A)	Incr	9,000	
Bank Loan Payable (L)		Incr	9,000

Transaction E: Purchased store equipment for a total of $10,000 cash.

Store Equipment (A)	Incr	10,000	
Cash (A)		Decr	10,000

Transaction F: Cash sales amounted to $30,300.

Cash (A)	Incr	30,300	
Retained Earnings (OE) – (Cash Sales)		Incr	30,300

Transaction G: Credit sales amounted to $45,500.

Accounts Receivable (A)	Incr	45,500	
Retained Earnings (OE) – (Credit Sales)		Incr	45,500

Transaction H: Customers returned merchandise that they previously had purchased in the amount of $1,300. Of this, $500 had been cash sales and $800 had been credit sales.

Retained Earnings (OE) – (Sales Returns)	Decr	1,300	
Cash (A)		Decr	500
Accounts Receivable (A)		Decr	800

Transaction I: Collections of accounts receivable totaled $40,500.

Cash (A)	Incr	40,500	
Accounts Receivable (A)		Decr	40,500

Transaction J: Payments for merchandise previously purchased on credit amounted to $53,600.

Accounts Payable (L)	Decr	53,600	
Cash (A)		Decr	53,600

Transaction K: Paid cash for rent totaling $3,600. This amount is the total rent due to the owner of the building for its use for the entire year.

Retained Earnings (OE) – (Rent)	Decr	3,600		
Cash (A)			Decr	3,600

Transaction L: Paid cash wages to employees totaling $14,600. As of March 31, 1979, wages earned by employees but not yet paid were $700.

Retained Earnings (OE) – (Wages)	Decr	15,300		
Cash (A)			Decr	14,600
Wages Payable (L)			Incr	700

Transaction M: Paid cash for utilities in the amount of $450. As of March 31, 1979, Corner Drugstore owed an additional $200 for utilities.

Retained Earnings (OE) – (Utilities)	Decr	650		
Cash (A)			Decr	450
Utilities Payable (L)			Incr	200

Transaction N: Estimated federal and state income taxes paid during the year amounted to $600. At fiscal year-end, an additional tax of $2,300 was due on the income actually earned during the year, suggesting that the drugstore was more profitable during its first year than the owners expected.

Retained Earnings (OE) – (Income Taxes)	Decr	2,900		
Cash (A)			Decr	600
Income Taxes Payable (L)			Incr	2,300

Transaction O: Paid cash for "other expenses" in the amount of $500.

Retained Earnings (OE) – (Other Expenses)	Decr	500		
Cash (A)			Decr	500

Transaction P: On March 31, paid the first installment due on the bank loan, totaling $1,950. Of this amount, $1,500 was repayment of the principal, and $450 was interest expense.

Bank Loan Payable (L)	Decr	1,500		
Retained Earnings (OE) – (Interest)	Decr	450		
Cash (A)			Decr	1,950

Transaction Q: $1,000 of the original cost of the store equipment was "written-off" the balance sheet and allocated to expense. An expense of this type is known as "depreciation."

Retained Earnings (OE) – (Depreciation)	Decr	1,000		
Store Equipment			Decr	1,000

Transaction R: The cost to corner Drugstore of the merchandise that was sold and not returned during the year totaled $44,700.

Retained Earnings (OE) – (Cost of Merchandise Sold)	Decr	44,700		
Merchandise Inventory (A)			Decr	44,700

Transaction S: Cash dividends of $1,500 were declared and paid.

At date of declaration:

Retained Earnings (OE) – (Dividends)	Decr	1,500		
Dividends Payable (L)			Incr	1,500

At date of payment:

Dividends Payable (L)	Decr	1,500		
Cash (A)			Decr	1,500

Illustration 3-4

Transactions Entered in Corner Drugstore's Ledger
Fiscal Year Ended March 31, 1979

Cash (A)

3-31-78 Balance	-0-		(E)	10,000
(A)	10,000		(H)	500
(D)	9,000		(J)	53,600
(F)	30,300		(K)	3,600
(I)	40,500		(L)	14,600
			(M)	450
			(N)	600
			(O)	500
			(P)	1,950
			(S)	1,500
				87,300
			To balance	2,500
	89,800			89,800
3-31-79 Balance	2,500			

Accounts Receivable (A)

3-31-78 Balance	-0-		(H)	800
(G)	45,500		(I)	40,500
				41,300
			To balance	4,200
	45,500			45,500
3-31-79 Balance	4,200			

Merchandise Inventory (A)

3-31-78 Balance	-0-		(R)	44,700
(C)	57,400			44,700
			To balance	12,700
	57,400			57,400
3-31-79 Balance	12,700			

Store Equipment (A)

3-31-78 Balance	-0-		(Q)	1,000
(E)	10,000			1,000
			To balance	9,000
	10,000			10,000
3-31-79 Balance	9,000			

Accounts Payable (L)

(J)	53,600	3-31-78 Balance	-0-
		(C)	57,400
	53,600		
To balance	3,800		
	57,400		57,400
		3-31-79 Balance	3,800

Wages Payable (L)

To balance	700	3-31-78 Balance	-0-
		(L)	700
		3-31-79 Balance	700

Utilities Payable (L)

		3-31-78 Balance	-0-
To balance	200	(M)	200
		3-31-79 Balance	200

Taxes Payable (L)

		3-31-78 Balance	-0-
To balance	2,300	(N)	2,300
		3-31-79 Balance	2,300

Bank Loan Payable (L)

(P)	1,500	3-31-78 Balance	-0-
		(D)	9,000
	1,500		
To balance	7,500		
	9,000		9,000
		3-31-79 Balance	7,500

Dividends Payable (L)

(S)	1,500	3-31-78 Balance	-0-
		(S)	1,500
		3-31-79 Balance	-0-

Capital Stock (OE)

To balance	10,000	4-1-78 Balance (A)	-0- 10,000
		3-31-79 Balance	10,000

Retained Earnings (OE)

(H) Sales returns	1,300	3-31-78 Balance	-0-
(K) Rent expense	3,600	(F) Cash sales	30,300
(L) Wages expense	15,300	(G) Credit sales	45,500
(M) Utilities expense	650		
(N) Taxes expense	2,900		
(O) Other expenses	500		
(P) Interest expense	450		
(Q) Depreciation expense	1,000		
(R) Cost of merchandise sold	44,700		
(S) Dividends	1,500		
	71,900		
To balance	3,900		
	75,800		75,800
		3-31-79 Balance	3,900

dollar amount of the account balance at the beginning of the new fiscal year.

2. Sometimes the year-end balance of an account is zero.
3. All revenues cause retained earnings to increase. All expenses and all contra-revenues (such as sales returns) cause retained earnings to decrease.
4. All of the data needed to prepare an income statement and a retained earnings statement are contained in the retained earnings account. Each entry to retained earnings must be identified to facilitate these statements' preparation.
5. Not all of the entries in the retained earnings account pertain to transactions affecting the income statement. For example, transaction S pertaining to cash dividends decreased retained earnings, yet dividends are not an expense and therefore do not affect the calculation of net income.

TRIAL BALANCE

Now that we have determined the balance in each ledger account as of March 31, 1979, we need to make sure that the total of the left-hand account balances equals the total of the right-hand account balances. We know that this equality existed as of the beginning of the first fiscal year (all balances were zero), and we attempted to record each transaction so that equal left-hand and right-hand entries were made. Therefore, we can be reasonably confident that at year-end the ledger accounts are *in balance*; that is, total left-hand and right-hand balances are equal.

To prove the company's ledger is in balance, we will prepare a *trial balance*. From the one presented in Illustration 3-5, we can see that:

1. Accounts are listed on the trial balance in the same order that they appear on the balance sheet.
2. No dollar signs are used because the trial balance is not an actual financial statement, just a convenient means of proving that the ledger accounts are in balance.
3. The trial balance proves only the mathematical equality of the left-hand and right-hand entries in the accounts. The trial

Illustration 3-5

Corner Drugstore, Inc.
Trial Balance
March 31, 1979

Account Name	Left-Hand Balance	Right-Hand Balance
Cash	2,500	
Accounts Receivable	4,200	
Merchandise Inventory	12,700	
Store Equipment (Cost $10,000)	9,000	
Accounts Payable		3,800
Wages Payable		700
Utilities Payable		200
Taxes Payable		2,300
Bank Loan Payable		7,500
Dividends Payable		-0-
Capital Stock		10,000
Retained Earnings		3,900
Total	28,400	28,400

balance does not prove that the transactions were properly analyzed or that they were entered in the proper accounts.

THE REPORT FORM OF BALANCE SHEET

We are now ready to prepare the basic financial statements of Corner Drugstore. In Chapter 2, we illustrated the *account form* of balance sheet. Several other forms of balance sheet presentation are also used by businesses. Illustration 3-6 presents Corner Drugstore's March 31, 1979 balance sheet in the *report form*, wherein liabilities and owners' equity are shown below assets. A variation of the report form shows a downward sequence of total assets minus total liabilities equal to total owners' equity. Another form used occasionally is the *financial position form*. This form of balance sheet shows current assets less current liabilities equal to working capital (net current assets). Noncurrent assets are then added and noncurrent liabilities deducted

Illustration 3-6

Corner Drugstore, Inc.
Balance Sheet
March 31, 1979

Assets

Cash	$ 2,500
Accounts receivable	4,200
Merchandise inventory	12,700
Store equipment (cost $10,000)	9,000
Total assets	28,400

Liabilities and Owners' Equity

Accounts payable		3,800
Wages payable		700
Utilities payable		200
Income taxes payable		2,300
Bank loan payable		7,500
Total liabilities		14,500
Capital stock	$10,000	
Retained earnings	3,900	13,900
Total liabilities and owners' equity		$28,400

from working capital to arrive at the total amount of net assets (total assets less total liabilities). Owners' equity is shown last, the total of which is equal to the amount of the net assets. The balance sheet of Caterpillar Tractor Company illustrated in subsequent chapters is an example of the *financial position form*.

COMBINED STATEMENT OF INCOME AND RETAINED EARNINGS

In Chapter 2, we mentioned that the income statement and the statement of retained earnings are often combined into a single statement. This combination is possible because both statements cover the same period of time and because both statements reflect

---

Illustration 3-7

Corner Drugstore, Inc.
Statement of Income and Retained Earnings
For the Fiscal Year Ended March 31, 1979

Gross sales		$75,800
Less: Sales returns		1,300
Net sales		74,500
Less: Cost of merchandise sold		44,700
Gross margin on sales		29,800
Less Operating expenses:		
Employees wages	$15,300	
Rent	3,600	
Utilities	650	
Allocated cost of store equipment	1,000	
Other	500	
Total operating expenses		21,050
Income from operations		8,750
Less: Interest on bank loan		450
Income before income taxes		8,300
Less: Federal and state income taxes		2,900
Net income		5,400
Add: Retained earnings, March 31, 1978		-0-
		5,400
Less: Cash dividends		1,500
Retained earnings, March 31, 1979		$ 3,900

transactions affecting retained earnings. Illustration 3-7 contains a combined statement of income and retained earnings for Corner Drugstore's first fiscal year prepared solely from the data provided by the retained earnings ledger account in Illustration 3-4.

COMPARATIVE FINANCIAL STATEMENTS

Companies customarily provide external users of their financial statements with information pertaining to more than one fiscal year through the preparation of comparative financial statements. A comparative balance sheet shows a company's financial position as of two or more consecutive fiscal year-ends. A comparative statement of income and retained earnings presents the results of a company's activities during two or more consecutive fiscal years.

Representative comparative financial statements for Corner Drug-

Illustration 3-8

Corner Drugstore, Inc.
Comparative Balance Sheet
March 31, 1980 and March 31, 1979

Assets	3/31/80	3/31/79
Cash	$ 575	$ 2,500
Accounts receivable	7,400	4,200
Merchandise inventory	18,000	12,700
Store equipment (cost $15,000; $10,000)	12,500	9,000
Total assets	38,475	28,400
Liabilities and Owners' Equity		
Accounts payable	6,200	3,800
Wages payable	900	700
Utilities payable	100	200
Income taxes payable	1,800	2,300
Bank loan payable	6,000	7,500
Total liabilities	15,000	14,500
Capital stock	13,000	10,000
Retained earnings	10,475	3,900
Total liabilities and owners' equity	$38,475	$28,400

Illustration 3-9

Corner Drugstore, Inc.
Comparative Statement of Income and Retained Earnings
For the Fiscal Years Ended March 31, 1980 and March 31, 1979

		1980		1979
Gross sales		$103,700		$75,800
Less: Sales returns		3,200		1,300
Net sales		100,500		74,500
Less: Cost of merchandise sold		60,300		44,700
Gross margin on sales		40,200		29,800
Less Operating expenses :				
Employees wages	$18,500		$15,300	
Rent	3,600		3,600	
Utilities	850		650	
Depreciation of				
store equipment	1,500		1,000	
Other	750		500	
Total operating expenses		25,200		21,050
Income from operations		15,000		8,750
Less: Interest on bank loan		375		450
Income before income taxes		14,625		8,300
Less: Federal and state income taxes		6,050		2,900
Net income		8,575		5,400
Add: Beginning retained earnings		3,900		-0-
		12,475		5,400
Less: Cash dividends		2,000		1,500
Ending retained earnings		$ 10,475		$ 3,900

store for its 1980 and 1979 fiscal years are shown in Illustrations 3-8 and 3-9. A summary of the drugstore's transactions for its fiscal year ended March 31, 1980 is intentionally omitted from this chapter for reasons that will become evident (perhaps painfully so) in Chapter 4.

REMARKS ABOUT THE APPROACH

At this point in the development of accounting fundamentals, we wish to distinguish between the manner in which we have presented certain aspects of the accounting process and the more traditional method of presentation. The first such difference pertains to the recording of amounts in the ledger accounts. In our discussion, we stated that each account has a left-side and a right-side, and that accountants have developed rules requiring that changes in asset accounts be recorded in a manner opposite from changes in liability and owners' equity accounts. The more traditional presentation of changes in account balances introduces the terms "debit" and "credit." Notwithstanding that these terms are part of the accounting language, we avoid their use for two reasons. First, preconceived notions about these terms are often wrong and are very difficult to change. Second, debit means nothing more than the left side of an account, and credit means nothing more than the right side of an account. Omitting their use gives up little in terms of substance but avoids a considerable amount of confusion.

Another difference between our presentation and a more traditional one pertains to the retained earnings account. Whereas we recorded all of Corner Drugstore's revenues and expenses directly in its retained earnings account, the more traditional method (and the one actually used by businesses) establishes separate accounts for each revenue and for each expense. The net difference between the revenues and the expenses is then recorded periodically in the retained earnings account.

As we have presented it, then, the *accounting process* can be described as follows:

1. Transactions are identified and chronologically recorded in a journal through an analysis of transactions.
2. Periodically, the chronologically recorded data are entered in the appropriate ledger accounts. These entries are made at least every fiscal year-end.
3. A trial-balance is prepared to prove the mathematical equality of the left-hand and right-hand balances in the ledger accounts.
4. The basic financial statements are prepared.

SUMMARY

Business financial records are kept in accordance with the requirements of the double-entry system of accounting. The account is used to collect financial information about business transactions. Each account has a left side and a right side, and the rules are such that increases in assets are recorded in the left side of an account whereas decreases in assets are recorded in the right side of an account. The reverse is true for recording changes in liabilities and owners' equity. Prior to the preparation of financial statements, a trial balance is prepared to make sure that the total of the left-hand account balance is equal to the total of the right-hand account balance. Comparative financial statements for two or more years are usually prepared for external reporting purposes.

QUESTIONS AND PROBLEMS

1. Name the three parts of an account.
2. Explain the double-entry system of accounting.
3. Why aren't transactions entered directly in the ledger accounts?
4. Is it possible to recognize revenue prior to the time a product is sold? For example, could revenue be recognized at the time of production rather than at the time of sale? Explain.
5. Is it necessary to prepare a trial balance prior to the preparation of financial statements? If not, then why is it a common practice to do so? List three types of errors that would not be discovered as a result of preparing a trial balance.
6. Companies frequently state that their employees are their most valuable asset. If that is true, then why aren't a company's employees shown as an asset on its balance sheet?
7. Why are comparative financial statements more useful to external users than single year financial statements?
8. Indicate the effect of each of the following transactions on the accounts listed below by placing a plus (+) or a minus (−) in the appropriate columns.

| | Assets | | | Liabilities | | Owners' Equity | |
Transactions	Cash	Accounts Receivable	Supplies	Accounts Payable	Notes Payable	Capital Stock	Retained Earnings
a. Sold additional shares of capital stock.	+					+	
b. Borrowed money from a local bank and signed a note.	+				+		
c. Purchased supplies for cash.	−		+				
d. Rendered services and collected cash for those services.	+		−				
e. Rendered services to customers who agreed to pay for those services within 30 days.		+	−				

Transactions	Cash	Accounts Receivable	Supplies	Accounts Payable	Notes Payable	Capital Stock	Retained Earnings
f. Purchase supplies on account.			+	+			
g. Paid salary expense.	−						−
h. Paid office rent.	−						−
i. Collected cash from customers for whom services were previously performed.	+	−					
j. Paid interest on the loan.	−						−
k. Used supplies in connection with performing services.			✕	−			(−?)
l. Repaid part of the bank loan principal.	−				−		
m. Paid cash dividends to stockholders.	−					+	−

9. The following financial information was obtained from the books of the Kirsch Corporation:

Total assets-Beginning	$ 85,000
Total assets-Ending	102,000
Total liabilities-Beginning	50,000
Revenues for the period	63,000
Expenses for the period	49,000
Dividends declared and paid	8,000
Proceeds from sale of additional Capital Stock	5,000
Purchase of equipment	7,000

Required: Calculate the total liabilities-Ending. ⟶ 54,000

10. The books of the Aztec Corporation contain the following information for the month of February:

Collections from cash customers	$ 18,000
Proceeds from bank loan	10,000
Dividends to stockholders	4,000
Collections from credit customers on January sales	15,000
Depreciation on building for February	400
Cost of merchandise sold	32,000
Merchandise sold on account in February	29,000
Salaries paid to employees in February	6,500

Paid for a one-year insurance policy
(policy effective February 1)   3,000
Signed a contract to deliver merchandise
in March   2,000

Required: Prepare an income statement for the Aztec Corporation for the month of February. (Ignore income taxes.)

11. The following changes occurred in the account balances of the Falcon Company during 1980:   *Assets*

Cash	Increased	$ 7,000 +
Accounts receivable	Increased	4,000 +
Merchandise inventory	Decreased	5,000 −
Office supplies	Increased	1,000 − +
Building (net)	Decreased	2,000 + − = + 5000
Accounts payable	Increased	5,000 − +

During the year, dividends of $6,000 were declared and paid and $7,000 + was received from the sale of additional capital stock.   (1000)

Required: How much was Falcon Company's net income or loss for 1980?   5000

12. On July 1, 1980, Tom and Sam Parks formed a window washing business. The following information pertains to their first month's operations:

Total cash received (including $600 from Budget Shoe Store)	$ 2,400
Cash paid out:	
Purchase of supplies	90
Purchase of used truck	800
Paid employees	550
Paid July rent for office space	150

Although the Parks brothers expected most of their work to come from single engagements, they did enter into two contracts early in July. The first contract was with Budget Shoe Store, and it specified that Tom and Sam were to wash the shoestore's windows at a rate of $50 per month for a period of one year. During July, Budget Shoe Store paid the Parks brothers six-months cash in advance. The second contract was with Economy Drugs. This contract was also for a one-year period and called for Tom and Sam to wash the drugstore's windows at a rate of $40 per month to be paid on the 10th of the month following when the services were performed. The $40 payment for July services was subsequently received on August 10th. There were no supplies on hand as of July 1 and supplies on hand at July 31 had cost $40. Depreciation on the truck for July amounted to $35.

Required: Prepare an income statement for the Parks Brothers for the month of July.

13. The Rex Carrs Corporation was formed on January 2, 1980. During the

month of January, the corporation entered into *seven* different business transactions. At the end of the month, Rex Carrs Corporation prepared the following trial balance:

Rex Carrs Corporation
Trial Balance
January 31, 1980   *DR*   *CR*

	Left	Right
Cash	18,500	
Accounts Receivable	1,500	
Office Supplies	400 *-BGT.SUP.*	
Office Furniture	5,875	
Salaries Payable		800
Capital Stock		25,000
Revenue from Services		1,500
Supplies Expense	100 *-USED SUP*	
Salaries Expense	800	
Depreciation Expense	125	
	27,300	27,300

Required: Based on the data contained in the trial balance, prepare an analysis of transactions for the seven transactions that occurred during January.

14. Early in January, Mr. Harold Betz began a new business called Quick Delivery Service. His initial investment consisted of $100 in cash and a motorcycle having a fair market value of $500. He kept no formal accounting records throughout the year and now has engaged you to determine the amount of his net income or loss for the year. You find that the year-end bank balance for Quick Delivery Service is $775 and that there is $15 in the office cash box. The motorcycle is still in reasonably good shape and you expect that it will last another four years. Early in July, the company bought a delivery truck at a cost of $3,000. Its estimated useful life was 5 years. In order to purchase a truck, Quick Delivery Service borrowed $2,600 from a local bank. Terms of the loan called for monthly interest to be paid at 10% and the principal to be repaid in three equal yearly installments beginning one year after the date of the loan. During the year, Mr. Betz withdrew a total of $5,000 from the business to use for his personal living expense.

Required: Ignoring income taxes, determine the net income or loss for the Quick Delivery Service for the year.

15. Determine the effect of each of the following transactions on a company's income statement and its cash balance. Under the column headed "Income Statement," indicate whether the transaction results in a revenue or an expense and also the dollar amount involved. Under the "Cash Balance" column, indicate whether the cash balance would increase or decrease and also indicate the dollar amount involved. If a transaction has no effect on the

income statement or the cash balance, then so indicate in the appropriate column.

Transaction	Income Statement		Cash Balance	
(x) Purchased land for $5,000 cash.	N. E.	$----	Dec.	$5,000
(a) Paid salaries of $700.	EXP.	700	Decr	700
(b) Purchased a $23,000 machine, giving a $23,000 note payable in exchange. The note carried an interest rate of 12%.	N.E		NE	
(c) Paid dividends of $2,500.	NE		Decr.	2500
(d) Paid rent of $600.	EXP	600	"	600
(e) Sold additional capital stock for $8,000 cash.	NE		INC	8000
(f) Used $300 worth of supplies previously purchased.	EXP	300	NE	
(g) Recorded depreciation expense of $200.	EXP	200	NE	
(h) Collected a $75 account receivable.	NE		INCR	75

[handwritten annotations near (b): "AN EXPENSE & DISTRIB. of CAPITAL" and "NOT AN EXPENSE BUT A DISTRIB. of CAPITAL"]

16. In January of 1980, Mary Jane Bowers was reviewing her plans for the April 1 opening of a garden center in Lynchburg, Virginia. Mrs. Bowers was a college graduate and had worked for three years for a wholesale nursery in Richmond. Her husband, John, an electrical engineer with a large multinational company, was transferred to Lynchburg in October, 1979. Mary Jane wanted to continue a career in a horticultural related field and after surveying the opportunities in Lynchburg, decided to open a store, The Garden Center, Inc., to sell plants, trees, and shrubs.

   Mary Jane accumulated information on retail garden stores from a number of sources, talked to suppliers, looked at potential locations, and established a banking relationship with the Campbell National Bank. Mary Jane wanted to make sure that she had enough money to get the business off to a good start. She had heard that many small businesses failed because they were under-capitalized.

   After careful study and analysis, Mary Jane made the following projections for the first year of operations of The Garden Center, Inc.:

   (1) April 1, 1980—The business would be incorporated and Mary and John would buy $30,000 capital stock.

   (2) April 1, 1980—The Campbell National Bank would loan the Garden Center, Inc. $16,000 to be repaid in equal principal payments over 4 years. The interest rate was 13% and payable at the end of each year when the principal payment was made.

(3) April 1, 1980—A pick up truck would be purchased for $6,000,
     $5,000 to be financed by the Campbell National Bank. The loan
     would be repaid over 3 years at the rate of $168 per month or a
     total of $6050.
(4) April 1, 1980—Purchase display equipment for $3,000 cash.
(5) April 1, 1980—Purchase a roto-tiller for $200 cash.
(6) April 1, 1980—Purchase a cash register for $1800 cash.
(7) April 1, 1980—Purchase inventory of plants, trees, and shrubs for
     $30,000 cash.

The following transactions were projected between April 1, 1980 and
March 31, 1981:

(8) Cash sales $170,000
     Charge sales $ 30,000
(9) Additional purchase of plants, trees, and shrubs $120,000. Mary
     Jane planned to price all items to give her a 40% gross margin, i.e.,
     if an item cost $6.00, it would sell for $10.00.
(10) Advertising expenses projected at 5% of sales or $10,000 for the
     year.
(11) Mary Jane categorized a group of expenses as "on-going." They
     were projected at:
     Rent $3600 ($300 per month)
     Telephone   600 ($50.00 per month)
     Utilities $2400 ($200 per month)
     Payroll $56,000 ($20,000 for Mary Jane
                                   and $36,000 for three regular and
                                   four part time employees)
(12) Monthly payments of $168.00 to be made on the truck loan de-
     scribed in (3).
(13) Principal payment of $4000 on the bank loan described in (2) and
     interest of $2,080.

Required:
1. Prepare transaction analysis for items (1)-(13).
2. Post to "T" accounts.
3. Prepare a projected balance sheet as of the end of the day on April 1, 1980.
4. Prepare a projected cash receipts and disbursements statement for the peri-
    od April 1, 1980-March 31, 1981.
5. How much profit (approximately) do you think Mary Jane will make in her
    first year of business if things go as planned.
6. Make a list of the information you think you need to prepare a projected
    income statement for the year ending March 31, 1981 and a balance sheet as
    of March 31, 1981. Why do you need the information?
7. What will be the break-even point in sales dollars for The Garden Center,
    Inc.?

4

Statement of Changes
in Financial Position

*For external reporting purposes, the presentation
of a statement of changes in financial position has
been required only since 1971. Although most accounting texts do not discuss this relatively new
financial statement until much later on, we believe
that its importance and usefulness are such that
earlier treatment is both necessary and desirable.
This chapter is, therefore, devoted primarily to the
illustration and discussion of the preparation and
purpose of this informative financial statement.
The latter part of this chapter addresses some of
the limitations of all of the basic financial statements.*

With the issuance of Accounting Principles Board (APB) Opinion
No. 19 in March 1971, the accounting profession adopted the *statement of changes in financial position* as a basic financial statement
that must be presented whenever financial statements purporting to
disclose both financial position and results of operations are made
available to external users. The APB believed that this statement
would provide additional relevant financial information useful in
making economic decisions.

The belief that a financial statement disclosing all significant changes in a company's financial position would be externally useful dates back to the development of a "where-got, where-gone" statement by William M. Cole in the early 1900s. Then about 1920, an accounting educator and author named H. A. Finney advocated that a financial statement entitled the "statement of sources and uses of funds" be a required financial statement for external reporting purposes. Whereas Cole's financial statement disclosed changes in all balance sheet accounts, Finney's financial statement discussed only changes in a company's working capital position. *Working capital* is defined as the excess of a company's *current assets* over its *current liabilities*. In equation form, this relationship is:

$$\text{Working Capital} = \text{Current Assets} - \text{Current Liabilities}$$

or

$$\text{W.C.} = \text{C.A.} - \text{C.L.}$$

Current assets are cash and other assets that normally will be converted into cash or sold or consumed within one year from the date of the balance sheet. *Current liabilities* are debts or obligations due within one year of the balance sheet date. Current assets include cash, accounts receivable, and inventory; current liabilities include accounts payable, wages payable, and the current portion due of any long-term obligation.

A company's working capital position is generally regarded as a measure of the company's ability to meet its short-term financial obligations, that is, those obligations due within the next year. Finney's statement of sources and uses of funds, where "funds" meant "working capital," was an early predecessor to the statement of changes in financial position required by APB Opinion No. 19.

THE STATEMENT'S FORM AND CONTENT

The statement of changes in financial position summarizes *all* significant *changes* that have occurred between the beginning and end of a company's accounting period (generally a fiscal year for external reporting purposes). In accordance with APB Opinion No. 19, the statement must:

1. Be based on a broad concept embracing all significant changes in financial position.
2. Prominently disclose *either* working capital *or* cash provided from or used in operations for the period.
3. Begin with income or loss and add back (or deduct) items recognized in determining that income or loss that did not use or provide working capital or cash during the period.
4. Disclose, either on the statement or a related tabulation, the net changes in each element of working capital (i.e., each current asset and current liability) for the period.

Within these guidelines, companies are permitted considerable flexibility in the statement's preparation. In each case, management should adopt the presentation that is most informative for the circumstances.

Although Opinion No. 19 permits the statement of changes in financial position to be prepared so as to disclose either changes in working capital or changes in cash, most companies choose the "working capital" format. We believe that much of the popularity of disclosure of working capital changes over disclosure of cash changes is due to the accounting profession's familiarity with H. A. Finney's "working capital-based" funds statement. There are indications, however, that the "cash-based" funds statement may increase in popularity during the 1980s due to the increased importance of cash flow analysis.

PREPARATION OF THE STATEMENT

Regardless of whether the statement is prepared to disclose working capital changes or cash changes, it is based on data obtained from a company's comparative balance sheet, its current year's statement of income and retained earnings, and from various internal accounting records. Thus, much of what is contained in the statement of changes in financial position could be extracted by external users from the other basic financial statements. Its real values, then, are its disclosure of data not found on the other statements and the manner in which it presents a company's significant financial changes.

In this chapter, we address only the preparation of the statement of changes in financial position designed to disclose changes in *working capital*. We do so, first, because the working capital approach is most commonly used and, second, because the disclosure of significant changes in cash will be discussed in Chapter 5. From the data presented in Illustration 3-8 and 3-9, we will complete the Corner Drugstore's set of basic financial statements by preparing a statement of changes in financial position for the fiscal year ending March 31, 1980.

A statement of changes in financial position prepared on the working capital basis has three major objectives. These are:

1. To disclose the manner in which a company's working capital position changed during the period. Thus, the statement lists all *working capital accounts* (i.e., all current assets and current liabilities), their balances at the beginning and end of the period, and the effect that each of these account balance changes had on the company's working capital position. Such a listing is often called a *schedule of working changes* and usually appears at the bottom of or as an attachment to the statement of changes in financial position.
2. To disclose the *reasons* for the change in a company's working capital position.
3. To disclose all other significant changes in financial position that did not affect working capital, citing the reasons for these changes. (Corner Drugstore did not have any such changes.)

To summarize, the primary goal of the statement of changes in financial position is to report all financially significant changes in a company's financial position that occurred during the period covered by the statement and to disclose the causes of these changes. In a working capital-based statement, the changes in financial position are organized into two categories: changes that affected working capital, and changes that did not. (Corner Drugstore had no changes in the second category.)

The first step in preparing the statement is to determine the amount by which Corner Drugstore's working capital position changed during its 1980 fiscal year. We do so by developing the schedule of working capital changes shown in Illustration 4-1. The right-hand column shows the *effects* on *working capital* of the changes in each current asset and current liability account balance. Notice that increases

Illustration 4-1

Corner Drugstore, Inc.
Schedule of Working Capital Changes
For the Fiscal Year Ended March 31, 1980

	Balance 3/31/80	Balance 3/31/79	Working Capital Incr. or (Decr.)
Current Assets:			
Cash	$ 575	$ 2,500	$(1,925)
Accounts receivable	7,400	4,200	3,200
Merchandise inventory	18,000	12,700	5,300
	25,975	19,400	6,575
Current Liabilities:			
Accounts payable	6,200	3,800	(2,400)
Wages payable	900	700	(200)
Utilities payable	100	200	100
Taxes payable	1,800	2,300	500
Bank loan payable (current)	1,500	1,500	-0-
	10,500	8,500	(2,000)
Working Capital	$15,475	$10,900	$ 4,575

in current assets increase working capital; decreases in current assets decrease working capital. The reverse is true, however, for current liabilities. Increases in current liabilities cause working capital to decrease; decreases in current liabilities cause working capital to increase. The logic of these relationships is based on the definition of working capital: W.C. = C.A. − C.L. A direct relationship exists between changes in current assets and changes in working capital. An inverse relationship exists between changes in current liabilities and changes in working capital.

Now that we have determined that during the 1980 fiscal year the working capital for Corner Drugstore increased by $4,575, our next step is to prepare a statement of changes in financial position for the purpose of explaining what caused the increase. The fundamental concept underlying the statement's preparation, although not particularly difficult, is somewhat elusive and requires considerable thought. The only way to determine what caused a change in a company's working capital position is to analyze the changes in all of the company's *nonworking capital accounts*. Nonworking capital accounts are all accounts *other than* the current assets and current liabilities. Changes in current accounts establish the *amount* and *direction* of a change in working capital. Changes in noncurrent accounts reveal the *reasons* for the change in working capital.

To analyze changes in a company's nonworking capital accounts means examining each such account to determine the specific cause of every increase or decrease recorded in the account throughout the reporting period. The specific reasons for changes in the noncurrent accounts must be identified, because *every transaction that causes a company's working capital position to change also causes the balance in one or more of a company's noncurrent accounts to change by an equal amount*. Therefore, a transaction must affect both a current and a noncurrent account to affect working capital. Transactions affecting only current accounts have *no* effect whatsoever on working capital. Similarly, transactions affecting only noncurrent accounts have *no* effect on working capital. Perhaps the best way to explain these ideas is to describe several different types of business transactions, to analyze them, and to test the results against the rationale just described.

Because an analysis of nonworking capital accounts entails identifying the specific causes of all significant increases or decreases in their balances, it is helpful to become familiar with some of the common transactions that affect the typical noncurrent accounts found on the balance sheets of most corporations. Some examples are as follows:

Nonworking Capital Account	Type of Account	Common Causes of Changes in the Account Balance
Machinery and Equipment	Asset	Acquistion Sale or disposal Depreciation
Long-Term Debt	Liability	Incur additional debt Repay debt Portion of long-term debt becomes current (due within the next year)
Capital Stock	Owners' Equity	Sell additional stock Purchase and retire existing stock
Retained Earnings	Owners' Equity	Net income or loss Dividends

We are now ready to examine all of Corner Drugstore's noncurrent accounts so that we can prepare its statement of changes in financial position. From the comparative balance sheet presented in Illustration 3-8, we can identify the noncurrent accounts as Store Equipment, the noncurrent portion of the Bank Loan Payable, Capital Stock, and Retained Earnings. Identifying the transactions affecting the balances in these four noncurrent accounts will provide us all the information needed to prepare the Corner Drugstore's statement of changes in financial position.

RECONSTRUCTION OF ACCOUNTS

The easiest way to identify the transactions affecting a company's noncurrent accounts is to gain access to the company's ledger and to observe the individual changes that occurred in these accounts during the period. Without such access, it is usually possible to reconstruct the activity in each noncurrent account by applying transaction analysis to the data provided by a company's comparative balance sheet and its combined statement of income and retained earnings.

We mentioned earlier in the chapter that, according to APB Opinion No. 19, the statement of changes in financial position should begin with the company's income. The net income figure must then be adjusted to eliminate the effects of any revenues or expenses that did not alter working capital. The logical place to start our reconstruction of accounts, then, is with an analysis of the retained earnings account. Illustration 4-2 was prepared solely from the data contained in Illustrations 3-8 and 3-9.

Because the difference between the left and right-side amounts in our reconstructed retained earnings account agrees with its 3-31-80 balance, we know that we have not omitted anything in our reconstruction. In other words, nothing affected retained earnings during the fiscal year other than net income and dividends, both of which

Illustration 4-2

Corner Drugstore, Inc.
Reconstruction of Retained Earnings Account
For the Fiscal Year Ended March 31, 1980

Retained Earnings

Dividends for the year	2,000	3-31-79 Balance	3,900
		Net income for the year	8,575
		3-31-80 Balance	10,475

Illustration 4-3

Corner Drugstore, Inc.
Reconstruction of Three Accounts
For the Fiscal Year Ended March 31, 1980

Store Equipment

3-31-79 Balance	9,000	Depreciation for the year	1,500
Plug	5,000		
3-31-80 Balance	12,500		

Bank Loan Payable (Noncurrent portion)

Plug	1,500	3-31-79 Balance	6,000
		3-31-80 Balance	4,500

Capital Stock

		3-31-79 Balance	10,000
		Plug	3,000
		3-31-80 Balance	13,000

are shown in our account reconstruction.

Once again using the financial information from Illustrations 3-8 and 3-9, we prepared a reconstruction of the other three noncurrent accounts of Corner Drugstore. The results are shown in Illustration 4-3.

Unlike the retained earnings account reconstruction, our reconstruction of the remaining three noncurrent accounts requires a "plug" figure to reach the 3-31-80 balances in the accounts. Each plug figure represents *one or more transactions* that occurred during the year and affected the account balance, the substance of which could *not* be obtained from the data presented in Illustrations 3-8 and 3-9. We must therefore apply some business logic.

The $5,000 plug figure in the store equipment account is a left-side entry, so we know that something occurred during the year to increase this account balance. We can conclude that the cost of equipment acquired exceeded the cost of the equipment disposed of by $5,000.

The $1,500 plug figure in the bank loan payable (noncurrent portion) account is also a left-side entry, but in this case it represents a transaction that reduced the long-term liability. This reduction can only be explained by a principal payment to the bank in the amount of $1,500 or by the reclassification of this amount from a noncurrent liability to a current liability.

In the case of the capital stock account, the $3,000 plug figure represents a transaction that caused this account balance to increase. The increase is explicable only by the issuance of additional capital stock in the amount of $3,000.

A SINGLE YEAR'S STATEMENT ILLUSTRATED

We can now prepare a statement of changes in financial position for Corner Drugstore for its 1980 fiscal year. Illustration 4-4 contains this statement prepared in accordance with the requirements set forth in APB Opinion No. 19.

The most difficult process to understand in Illustration 4-4 is undoubtedly the addition of depreciation to net income to reach the amount of working capital provided by operations. The net income figure of $8,575 represents the excess of Corner Drugstore's revenues over its expenses for the 1980 fiscal year. This amount is treated as a source of working capital because almost all revenues cause working capital to increase (through the receipt of cash or accounts receivable), and almost all expenses cause working capital to decrease (through the payment of cash or incurrence of a current liability).

If a company earns a revenue that does not increase working capital or incurs expenses that do not decrease working capital, the net income figure in the income statement does not represent the net change in working capital resulting from operations. To determine the true change, we must deduct from the net income figure any "nonworking capital" revenues, and add to it any "nonworking capital" expenses. Corner Drugstore had no such revenues and only one such expense—depreciation. When the drugstore recorded its depreciation expense of $1,500 for fiscal 1980, the two accounts affected were Store Equipment and Retained Earnings. Because neither of these is a current account, working capital was unaffected. Thus, depreciation represents a "nonworking capital" expense that must be added back

Illustration 4-4

Corner Drugstore, Inc.
Statement of Changes in Financial Position
For the Fiscal Year Ended March 31, 1980

Sources of Working Capital:

Net income	$ 8,575	
Add: Depreciation	1,500	
Working capital provided from operations	10,075	
Other sources of working capital:		
Issuance of capital stock	3,000	
Total sources of working capital		$13,075

Uses of Working Capital:

Payment of bank loan installment	1,500	
Purchase of store equipment (in excess		
of dispositions)	5,000	
Payment of dividends	2,000	
Total uses of working capital		8,500
Increase in working capital		$ 4,575

Schedule of working capital changes:

	Balance 3-31-80	Balance 3-31-79	Working Capital Incr. or (Decr.)
Current Assets:			
Cash	575	2,500	(1,925)
Accounts receivable	7,400	4,200	3,200
Merchandise inventory	18,000	12,700	5,300
	25,975	19,400	6,575
Current Liabilities:			
Accounts payable	6,200	3,800	(2,400)
Wages payable	900	700	(200)
Utilities payable	100	200	100
Taxes payable	1,800	2,300	500
Bank loan payable (current)	1,500	1,500	-0-
	10,500	8,500	(2,000)
Working Capital	$15,475	$10,900	$ 4,575

to net income to arrive at the amount of *working capital* actually
provided from operations.

A COMPARATIVE STATEMENT ILLUSTRATED

Companies customarily publish comparative statements of changes
in financial position. A comparative statement for Corner Drugstore

for its 1979 and 1980 fiscal years is presented in Illustration 4-5.

The only new item introduced by the fiscal 1979 statement of changes in financial position is the $7,500 source of working capital from the long-term bank loan. Because we know from previous chapters that the amount of the loan was $9,000, it may seem strange that working capital increased by only $7,500. The reason for this discrepancy lies in the terms of the loan. The loan agreement required

---

Illustration 4-5

Corner Drugstore, Inc.
Statement of Changes in Financial Position
For the Fiscal Years Ended March 31, 1980 and March 31, 1979

	1980	1979
Sources of Working Capital:		
Net income	$ 8,575	$ 5,400
Add: Depreciation	1,500	1,000
Working capital provided from operations	10,075	6,400
Other sources of working capital:		
Issuance of capital stock	3,000	10,000
Proceeds from bank loan		7,500
Total sources of working capital	$13,075	$23,900
Uses of Working Capital:		
Purchase of store equipment (in excess of dispositions)	5,000	10,000
Payment of dividends	2,000	1,500
Payment of bank loan installment	1,500	1,500
Total uses of working capital	8,500	13,000
Increase in working capital	$ 4,575	$10,900

Schedule of working capital changes:	Balance 3-31-80	Balance 3-31-79	Balance 3-31-78	1980 Working Capital Incr. or (Decr.)	1979 Working Capital Incr. or (Decr.)
Current Assets:					
Cash	$ 575	$ 2,500	-0-	$(1,925)	$ 2,500
Accounts receivable	7,400	4,200	-0-	3,200	4,200
Merchandise inventory	18,000	12,700	-0-	5,300	12,700
	25,975	19,400	-0-	6,575	19,400
Current Liabilities:					
Accounts payable	6,200	3,800	-0-	(2,400)	(3,800)
Wages payable	900	700	-0-	(200)	(700)
Utilities payable	100	200	-0-	100	(200)
Taxes payable	1,800	2,300	-0-	500	(2,300)
Bank loan payable (current)	1,500	1,500	-0-	-0-	(1,500)
	$10,500	$ 8,500	-0-	(2,000)	(8,500)
Change in Working Capital				$ 4,575	$10,900

that repayment be made in six installments beginning on March 31, 1979. The $1,500 amount of the principal repayment due in 1979 represented a *current* liability at the time the loan was granted. Therefore, the $9,000 cash received from the bank gave rise to a corresponding long-term liability of $7,500 and a current liability of $1,500. The net result was an increase in working capital (net current assets) of $9,000 minus $1,500, or $7,500.

LIMITATIONS OF EXTERNAL FINANCIAL STATEMENTS

Having discussed and illustrated all of the basic financial statements presented annually to external users, it is useful to indicate the limitations of such financial reports and to illustrate these limitations by referring to Corner Drugstore's statements.

1. The statements reflect only those transactions that have been accorded accounting recognition.

   According to generally accepted accounting principles, transactions given accounting recognition *exclude* sales backlogs, authorized future expenditures, contracts signed but not yet executed, accumulated customer goodwill, and the potential value of research discoveries. External financial reports, therefore, do not reflect such transactions.

2. Preparation of the statements requires estimation and judgment.

   To prepare the statements for the Corner Drugstore, *management* had to make estimates and judgments concerning:
   • How much of the cost of store equipment should be allocated as an expense of doing business for the year.
   • What unit costs should be used in determining the cost of the inventory, and what items of merchandise, if any, should be considered obsolete and eliminated from inventory.
   • What federal and state income tax expenses were incurred by the store on the year's operations.
   Conventional accounting statements are beguiling in their illusion of mathematical precision, as their preparation requires considerable estimation and judgment.

3. The statements are prepared on the assumption that the business will continue to operate indefinitely.

Accordingly, because Corner Drugstore planned to use its store equipment rather than to sell it, the current market value of its store equipment is ignored in the company's external financial statements.

4. The accounting for assets is based upon acquisition cost rather than upon replacement cost.

Store equipment is shown on the drugstore's balance sheet at cost of acquisition, less the portion of that cost previously allocated to expense. Inventory also is shown by the Corner Drugstore at acqustion cost, although inventory is sometimes reduced to current replacement cost for the sake of conservatism (see No. 5).

5. The statements are prepared conservatively.

For example, inventories are shown on the balance sheet at the "lower of cost or market," where "market" is defined as "current replacement cost." This departure from the acquisition cost policy is deemed justified by the principle of conservatism. This principle holds: "Provide for all foreseeable losses, but do not recognize gain until it is realized by sale."

6. The statements ignore changes in the dollar's purchasing power.

Corner Drugstore's investment in store equipment represented equipment acquired in different years with dollars of different purchasing power. At present, the accounting profession assumes that "dollars are dollars are dollars" and that they can be added together regardless of their vintage and their varying purchasing powers. When a portion of the "mixed vintage" investment in store equipment is allocated as depreciation expense of a given year, the depreciation expense is also expressed in dollars of mixed vintage and varying purchasing powers.

7. Companies may select from among several generally accepted accounting principles with respect to certain items contained in the financial statements.

Although companies are required to apply their accounting principles on a consistent basis from year to year, different companies are free to choose different generally accepted accounting principles. Two common examples pertain to inventory valuation and depreciation. When making comparisons among companies, external users must understand the accounting principles upon which each company's financial statements were based. To do so requires users to read the "notes to the financial statements" carefully.

Corner Drugstore's financial statements have limitations. They are not as precise as they appear to be. The balance sheet does not express current market values. The owners' equity section of the balance sheet does not express the current market value of the owners' interests. The statement of income is expressed in more current dollars than is the balance sheet, but at least one of its expense deductions, depreciation, is expressed in dollars of mixed vintage. Many matters affecting the financial condition of the enterprise are not shown in the conventional accounting statements. Yet, despite their limitations, these statements are the accepted means for reporting to outsiders a corporation's financial activities and positions. Accordingly, their limitations must be fully recognized.

SUMMARY

Commencing in 1971, corporate external reports are required to include a statement of changes in financial position whenever financial statements purporting to present both financial position (balance sheet) and results of operations (statement of income and retained earnings) are issued. Although this newly required statement may be prepared to disclose either changes in cash or changes in working capital, most companies seem to choose the working capital approach. The major objective of the statement is to show what caused a change in a company's cash or in its working capital. As with the other required financial statements, the statement of changes in financial position has its limitations, and these limitations must be kept in mind when using the data contained therein.

QUESTIONS AND PROBLEMS

1. What can be learned from a company's statement of changes in the financial position?

2. Describe the content of a schedule of working capital changes. How does a schedule of working capital changes relate to a statement of changes in a financial position?

3. Is a funds statement the same thing as a statement of changes in the financial position?

4. What does the term "working capital" mean? Do companies have any "nonworking capital"? Explain.

5. List several major sources and several major uses of working capital.

6. If a company reported a net income for its most recent fiscal year, would you expect its working capital to have increased or decreased during the year? Explain.

7. Is it possible for a company's cash balance to increase during the same period that its working capital position decreases? Explain.

8. Why is a company's working capital position important? What problems might a company encounter that are working capital-related?

9. Are increases in working capital good or bad? What about decreases in working capital? Explain.

10. Can a company have too much working capital? Explain.

11. Why does a statement of changes in financial position begin with net income for the year? Why is depreciation expense added back to the net income figure? Is depreciation a source of working capital? Is it a source of cash?

12. A company purchased a $50,000 machine, paying $25,000 in cash and signing a 10%, two year note for the balance. How was the company's working capital position affected by the purchase?

13. Indicate the effect that each of the following transactions has on (1) working capital, and (2) cash:

   (a) Purchased $15,000 of merchandise on account. Payment to be made within 30 days.
   (b) Sold merchandise costing $500 for $700 cash.
   (c) Borrowed $75,000 cash, issuing a 90-day, 12% note.
   (d) Collected a $150 account receivable.
   (e) Purchased equipment for $10,000 cash.
   (f) Sold 1,000 shares of common stock at a price of $10/share.
   (g) Sold for $4,000 a long-term investment that had cost $5,000.
   (h) Paid cash dividends of $2,000.
   (i) Borrowed $100,000, issuing a 5-year, 10% note.
   (j) Paid a $1,200 account payable.

14. The following information was taken from the books of a small business:

Assets:	12/31/80	12/31/79	Increase (Decr.)
Cash	$ 10	$ 24	$(14)
Accounts Receivable	16	12	4
Inventory	21	16	5
Office Equipment (net)	33	36	(3)
Total Assets	$ 80	$ 88	$(8)

Liabilities and Stockholders' Equity:

Accounts Payable	$ 4	$ 26	$(22)
Wages Payable	6	19	(13)
Long-Term Notes Payable	12	10	2
Capital Stock	26	20	6
Retained Earnings	32	13	19
Total Liabilities and Stockholders' Equity	$ 80	$ 88	$(8)

Additional information for 1980:

1. Depreciation on office equipment was $7.
2. Cash dividends of $4 were declared and paid.

Required: Prepare a schedule of working capital changes and a statement of changes in financial position to explain the net increase or the net decrease in working capital.

15. The following information pertains to a corporation's fiscal year ended December 31, 1980:

Assets:	12/31/80	12/31/79	Increase (Decrease)
Cash	$ 20	$ 62	$(42)
Accounts Receivable	32	24	8
Inventory	42	32	10
Office Equipment (net)	66	58	8
Total Assets	$160	$176	$(16)
Liabilities & Stockholders' Equity:			
Accounts Payable	$ 8	$ 52	$(44)
Wages Payable	12	38	(26)
Long-Term Debt	24	28	(4)
Capital Stock	52	40	12
Retained Earnings	64	18	46
Total Liabilities and Stockholders' Equity	$160	$176	$(16)

During the year 1980:

1. Office equipment costing $18 with a book value of $4 was sold at a $2 gain.
2. Additional office equipment costing $19 was acquired for cash.
3. Cash dividends of $8 were paid.
4. Long-term debt of $4 was paid-off prior to maturity.

Required: Prepare a statement of changes in financial position for the year 1980.

16. The following information was taken from the books of the Waters Company:

The Waters Company
Comparative Balance Sheet
December 31, 1980 and 1979

	1980	1979	Increase (Decrease)
Assets:			
Cash	$ 16,000	$ 2,000	$ 14,000
Accounts Receivable	15,000	14,000	1,000
Inventory	8,000	18,000	(10,000)
Equipment (net)	100,000	81,000	19,000
Total Assets	$139,000	$115,000	$ 24,000
Liabilities and Stockholders' Equity			
Accounts Payable	$ 6,000	$ 8,000	$ (2,000)
Accrued Expenses Payable	5,000	2,000	3,000
Long-Term Debt (Due 1985)	16,000	15,000	1,000
Capital Stock	40,000	15,000	25,000
Retained Earnings	72,000	75,000	(3,000)
Total Liabilities and Stockholders' Equity	$139,000	$115,000	$ 24,000

Additional information:

1. Net income for 1980 was $13,000.
2. Depreciation for 1980 was $9,000.
3. Equipment costing $17,000 that had a book value of $11,000 was sold for $9,000.

Required: (a) Compute the amount of working capital at December 31, 1980.

(b) Did working capital increase or decrease during 1980? By what amount?

(c) Prepare a statement of changes in financial position for 1980.

17. Prepare a statement of changes in financial position for 1980 based on the following data:

	Dec. 31	
	1980	1979
Assets:		
Cash	$150	$200
Marketable Securities	50	25
Accounts Receivable	285	250
Inventory	250	200
Prepaid Expenses	75	100
Machinery and Equipment (net)	140	125
Total	$950	$900

Liabilities and Owners' Equity:

Accounts Payable	$125	$175
Salaries Payable	30	25
Accrued Interest Payable	40	25
Income Taxes Payable	25	25
Long-Term Debt (Due 1990)	125	100
Capital Stock	480	450
Retained Earnings	125	100
Total	$950	$900

Additional information:

1. No machinery and equipment was sold or written-off, but $30 of new equipment was purchased.
2. Net income for 1980 was $75.
3. Dividends of $50 were declared and paid in cash.

18. On the basis of the following data for Hess Company, prepare a statement of changes in financial position. Assume that (1) no items of equipment were disposed of during the year; (2) the capital stock was issued for cash; (3) that the only entries in the retained earnings account were for the net income of $40,000 and cash dividends declared and paid of $25,000; and (4) depreciation for the year was $9,000.

	June 30	
	1981	1980
Assets:		
Cash	$ 45,000	$ 30,000
Accounts Receivable	60,000	50,000
Inventory	81,000	60,000
Equipment (net)	100,000	78,000
Land	45,000	30,000
Total	$331,000	$248,000
Equities:		
Accounts Payable	$ 60,000	$ 52,000
Capital Stock	210,000	150,000
Retained Earnings	61,000	46,000
Total	$331,000	$248,000

19. Using the following data, prepare a statement of changes in financial position for the Patton Corporation for 1980:

Patton Corporation
Summary of Balance Sheet Changes
From December 31, 1979 to December 31, 1980

	Increase	Decrease
Assets:		
Cash	$ 20,220	
Temporary investments		$ 5,000
Notes receivable (short-term)	3,000	
Accounts receivable	12,000	
Inventories	1,900	
Prepayments		900
Property, Plant, and Equipment:		
Land	–	–
Buildings and equipment (cost)	15,000	
Deduct: Increase in accumulated		
depreciation	3,800	
Liabilities & Owners' Equity:		
Notes payable (short-term)		6,200
Accounts payable		9,000
Taxes payable	1,000	
Long-term liabilities:		
Notes payable	21,000	
Stockholders' Equity:		
Capital stock	25,000	
Retained earnings	10,620	
	$112,540	$21,100

Additional information:

1. Cash dividends of $12,000 were declared and paid during 1980.
2. Equipment which had cost $2,000 was sold during 1980 for an amount equal to its book value of $1,000.

5

Cash, Cash Equivalent, and Cash Flow

In this chapter we consider the accounting, report-ing, and management of cash on hand, cash in bank, and cash temporarily invested in short-term debt securities. We explain the statement of cash receipts and disbursements and the cash flow statement— statements that can be used to summarize changes in cash for the past or to forecast them for the fu-ture. The chapter opens with a brief look at the relationship among cash, receivables, inventories, plant and equipment, and long-term investments— the five kinds of assets to be discussed, successive-ly, in the chapters to follow.

The funds invested in a business by creditors and stockholders are invested by its management in five types of assets:

1. Cash and cash equivalent
2. Trade receivables
3. Inventories
4. Property, plant, and equipment
5. Long-term investments and other assets.

In a trading company, such as Corner Drugstore, daily transactions cause a continual shifting among cash, receivables, and inventory. In a manufacturing company, daily transactions cause a more complex pattern of changes among cash, receivables, inventories (in various stages of manufacture), and plant, property, and equipment.

CHANGES IN ASSETS: A TRADING COMPANY

For a trading company, the typical sequence of changes in assets is shown graphically in Illustration 5-1. Note these changes:

1. From cash to merchandise inventory when the company buys merchandise for sale.
2. From merchandise inventory to receivables when the company sells merchandise to customers on account.
3. From receivables to cash when the company collects customer accounts.

When Corner Drugstore (Chapter 3) purchased merchandise on account, a lapse of time occurred between the receipt of the merchandise and the outgo of cash to the suppliers. Ultimately, however, the change was from cash to merchandise. When the drugstore made sales for cash rather than on credit, the change was direct from merchandise to cash—rather than from merchandise to receivables to cash. The typical operating cycle, however, is from cash to merchandise to receivables and back to cash.

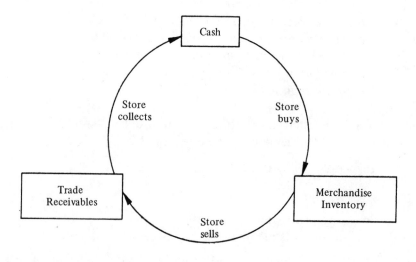

Illustration 5-1. Typical sequence of changes in assets for a trading company.

CHANGES IN ASSETS: A MANUFACTURING COMPANY

For a manufacturing company, goods to be sold are manufactured rather than purchased, and the typical sequence of changes among assets is much more complex than that for a trading company. Note, in Illustration 5-2, these changes:

1. From (a) cash to materials when the company buys materials (including purchased parts) and (b) materials to finished goods when the company uses materials to produce finished goods.
2. From cash to finished goods when the company pays for factory labor to convert materials into finished goods.
3. From cash to finished goods when the company pays for such factory costs as heat, light, power, building and equipment repairs, property taxes and insurance used in the conversion of materials into finished goods.
4. From (a) cash to property, plant, and equipment when the company acquires factory buildings, and (b) property, plant, and equipment to finished goods when the company periodically allocates part of its investment in factory buildings and equipment to the cost of producing finished goods.
5. From finished goods to receivables when the company sells finished goods to customers on account.
6. From receivables to cash when the company collects customer accounts.

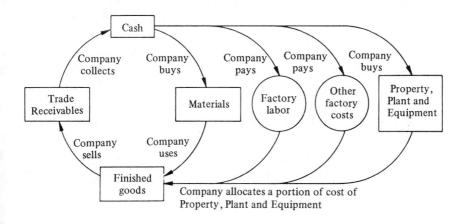

Illustration 5-2. Typical sequence of changes in assets for a manufacturing company.

A Note on Cost Accounting Practice

In the physical process of production, the usual progression is from materials to work-in-process to finished goods. In cost accounting, an account is usually set up for work-in-process. All factory costs of production are accumulated in this account before transfer to the finished goods account. In Illustration 5-2, we did not show work-in-process because for our present purposes it was simpler to omit it.

MANAGING CHANGES IN ASSETS

The job of management is to manage the changes in assets to accomplish the company's objectives. Management may set as the company's objectives:

1. To earn a satisfactory return on investment in assets.
2. To accommodate the business to seasonal, cyclical, growth, and random changes.
3. To aim for a pattern of investment in assets consistent with the sources of funds used to finance the business.
4. To assure continuity of the enterprise.
5. To assure continuity of management.

The relative weight given to each of these objectives will govern management in the patterns of asset investment it plans for the business. For example, if earning a satisfactory return on investment in assets is the controlling objective, managers will plan the minimum investment in each type of asset that will bring the highest rate of return. Our corner druggist will begin by asking himself why he should have more than a "zero" investment in cash, receivables, inventories, or equipment. He would maintain only the minimum cash required to operate the store. He would weigh any additional investment in receivables and inventories against the additional net income to be realized. For equipment, he would weigh the additional cost of short-term leasing against the additional investment required for acquisition by purchase.

If management needs to give more weight to accommodating the business to seasonal changes, the company may resort to seasonal borrowing for peak needs. Such borrowing may require that the company maintain "compensating" bank balances. Thus the source of financing would affect the pattern of asset investment. The more our corner druggist resorts to bank credit, the larger the related bank balance he will have to maintain.

If more weight is given to assuring continuity of present management or continuity of the enterprise, management may seek to finance the business more with equity capital than with debt. If, for example, our corner druggist wishes to forego borrowing from the bank, he will have to provide a buffer of cash to accommodate the store's operations to seasonal and cyclical fluctuations.

This brief discussion is illustrative rather than comprehensive. It is enough at this point for us to be aware of the effect of management objectives upon the pattern of asset investment and to be wary of looking for a standard pattern for all kinds of businesses.

CURRENT ASSETS, THE OPERATING CYCLE, AND THE CURRENT RATIO

In the glossary at the end of this book, we define *current assets* as cash and other assets that normally will be converted into cash or utilized within a year (or within the operating cycle of the particular business entity if this is longer than a year). We can now define the *operating cycle* as the average time period between the purchase of merchandise (or materials) and the collection of cash from customers after the merchandise (or manufactured product) has been sold. The operating cycle is indicated graphically in Illustrations 5-1 and 5-2. The *current ratio* is a comparison between the company's investment in current assets and the funds supplied by short-term creditors, shown as current liabilities. In Illustration 4-1, the Corner Drugstore at March 31, 1979, had current assets of $19,400 and current liabilities of $8,500, so its current ratio was $19,400 to $8,500, or 2.3 to 1; at March 31, 1980, the ratio was $25,975 to $10,500, or 2.5 to 1.

THE NATURE OF CASH AND CASH EQUIVALENT

Cash and cash equivalent consist of cash on hand, cash in bank, and marketable securities representing a temporary investment of cash.

Cash on hand may be in the form of special cash funds for operating purposes, such as change funds maintained by retail stores, or cash collections (currency, coins, and checks), received from customers and others, on hand awaiting deposit in bank.

Cash in bank represents the balances on deposit with banks. The bank may not record deposit and check transactions on the same date that the company records them. Thus, the balance shown by the company's books usually differs from that shown by the bank's, although the two are reconcilable. On the company's balance sheet, cash in bank is stated at the balance shown on the company's books, not the bank's.

Marketable securities, representing a temporary investment of cash, are usually in the form of readily salable short-maturity fixed obligations on which the company earns interest.

CASH MANAGEMENT AND COMPENSATING BALANCES

The company maintains its investment in cash in bank for one or more of the following reasons:

1. To cover the amount of customer checks in process of collection.
2. To provide a margin or "safety-valve" against possible errors in cash forecasting.
3. To assure freedom from the necessity of borrowing from the bank.
4. To meet the bank's requirement for a *compensating balance* (a) against the bank's loan(s) or line of credit extended to the business and (b) to "pay" the bank for servicing the checking account and for other bank services.

Let's discuss each of these reasons.

The company maintains a balance at least equal to the amount of customer checks in process of collection. When our corner drugstore deposited its customers' checks in the bank, the bank undertook to collect them through the check collection facilities of the banking system. The period needed to collect checks deposited varies according to the location of the banks upon which they are drawn. Customer checks drawn on the bank in which they are deposited are "collected" the same day that they are deposited, those drawn on other local banks may be collected the day following deposit; while those drawn on out-of-town banks may take two, three, or even four days to collect.

Despite the lag in collecting deposited checks, normal banking practice is to credit the depositor's account in full the day that the checks are deposited. In the case of Corner Drugstore and its bank, neither the store's nor the bank's books showed that a part of the store's recorded balance represented checks in the process of collection. But both the store and the bank operated on the basis that the recorded balance would be sufficient to cover the amount of customer checks in process of collection.

The bank balance is maintained to provide against errors in cash forecasting. Ideally, if the Corner Drugstore could forecast its cash receipts and disbursements exactly, it could keep its investment in cash in bank to a minimum. The less precisely it can forecast, the larger the safety valve or buffer it must maintain in the form of cash in bank.

The company may maintain a bank balance sufficient to avoid borrowing from the bank. The objective of some companies may be to "keep out of the bank," that is, to avoid borrowing from the bank. To avoid borrowing, these companies must have cash in excess of needs in periods of seasonal and cyclical slack. When a company uses its cash balance as a buffer for seasonal and cyclical fluctuations, its return on investment in assets is usually lower than if it borrowed for peak needs. Companies may, however, have valid reasons for maintaining buffer cash balances and for refusing to borrow, despite the lowered return on investment.

The bank balance is maintained (a) to meet the bank's requirements for a compensating balance against loans or line of credit, and (b) to cover cost of bank services. When a company opens a bank account, the bank will usually acquaint the company's officers with the bank's requirements for a compensating balance sufficiently large to meet the compensating balance requirement against loan(s) or line of credit extended and to cover the cost of bank services.

When a company negotiates an agreement with its bank for a *line of credit*—the bank's agreement to lend the company funds up to an agreed amount during, say, the next calendar year—the bank may require that the company maintain a *collected balance* of 10 percent of the line of credit, or 20 percent of the loans actually made. From time to time, the bank will calculate the *collected balance* of each business customer in the following manner:

Average daily book balance for the month.	$10,000
(This balance is computed by adding together the balance for each day in the month as shown on the bank's account for the customer and by dividing the total by the number of days in the month.)	
Deducting average daily "float" for the month	400
(The bank determines for each check deposited the number of days required to collect the check, multiplies dollars by days, sums for the month, and then divides by number of days in the month.)	
Average daily collected balance for the month	$ 9,600

Disclosure of compensating balance requirements is required by the Securities and Exchange Commission. Dan River, Inc., made the following disclosure in its annual report for 1978:

Compensating Balances—Informal lines of credit agreements with several banks require the company to maintain average cash compensating balances principally equal to 20 percent of the average outstanding short-term bank loans or 10 percent of the amount of the credit line, whichever is higher. . . . In 1978 the average compensating balance required to be maintained amounted to $4,354,000 and the amount required at December 30, 1978 was $4,008,000 after adjustment for estimated average float.

CASH IN BANK: CHECKS AND DEPOSITS

Conventional accounting for cash in bank is not complex. Deposits are recorded as increases, checks as decreases, in the Cash in Bank account.

The time for accounting recognition of a check is the date the company issues the check. This brings the check immediately under accounting control. If the company draws a check to an out-of-town supplier on August 27, the check is recorded as of that date, even though several days may elapse before the check gets to, and is paid by, the company's bank. When a company issues a check in payment of a bill to an out-of-town supplier, time elapses (1) in the transmission of the check to the supplier, (2) in the supplier's recording and depositing the check, and (3) in the transmission of the check through the banking system from the supplier's bank to the company's bank. A study by one company indicated that the average time lapse between the dates checks were drawn and the dates they were ultimately paid by the company's bank was eight days for checks drawn to out-of-town suppliers and three days for checks drawn to employees (for weekly wages).

The time lags that exist between the company's records and the bank's records explain why the daily balances shown in the company's cash in bank account may differ considerably from the "average collected balance" used by the bank in its analysis of the company's account for service charges and for compensating balance requirements against borrowings. Furthermore, whenever the company receives a bank statement, usually at a month-end, it should prove its accounting record of cash in bank with the bank's record by preparing a reconciliation of the bank account.

Bank Reconciliation

To prepare a reconciliation of the bank account as of the month-end, the company compares the checks it receives from the bank against its check disbursement record and prepares a list of outstanding checks. It then compares the deposits shown on the bank statement with those in the company's records, and notes any deposits not on the bank statement, or vice versa. Notes are made of any special bank "Debit Memos" or "Credit Memos" that have not been recorded by the company. One form of bank reconciliation, Illustration 5-3, is in two parts. The first begins with the month-end balance shown by the bank statement and works to an *adjusted balance*. The second part begins with the month-end balance shown by the cash in bank account in the company's ledger and works to an adjusted balance. The adjusted balance should be the same in both parts.

Note, in Illustration 5-3, that the second part of the reconciliation provides the data for entries to be made for any bank Debit Memos or Credit Memos not previously recorded by the company, and for correction of any company errors discovered in the reconciliation. The second part of Illustration 5-3 shows the following entries to be in order:

Cash in Bank (A)	Incr 234.00	
Notes Receivable (A)		Decr 225.00
Accounts Payable (L)		Incr 9.00
Trade Receivables (A)	Incr 63.27	
Cash in Bank (A)		Decr 63.27

CASH AND CASH EQUIVALENT ON THE BALANCE SHEET

Balance sheet treatment of cash and cash equivalent raises two questions. First, at what value should the items comprising cash and

---

Illustration 5-3

Two-Part Form for Reconciliation of Bank Account

Bank's Records

Balance at month-end, per bank statement		$3,481.93
Add:		
Deposits in transit at month-end (per list)	$688.05	
Bank error in charging our account with check		
drawn by another company	85.00	773.05
		$4,254.98
Deduct:		
Checks outstanding at month-end (per list)		1,882.70
Adjusted Balance at month-end		$2,372.28

Our Records

Balance at month-end, per our records		$2,201.55
Add:		
Bank Credit Memo for collection of customer note		
not yet recorded by us		225.00
Error on our check #1465 drawn for $123.00 but		
recorded by us as $132.00		9.00
		$2,435.55
Deduct:		
Bank Debit Memo for check of our customer, J. A. Best,		
returned for "Insufficient Funds," not yet entered on		
our records.		63.27
Adjusted Balance at month-end		$2,372.28

---

cash equivalent be shown? Second, under what classification should the items be shown?

Valuation

Cash on hand and cash in bank are shown at realizable value. For cash on hand, the realizable value is the amount of the change fund, petty cash fund, cash on hand awaiting deposit, etc. For cash in bank, realizable value is the amount of the adjusted balance shown on the reconciliation of the bank account at the balance sheet date.

Marketable securities representing a temporary investment of cash in the form of readily salable short-maturity debt instruments are carried at cost, if cost is less than market value at the balance sheet date. (In such cases, market value may be disclosed parenthetically.) When market value is substantially less than cost, this difference should be disclosed, and in such case the securities should be shown at market. If cost is slightly less than market, the securities may continue to be shown at cost with disclosure of the market value.

Classification

Cash on hand and cash in bank available for current operations are usually shown simply as Cash in the current asset section of the balance sheet. Cash not available for current operations is not shown in the current asset section.

The *Restatement and Revision of Accounting Research Bulletins*, issued in 1953 by the American Institute of Certified Public Accountants (Chapter 3), discusses the nature of current assets and indicates that there should be *excluded* from current assets "cash and claims to cash which are restricted as to withdrawal or use for other than current operation, are designated for expenditure in the acquisition or construction of noncurrent assets, or are segregated for the liquidation of long-term debts." Such assets should be shown elsewhere on the balance sheet.

Cash advances to suppliers and others, and cash deposits for specific purposes (insurance, public utilities, etc.) are not shown as Cash. Such advances and deposits are classified sometimes as current assets, sometimes as noncurrent.

Marketable securities in the form of short-term fixed obligations and representing an investment of temporarily unneeded cash, are sometimes combined with cash and shown as Cash and Cash Equivalent under current assets. Normally, marketable equity securities are not considered as cash equivalent. In those cases when marketable equity securities are included in current assets, FASB statement No. 12 requires (1) that they be carried at the lower of aggregate cost or market value and (2) that the aggregate cost and aggregate market value be disclosed.

Marketable securities, either equity or fixed-obligation, bought for purposes other than temporary investment of unneeded cash, are generally shown under long-term investments in the noncurrent section of the balance sheet. (See Chapter 11.)

STATEMENT OF CASH RECEIPTS AND DISBURSEMENTS

At the end of an accounting period a statement of cash receipts and disbursements can be prepared. This statement is based upon a summary of the transactions recorded in the cash account in the company's ledger.

A summary of the Corner Drugstore's cash account for the fiscal year 1979 is reproduced in Illustration 5-4.

Illustration 5-4

Corner Drugstore's Ledger Account for Cash for Fiscal 1979
(Source: Illustration 3-4)

Cash (A)

4-1-78 Balance	-0-	(E) Pd. for store eq.	10,000
(A) From capital stock	10,000	(H) Cash sales returned	500
(D) Bank loan payable	9,000	(J) Pd. mdse. suppliers	53,600
(F) Cash sales	30,300	(K) Paid rent	3,600
(I) Collections of receiv.	40,500	(L) Paid employees	14,600
		(M) Paid for utilities	450
		(N) Pd. est. income tax	600
		(O) Pd. other expenses	500
		(P) Pd. on bank loan—On principal $15,000, Interest $450	1,950
		(S) Paid dividends	1,500
		3-31-79 To balance	2,500
	89,800		89,800
3-31-79 Balance	2,500		

A simple form of cash receipts and disbursements for the drug-store would show:

Cash balance at beginning of fiscal year (4/1/78)	$	0
Add: Cash receipts during the year (In order summarized in Illustration 5-4.)		89,800
		89,800
Deduct: Cash disbursements during the year (In order summaraized in Illustration 5-4.)		87,300
Cash balance at the end of fiscal year (3/31/79)	$	2,500

In Illustration 5-5, we have presented the same information in a more orderly format.

The format used in Illustration 5-5 permits a ready conversion to a "cash flow statement" that shows:

1. "Cash internally generated" from transactions associated with purchasing, selling, and collecting.

Illustration 5-5

Corner Drugstore, Inc.
Statement of Cash Receipts and Disbursements
For the Year Ended March 31, 1979

Cash Receipts:

Cash sales (less $500 paid for cash sales returned)		$29,800
Collections on customer accounts.		40,500
Cash received from customers.		70,300
Proceeds from issue of capital stock		10,000
Borrowing from bank.		9,000
Total Cash Receipts.		89,300

Less Cash Disbursements:

For payments on supplier accounts.	$53,600	
For payments to employees	14,600	
For rent, utilities and other expenses.	4,550	
For payments of interest on bank loan.	450	
For payments on estimated income taxes	600	
Sub-total	73,800	
For acquisition of store equipment	10,000	
For dividends to stockholders.	1,500	
For reduction in principal of bank loan	1,500	
Total Cash Disbursements		86,800
Net increase in cash account in fiscal 1979		2,500
Add: Cash balance, April 1, 1978.		-0-
Cash balance, March 31, 1979.		$ 2,500

---

2. Cash outflow for

    Acquisition of property, plant, and equipment (in excess
    of any dispositions).
    Dividends to stockholders.

3. Financing and other cash inflows and outflows.

Converting Illustration 5-5, we arrive at the following "cash flow"
summary for the Corner Drugstore:

1. Cash received from customers, *$70,300*, was less than cash paid out to
    suppliers and employees and cash paid for store expenses, interest, and
    income tax, (*$73,800*).
    Thus "cash internally generated" was a *minus*. . . . . ($ 3,500)

2. Payments for acquisition of store equipment, (*$10,000*),
    and for dividends to stockholders, (*$1,500*),
    amounted to. . . . . (11,500)

3. Cash received from financing transactions:
    From issue of capital stock $10,000
    From net increase in bank loan   7,500
          A total of.   17,500

    So the increase the store's cash balance from *zero* at 4/1/79
    to *$2,500* at 3/31/80 was · $ 2,500

(Note that for the purposes of the above summary we have shown uses of cash
enclosed in parentheses, sources without parentheses.)

The cash receipts and disbursements statement is prepared for internal use only, primarily for cash management and cash forecasting.
The *form* of the statement serves as one model for cash forecasting.
Cash forecasting begins with a forecast of sales, from which forecasts of cash sales and collections on account can be made. The forecast of sales volume aids in forecasting cash outlays for operating
expenses and income tax payments. All these items combined go to
make up what we have termed "cash internally generated." There
then remain the tasks of forecasting cash dividends to stockholders,
cash outlays for property, plant, and equipment, cash receipts from
borrowing and issue of capital stock, and cash payments on debt
principal.

CASH FLOW STATEMENT

A cash flow statement, developed from a published statement of changes in financial position, can give substantially the same information as the statement of cash receipts and disbursements prepared for internal use from the cash account in the ledger.

As indicated in Chapter 4, the statement of changes in financial position "may be prepared so as to disclose either changes in working capital or changes in cash." If the statement uses the working capital format, our first task is to analyze the schedule of working capital changes to determine, within this schedule, which items represent Uses of cash and which represent Sources of cash, according to the following scheme:

Uses	Sources
Increase in a current asset	Decrease in a current asset
Decrease in a current liability	Increase in a current liability

Apply this analysis to the statement of changes in financial position for Corner Drugstore for fiscal 1979, shown in Illustration 4-5.

From Illustration 4-5

1979

	Working Capital Incr. or (Decr.)	Use or Source	Why Use or Source
Current Assets:			
Cash	$ 2,500	Use	Incr. in current asset
Trade receivables	4,200	Use	Incr. in current asset
Merchandise inventory	12,700	Use	Incr. in current asset
Current Liabilities:			
Accounts, wages, and utilities payable	(4,700)	Source	Incr. in current liab.
Income tax payable	(2,300)	Source	Incr. in current liab.
Bank loan (current)	(1,500)	Source	Incr. in current liab.
Increase in Working Capital	$10,900		

The next step, in converting the published statement of changes in financial position to the cash flow statement format is to group the various Sources and Uses into four categories:

1. Net Income Adjusted (NIA)—that is, net income (after income tax) before deduction of noncash expenses and before addition of noncash revenue.

    In Illustration 4-5, the NIA figure is $6,400 — net income, $5,400, plus noncash expense for depreciation, $1,000.

2. Changes in receivables, inventories, payables and accruals, and income tax liability (RIPT) which changes act as adjustments of Net Income Adjusted to give "cash internally generated."

    In Illustration 4-5, these items are found in the schedule of working capital changes:

Increase in receivables	(4,200) a Use
Increase in merchandise inventory	(12,700) a Use
Increase in accounts, wage, and utilities payable	4,700 a Source
Increase in income tax payable	2,300 a Source
A net adjustment of	(9,900) a Use

3. Discretionary Outgoes (D. O.)—for acquisitions of property, plant, and equipment (in excess of dispositions), and for cash dividends to stockholders.

    In Illustration 4-5, these items are:

Acquisition of store equipment	(10,000) a Use
Payment of dividends	(1,500) a Use
A total of	(11,500) a Use

4. Financing and Other (F. & O.)—for financing and all other changes (except the change in Cash itself).

    In Illustration 4-5, these items are:

Issuance of capital stock	10,000 a Source
Net increase in bank loan in fiscal 1979	7,500 a Source

This information, taken from the statement of changes in financial position (Illustration 4-5), can now be brought together in a cash flow statement. Note that this form carries the instruction that "changes that decrease cash are shown in parentheses," so we will show *Uses* in parentheses and *Sources* without.

Ideally we should "checkoff" with a check mark, each item on the statement of changes in financial position as we use it in preparing the cash flow statement to make sure that we leave out no item and that the statement will prove, at the bottom, with the change in Cash.

The Cash Flow Statement for the Corner Drugstore, Inc., for its fiscal year ended March 31, 1979, is shown as Illustration 5-6. Trace each item shown in the previous discussion of the four categories to its entry on the cash flow statement.

Note that Illustration 5-6 agrees, in summary, with the statement of cash receipts and disbursements (Illustration 5-5), with respect to

Cash internally generated	($ 3,500)
Discretionary outgoes	(11,500)
Financing and other	17,500
Increase in cash	$ 2,500

CASH FLOW STATEMENTS DERIVED FROM COMPANY ANNUAL REPORTS

It is useful in interpreting published statements of changes in financial position to convert such statements to a cash flow statement by using the form in Illustration 5-6.

The following discussion considers in more detail the four categories of changes which affect cash and cash equivalent.

1. *Net income (after tax) before deduction of noncash expenses and before addition of noncash revenue.*

Until recent years, the most common adjustment to net income after tax was the addition of depreciation as a source. Depreciation is deducted as an expense in determining net income, but depreciation does not involve a cash outlay. (The cash outlay involved is, of course, the capital expenditure which went for acquiring the assets being depreciated.) The addition of depreciation here simply reverses the earlier deduction—to convert the net income figure into a cash income figure.

Other kinds of noncash expenses and revenues have appeared in recent years to make the translation of reported net income to cash net income more complex. Some of these other adjustments are:

Deferred income taxes. This tax expense is reported on the income statement but does not involve a cash outlay. The amount of

Illustration 5-6

CASH FLOW STATEMENT
(Changes that decrease cash are shown in parentheses)

Company Corner Drugstore, Inc. in - - - - - - - - of Dollars	Year Sales	1979 74,500		
I. Net Income		5,400		
Add: Depreciation		1,000		
Add: Other noncash expenses				
Subtract: Noncash revenues				
Net income before depreciation and other noncash expenses and revenues		6,400		
II. This could have represented cash inflow but it did not happen this way because the company:				
A. Collected (less than) more than it billed customers, as shown in *Receivables* (incr.) decrease		(4,200)		
B. Bought and mfd. (more than) less than the cost of goods shipped, as shown in *Inventories* (incr.) decrease		(12,700)		
C. Paid out (more than) less than the costs it incurred, as shown in *Payables & Accruels* (decr.) increase		4,700		
D. Paid out (more than) less than income tax incurred as shown in *Income Tax Liabilities* (decr.) increase		2,300		
Total four items:		(9,900)		
so that "cash internally generated" was		(3,500)		
III. There were "discretionary" outgoes of cash for:				
Acquisitions of property, plant and equipment (in excess of dispositions)		(10,000)		
Dividends to stockholders		(1,500)		
Total discretionary outgoes		(11,500)		
Cash internally generated less discretionary outgoes		(15,000)		
IV. Financing and other cash inflows and outgoes were:				
Issue of Capital Stock		10,000		
Net Increase in Bank Loan Payable		7,500		
Total financing and other flows		17,500		
With the effect on the company's cash (and cash equivalent) being an increase (decr.) of		2,500		

this expense each year becomes an addition to deferred income tax liability on the balance sheet.

Equity in profits in nonconsolidated affiliated or subsidiary companies. This equity occurs when the parent company takes its share of the affiliated or subsidiary company's profit into its income statement. This, then, is noncash revenue, and so for computing cash net income, the transaction must be reversed. If dividends are received from affiliated or subsidiary companies, they show up later under the Financing and Other category. (This is known as the *equity method* of accounting for affiliates and unconsolidated subsidiaries.)

2. *Changes in receivables, inventories, payables and accruals, and income tax liability* (the current liability, not deferred tax liability) are in effect uses and sources of cash that are closely tied to operating policies, practices and results.

3. *Discretionary outgoes*, capital expenditures and dividends, are two major uses of cash that are not a part of current operations. These outgoes are authorized not by the company's operating management, but by the board of directors.

4. *Financing and Other* is a group of cash sources and uses that shows the major financing flows and other flows not shown elsewhere. The short-term portion of long-term debt is combined with the long-term portion to show the flows that result from total change in long-term debt.

Let us derive cash flow statements for Caterpillar Tractor Co. for 1978 and 1979, based upon its statement of changes in financial position, Statement 3, 1979 Annual Report (reproduced in Chapter 15).

1. Since Caterpillar uses the net current assets (working capital) format, we go to the schedule of net current asset changes and indicate by (U) or S whether each change represents a Use or Source according to the following scheme:

Use	Source
Increase in a current asset	Decrease in a current asset
Decrease in a current liability	Increase in a current liability

Then we indicate for each item whether it is RIPT, DO, or F&O. In Illustration 5-7, we show the designations (U), S, RIPT, and F&O for Caterpillar's schedule of net current asset changes.

2. Now we go to the top of Caterpillar's Statement 3, and indicate whether the change should be included as NIA, RIPT, DO, or F&O. We also show whether each change is (U) or S. See Illustration 5-8.

3. Using our annotated version of Caterpillar's statement of changes in financial position, Illustrations 5-7 and 5-8, we enter the figures appropriately on the cash flow statement. As we enter each figure, we check it off on the statement of changes in financial position. The completed cash flow statement form is shown as Illustration 5-9. Trace the figures on Illustration 5-9 from Illustrations 5-7 and 5-8.

LEARNING FROM THE CASH FLOW STATEMENT

The form should help you to grasp the significant factors in the way a company has managed its cash flows in the changing economic environment from year to year. It should help you also to reconcile a

---

Illustration 5-7

Analysis of Schedule of Net Current Assets (Working Capital)
Changes of Caterpillar Tractor Co. for 1979 and 1978
(In millions of dollars)

		1979		1978	
Cash and short-term investments	Cash	(97.3)	S	35.1	(U)
Receivable from customers and others . . .	RIPT	(75.1)	S	119.7	(U)
Prepaid expenses, etc.	F&O	3.1	(U)	(12.5)	S
Inventories.	RIPT	147.9	(U)	233.7	(U)
Net change in current assets		(21.4)		376.0	
Notes payable	F&O	291.6	S	25.3	S
Payable to material suppliers and others . .	RIPT	(64.0)	(U)	175.8	S
Taxes based on income.	RIPT	(103.3)	(U)	58.5	S
Long-term debt due within one year	F&O	24.7	S	21.7	S
Net change in current liabilities		149.0		281.3	
Increase (or decrease) in net current assets during year		(170.4)		94.7	

Illustration 5-8

**Analysis of Top Part of Caterpillar Tractor Co.'s
Changes in Consolidated Financial Position
(In millions of dollars)**

		1979		1978	
Additions to net current assets:					
Operations:					
Profit for year	NIA	$491.6		$566.3	
Items affecting profit for the year, but not affecting net current assets:					
Depreciation.	NIA	311.8		257.1	
Deferred taxes based on income. . .	NIA	(47.4)		(12.1)	
Equity in profit of affiliated companies.	NIA	(30.2)		.8	
Profit of subsidiary credit companies.	NIA	(3.5)		(1.1)	
Net current assets provided from operations	NIA	722.3	S	811.0	S
Long-term debt	F&O	2.8	S	91.4	S
Capital assets sold or scrapped.	DO .	4.2	S	2.8	S
Common stock sold for cash under stock options.	F&O	3.1	S	4.5	S
Common stock issued upon conversion of convertible debentures	F&O	–		.3	S
Dividends from affiliated companies	F&O	6.0	S	7.1	S
Dividends from subsidiary credit companies	F&O	1.0	S	–	
Reduction in advances to subsidiary credit companies	F&O	–		8.7	S
Reclassification of other assets	F&O	10.8	S	–	
Other.	F&O	5.7	S	(4.7)	(U)
		755.9		921.1	
Reduction of net current assets for:					
Cash dividends.	DO	181.5	(U)	161.8	(U)
Land, buildings, machinery, and equip. . .	DO	675.9	(U)	543.4	(U)
Long-term debt	F&O	68.9	(U)	84.4	(U)
Reclassification of receivables.	F&O	–		36.8	(U)
		926.3		826.4	
Increase (or decrease) in net current assets during year		(170.4)		94.7	
Net current assets at beginning of year		1,391.2		1,296.5	
Net current assets at end of year		$1,220.8		$1,391.2	

company's reported net income with the change in its cash balance. Several interesting analyses can be made:

1. The percentage change of the four RIPT items can be compared to changes in sales and net income. One would expect receiv-

Illustration 5-9

CASH FLOW STATEMENT
(Changes that decrease cash are shown in parentheses)

	Year	1979	1978	
Company Caterpillar Tractor Co.				
in millions of Dollars	Sales	7,613.2	7,219.2	
I. Net Income		491.6	566.3	
Add: Depreciation		311.8	257.1	
Add: Other noncash expenses – Deferred inc. tax		(47.4)	(12.1)	
Subtract: Noncash revenues – Equity in Pft. subs. & Affil.		(33.7)	(.3)	
Net income before depreciation and other noncash expenses and revenues		722.3	811.0	
II. And this could have represented cash inflow but it did not happen this way because the company				
A. Collected (less than) more than it billed customers, as shown in *Receivables* (increase) decrease		75.1	(119.7)	
B. Bought and mfd. (more than) less than the cost of goods shipped, as shown in *Inventories* (increase) decrease		(147.9)	(233.7)	
C. Paid out (more than) less than the costs it incurred, as shown in *Payables & Accruals* (decrease) increase		(64.0)	175.8	
D. Paid out (more than) less than income tax incurred, as shown in *Income Tax Liabilities* (decrease) increase		(103.3)	58.5	
Total Four Items		(240.1)	(119.1)	
so that "cash internally generated" was		482.2	691.9	
III. There were "discretionary" outgoes of cash for: Acquisitions of property, plant & equipment (in excess of dispositions)		(671.7)	(540.6)	
Dividends to stockholders		(181.5)	(161.8)	
Total Discretionary Outgoes		(853.2)	(702.4)	
Cash internally generated less discretionary outgoes		(371.0)	(10.5)	
IV. Financing & other cash inflows & outgoes were: Net increase (decrease) in L-T debt (<&> 1 yr.)		(41.4)	28.7	
Increase in S-T notes payable		291.6	25.3	
Common Stock issued		3.1	4.8	
Dividends & advances to/from affil. & sub. co.		7.0	15.8	
Reclassification of receivables		–	(36.8)	
Other (1979–16.5-3.1) (1978–12.5-4.7)		13.4	7.8	
Total Financing and Other Flows		273.7	45.6	
With the effect on the company's cash (and cash equivalent) being an increase (decrease) of		(97.3)	35.1	

ables, inventory, and payables to fluctuate with sales, and tax liabilities to follow net income. Analysis of these four items should indicate whether variations are as expected or out of line, and if the latter, what the likely reasons may be.

2. A comparison of Cash Internally Generated with Discretionary Outgoes shows the extent to which the company was able to pay dividends and cover capital expenditures from internal sources.

3. The Financing and Other category shows how the firm is covering a cash deficit (or disposing of a cash surplus) resulting from cash internally generated less discretionary outgoes. One can check whether long-term sources are being matched with long-term needs, whether debt or equity is being used, and whether there are any other major sources or uses of cash.

4. One can also use this format for cash forecasting by filling in expected changes for the coming year. When the projections called for by the cash flow form have been made, one can see the major outlines of the projected cash flow pattern for the firm. By putting all this information on one page, one can discern the important interdependence of the several parts of the cash flow process.

FRAUD AND INTERNAL CONTROL

One of management's responsibilities is to safeguard the assets of the business against fraud by employees and others. Because cash and marketable securities are easily negotiated, safeguarding these assets is more difficult than safeguarding other kinds of assets.

Internal control is the principal means of safeguarding cash and marketable securities. By the term *internal control* we mean an allocation of duties among employees so that no one employee has complete responsibility for handling and recording a transaction from initiation to completion, the work of one employee checks against the work of another, and the subdivision of duties affords an automatic internal control over cash, securities, and other assets.

For example, in handling and recording of checks received from customers through the mail,

- One employee may receive the mail, open it, list the checks received, and arrive at the total, say $736.05.
- Another employee may prepare the deposit but, before taking

it to the bank, he will check the total of $736.05 against the total determined by the first employee.

- A third employee may record the amount received from each customer on the customer's account in the subsidiary ledger, and prove the total of the day's entries with the summary total of $736.05.

At times, management may find that internal control procedures conflict with other operating considerations. This conflict occurs most frequently in the area of customer relations. For example, in handling a cash sale, it might be good internal control for the sales clerk to send the cash to the cashier; yet, for good customer service, it might be better for the sales clerk to handle the whole transaction.

The job of management is to arrange an internal control that does not unduly interfere with the major operating activities of buying, manufacturing, selling, and collecting. Some years ago, Sir Simon Marks of England's Marks & Spencer stores resolved the dilemma for his organization by cutting out much of the internal paperwork, thus providing better customer service at lower cost. At the other extreme are instances where the discovery of employee fraud may bring about cumbersome internal control procedures which markedly affect customer relations. Balancing good relations with customers and adequate internal control among employees can be difficult.

Computer-based accounting and information systems have changed the nature of internal control. They have not changed the potential for fraud or the need for internal procedures to forestall it.

SUMMARY

Conventional accounting for cash and cash equivalent is not complex, although some problems are encountered in accounting for Cash in Bank. Both the company and the bank record deposits when the deposits are made, despite the fact that there may be a lag of several days before customer checks are collected by the bank. The time for accounting recognition of a check disbursement is the date the check is drawn. The bank records a check when it pays the check, and this may be a number of days after the business records the check. This lag introduces a continuing difference between the records of the company and the records of the bank, as indicated by the amount of outstanding checks in the reconciliation of the bank account.

In the management of bank balances, supplementary information to that afforded by the usual accounting records may be required. For example, a company may determine the time lag between the date it draws checks to its larger suppliers and the date these checks are paid by the bank, and take this time lag into account in managing the company's bank account. The reason that conventional accounting provides for the recording of checks when they are issued is to bring them under accounting control immediately as a matter of internal control. This, nevertheless, creates a gap between the data afforded by conventional accounting and the data needed by management to manage the company's bank balances.

In managing the changing mix of its investment in assets, management has the problem of determining how much investment in cash and cash equivalent it should maintain. This will be governed in part by how the business is financed, how much it is subjected to seasonal and cyclical swings, how much it desires to "stay out of the bank," and how well it can forecast its cash changes. In managing the company's bank balances, management needs to know (1) how the banks administer their requirements for compensating balances against loans and lines of credit, (2) what service charges the banks make, and (3) how much the company must rely upon its banks as a source of financing. There may be a conflict between strict return on investment considerations on the part of business management and the desire for substantial customer deposit balances on the part of bank management.

The cash receipts and disbursements statement is prepared for internal use only, primarily for cash management and cash forecasting. The form of the statement can be designed to show cash internally generated, discretionary outgoes for capital expenditures and dividends, and financing and other flows. A cash flow statement embodying this same information can be developed from a company's published statement of changes in financial position. The cash flow statement can help the user understand

- how a company has managed its cash flows,
- how changes in receivables, inventories, payables and accruals, and income tax liability have affected cash internally generated,
- the extent to which cash internally generated has covered discretionary outgoes for dividends and capital expenditures.
- the extent to which external financing via debt and equity has been used, and
- how all this ties into the change in the company's cash balance.

The format for the cash flow statement serves as a convenient model for cash forecasting.

The responsibility of management to safeguard assets is especially acute in the matter of cash and cash equivalent. Internal control is a main defense against employee fraud. But a proper balance needs to be struck between the requirements of internal control and the way in which the business performs its primary functions of buying, manufacturing, selling, and collecting.

QUESTIONS AND PROBLEMS

1. From whom, and how does a trading company get back the cash it invests in inventory? Does it always get it back? When it gets it back, what can it do with it?
2. From whom, and how does a manufacturing company, or a public utility, get back the cash it invests in buildings and machinery? Does it always get it back? When it gets it back, what can it do with it?
3. Is a change fund a "current asset"?
4. In Chapter 5, five company objectives were listed under "Management's Concern with Changes in Assets." Consider each of these and point out what effect it would have on the management of a company's investment in cash and cash equivalent.
5. The text states that "For a manufacturing company,. . . the typical sequence of changes in assets is much more complex than for a trading company." In what respects, and why, would this be so?
6. Why would a manufacturing company periodically allocate a "part of its investment in factory buildings and equipment to the cost of producing finished goods"?
7. (A) Why might you expect "the pattern of asset investment" to be different among companies in the same industry? To be different between companies in different industries?

    Assignment: Compare recent balance sheets for five companies—three in the same industry, the other two in different industries. For each company, determine the percentage of total assets represented by cash and cash equivalent, receivables, inventories, plant and equipment, and long-term investments and other assets; then explain the similarities, and differences, in the patterns of asset investment.

   (B) Why might the current ratio be different for the five selected companies in (A)?

    Assignment: Calculate the current ratio for each of the five selected companies, and then explain what the ratio tells you about each company.

8. (A)   What are the arguments for, and against, a company using the "time for accounting recognition" for bank deposits:

    1.   The date the checks of customers are received.
    2.   The date the bank records the deposit.
    3.   The date the bank "collects" the checks deposited.

    For checks drawn on the bank by the company:

    1.   The date a check is drawn.
    2.   The date a check is mailed.
    3.   The date a check is paid by the bank.

  (B)   For conventional accounting purposes, what is the "time for accounting recognition" for bank deposits? For checks drawn?

  (C)   Does conventional accounting for cash in bank serve all of management needs? If so, how? If now, why not?

9. "Cash receipts and disbursements over the long run (twenty years or more) tend to approximate the long-run income statement." To what extent is this true? Under what conditions? Specifically? *Hint*: Use format of cash flow statement as an outline for your answer.

10. (A)   The text refers to marketable securities as "representing a temporary investment of cash in the form of readily salable short-maturity debt instruments." Why not include in "marketable securities" investment in long-term bonds, preferred stocks, and common stocks?

  (B)   If you were the manager of a company's portfolio of marketable securities, representing a temporary investment of cash, in what kinds of securities would you consider investing? For example, would you invest in interest-bearing certificates of deposit issued by a bank, prime commercial paper, U.S. government debt issues, state and municipal bonds, corporate debt issues, etc.?

  (C)   At what value should a company's temporary investment in marketable securities be stated on the balance sheet? Why so?

11. In its *Notes to Financial Statements*, American Hospital Supply Corporation observed: "American has agreed to maintain average collected balances amounting to 10 percent of most domestic lines not in use and an additional 10 percent when in use. Although American has agreed to maintain such average collected balances during the year, these balances are not restricted and may be drawn down for daily operations as needed. Balances maintained in domestic line banks compensate those banks for services performed as well as for the lines of credit. Banks outside the United States are generally compensated for services with fees rather than balances and no charges or fees are being paid for lines with those banks."

  (A)   What are "compensating balances"?

  (B)   What purpose(s) do they serve?

  (C)   How would you answer a foreign student who, puzzled by an explanation that compensating balances were related to borrowing from the bank, asked: "If you have a balance, why do you need a loan"?

12. A summary of the cash account of Zelma Manufacturing Co. for 1979, in thousands of dollars, is shown below:

Cash (A)

12/31/78 Balance	244			
(A) Collected on customer		(G)	Pd. employees	2,563
accounts	7,688	(H)	Pd. suppliers, etc.	4,128
(B) Sale of property	4	(I)	Pd. int. on debt	130
(C) Short-term loans	292	(J)	Pd. dividends	182
(D) Dividends from		(K)	Cap. expenditures	672
affiliated co.s	7	(L)	Pd. L-T debt	41
(E) Sale-Com. stock	3	(M)	Pd. inc. tax	376
(F) Sundry	1		12/31/79 To Balance	147
	8,239			8,239
12/31/79 Balance	147			

Required: (A) A statement of cash receipts and disbursements in a format similar to Illustration 5-5.

(B) A conversion of your statement to a "cash flow" summary, similar to the conversion, done for the Corner Drugstore (based upon Illustration 5-5).

(C) Brief comments on what your cash flow summary tells you.

13. *An exercise in reconstruction of accounts using a published annual report.* Refer to Chapter 15 which shows excerpts from Caterpillar Tractor's 1979 Annual Report, and reconstruct accounts for 1979 for:

(A)   Receivables

(B)   Land, buildings, machinery, and equipment (Net). Note: Page 2 of Caterpillar's annual report shows "capital expenditures for land, buildings, machinery, and equipment" at $675.9 million, and you may use this figure in your reconstruction.

(C)   Current liability for taxes based on income. Note: Caterpillar's Note 5 shows 1979 income tax "currently paid or payable" at $271.6 million.

(D)   Retained earnings

As a guide for your reconstructing, Caterpillar's reconstructed account for Long-Term Debt (< and > 1 yr.)" is shown below:

Long-Term Debt (< and > 1 yr.) – (Liability)

12/31/79 < 1 yr.	59.0*	12/31/78 < 1 yr.	34.3*
12/31/79 > 1 yr.	951.9*	12/31/78 > 1 yr.	1,018.0*
"PLUG" to Balance–Net Decr. in 1979	41.4		
	1,052.3		1,052.3
		12/31/79	1,010.9

Notes: (1) 12/31/79 and 12/31/78 balance figures, asterisked, were obtained from Caterpillar's Statement 2.

(2) The net decrease figure of *$41.4* million reconciles exactly with the *41.4* figure shown in Illustration 5-9. Illustration 5-9 $41.4 figure was obtained from three figures in Caterpillar's Statement 3 (reproduced in Illustrations 5-7 and 5-8):

Additions to net current assets:		
Long-term debt (Illn. 5-8)	2.8	S
Reductions in net current assets:		
Long-term debt (Illn. 5-8)	(68.9)	(U)
Increase (or decrease) in components of net current assets: Long-term debt due within one year.	24.7	S
Net decrease in long-term debt	(41.4)	(U)

Required: For each of the four accounts you reconstruct, add a note, similar to Note (2) just above, to show how the information you have developed reconciles with the relevant figure (A) shown in Illustration 5-9. If you have a difference of *3.5* in trying to reconcile land, buildings, machinery, and equipment, leave it be.

14. (A) If a company's statement of retained earnings were to contain any of the following items:

(1) Loss on sale of fixed assets
(2) Non-recurring plant expenses
(3) Additional taxes for prior years
(4) Charge for a dividend payable in common stock—a "stock dividend"
(5) Gain on the sale of a long-term investment

how would you treat them in preparing a statement of changes in financial position or a cash flow statement.

(B) If you are given year-end balance sheets and annual income statements, together with a record of dividends declared, for a company over a series of years—and were asked to prepare cash flow statements for the company—what additional information concerning retained earnings, income taxes, investments in subsidiary and affiliated companies, and property, plant, and equipment (net) would you like to have? What would you do if you could not get such additional information?

15. Suppose a company included the following statement (in thousands of dollars) in its report for internal management use:

I. For the first nine months of FY 1981, net income (based on annual sales and other revenue of $296,466) was $ 6,514

II. And there would have been a net inflow of cash in this amount *if*:

Forwarded $ 6,514

a. Depreciation expenses were a cash outflow;
b. Deferred credits were cash inflows;
c. The company's (730) of the earnings of its subsidiary company were *all* cash inflows;
d. Collections from customers had been the same as sales;
e. The company had bought and manufactured exactly the cost of the goods it shipped to customers;
f. The company maintained its investment in miscellaneous assets;
g. The company paid out exactly the costs it incurred;
h. The company paid exactly the income taxes it incurred (on the books).

But these conditions did not prevail, for the company:

a. Charged depreciation as an expense, thereby reducing income without an outflow of cash $10,470

b. Increased income through amortization of its deferred credit without receiving an inflow of cash   (1,242)

c. Increased income with its share of the profits of its subsidiary company: However, a majority of these earnings did not result in an inflow of cash   (530)

d. Collected less than it billed, as shown as an increase in Receivables   (9,754)

e. Bought and manufactured more than the cost of the goods it shipped, as shown in the increase in inventories   (3,942)

f. Reduced its investment in miscellaneous assets, freeing cash   736

g. Paid out less than the costs it incurred, as shown in the changes in payables and accruals   20,704

h. Paid out less than the income taxes it incurred, as shown in the increase in the Income Tax Liability   102

The net effect of these eight items being $16,544

So that inflow of cash which may be termed *Cash Internally Generated* was $23,058

Forwarded		$23,058

III. There were *"discretionary"* outgoes of cash for:

a.	Dividends to stockholders	$ 5,638	
b.	Acquisition of Plant, Property and Equipment (in excess of dispositions)	17,914	
c.	Investment of temporarily unneeded cash in short-term securities	1,840	$25,392

Resulting in a decrease in the company's cash between June 30, 1980 and March 31, 1981 of	($2,334)

(A) Convert this statement to the form used in Illustration 5-9.

(B) Comment on the usefulness of this information to management (including directors).

16. Select a published annual report, and from the statement of changes in financial position presented therein, prepare a cash flow statement for two years by following the procedure set forth in Illustrations 5-7, 5-8, and 5-9. Outline what one learns about the company from your cash flow statement, with numbers put on your ideas.

6

Trade Receivables and Sales Revenue

Selling goods and services on credit plays an important role in most business enterprises. Credit may be granted on open account or on the basis of a formal instrument of credit such as a promissory note.

In this chapter we will consider the accounting for trade receivables and sales revenue arising from the sale of goods and services. Special topics include a comparison of the write-off and reserve methods for handling uncollectible accounts, factors affecting a company's investment in trade receivables, the receivables/sales ratio, and the percentage-of-completion method in recording income under long-term contracts. A brief explanation of present value is given in the Appendix.

TRADE RECEIVABLES AND NONTRADE RECEIVABLES

Trade receivables are amounts due from customers arising from sales of a company's products and services. The receivables may be in the form of open accounts, notes receivable, or installment obligations.

Nontrade receivables include advances to employees and to affiliated companies, claims for insured losses, claims for tax refunds, and receivables arising from sales of property, plant, and equipment no longer needed by the company.

Trade receivables (net) are trade receivables shown at the amount the company expects to collect on them. Accordingly, the total amount due from customers as of the balance sheet date is reduced by an estimate of the portion the company expects not to collect because of bad debt losses, cash discounts to be taken by customers when they pay, and sales returns and allowances to be authorized.

SALES REVENUE AND NONSALES REVENUE

Sales revenue arises from the sale of products and services for cash or on account, and is measured by the total of the charges made to customers for the products and services sold them during an accounting period.

Nonsales revenue includes "gains from the sale or exchange of assets (other than stock in trade), interest and dividends earned on investments, and other increases in the owners' equity except those arising from capital contributions and capital adjustments."[1]

Sales revenue (net), or *net sales*, is sales revenue less sales adjustments recorded during an accounting period. Sales adjustments include cash discounts on sales, sales returns, and sales allowances.

SALES AND COLLECTIONS ON ACCOUNT

Sales on account are recorded as increases in trade receivables at the selling prices of the goods, *plus*, when applicable, (a) excise and sales taxes and (b) charges for transportation, installation, maintenance service, etc. A $200 sale plus an $8 sales tax is recorded thus:

Trade Receivables (A)	Incr 208	
Retained Earnings (OE)–(Sales Revenue)		Incr 200
Sales Tax Payable (L)		Incr 8

[1] *Accounting Terminology Bulletin* No. 2, 1955. Reprinted by permission of the American Institute of Certified Public Accountants.

The time for accounting recognition of a sale is the date of the sales invoice. The sales invoice is usually dated, in the case of a store sale, when the sale is made; in the case of a warehouse shipment, when the goods are shipped to the customer in response to an order. (This dating accords with the basic concept of realization discussed in Chapter 1.)

Complete accounting for a sales transaction involves two entries. One entry shows the *selling price* of the goods sold, the other shows the *cost*. At the time of each sale, an entry is made at the *selling price* to show the increase in trade receivables (or in cash, if a cash sale) and the corresponding increase in retained earnings:

Trade Receivables (A)	Incr xxx	
Retained Earnings (OE)–(Sales Revenue)		Incr xxx

At the end of the accounting period or at the time of each sale, an entry is made at the *cost* of the goods sold to show the outgo of merchandise to customers and the corresponding decrease in retained earnings:

Retained Earnings (OE)–(Cost of Goods Sold)	Decr xxx	
Merchandise Inventory (A)		Decr xxx

Thus, at the end of the accounting period, the retained earnings account shows both the *total selling price* of the goods sold during the period and the *total cost* of these goods.[2]

In this chapter we are concerned with the accounting for the *selling price* of goods sold. In Chapters 8 and 9 we shall deal with the accounting for the *cost* of the goods sold.

ACCOUNTING FOR COLLECTIONS ON ACCOUNT

Collections on account are recorded as decreases in trade receivables:

Cash in Bank (A)	Incr 100	
Trade Receivables (A)		Decr 100

[2] In the Corner Drugstore illustration, Chapter 3, an entry for the total cost of all goods sold during the year was made after a physical inventory had been taken at the year-end. In some companies, cost of the goods sold can be determined for each sale.

When a company grants cash discounts and a customer pays his account within the specified discount period, the amount that the company deposits in the bank is less than the amount of the decrease entered in the trade receivables account. The entry is then

Cash in Bank (A)	Incr 98	
Retained Earnings (OE)–Cash discounts on sales)	Decr 2	
Trade Receivables (A)		Decr 100

SALES DISCOUNTS, RETURNS, AND ALLOWANCES

Sales adjustments include

- Cash discounts for customer payment within a specified discount period.
- Sales returned by the customer.
- Other sales allowances.

When a company's credit terms are expressed as "2%/10, net 30," a customer can deduct 2% if he pays within 10 days after the invoice date, but if he does not, he is to pay the total amount within 30 days after the invoice date. If the credit terms are "2%/10, net 30, E.O.M." the customer gets the discount if he pays within 10 days after the end of the month. Thus, if a customer pays a $100 invoice within the 10-day discount period, he sends his check for $98 in full payment of the invoice. The entry (as previously shown) is

Cash in Bank (A)	Incr 98	
Retained Earnings (OE)–(Cash discounts on sales)	Decr 2	
Trade Receivables (A)		Decr 100

Cash discounts are distinguished from trade discounts, which are merely deductions made from the list price to arrive at the effective price billed the customer.

When a sale made on account is returned by a customer, a Returned Sales Memo, authorizing the amount allowed the customer, is issued and serves as the basis for the following entry:

Retained Earnings (OE)–(Returned Sales)	Decr 150	
Trade Receivables (A)		Decr 150

If the returned goods are salable, they are put back into stock. No entry need be made for the cost of the goods returned to inventory unless the company recognizes changes in its inventory account at the time each sale is made.

Other Sales Allowances

Special allowances may be made to customers for imperfections or damage to merchandise retained by the customer, for trade discounts allowed after initial billing, etc. The entry for sales allowances is similar to that for returned sales:

Retained Earnings (OE)–(Sales Allowances)	Decr 25	
Trade Receivables (A)		Decr 25

Summary Illustrations of Sales Adjustment Entries

To give a more complete picture of sales adjustment entries and their effect on T-accounts, see Illustrations 6-1 and 6-2. Illustration 6-1 shows the sales, collections, and sales adjustment transactions of the JKL Company in 1980, and Illustration 6-2 shows the effect of these transactions on the company's ledger accounts.

Illustration 6-1

**Summary of Sales, Collections, and Sales Adjustments
Transactions of the JKL Company in 1980
(In Thousands of Dollars)**

(A)				
Trade Receivables (A)	Incr	700.0		
Retained Earnings (OE)–(Sales Revenue)			Incr	700.0
Sales on account in 1980				
(B)				
Cash in Bank (A)	Incr	662.3		
Retained Earnings (OE)–(Sales Discounts)	Decr	12.1		
Trade Receivables (A)			Decr	674.4
Collections on account in 1980				
(C)				
Retained Earnings (OE)–(Sales Returns & Allowances)	Decr	3.6		
Trade Receivables (A)			Decr	3.6
Sales returns and allowances authorized in 1980				

Illustration 6-2

Selected T-Accounts of JKL Company for 1980
(In Thousands of Dollars)

Cash in Bank (Asset)

(Showing only the entry for transactions in Illustration 6-1)

B-1980 Collection on a/c	662.3		

Trade Receivables (Asset)

12/31/79 Balance	155.0	B-1980 Collections on a/c	674.4
A-1980 Sales on a/c	700.0	C-1980 Returns & allow.	3.6
		12/31/80 To balance	177.0
	855.0		855.0
12/31/80 Balance	177.0		

Retained Earnings (Owners' Equity)

(Showing only the entries for transactions in Illustration 6-1)

B-1980 Sales discounts	12.1	A-1980 Sales on a/c	700.0
C-1980 Returns & allow.	3.6		

Note from Illustration 6-2 that the company would show net sales at
$684.3M in its income statement for 1980:

Gross sales	$700.0M
Deduct sales adjustments	15.7M
Net sales for 1980	$684.3M

The $15.7M shown for sales adjustments is the total of the dis-
counts, returns, and allowances taken or granted in 1980. They arose
in part out of sales made in 1979, in part out of sales made in 1980.
To relate the amount deducted for sales adjustments to the year of
the original sales, some companies make appropriate year-end adjustments.

ACCOUNTING FOR UNCOLLECTIBLE ACCOUNTS

There are two methods of accounting for uncollectible accounts,
the *write-off* method and the *reserve* method.

Under the *write-off method*, a company "writes off" a specific customer's account when it determines the account to be uncollectible:

Retained Earnings (OE)–(Uncollectible Accounts   Decr 140
                           Written Off)
    Trade Receivables (A)   Decr 140
    Account of Joseph Snidow determined to be
    uncollectible and written off

Note that loss is recognized in the retained earnings account only when a specific customer's account—Mr. Snidow's in the entry above—is written off as uncollectible.

If it should happen that Mr. Snidow's account is subsequently determined to be collectible, the company would restore to Trade Receivables the amount owed by Snidow:

Trade Receivables (A)   Incr 140
    Retained Earnings (OE)–(Recovery of   Incr 140
    Accounts Previously Written Off)

Thereafter the company would record collections on the customer's account in the usual way.

With the *reserve method*, the company at the end of each year makes an estimate of the portion of the year's sales on account that it expects not to collect. This estimate may be expressed as a percentage of the total sales on account for the year, the percentage being determined on the basis of the company's past collection experience as modified by any prospective changes. The entry for the year-end estimate utilizes a *Contra Asset* account, Deduction for Estimated Uncollectible Accounts:

Retained Earnings (OE)–(Portion of this
    year's sales estimated uncollectible)   Decr 3,500

Deduction for Estimated Uncollectible
    Accounts (Contra Asset)   Incr 3,500

The *Contra Asset* account, Deduction for Estimated Uncollectible Accounts, is located in the ledger adjacent to the Trade Receivables account with which it is inseparably linked. The balance of the Contra Asset account is on the right, so increases are entered on the right and decreases on the left—all "contra" to the rule for entering increases and decreases in Asset accounts. The Contra Asset account is a device that permits the company to record a decrease in Trade Receivables for its year-end estimate of uncollectible receivables, although the company is unable to indicate which specific accounts will be written off.

Whenever a specific customer's account is determined to be uncollectible, the entry is:

Deduction for Estimated Uncollectible Accounts (Contra Asset)	Decr 140	
Trade Receivables (A)		Decr 140
Account of Joseph Snidow determined to be uncollectible and written off.		

The Deduction for Estimated Uncollectible Accounts is decreased for write-offs because the balance in this account has been accumulated to serve just this purpose. With the reserve method, loss is recognized in the Retained Earnings account when the annual estimate is made, not when specific accounts are determined to be uncollectible and written off.

If it should happen that Mr. Snidow's account is subsequently determined to be collectible, the company would restore the amount due to both the Trade Receivables account and its *Contra Asset* account:

Trade Receivables (A)	Incr 140	
Deduction for Estimated Uncollectible Accounts (Contra Asset)		Incr 140

The company would thereafter record collections on the customer's account in the usual way.

Extended Illustration. To compare the write-off and reserve methods, let us extend the summary of transactions of the JKL Company for 1980, Illustration 6-1, to include:

(D) Specific accounts totaling $2.4 M written off during 1980.

(E) Accounts previously written off totaling $.3 M restored to Trade Receivables account in 1980.

(F) The Company's year-end estimate of the portion of the year's sales it expects not to collect—$3.5 M, representing ½ of 1% of sales of $700.0 M.

The analyses of these transactions are shown in Illustration 6-3. Part A shows how the transactions are analyzed with the write-off method, and Part B shows how they are analyzed with the reserve method. Illustration 6-4 shows the effect on the ledger accounts of the JKL

Illustration 6-3

**Summary of Uncollectible Accounts Transactions of
the JKL Company in 1980
(In Thousands of Dollars)**

PART A IF WRITE-OFF METHOD USED

(D)
Retained Earnings (OE)–(Uncollectible Accounts Written Off)   Decr 2.4
    Trade Receivables (A)   Decr   2.4
  Specific accounts written off as uncollectible.

(E)
Trade Receivables (A)   Incr   .3
    Retained Earnings (OE)–(Recovery of Accounts
      Previously Written Off)   Incr   .3
  Accounts previously written off now deemed good.

(F)
No Entry

PART B IF RESERVE METHOD USED

(D)
Deduction for Estimated Uncollectible Accounts
  (Contra Asset)   Decr 2.4
    Trade Receivables (A)   Decr   2.4
  Specific accounts written off as uncollectible.

(E)
Trade Receivables (A)   Incr   .3
    Deduction for Estimated Uncollectible Accounts
      (Contra Asset)   Incr   .3
  Accounts previously written off now deemed good.

(F)
Retained Earnings (OE)–(Portion of 1980 sales estimated
  uncollectible)   Decr 3.5
    Deduction for Estimated Uncollectible Accounts
      (Contra Asset)   Incr   3.5
  Estimate of uncollectible accounts in 1980 sales.

Illustration 6-4

Selected T-Accounts of JKL Company for 1980 Showing Effects
of Transactions Analyzed in Illustration 6-1
and in Part A (Write-off Method) of Illustration 6-3
(In Thousands of Dollars)

Cash in Bank (Asset)

(Showing only the entry for transactions in Illustration 6-1)			
B-1980 Collections on a/c	662.3		

Trade Receivables (Asset)

12/31/79 Balance	155.0	B-1980 Collections on a/c	674.4
A-1980 Sales on a/c	700.0	C-1980 Returns & Allow.	3.6
E-A/c's Recovered in 1980	.3	D-A/c's written off in 1980	2.4
		12/31/80 To balance	174.9
	855.3		855.3
12/31/80 Balance	174.9		

Retained Earnings (Owners' Equity)

(Showing only the entries for transactions in Illustrations 6-1 & 6-3)			
B-1980 Sales discounts	12.1	A-1980 Sales on a/c	700.0
C-1980 Returns & Allow.	3.6	E-A/c's Recovered in 1980	.3
D-A/c's Written Off in 1980	2.4		

Company of the transactions analyzed in Illustration 6-1 and in Part A (write-off method) of Illustration 6-3.

Note, in Illustration 6-4, that the JKL Company, using the write-off method, would show Trade Receivables on its 12/31/79 and 12/31/80 balance sheets as follows:

	12/31/79	12/31/80
Trade Receivables	$155.0 M	$174.9 M

Its income statement for 1980 would show:

Net Sales for 1980 ($700.0 M less $15.7 M) at . . . . $684.3 M
Loss from uncollectible accounts ($2.4 M less $.3 M) at . . . . . $ 2.1 M

Illustration 6-5 shows the effect on the ledger accounts of the JKL Company analyzed in Illustration 6-1 and in Part B (reserve method) of Illustration 6-3.

Note in Illustration 6-5 that the JKL Company, using the Reserve

Illustration 6-5

Selected T-Accounts of JKL Company for 1980
Showing Effects of Transactions Analyzed in Illustration 6-1 and
in Part B (Reserve Method) of Illustration 6-3
(In Thousands of Dollars)

Cash in Bank (Asset)

(Showing only the entry for transactions in Illustration 6-1)	
B-1980 Collections on a/c	622.3

Trade Receivables (Asset)

12/31/79	155.0	B-1980 Collections on a/c	674.4
A-1980 Sales on a/c	700.0	C-1980 Returns & Allow.	3.6
E-A/c's Recovered in 1980	.3	D-A/c's Written off in 1980	2.4
		12/31/80 To balance	174.9
	855.3		855.3
12/31/80 To balance	174.9		

Deduction for Estimated Uncollectible Accounts (Contra Asset)

D-A/c's Written off in 1980	2.4	12/31/79 Balance	4.5
12/31/80 To balance	5.9	E-A/c's Recovered in 1980	.3
		F-Est. Uncollectible on	
		1980 sales	3.5
	8.3		8.3
		12/31/80 Balance	5.9

Retained Earnings (Owners' Equity)

(Showing only the entries for transactions in Illustrations 6-1 & 6-3)			
B-1980 Sales discounts	12.1	A-1980 Sales on a/c	700.0
C-1980 Returns & Allow.	3.6		
F-Estimated Uncollectible			
on 1980 Sales	3.5		

Method, would show Trade Receivables — Net on its 12/31/79 and 12/31/80 balance sheets as follows:

	12/31/79	12/31/80
Trade Receivables	$155.0 M	$174.9 M
Deduct Estimated Uncollectibility	4.5 M	5.9 M
Trade Receivables—Net	$150.5 M	$169.0 M

Its income statement for 1980 would show:

Net Sales for 1980 ($700.0 M less $15.7 M) at . . . . . . $684.3 M
Loss from uncollectible accounts at . . . . $ 3.5 M

In the extended illustration for the JKL Company, the different results obtained by the two methods may be summarized:

	Write-Off Method	Reserve Method	Difference
Income statement for 1980:			
Net sales	$684.3M	$684.3M	-0-
Loss from uncollectible accounts shown			
as a part of Operating Expenses	2.1	3.5	1.4
Balance Sheet 12/31/79:			
Trade Receivables (Net)	155.0	150.5	(4.5)
Retained Earnings	Not given	Not given	(4.5)
Balance Sheet 12/31/80:			
Trade Receivables (Net) . . . :	174.9	169.0	(5.9)
Retained Earnings	Not given	Not given	(5.9)

The two essential differences between the two methods deal with (1) when the loss from uncollectible accounts is recognized in the income statement:

Under the write-off method, loss is recognized only when specific accounts are written off. Thus, revenue from a sale on account may be shown in one year and the loss from its uncollectibility in another.
Under the reserve method, loss because of uncollectibility is recognized in the year in which the related sales revenue is recognized.

and (2) whether recognition is accorded on the balance sheet to the expected uncollectibility of receivables outstanding:

Under the write-off method, this is not done.
Under the reserve method, it is.

In summary, the write-off method is appropriate for those companies whose bad debt losses are relatively insignificant. The reserve method is appropriate for those companies whose bad debt losses are significant, and whose collection experience permits the required estimating to be done. For federal income tax purposes either method may be used, *if* used consistently from year to year. Note, however, that the reserve method gives a company a continuing deferral of taxes that is equivalent to the balance in the contra asset account multiplied by the income tax rate.

Year-End Estimating Under the Reserve Method

All the information that a company needs to convert its accounting for uncollectible accounts from the write-off method to the reserve method is the year-end estimating of uncollectibility. Let us consider how this estimating may be done and how its reliability may be tested.

The JKL Company arrived at its year-end estimate for 1980 by taking ½ of 1 percent of the sales made on account in 1980. How would the company determine this percentage? Ideally, it should first determine the ratio of its losses to sales over a complete business cycle, and modify this ratio by its judgment of prospective changes in credit and collections. Practically, a company can determine the loss/sales ratio for its past five years, and then base the percentage it uses upon this experience.

Not all companies using the reserve method make a percentage-of-sales computation. Some appraise the uncollectibility of receivables outstanding at the year-end, and then adjust the accounts in accordance with this appraisal.

Illustration 6-6

Trade Receivables of JKL Company at 12/31/80 Classified
According to Age of Uncollected Charges
(In Thousands of Dollars)

Uncollected charges on account:

Less than 31 days old.	$119.4
31 to 60 days old	36.2
61 to 90 days old	11.3
Over 90 days old	8.0
Total Trade Receivables Outstanding at 12/31/80	$174.9

The judgment of the JKL's accounting staff, aided by the counsel of the company's credit manager, may be that

A percentage of ½ of 1 percent be applied to the $119.4M of charges less than 31 days old	$ .6M
A percentage of 2 percent to the $36.2M of charges 31 to 60 days old	.7M
And, on the basis of a detailed review of the $19.3M of charges over 60 days old, their uncollectibility approximates	4.0M
A total of	$5.3M

Companies using the percentage-of-sales computation can test the reliability of their estimating each year-end by comparing their trade receivables (net), according to their ledger accounts, against an independent appraisal of their collectibility. This independent appraisal may be accomplished by a detailed evaluation of each customer's account. A more practical approach begins with "aging" the receivables outstanding, as in Illustration 6-6.

This independent appraisal of $5.3M might then be considered close enough to the $5.9M shown in the JKL Company's Contra Asset account to warrant no adjustment.

FINANCIAL STATEMENT PRESENTATION

Balance Sheet Valuation

Trade receivables are shown on the balance sheet at their "net realizable value." Burlington Industries, Inc. presented trade receivables in the current asset section of its balance sheet as follows:

	9/29/79	9/30/78
Customer accounts receivable after deduction of $21,554M in 1979 and $18,597 in 1978 for doubtful accounts, discounts, returns and allowances	$477,497M	$411,894M

A special problem in valuation of receivables arises when a company receives a promissory note bearing no interest or an interest rate less than the prevailing rate. In such cases, the note is valued at the fair value of the property or services exchanged for the note or at the fair market value of the note. If neither of these values are readily determinable, the note should be valued at the *present value* of all future cash receipts discounted at the debtor's borrowing rate.[3] Present value is discussed in the Appendix to this chapter.

Classification

Trade receivables are usually shown in the current asset section only, since they normally meet the requirements of being due within one year or within the "normal operating cycle" of the business.

[3] AICPA Accounting Principles Board Opinion No. 21, Interest on Receivables and Payables, October 1, 1971.

Income Statement

In published annual reports to stockholders, the income statement usually shows only the net sales figure with no reference to the amount of gross sales or the amount of the deduction for discounts, returns, and allowances. In reports prepared for internal use only, the income statement normally begins with gross sales, from which discounts, returns, and allowances are deducted to arrive at net sales.

Three other items, in addition to discounts, returns, and allowances, are related to gross sales revenue:

- The annual provision for bad debts,
- Sales and excise taxes, and
- Freight cost incurred on goods shipped to customers.

The annual provision for bad debts is normally included in operating expenses rather than being deducted directly from gross sales to arrive at net sales.

Sales and excise taxes may be (1) deducted from gross sales in arriving at net sales, or (2) included in the reported net sales figure and then deducted as part of operating expenses. With either of these methods, companies for whom sales and excise taxes are sizable amounts, in particular, tobacco, whiskey, and oil companies, may give additional information on their sales and excise taxes in a footnote.

The freight cost incurred on goods shipped to customers, called *freight out* in accounting terminology, is normally included in operating expenses. In some cases, however, freight out is deducted from gross sales in arriving at net sales.

Whenever reported sales figures for two or more companies are compared, one should be aware of these possible variations in reporting practice.

INVESTMENT IN TRADE RECEIVABLES

Factors affecting a company's investment in trade receivables include:

- Seasonal, cyclical, and growth changes in volume of sales.

- The market the company serves.
- The company's credit and collection policies.
- Inflation.

Receivables investment is closely related to the volume of sales for the month or quarter immediately preceding the balance sheet date. Thus, for businesses with wide seasonal fluctuations in sales, there are corresponding swings in receivables investment. Fluctuations in sales volume because of cyclical or growth changes similarly cause changes in the related receivables investment.

The market a company serves has a bearing on its receivable investment. This relationship is particularly noticeable when a company makes a change in the market it serves. In such cases, management needs to consider the financial implications of the changes on receivables investment.

The company's credit and collection policies also affect its receivables investment. Some years ago Montgomery Ward and Company introduced a revolving credit plan, similar to Sears', to further "more aggressive promotion of credit sales." As a result, in the year of change, the company's fourth quarter sales increased 23 percent, year-end receivables 57 percent. Increasing use of national credit cards for retail sales has reduced receivables investment for retail stores.

The effect of inflation on receivables investment is particularly noticeable in years of double-digit inflation. So much so, that many companies experience severe financing difficulties, because inflationary increases in dollar sales bring about increases in receivables.

Receivables/Sales Ratio

The relationship between a company's year-end receivables and its sales for the year (or for the fourth quarter) is an important ratio for credit analysts. The ratio may be expressed as a *percentage* of year-end receivables to sales, or as the *receivable collection period*.

For example, here are Caterpillar Tractor Co.'s receivables/sales percentages for 1979 and 1978:

	1979	1978
Annual Sales basis:		
Year-end receivables/Annual sales	692.7/7,613.2	767.8/7,219.2
Receivables/Sales	9.1%	10.6%
4th Quarter Sales basis:		
Year-end receivables fourth quarter sales	692.7/1,320.6	767.8/1,928.6
Receivables/Sales percentage	52.5%	39.8%

Caterpillar's *receivable collection period* is determined by multiplying the receivables/sales percentage by the number of days in the year (or in the fourth quarter):

	1979	1978
Annual Sales basis:		
Receivable/Sales percentage times 365 days	9.1% × 365	10.6% × 365
Receivable collection period	33 days	39 days
4th Quarter Sales basis:		
Receivables/Sales percentage times 92 days	52.5% × 92	39.8% × 92
Receivable collection period	48 days	37 days

It should be emphasized that fourth quarter sales figures, if available, are a more reliable basis than annual sales figures for determining the receivables/sales percentage and receivable collection period. Year-end receivables are more closely related to fourth quarter sales than to sales for the entire year.[4] The number of days in the receivable collection period can be compared (1) with the company's figure for a previous date, (2) with the company's credit terms, and (3) with the receivable collection period of similar companies.

MEETING MANAGEMENT'S NEEDS

Conventional accounting for trade receivables and sales revenue is concerned with:

[4] Caterpillar's figures for 1979 substantiate this observation. Sales for the fourth quarter were adversely affected by an extended strike by the United Auto Workers union. In the first three quarters of 1979, sales were 1924, 2137, and 2232, and in the fourth quarter 1321 —whereas, in 1978, sales were 1630, 1844, and 1817 in the first three quarters, 1929 in the fourth.

- Recording legal claims against customers when they arise.
- Recording settlement of those claims by collection, discounts, and other allowances.
- Maintaining records of customer accounts for billing.
- Determining the net realizable value of sales revenue for a period and of receivables at the period's end for the income statement and the balance sheet.

But management's needs for information extend beyond these areas. For example, in the area of sales management, there is a need for up-to-date analyses of sales orders received, by salesman and by product, for comparison with sales quotas and forecasts. When there is a time lag between receipt of sales orders and their fulfillment, a need for "backlog" analysis arises. Then again, when a management is considering changes in discount terms or in type of credit services offered customers, special studies are necessary.

PERCENTAGE-OF-COMPLETION METHOD

As we have indicated earlier in this chapter, the gross profit on a sale—that is, the selling price less cost of goods sold— is usually recognized in full the year the sale is made. An exception to this general rule is the percentage-of-completion method for reporting income under long-term contracts. Contractors under long-term contracts (such as construction contracts) may use either (1) the percentage-of-completion method or (2) the completed-contract method. The percentage-of-completion method recognizes income (or loss) as the work progresses. The percentage of income from the whole contract that this work provides is estimated (a) on the basis of total costs to date compared to the estimated total costs for the completed contract or (b) on such other measures of progress toward completion as may be appropriate. The completed-contract method recognizes income (or loss) only when the contract is completed. The percentage-of-completion method is preferable whenever reliable estimtes of progress toward completion can be made. For a more detailed discussion, see Accounting Research Bulletin No. 45 published by the AICPA in October 1955.

SUMMARY

Trade receivables and sales revenue arise from the sale of goods and services to customers on account. (Sales revenue arises also from cash sales to customers.) On the balance sheet, trade receivables are shown at their net realizable value after deduction for estimated uncollectibility and, when feasible, for estimated discounts, returns, and allowances. In the income statement, sales revenue is shown net of discounts, returns, and allowances. Provision for uncollectible accounts is shown as an operating expense. Sales taxes, excise taxes, and freight out are deducted from gross sales in determining net sales, or are included in operating expenses.

The factors affecting a company's investment in trade receivables are (1) seasonal, cyclical, and growth changes in sales volume, (2) the market the company serves, (3) the company's credit and collection policies, and (4) inflation.

The receivables/sales ratio may be expressed either (1) as a percentage or (2) as the receivable collection period (in days). If appropriate consideration is given to the presence of any unusual account balances in the year-end receivables, to seasonal and other fluctuations in sales, and to elimination of any cash sales from the sales figure used in the computation, the relationship between receivables and sales can be a most useful ratio for credit analysis.

An exception to the general rule that gross profit on a sale is recognized in full the year the sale is made is the percentage-of-completion method.

APPENDIX A: PRESENT VALUE

Let us suppose that on December 31, 1980, JKL Company received from its customer, Wilson Company, a noninterest bearing note for $1,000 due December 31, 1982, The company ascertained that Wilson Company's borrowing rate at December 31, 1980 was about 10 percent.

Problem. At what figure should the Wilson note be shown on the JKL Company's December 31, 1980 balance sheet?

Answer. 1. At the cash equivalent value of the note on December 31, 1980.
2. Obviously this is less than the $1,000 to be received on December 31, 1982.
3. $1 lent to Wilson Company at 10 percent would become $1.10 at the end of one year, and this $1.10 would become $1.21 at the end of a second year (if interest is compounded annually).
4. The "present value" of Wilson's $1,000 noninterest bearing two-year note would bear then the same relationship to $1,000 as $1.00 to $1.21.
5. So $PV: $1,000 = 1.00 : 1.21
$$\$PV \times 1.21 = \$1,000 \times 1.00$$
$$\$PV = \$1,000 \times 1.00/1.21$$
6. The "present value" factor of 10 percent compounded annually for two years is 1.00/1.21, or 0.82645.
7. $1,000 times 0.82645 is $826.45, the figure at which the note should be shown on JKL Company's 12/31/80 balance sheet.

Proof. If we lend Wilson Company $826.45 on December 31, 1980, at 10 percent, the compound amount owed one year later, at December 31, 1981, would become $909.09 ($826.45 × 1.10), and two years later, at December 31, 1982, would become $1,000 ($909.09 × 1.10). The $826.45 at December 31, 1980 is equivalent, at 10 percent compounded annually, to $1,000 two years later.

Present Value Calculations and Inflation

The calculations we have just made illustrate the fact that, given a choice, we would rather have a dollar today than a dollar two years from now. The timing of the receipt makes a difference because money has a time value. One reason for preferring a dollar now compared to a dollar two years from now is the probability that, with continuing inflation, the dollar will decline in purchasing power.

The present value techniques explained in this Appendix are based upon compound interest factors and their reciprocal present value factors. These techniques apply irrespective of inflation. Some acknowledgement of inflation effects may be made through our choice of discount interest rates. In the example of the Wilson Company note, the company's 1980 10 percent borrowing rate reflects in part the prospect of continuing inflation. But the choice of discount rate is only a rough tool. If more refined adjustments for inflation effects are desired, these are outside the scope of this Appendix.

In this Appendix our present value calculations deal with dollars as dollars with no discrimination as to possible differences in their purchasing power.[5]

Present Value is the Reciprocal of Compound Interest

A present value factor—for a specified rate and number of years—is the reciprocal of the compound amount factor.[6] In our Wilson Company example, the compound interest factors, at 10 percent, are *1.10* for one year and *1.21* for two years. The corresponding present value factors are *0.90909* (1/1.10) for one year and *0.82645* (1/1.21) for two years.

If one has a hand calculator with (1) a reciprocal key and (2) a key for raising a number to any power, determining a present value factor for a specified rate and number of years is simple. First, enter 1, decimal point, interest rate, then raise to power (number of years), then hit reciprocal key. For example, a 10 percent rate for 3 years, enter 1.10 and raise to 3rd power, and get *1.331*, then find reciprocal, *0.751314801*.

Factors for determining the present value of a single future amount based upon the equation $PV = 1 \div (1 + i)^n$ are set forth in Table A-I. In Table A-I, the present value factors for the specified rates and years have been "rough-rounded" to two decimal places.[7] For many

---

[5] In the Wilson Company example, the company promised only to pay $1,000 on December 31, 1982, with no adjustment for the difference in purchasing power of the dollar that might occur between 12/31/80 and 12/31/82.

[6] The compound amount factor, s, is determined:

$$s = (1 + i)^n$$

where i is the interest rate and n is the number of periods.

[7] Since compound amount factors and present value factors are reciprocals of each other, rough-rounded compound amount factors may be derived by taking the reciprocals of Table A-I's factors. For example, rough compound amount factors, at a 10 percent rate, would be:

1 End of Year	2 Table A-I Factor	3 Reciprocal of Column 2
1	.91	1.099
2	.83	1.205
3	.75	1.333
10	.39	2.564

The "rough" factors shown in Column 3 compare with factors more precisely derived from the compound amount formula $(1 + i)^n$: 1.100, 1.210, 1.331, 2.594.

problems, when the future amount, the interest rate, or the number of years are approximations, the use of Table A-I's two decimal factors should give answers as valid as the rough, raw data warrant. In the Wilson Company note example, the 10 percent rate specified as the company's borrowing rate at December 31, 1980 is a rough approximation, and our precisely calculated *$826.45* is perhaps no more valid than *$830*, approximated by Table A-I's .83 factor.

Present Value of an Annuity

Now let us suppose we wished to know the present value, at 8 percent, of $5,000 receivable at the end of one year, another $5,000 receivable at the end of two years, and another $5,000 receivable at the end of three years. A uniform amount receivable each year for a stated number of years is called an annuity. To find the present value of an annuity of $5,000 for three years, we could figure the present value of each installment, and then sum the three *PV* amounts, as in Column 4:

1 End of Year	2 Compound Amount Factor $(1 + i)^n$	3 Present Value Factor $1 \div (1 + i)^n$	4 Present Value of $5,000 Receivable
1	1.08	.92593	$ 4,629.65
2	1.1664	.85734	4,286.70
3	1.2597	.79384	3,969.20
		2.57711	$12,885.55

A shorter way of figuring the present value would be to go to an annuity present value table which shows successive sums of present value factors, find the appropriate factor, and apply to the uniform annual amount receivable each year. A 5-place annuity table would show a factor of 2.57710 for three years at 8 percent, and this times $5,000 would give us the present value figure of $12,885.50.

Proof. If a financial institution could lend $12,855.55 at 8 percent, payable in three annual installments of $5,000 each, it could use the $5,000 received each year to pay the annuitant. The amortization table would work out as follows:

Year	Loan Principal Beginning of Year	Portion of $5,000 Applied to	
		Interest at 8%	Principal Curtail
1	$12,885.55	$1,030.84	$3,969.16
2	8,916.39	713.31	4,286.69
3	4,629.70*	370.38	4,629.62*

*Does not come out exactly because of rounding.

Another way to prove would call for splitting the $12,885.55 into three parts—$4,629.65, $4,286.70, and $3,969.20. Then lend each of these amounts at 8 percent, compounded annually, for 1, 2, and 3 years, respectively:

Term of Loan	Amount of Loan	Compound Amount Factor	Amount Payable at Due Date
1 Year	$4,629.65	1.08	$5,000
2 Years	4,286.70	1.1664	5,000
3 Years	3,969.20	1.2597	5,000

Present value factors for an annuity, uniform amounts payable at the end of each year, for a series of years, are shown in Table A-III—rough-rounded to two decimal points—for specified rates and years. Note that Table A-III shows merely the successive sums of Table A-I's factors.[8]

Middle-of-the-Year Present Value Factors

Table A-I and A-III provide present value factors to be applied to amount(s) received in one lump sum at year-end(s). What if the annual amounts we deal with are received continuously throughout the year as is the case with sales revenue, cash operating expenses, etc.? Tables A-II and A-IV show present value factors for annual amounts received at the middle-of-the-year, and thus approximate more closely cash flows received, or paid, throughout the year.

Table A-II is based upon the formula, $1/(1 + i)^{n - \frac{1}{2}}$, with factors

[8] By hand calculator, the present value factor of an annuity for a specified rate and number of years can be determined by solving the formula, $1/i \ [1-1/(1 + i)^n]$. To find the *PV* factor for an annuity for 3 years at 8 percent: (1) Enter 1.08, (2) raise to 3rd power (1.259712), (3) get reciprocal (0.793832241), (4) subtract 1 (−0.206167759), (5) divide by .08 (−2.577096988). Change sign and round (2.5771). Compare this with Table A-III's 2-decimal figure of 2.58.

rough-rounded to two decimal places. Table A-IV shows present value factors for an annuity payable at the middle of the year for a
series of years, rough-rounded to two decimal places. Note that Table
A-IV merely shows the successive sums of Table A-II's factors.[9]

To illustrate the derivation of Table A-II and Table A-IV factors,
at a 10 percent rate:

1	2	3	4
Middle of Year	Compound Amount Factor $(1 + i)^{n-\frac{1}{2}}$	Present Value Factor $1/(1 + i)^{n-\frac{1}{2}}$	Successive Sums of Column 3 Factors
1	1.04881	0.95346	0.95346
2	1.15369	0.86678	1.82024
3	1.26906	0.78798	2.60822

Some Examples of the Use of Present Value

Example A. A Bond: Suppose a business were to raise money by
issuing bonds. Let's assume the bond issue is for $20 million princi-
pal payable 5 years from date, with 10 percent interest payable annually. Suppose the net proceeds the company receives from the issuance of the bonds is $20,000,000, what liability should the company
show? The company will pay out $30,000,000 over the five-year
period—but the present value, at 10 percent, is $20,000,000.

---

[9] Note that Table I factors may be converted to Table II factors, and Table III factors to
Table IV factors, if we divide Tables A-I and A-III factors by $1/(1 + i)^{\frac{1}{2}}$. For example, at 10
percent:

Year	Correction Factor $1/(1 + i)^{\frac{1}{2}}$	Table A-I Factor	Table A-II Factor Col 2 ÷ Col 1	Table A-III Factor	Table A-IV Factor Col 4 ÷ Col 1
1	0.95346	.91	.95	.91	.95
2	0.95346	.83	.87	1.74	1.82
3	0.95346	.75	.79	2.49	2.61

			($ in Millions)	
	Interest	Principal	Present Value	
Year	End of Year	End of Year	Factor at 10%	PV Amount
1	$ 2.0	–	.90909	$ 1.81818
2	2.0	–	.82645	1.65290
3	2.0	–	.75131	1.50262
4	2.0	–	.68301	1.36602
5	2.0	–	.62092	1.24184
		20.0	.62092	12.41840
Totals	$10.0	20.0		$19.99996
			Rounded	$20.0 Million[10]

Note. The present value of any interest-bearing obligation, discounted at its stated interest rate, is the same as the principal amount of the obligation.

Now, let us suppose two years after the above bonds were issued an investor wished to buy $10,000 of the bonds at a price which would yield a 12 percent return, how much must the investor pay?

Answer. Graph the $1,000 interest to be received annually, and the $10,000 principal to be received at the end of three years, and calculate present value:

				Present Value	
				Factor at 12%	Amount
1,000				.89286	$ 892.86
	1,000			.79719	797.19
		1,000		.71178	711.78
		10,000		.71178	7,117.80
					$9,519.63

Note. We have used 5-place factors for this problem to facilitate precise proof. Using Tables A-I and A-III factors, we would obtain $9,500 as our answer.

---

[10] A shorter way to do this problem would be to use a Table A-III type factor: 3.79078 (10% – 5 yrs.) times $2 million interest equals $7,581,560, and this plus $12,418,400, present value of $20 million principal, gives $19,999,960.

Proof.

Year	Investment at Beginning of Year	Interest at 12%	Amount Received	Added to Investment
1	9,519.63	1,142.36	1,000	142.36
2	9,661.99	1,159.44	1,000	159.44
3	9,821.43	1,178.57	11,000	-0-

Example B.   A Cost Savings Proposal: It is proposed that we purchase a machine costing $9,000 that will give cash savings in labor
costs of $3,000 a year for 5 years. Assume no terminal value for
machine and ignore effect of income taxes. What rate of return would
we get?

Answer.   Divide initial outlay, $9,000, by annual cash savings,
$3,000, and get 3.00 as "payback factor." Look in Table A-IV, at
five-year line, for factor of 3.00. At 25 percent, factor is 3.01. Therefore, rate of return is just slightly over 25 percent.

Proof.   Present value factor at 25 percent, for cash savings to be
received during the year, each year for 5 years is, per Table A-IV,
3.01. 3.01 times $3,000 gives present value amount of $9,030, which
approximates the $9,000 present value of initial outlay for machine.

Example C.   Monthly Payments on Real Estate Mortgage and on
a Lease. An article in the *Richmond Times-Dispatch* of August 3,
1980, "Mortgage Rates Have Inched Up," noted as one of the factors contributing to the rise in rates ". . . continued high inflation
that lenders try to outpace by seeking yields that are higher than the
inflation rate." One lender was charging a 12 percent annual rate for
a 360-month (30-year) mortgage when the borrower had made a 25
percent down payment.

Problem.   What would be the monthly payment on a $45,000
loan if the borrower had made a 25 percent down payment on the
$60,000 purchase price?

Answer. The 12 percent annual rate is 1 percent a month. The uniform monthly payments are to be made at the end of each month. Therefore, we can use the formula, $1/i\,[1 - 1/(1 + i)^n]$. On hand calculator, (1) enter 1.01, (2) raise to 360th power (35.94964151), (3) get reciprocal (0.027816689), (4) subtract 1 (−0.972183311), (5) divide by .01 (−97.21833109). Change sign and divide into $45,000 ($462.8756686). The answer then is that a monthly payment of *$462.88* will amortize the $45,000 over 360 months.

Note. This $462.88 is the same figure cited in the news article.

Now, let us suppose a manufacturing company has acquired the use of a plant through a 20-year noncancellable lease calling for the payment of $10,000 a month at the end of the month. The lease meets all the requirements to be considered as a "capital lease" and therefore the company's interest in the property is to be recognized as an asset and the lease obligation as a liability, at the capitalized value of the lease. The company's marginal borrowing rate is about 12 percent a year.

Problem. What is the capitalized value?

Answer. Determine present value factor by formula for annuity, $1/i\,[1 - 1/(1 + i)^n]$. On hand calculator, (1) enter 1.01, (2) raise to 240th power (10.89255369), (3) get reciprocal (0.091805836), (4) subtract 1 (−0.908194164), (5) divide by .01 and change sign (90.8194164). This is the present value factor. Multiply monthly lease payment, $10,000, by present value factor—get *$908,194*. This is the "capitalized value" of the 240 monthly lease payments of $10,000 each.

Preliminary Analysis of Present Value Problems

Present value problems involve the calculation of the current cash equivalent of future cash flow(s). The elements involved in the calculations are (1) present value amount, (2) amount(s) of future cash flows, (3) timing of future cash flows, and (4) interest rate (sometimes called discount rate). If we know, or can approximate, three of these four elements, we should be able to calculate the fourth.

The first step is to determine which of the four elements we are trying to calculate. In the cost savings example, the amount of annual savings rather than the rate of return may have been the uncertain factor; if so, given a desired return of 20 percent, the $9,000 purchase price can be divided by the present value factor 3.27 (Table A-IV: 5 years–20 percent), and a figure of $2,750 determined for the annual savings.

The next step is to determine the appropriate interest rate or "discount" rate to use. The rate should be appropriate to the risk and certainty of the future payments (or receipts). For example, the lease payments on the 20-year noncancellable lease are similar in certainty to the borrowing rate on a mortgage loan. By contrast, the annual savings in the cost savings example are less certain and more risky, and should therefore warrant a higher rate.

Finally, we need to determine the timing and amount of the future cash flows. Are we dealing with a single future cash flow, as with the Wilson note, or a series of uniform cash flows, as in mortgage example, or a series of nonuniform cash flows?[11] Do the future cash flows come at the end of the period (lease example) or during the period (cost savings example)? Has consideration been given to income taxes which affect net cash flows?

---

[11] When cash flows vary from year to year, we cannot use Table A-III or Table A-IV. If the rate is specified, say 10 percent, we can determine the present value as follows:

End of Year	End-of-year Cash Flow	*PV* Factor at 10% (Table A-I)	Present Value Amount
1	$5,000	.91	$4,550
2	4,000	.83	3,320
3	2,000	.75	1,500
			$9,370

If, without the rate specified, we were asked to determine the rate of return for an initial outlay of $9,000 to obtain cash savings of $5,000, $4,000, and $2,000 as above, we would have to determine by making additional calculations on a trial-and-error basis. There are computer programs, and hand calculator programs, which calculate rate-of-return for variable cash flows.

APPENDIX

Table A-I
Present Value of $1 Received at End of Year Indicated
$$PV = 1 \div (1 + i)^n$$
$$PV = 1 \div (1 + i)^n$$

End of Year	2%	4%	6%	8%	10%	12%	14%	16%	18%	20%	25%	30%
1	.98	.96	.94	.93	.91	.89	.88	.86	.85	.83	.80	.77
2	.96	.92	.89	.86	.83	.80	.77	.75	.71	.70	.64	.59
3	.94	.89	.84	.79	.75	.71	.67	.64	.61	.58	.51	.46
4	.93	.86	.79	.73	.68	.63	.59	.55	.52	.48	.41	.35
5	.90	.82	.75	.68	.62	.57	.52	.47	.44	.40	.33	.27
6	.89	.79	.71	.63	.56	.51	.46	.41	.37	.34	.26	.20
7	.87	.76	.66	.59	.51	.45	.40	.36	.31	.28	.21	.16
8	.85	.73	.63	.54	.47	.41	.35	.30	.27	.23	.17	.12
9	.84	.70	.59	.50	.42	.36	.31	.26	.22	.19	.13	.10
10	.82	.68	.56	.46	.39	.32	.27	.23	.19	.16	.11	.07
11	.81	.65	.52	.43	.35	.29	.23	.20	.16	.14	.09	.06
12	.79	.63	.50	.40	.32	.26	.21	.17	.14	.11	.07	.04
13	.77	.60	.47	.37	.29	.23	.18	.14	.12	.09	.05	.03
14	.76	.58	.44	.34	.26	.20	.16	.13	.10	.08	.04	.03
15	.74	.55	.42	.31	.24	.18	.14	.11	.08	.07	.04	.02
20	.67	.45	.31	.22	.15	.10	.07	.05	.04	.03	.01	.01
25	.61	.37	.23	.15	.09	.06	.04	.03	.02	.01	*	*
30	.55	.31	.17	.10	.06	.03	.02	.01	.01	*	*	*
35	.50	.25	.13	.07	.04	.02	.01	.01	*	*	*	*
40	.45	.21	.10	.05	.02	.01	*	*	*	*	*	*

Table A-II
Present Value of $1 Received at Middle of Year Indicated
$$PV = 1 \div (1 + i)^{n\ -\frac{1}{2}}$$

Middle of Year	2%	4%	6%	8%	10%	12%	14%	16%	18%	20%	25%	30%
1	.99	.98	.97	.96	.95	.95	.94	.93	.92	.91	.89	.88
2	.97	.94	.92	.89	.87	.84	.82	.80	.78	.76	.72	.67
3	.95	.91	.86	.83	.79	.75	.72	.69	.66	.63	.57	.52
4	.93	.87	.82	.76	.72	.67	.63	.60	.56	.53	.46	.40
5	.92	.84	.77	.71	.65	.60	.55	.51	.48	.44	.37	.31
6	.90	.81	.72	.65	.59	.54	.49	.44	.40	.37	.29	.23
7	.88	.77	.69	.61	.54	.48	.43	.38	.34	.31	.23	.18
8	.86	.75	.64	.56	.49	.43	.37	.33	.29	.25	.19	.14
9	.84	.71	.61	.52	.44	.38	.33	.28	.24	.21	.15	.11
10	.83	.69	.58	.48	.40	.34	.29	.25	.21	.18	.12	.08
11	.81	.66	.54	.45	.37	.31	.25	.21	.18	.15	.10	.07
12	.80	.64	.51	.41	.33	.27	.22	.18	.15	.12	.07	.05
13	.78	.61	.48	.38	.30	.24	.20	.15	.12	.10	.06	.04
14	.76	.59	.46	.36	.28	.22	.17	.14	.11	.09	.05	.03
15	.75	.57	.43	.33	.25	.19	.15	.11	.09	.07	.04	.02
20	.68	.47	.32	.22	.16	.11	.08	.05	.04	.03	.01	*
25	.61	.38	.24	.15	.10	.06	.04	.03	.02	.02	*	*
30	.56	.31	.18	.10	.06	.04	.02	.01	.01	.01	*	*
35	.50	.26	.13	.07	.04	.02	.01	.01	*	*	*	*
40	.46	.21	.10	.05	.02	.01	*	*	*	*	*	*

Table A-III
Present Value of $1 Received at End of Each Year for "N" Years
$$PV = 1/i\ [1 - 1/(1 + i)^n]$$

Period in Years	2%	4%	6%	8%	10%	12%	14%	16%	18%	20%	25%	30%
1	.98	.96	.94	.93	.91	.89	.88	.86	.85	.83	.80	.77
2	1.94	1.88	1.83	1.79	1.74	1.69	1.65	1.61	1.56	1.53	1.44	1.36
3	2.88	2.77	2.67	2.58	2.49	2.40	2.32	2.25	2.17	2.11	1.95	1.82
4	3.81	3.63	3.46	3.31	3.17	3.03	2.91	2.80	2.69	2.59	2.36	2.17
5	4.71	4.45	4.21	3.99	3.79	3.60	3.43	3.27	3.13	2.99	2.69	2.44
6	5.60	5.24	4.92	4.62	4.35	4.11	3.89	3.68	3.50	3.33	2.95	2.64
7	6.47	6.00	5.58	5.21	4.86	4.56	4.29	4.04	3.81	3.61	3.16	2.80
8	7.32	6.73	6.21	5.75	5.33	4.97	4.64	4.34	4.08	3.84	3.33	2.92
9	8.16	7.43	6.80	6.25	5.75	5.33	4.95	4.60	4.30	4.03	3.46	3.02
10	8.98	8.11	7.36	6.71	6.14	5.65	5.22	4.83	4.49	4.19	3.57	3.09
11	9.79	8.76	7.88	7.14	6.49	5.94	5.45	5.03	4.65	4.33	3.66	3.15
12	10.58	9.39	8.38	7.54	6.81	6.20	5.66	5.20	4.79	4.44	3.73	3.19
13	11.35	9.99	8.85	7.91	7.10	6.43	5.84	5.34	4.91	4.53	3.78	3.22
14	12.11	10.57	9.29	8.25	7.36	6.63	6.00	5.47	5.01	4.61	3.82	3.25
15	12.85	11.12	9.71	8.56	7.60	6.81	6.14	5.58	5.09	4.68	3.86	3.27
20	16.35	13.59	11.47	9.82	8.51	7.47	6.62	5.93	5.35	4.87	3.95	3.32
25	19.52	15.62	12.78	10.68	9.08	7.85	6.88	6.09	5.47	4.95	3.99	3.33
30	22.40	17.30	13.76	11.26	9.43	8.06	7.01	6.18	5.52	4.98	4.00	3.33
35	25.00	18.67	14.49	11.65	9.64	8.18	7.07	6.21	5.54	4.99	4.00	3.33
40	27.36	19.80	15.04	11.92	9.78	8.25	7.11	6.23	5.55	5.00	4.00	3.33

Table A-IV
Present Value of $1 Received at Middle of Each Year for "N" Years
$$PV = 1/i \ [1 - 1/(1 + i)^n] \times (1 + i)^{1/2}$$

Period in Years	2%	4%	6%	8%	10%	12%	14%	16%	18%	20%	25%	30%
1	.99	.98	.97	.96	.95	.95	.94	.93	.92	.91	.89	.88
2	1.96	1.92	1.89	1.85	1.82	1.79	1.76	1.73	1.70	1.67	1.61	1.55
3	2.91	2.83	2.75	2.68	2.61	2.54	2.48	2.42	2.36	2.30	2.18	2.07
4	3.84	3.70	3.57	3.44	3.33	3.21	3.11	3.02	2.92	2.83	2.64	2.47
5	4.76	4.54	4.34	4.15	3.98	3.81	3.66	3.53	3.40	3.27	3.01	2.78
6	5.66	5.35	5.06	4.80	4.57	4.35	4.15	3.97	3.80	3.64	3.30	3.01
7	6.54	6.12	5.75	5.41	5.11	4.83	4.58	4.35	4.14	3.95	3.53	3.19
8	7.40	6.87	5.39	5.97	5.60	5.26	4.95	4.68	4.43	4.20	3.72	3.33
9	8.24	7.58	7.00	6.49	6.04	5.64	5.28	4.96	4.67	4.41	3.87	3.44
10	9.07	8.27	7.58	6.97	6.44	5.98	5.57	5.21	4.88	4.59	3.99	3.52
11	9.88	8.93	8.12	7.42	6.81	6.29	5.82	5.42	5.06	4.74	4.09	3.59
12	10.68	9.57	8.63	7.83	7.14	6.56	6.04	5.60	5.21	4.86	4.16	3.64
13	11.46	10.18	9.11	8.21	7.44	6.80	6.24	5.75	5.33	4.96	4.22	3.68
14	12.22	10.77	9.57	8.57	7.72	7.02	6.41	5.89	5.44	5.05	4.27	3.71
15	12.97	11.34	10.00	8.90	7.97	7.21	6.56	6.00	5.53	5.12	4.31	3.73
20	16.51	13.86	11.81	10.20	8.93	7.91	7.07	6.38	5.81	5.33	4.42	3.78
25	19.72	15.93	13.16	11.09	9.52	8.30	7.34	6.56	5.94	5.42	4.45	3.80
30	22.62	17.64	14.18	11.70	9.88	8.53	7.48	6.65	5.99	5.46	4.46	3.80
35	25.25	19.04	14.93	12.11	10.11	8.66	7.55	6.69	6.02	5.47	4.46	3.80
40	27.63	20.19	15.50	12.39	10.26	8.73	7.58	6.71	6.03	5.48	4.47	3.80

QUESTIONS AND PROBLEMS

1. Distinguish between (a) trade receivables and nontrade receivables; and (b) trade receivables and accounts receivable.
2. Explain the difference between the direct write-off method and the reserve (allowance) method for accounting for bad debts. Are both methods acceptable for financial accounting and reporting purposes? For income tax purposes?
3. How might an external auditor test the reasonableness of a company's bad debt expense and its allowance for uncollectible accounts?
4. What is contained in a trade receivables aging schedule? Why do companies age their trade receivables?
5. How does inflation affect a company's trade receivables balance?
6. Distinguish between sales discounts and sales returns and allowances. Explain how each is treated in a company's income statement.
7. A local florist follows the policy of billing her customers at the end of each month. During the past six months, sales have remained steady but the company's accounts receivable balance has increased substantially. What steps might the owner consider taking to reduce the store's accounts receivable balance?
8. Distinguish between the percentage of completion method and the completed contract method for accounting for long-term construction contracts. Which method is preferable? Explain.
9. Sales discounts, returns, and allowances for an accounting period are treated in the income statement as "sales adjustments" and deducted from sales revenue to arrive at net sales.

   (A) Uncollectible accounts, however, are treated as an operating expense. What are the arguments, pro and con, for treating the uncollectibility of accounts in the income statement as a "sales adjustment"?

   (B) Sales and excise taxes are treated sometimes as operating expenses, sometimes as "sales adjustments." What are the arguments, pro and con?

   (C) Freight cost incurred on goods shipped to customers is normally considered to be an operating expense, yet it is sometimes treated as a "sales adjustment." What are the arguments, pro and con?

   (D) What difference does it make how all these items—cash discounts on sales, sales returns and allowances, uncollectibility of accounts, sales and excise taxes, and freight out—are treated in the income statement?

10. Suppose the Tentex Company had the following balances in certain of its accounts on December 31, 1979 (in thousands of dollars):

Trade Receivables.		$ 350.0
Deduction for estimated uncollectible accounts.		10.2

and that transactions during 1980 were (in thousands of dollars):

a.	Sales on account	$1,585.0
b.	Collections on account—$1,549.4 less cash	
	discounts of $27.4M.	1,522.0
c.	Sales returns and allowances authorized	
	in 1980	8.5
d.	Accounts written off in 1980 as uncollectible.	5.4
e.	Accounts previously written off now determined	
	to be collectible	0.7
f.	Portion of 1980 sales estimated uncollectible	8.0

Required: Prepare an analysis of the previous transactions. At what figure will Tentex show: (A) Net Sales in its 1980 income statement?; (B) Trade Receivables on its 12/31/80 balance sheet?

11. If the Texten Company described in Question 10 were to use the write-off method for uncollectible accounts:

(A) At what figure would it show Net Sales and Loss from Uncollectible Accounts in its 1980 income statement?

(B) At what figure would it show Trade Receivables on its 12/31/80 balance sheet?

(C) What difference would the use of the write-off method instead of the "reserve" method make in Tentex's federal income taxes? Assume Tentex's rate to be 46%.

12. If the Tentex Company were to relate sales discounts, returns, and allowances to the sales made each year, and assuming that the company's estimate of the discounts, returns, and allowances to be taken or granted on the receivables outstanding at 12/31/79 was $7,000, and at 12/31/80 was $7,800, at what figure would the company show Net Sales and sales adjustment for discounts, returns, and allowances in its 1980 income statement, and at what figure would it show Trade Receivables (net) on its 12/31/79 and 12/31/80 balance sheets?

13. The Buckeye Construction Company undertakes the construction of a tunnel at a contract price of $1,500,000. Construction begins in 1978 and is completed in 1980. Construction transactions are summarized below:

1978: Construction costs incurred total $500,000; remaining costs to complete the project are estimated at $1,020,000.

1979: Construction costs for the year total $676,000; remaining costs to complete the project are estimated at $294,000.

1980: Construction costs in completing the project total $280,000.

Required: Determine the profit (or loss) to be recognized by the Buckeye Construction Company for 1978, 1979, and 1980 under (a) the percentage of completion method; and (b) the completed con-contract method.

14. The following data were associated with the trade receivables and bad debts of CPL, Inc., during 1980:

(A) The opening balance in the Allowance for Doubtful Accounts was $710,000 at 1/1/80.

(B) During 1980, the company realized that specific trade receivable accounts totalling $820,000 had actually gone bad and were written off.

(C) A trade receivable of $50,000 was paid up during 1980. This account had previously been written off as a bad debt in 1979.

(D) The financial officer decided that the Allowance for Doubtful Accounts would need a balance of $920,000 at the end of 1980.

Required: 1. Do an analysis of transactions to show how these events would be recognized in an accounting system using:
   a. the reserve (allowance) method for bad debts.
   b. the write-off method for bad debts.
2. Discuss the advantages and disadvantages of each method with respect to the following accounting conventions:
   a. Matching
   b. Conservatism

15. The trial balance of the Aha Bra Company at the end of its 1980 fiscal year included the following account balances:

Account	Left	Right
Accounts Receivable	48,900	
Trade Notes Receivable	12,500	
Marketable Securities	15,000	
Allowance for Bad Debts	2,500	
Sales		500,000

The company has *not yet* recorded any bad debts expense for 1980.

Required: Determine the amount of bad debts expense to be recognized by the Aha Bra Company for 1980 assuming:

(A) Experience shows that 90 percent of all sales are credit sales and that an average of 1 percent of credit sales prove to be uncollectible.

(B) An analysis of the aging of trade receivables indicates that probable uncollectible accounts at year-end amount to $1,500.

(C) Company policy is to maintain a balance sheet provision for bad debts equal to 3 percent of outstanding trade receivables.

16. Moss Products, Inc. was formed in 1974. Sales have increased on the average of 5 percent per year during its first seven years of existence, with total sales for 1980 amounting to $350,000. Since incorporation, Moss Products has used the Allowance (reserve) Method of accounting for bad debts for both book and income tax purposes. The company's fiscal year is the calendar year.

On January 1, 1980, the company's "Allowance for Uncollectible Accounts" had a *right-hand* balance of $4,000. During 1980, accounts totaling $3,300 were written-off as uncollectible:

Required: (A) What does the 1-1-80 right-hand balance of $4,000 in the "Allowance for Uncollectible Accounts" represent?

(B) Since Moss products wrote-off $3,300 in uncollectible accounts during 1980, does this mean that their prior year's bad debts estimate was overstated?

(C) Do an analysis of transactions to record:

1. The $3,300 write-off during 1980
2. Moss Products' 1980 bad debts expense assuming: (a) Experience indicates that 1 percent of *Total* annual sales prove uncollectivle; and (b) an aging of the 12-31-80 accounts receivable indicates that potential uncollectible accounts at year-end total $4,000.

17. The following data are available regarding the Shoemaker Products Company for 1980: (In thousands of dollars)

	1st Quarter	2nd Quarter	3rd Quarter	4th Quarter	Total
Cash Sales	$ 872	$ 715	$1,186	$ 1,295	$ 4,068
Credit Sales	10,128	6,885	9,046	13,551	39,610
Sales Returns & Allowances (All related to credit sales)	125	110	97	122	454
Collections on Customer Accounts	12,742	9,843	7,436	10,148	40,169
Cash Discounts Taken by Customers	114	88	75	94	371
Bad Accounts Written Off	152	81	109	70	412
Cash Collected on Accounts Previously Written Off (To be reflected as "Other Income")	–	20	1	12	33

Shoemaker figures it's *ending* Deduction for Estimated Uncollectible Accounts balance to the sum of: (1-1-80 balance was $137)

½ of 1 percent of outstanding customer accounts less than 30 days old

2 percent of outstanding customer accounts between 31 and 60 days old

4 percent of all outstanding customer accounts greater than 60 days old

An analysis of all outstanding customer accounts at year-end 1980 showed:

	(Thousands)
Less than 30 days	$7,456
31 to 60 days	2,109
Greater than 60 days	739

Required: Prepare *one* yearly summary transaction for each of the following items:

(A) Cash Sales
(B) Credit Sales
(C) Sales Returns and Allowances
(D) Collections on Customer Accounts
(E) Cash Discounts Taken by Customer
(F) Bad Accounts Written Off
(G) Collections on Accounts Previously Written Off
(H) Bad debts expense

18. The 20th Century Engineering Associates undertakes the construction of a bridge at a contract price of $685,000. Construction begins in 1977 and is completed in 1979. Construction transactions are summarized below:

1977: Construction costs incurred total $125,000; remaining costs to complete the project are estimated at $500,000.

1978: Construction costs for the year total $475,000; remaining costs to complete the project are estimated at $125,000.

1979: Construction costs in completing the project total $65,000.

Required: Determine the profit (or loss) to be recognized by Engineering Associates for 1977, 1978, and 1979 under (a) the percentage of completion method; and (b) the completed contract method.

19. If you desired a 12 percent return on your investment, how much would you pay today for $200 received at the end of each year for the next 5 years and $100 at the end of each year for years 6 to 10, and nothing thereafter?

20. If you desired a 12 percent return on your investment, how much would you pay today for $100 received at the end of each year for the next 5

years and $200 at the end of each year for years 6 to 10, and nothing thereafter?

21. If you invested $10,000 today and received $18,000 ten years from now, what would be your return on investment?

22. R. H. Shay Motor Company offers a customer a car for his $4,000 cash. The customer has a $4,000 note, payable to his order, from his employer. The employer promises to pay $4,000 to the customer, "or his order," one year from now, and the customer offers to endorse the note to R. H. Shay Motor Company. R. H. Shay, recognizing that the employer is a prime credit risk, decides to accept the deal.

    (A) How should Shay Motor Company enter the transaction now?
    (B) One year from now if the employer pays?

23. (A) Find the *amount* of initial principal investment which a $100,000 *annual* level installment, payable at the *end* of each year for 5 years, will amortize over the 5-year period—at an interest rate of 10 percent.
    (B) Prepare an amortization schedule.

24. The January 5, 1981 issue of *Newsweek* included an article titled "Have Interest Rates Peaked"?, and the article contained the following passage:

    "Bonds. The old, high-grade Telephone bonds that used to be such a comfort to widows, orphans and retirees have become the province of the speculator. If investors are demanding a 15 percent return on their money, for example, a $1,000 bond paying a nominal rate of 7.5 percent is worth only $500 on the market. Because of the risks of locking up their money in long-term fixed-rate securities, investors are demanding ever higher interest premiums. Corporations, however, are equally reluctant to pay those high rates for years to come, and they are increasingly turning to short-term borrowing, even if that involves temporarily higher borrowing costs."

    Required: (A) Evaluate the validity of the *Newsweek* passage.
               (B) Can you verify the $500 figure mentioned in the passage?

7

Taxes: Their Impact and Recognition

The purpose of this Chapter is to discuss briefly those taxes that affect a business organization. The differences between accounting for tax and external reporting will be discussed and an illustration of a completed U.S. Corporation Income Tax Return will be shown.

A business organization is exposed to many different types of taxes; taxes are levied on:

- Income
- Sales
- Payrolls
- Property
- Consumption of specified products, such as gasoline and electricity

INCOME TAXES

Most business organizations of any significant size have an approximately equal partner to share in their profits—the federal government. Corporations have been subject to a federal income tax since 1908, individuals since 1913. In 1980 corporate taxable income over $100,000 was subject to a tax rate of 46 percent. Many states also levy a corporate income tax.

A corporation's income that is subject to tax may, and usually will, vary significantly from the income reported for financial accounting purposes. Taxable income is determined by:

- The Sixteenth Amendment to the Constitution.
- The various revenue acts passed by Congress as codified into the *Internal Revenue Code*.
- The interpretation of the *Internal Revenue Code* by the Federal Courts.
- The administration of the *Internal Revenue Code* by the Internal Revenue Service.

Congress, in passing tax laws, does not necessarily base these laws on "good accounting." Specific laws may be passed to raise revenue, stimulate investment, favor or penalize certain industries, or promote employment. Thus, financial accounting, based on generally accepted accounting principles, and tax accounting, based on tax law, vary in many respects.

DIFFERENCES BETWEEN TAX ACCOUNTING AND GAAP

The differences between tax accounting for federal purposes and generally accepted accounting principles and practices for external reporting may be grouped under four classifications:

1. Some items of gross income included in determining *accounting* net income are excluded in determining taxable income. For example, excluded items are interest on state and municipal bonds and life insurance proceeds received upon the death of an officer on whom the company has carried life insurance.
2. Some deductions used in determining *accounting* net income are excluded in determining *taxable* income. For example, deductions excluded from taxable income include life insurance premiums on the life of an officer paid by the corpora-

tion if the corporation is the named beneficiary and amortization of purchased goodwill.

3. Some deductions allowed in determining *taxable* income are not used in determining *accounting* net income. For example, percentage depletion for some oil and gas wells is allowed in determining *taxable* income but cost depletion is used in determining *accounting* net income. (See Chapter 10).

    Partial deduction (85%) for dividends received from other corporations is allowed in determining taxable income.

4. Some items of gross income and some deductions are taken into account for *tax* purposes at times different from the times that they are taken into account for *financial reporting* purposes. For example,

    a. Depreciation deducted for tax purposes may be based upon accelerated methods and "guideline lives," whereas depreciation deducted in determining accounting net income may be based upon the straight-line method and upon useful lives different from those shown in "guideline" regulations of the Internal Revenue Service.

    b. Rents and royalties received in advance are included in taxable income when received, whereas they are included in accounting income when they are earned.

    c. Warranty expense is deducted for tax purposes when the expense is actually incurred, whereas warranty expense deducted in determining accounting net income is based upon the expense expected to be incurred based on sales for the accounting period.

Despite the difference just outlined, a company can usually supplement the accounting it does for external reporting to meet its tax accounting needs as well. Two observations, however, are pertinent.

Many companies, given a choice of accounting procedures to handle a particular situation, will adopt the procedure which serves its tax accounting needs as well as its general accounting needs; thus, tax requirements in many cases do influence the accounting procedures.

And second, tax Form 1120, Schedule M-1, requires that a company reconcile its income per books with its income per tax return. Appendix A presents Schedule M-1, Form 1120, United States Corporation Income Tax Return (1979), for a hypothetical company that has the seven differences between taxable income and accounting net income cited as examples in the preceding discussion. The form has been completed with hypothetical information. A chronology of United States corporate income tax rates and dates of payment is outlined in Appendix B of this chapter.

PROPRIETORSHIPS AND PARTNERSHIPS

Unincorporated businesses are not subject to federal income tax, and only the owners of the business have taxable income. Thus, proprietorships and partnerships determine income that is then allocated to the owners to report on their personal tax returns. Partnerships do have to file an information return. The owners pay taxes on all the taxable income whether or not they take the income (in the form of cash, property, etc.) out of the business.

SUBCHAPTER S CORPORATIONS

Some corporations may elect not to be taxed as a corporation. In such cases, the corporation's income is *taxed* directly to its shareholders, as in a partnership. To make "an election under Subchapter S" (Subchapter S refers to a subchapter of the Internal Revenue Code), that is, to choose this option, a few of the specified requirements are:

1. Have no more than fifteen shareholders.
2. Have shareholders who are individuals or estates, not other corporations.
3. Have only one class of stock.
4. Derive at least 80 percent of its gross receipts from active businesses, rather than passive investments.

CAPITAL GAINS AND LOSSES

Varying tax rates apply to gains and losses on the sale or exchange of capital assets, that is, property. The maximum rate on long-term capital gains (requires one-year holding period) for an individual is 28 percent, and the maximum rate for a corporation with income over $100,000 is also 28 percent. An individual can offset capital losses in excess of capital gains against ordinary income to the extent of $3,000 per year. Corporations cannot offset capital losses against ordinary income. Corporations can carry capital losses back 3 years and forward 5 years to offset capital gains.

INVESTMENT TAX CREDIT

At various times since 1963, Congress has passed, terminated, reinstated, and changed the investment tax credit, "a credit against tax for the taxpayer's investment in certain depreciable property." The purpose of this credit is to stimulate the economy through increased business spending. In general, the credit ranges from 7-10 percent of the purchase price of the asset. The credit is a direct reduction in taxes payable. For example, if a corporation owed $17,260 in federal income taxes and has purchased a piece of equipment for $36,350 which is eligible for a 10 percent credit, then the corporation has a $3,635 credit against the $17,260 tax liability. Thus, $13,625 income taxes are payable rather than $17,260. (See line 11, Schedule J of Appendix A.)

The external reporting method of accounting for the investment credit may vary. The credit can be used to decrease the tax expense in the year received, or it can be spread over the useful life of the property. For tax return purposes, the credit must be used to directly reduce the tax liability in the year incurred.

OPERATING LOSS CARRY-BACK OR CARRY-FORWARD

When a company's federal income tax return (Form 1120, Appendix A) shows total operating deductions in excess of total revenue, it has an *operating loss* for tax purposes. Such operating loss may be carried back or forward a specified number of years and used as a deduction in computing taxable income of those years. If carried back, the operating loss results in a refund of past taxes paid. For external accounting purposes, the tax effect of a *loss carry-back* should be recognized in the determination of net income in the year the loss occurs. The tax effect of a *loss carry-forward* should normally be recognized as an extraordinary item in the year utilized.

INCOME TAXES AND DECISION MAKING

If a corporation is taxed at the maximum rate of 46 percent, incremental revenues are thus shared 46 percent with the government and any incremental tax deductible expenses are paid 46 percent by the government. Thus, taxes have to be a major factor in many business decisions. The only profit available to shareholders is after-tax profit. Thus, the taxability or nontaxability of revenue items, the deductibility or nondeductibility and the timing of the deduction of expense items, are important considerations in evaluating capital expenditures and investments.

In making business decisions, executives try to minimize taxes, just as they minimize other costs. Tax evasion is a crime—tax avoidance or minimization is good management.

OTHER TAXES

Sales taxes are levied by many states and municipalities, usually as a percentage of sales. For these taxes, the business in effect serves as a collection agent for the taxing authority. The same situation is true for *excise taxes*, which are taxes levied on the manufacture, sale, or consumption of a commodity.

Payroll Taxes

The most widely known and significant *payroll tax* is social security or FICA taxes. FICA taxes are levied on both the employer and the employee. In 1980, FICA taxes were 6.13 percent of the first $25,900 of earnings for both the employer and employee—a total of 12.26 percent on $25,900. In effect, the total outlay for an employee making \$25,900 is \$25,900 + (25,900 × 6.13%), or \$27,487.67, an expense to the business.

Unemployment Taxes

These taxes have become more significant in recent years. The employer pays a tax—part to the state and part to the federal government—based on the employer's record of stability of employment. This tax is an expense to the business.

Property Taxes

Such taxes are levied by many state and local governments. The rates vary significantly from one geographical area to another. The taxing authority assesses the taxable property; the rate is usually so much per \$100 of assessed value. The assessed value may or may not be the "market" value. Property tax is a consideration of businesses when deciding where to locate a plant or other facility.

Many other taxes are levied by the various levels of government. These taxes range from federal and state taxes on the consumption of gasoline, whiskey, and electricity to taxes on the mining of natural resources. Because these taxes are a direct cost of consuming and/or purchasing, they may be important in business decisions affecting the location of manufacturing and distribution facilities.

SUMMARY

It is necessary to distinguish between the purposes and requirements of accounting (1) to determine a company's taxable income for the year, (2) to report on behalf of management the company's financial position, income and retained income to third parties, and (3) to aid the company's management in the planning and control of the company's operations. Most business organizations must calculate their taxable income and pay federal tax (and state or local tax, if applicable) based on this income. Income tax accounting is governed by the Internal Revenue Code, and external financial reporting by generally accepted accounting principles. By contrast, there are no externally imposed constraints upon the way in which management information is obtained and presented.

APPENDIX A

Form **1120**	**U.S. Corporation Income Tax Return**	**1979**
Department of the Treasury Internal Revenue Service	For calendar year 1979 or other taxable year beginning ...., 1979, ending ...., 19	

Check if a— A Consolidated return ☐ B Personal Holding Co. ☐ C Business Code No. (See Page 8 of instructions) 2910	Use IRS label. Other-wise please print or type.	Name XYZ Corporation	D Employer Identification number (see instruction W) 12-3456789
		Number and street 123 Main Street	E Date incorporated 3/27/79
		City or town, State, and ZIP code City, State 12345	F Enter total assets (see instruction X) $ 836,842

Gross Income	1 (a) Gross receipts or sales $.................... (b) Less returns and allowances $.................... Balance ▶	1(c)	501,678
	2 Less: Cost of goods sold (Schedule A) and/or operations (attach schedule)	2	286,179
	3 Gross profit	3	215,499
	4 Dividends (Schedule C)	4	10,350
	5 Interest on obligations of the United States and U.S. instrumentalities	5	
	6 Other interest	6	
	7 Gross rents	7	93,200
	8 Gross royalties	8	
	9 (a) Capital gain net income (attach separate Schedule D)	9(a)	
	(b) Net gain or (loss) from Form 4797, line 11, Part II (attach Form 4797).	9(b)	
	10 Other income (see instructions—attach schedule)	10	66,409
	11 TOTAL income—Add lines 3 through 10	11	385,458
Deductions	12 Compensation of officers (Schedule E)	12	60,000
	13 (a) Salaries and wages ......113,620...... 13(b) Less WIN and jobs credit(s) .... Balance ▶	13(c)	117,031
	14 Repairs (see instructions)	14	11,246
	15 Bad debts (Schedule F if reserve method is used)	15	
	16 Rents	16	
	17 Taxes	17	3,675
	18 Interest	18	32,500
	19 Contributions (not over 5% of line 30 adjusted per instructions—attach schedule)	19	
	20 Amortization (attach schedule)	20	
	21 Depreciation from Form 4562 (attach Form 4562) ...., less depreciation claimed in Schedule A and elsewhere on return ...., Balance ▶	21	27,525
	22 Depletion	22	23,210
	23 Advertising	23	2,713
	24 Pension, profit-sharing, etc. plans (see instructions) (enter number of plans ▶ ....) . .	24	8,426
	25 Employee benefit programs (see instructions)	25	2,412
	26 Other deductions (attach schedule)	26	11,647
	27 TOTAL deductions—Add lines 12 through 26	27	300,385
	28 Taxable income before net operating loss deduction and special deductions (subtract line 27 from line 11) . .	28	85,073
	29 Less: (a) Net operating loss deduction (see instructions—attach schedule) . . 29(a)		
	(b) Special deductions (Schedule I) . . . . 29(b) 8,798	29	
	30 Taxable income (subtract line 29 from line 28)	30	76,275
Tax	31 TOTAL TAX (Schedule J)	31	13,625
	32 Credits: (a) Overpayment from 1978 allowed as a credit . . .		
	(b) 1979 estimated tax payments	8,000	
	(c) Less refund of 1979 estimated tax applied for on Form 4466 . ( )		
	(d) Tax deposited: Form 7004.................... Form 7005 (attach).... Total ▶		
	(e) Credit from regulated investment companies (attach Form 2439)		
	(f) Federal tax on special fuels and oils (attach Form 4136 or 4136-T)	32	8,000
	33 TAX DUE (subtract line 32 from line 31). See instruction G for depositary method of payment .	33	5,625
	(Check ▶ ☐ if Form 2220 is attached. See page 3 of instructions.) ▶ $....................		
	34 OVERPAYMENT (subtract line 31 from line 32)	34	
	35 Enter amount of line 34 you want: Credited to 1980 estimated tax ▶ Refunded ▶	35	

Please Sign Here	Under penalties of perjury, I declare that I have examined this return, including accompanying schedules and statements, and to the best of my knowledge and belief, it is true, correct, and complete. Declaration of preparer (other than taxpayer) is based on all information of which preparer has any knowledge.
	▶ Signature of officer Date ▶ Title

Paid Preparer's Information	Preparer's signature and date ▶	Check if self-employed ▶ ☐	Preparer's social security no.
	Firm's name (or yours, if self-employed) and address ▶	E.I. No. ▶	
		ZIP code ▶	

Form 1120 (1979) | **Schedule A** | **Cost of Goods Sold** (See Instructions for Schedule A) | Page **2**

1 Inventory at beginning of year	168,060
2 Merchandise bought for manufacture or sale	336,493
3 Salaries and wages	
4 Other costs (attach schedule)	
5 Total	504,553
6 Less: Inventory at end of year	218,374
7 Cost of goods sold—Enter here and on line 2, page 1	286,179

8 (a) Check all methods used for valuing closing inventory: (i) ☐ Cost (ii) ☒ Lower of cost or market as described in Regulations section 1.471-4 (see instructions) (iii) ☐ Writedown of "subnormal" goods as described in Regulations section 1.471-2(c) (see instructions)

(b) Did you use any other method of inventory valuation not described above? . . . . ☐ **Yes** ☒ **No**

If "Yes," specify method used and attach explanation ▶.................

(c) Check if this is the first year LIFO inventory method was adopted and used. (If checked, attach Form 970.) . . . .N/A. ☐

(d) If the LIFO inventory method was used for this taxable year, enter percentage (or amounts) of closing inventory computed under LIFO . . . .

(e) Is the corporation engaged in manufacturing activities? . . . . ☐ **Yes** ☒ **No**

If "Yes," are inventories valued under Regulations section 1.471-11 (full absorption accounting method)? . ☐ Yes N ☒ **No**

(f) Was there any substantial change in determining quantities, cost, or valuations between opening and closing inventory? . . . ☐ **Yes** ☒ **No**

If "Yes," attach explanation.

Schedule C	**Dividends** (See instruction 4)	
1 Domestic corporations subject to 85% deduction	10,350
2 Certain preferred stock of public utilities	
3 Foreign corporations subject to 85% deduction	
4 Dividends from wholly-owned foreign subsidiaries subject to 100% deduction (section 245(b))	
5 Other dividends from foreign corporations	
6 Includible income from controlled foreign corporations under subpart F (attach Forms 3646)	
7 Foreign dividend gross-up (section 78)	
8 Qualifying dividends received from affiliated groups and subject to the 100% deduction (section 243(a)(3)) .	
9 Taxable dividends from a DISC or former DISC not included in line 1 (section 246(d))	
10 Other dividends	
11 Total—Enter here and on line 4, page 1	10,350

Schedule E | **Compensation of Officers** (See instruction 12)

1. Name of officer	2. Social security number	3. Time devoted to business	Percent of corporation stock owned 4. Common	5. Preferred	6. Amount of compensation	7. Expense account allowances
Thomas P. Jones	987-65-4321	100%	20		60,000	—

Total compensation of officers—Enter here and on line 12, page 1 . . . . . .

Schedule F | **Bad Debts—Reserve Method** (See instruction 15)

1. Year	2. Trade notes and accounts receivable outstanding at end of year	3. Sales on account	Amount added to reserve 4. Current year's provision	5. Recoveries	6. Amount charged against reserve	7. Reserve for bad debts at end of year
1974						
1975						
1976						
1977						
1978						
1979						

Schedule I | **Special Deductions** (See instructions for Schedule I)

1 (a) 85% of Schedule C, line 1	8,798
(b) 59.13% of Schedule C, line 2	
(c) 85% of Schedule C, line 3	
(d) 100% of Schedule C, line 4	
2 Total—See instructions for limitation	8,798
3 100% of Schedule C, line 8	
4 Deduction for dividends paid on certain preferred stock of public utilities (see instructions)	
5 Deduction for Western Hemisphere trade corporations (see instructions)	
6 Total special deductions—Add lines 2 through 5. Enter here and on line 29(b), page 1	8,798

Form 1120 (1979)   Page **3**

Schedule J	Tax Computation

1 Taxable income (line 30, page 1)		76,275
2 (a) Are you a member of a controlled group? . . . . ☐ Yes ☒ No		
(b) If "Yes," see instructions and enter your portion of the $25,000 amount in each taxable income bracket:		
(i) $............................. (ii) $............................. (iii) $............................. (iv) $.............................		
3 Income tax (see instructions to figure the tax; enter this tax or alternative tax from Schedule D, whichever is less). Check if from Schedule D ▶ ☐		17,260
4 (a) Foreign tax credit (attach Form 1118)		
(b) Investment credit (attach Form 3468) 3,635		
(c) Work incentive (WIN) credit (attach Form 4874)		
(d) Jobs credit (attach Form 5884)		
5 Total of lines 4(a), (b), (c), and (d)		3,635
6 Subtract line 5 from line 3		13,625
7 Personal holding company tax (attach Schedule PH (Form 1120))		
8 Tax from recomputing prior-year investment credit (attach Form 4255)		
9 Tax from recomputing prior-year WIN credit (attach computation)		
10 Minimum tax on tax preference items (see instructions—attach Form 4626)		13,625
11 Total tax—Add lines 6 through 10. Enter here and on line 31, page 1		

Schedule K	Record of Federal Tax Deposit Forms 503 (List deposits in order of date made—See instruction G)		Date of deposit	Amount

Date of deposit	Amount	Date of deposit	Amount
4/15	2,000	12/15	2,000
6/15	2,000		
9/15	2,000		

	Yes	No
G (1) Did you claim a deduction for expenses connected with:		
(a) Entertainment facility (boat, resort, ranch, etc.)? . . .		X
(b) Living accommodations (except employees on business)? .		X
(c) Employees attending conventions or meetings outside the U.S. or its possessions?		X
(d) Employee's families at conventions or meetings? . . .		X
If "Yes," were any of these conventions or meetings outside the United States or its possessions?		X
(e) Employee or family vacations not reported on Form W-2? .		X

(2) Enter total amount claimed on Form 1120 for entertainment, entertainment facilities, gifts, travel, and conventions of the type for which substantiation is required under section 274(d). (See instruction Y.) ▶ 2,715

H (1) Did you at the end of the taxable year own, directly or indirectly, 50% or more of the voting stock of a domestic corporation? (For rules of attribution, see section 267(c).) . . . | | | X

If "Yes," attach a schedule showing: (a) name, address, and identifying number; (b) percentage owned; (c) taxable income (or loss) (e.g., if a Form 1120: from Form 1120, line 28, page 1) of such corporation for the taxable year ending with or within your taxable year; (d) highest amount owed by you to such corporation during the year; and (e) highest amount owed to you by such corporation during the year.

(2) Did any individual, partnership, corporation, estate or trust at the end of the taxable year own, directly or indirectly, 50% or more of your voting stock? (For rules of attribution, see section 267(c).) If "Yes," complete (a) through (e) . . . | | | X

  (a) Attach a schedule showing name, address, and identifying number; (b) Enter percentage owned ▶

  (c) Was the owner of such voting stock a person other than a U.S. person? (See instruction S.) . . . . . .

  If "Yes," enter owner's country ▶

  (d) Enter highest amount owed by you to such owner during the year ▶

  (e) Enter highest amount owed to you by such owner during the year ▶

(Note: For purposes of H(1) and H(2), "highest amount owed" includes loans and accounts receivable/payable.)

	Yes	No
I Did you ever declare a stock dividend?		X

J Taxable income or (loss) from Form 1120, line 28, page 1, for your taxable year beginning in:
1976 _10,615_ , 1977 _27,214_ , 1978 _52,311_

K If you were a member of a controlled group subject to the provisions of section 1561, check the type of relationship:
(1) ☐ parent-subsidiary   (2) ☐ brother-sister
(3) ☐ combination of (1) and (2) (See section 1563.)

L Refer to page 8 of instructions and state the principal:
Business activity ....
Product or service ....

	Yes	No
M Did you file all required Forms 1087, 1096 and 1099? . . .	X	
N Were you a U.S. shareholder of any controlled foreign corporation? (See sections 951 and 957.) If "Yes," attach Form 3646 for each such corporation		X
O At any time during the tax year, did you have an interest in or a signature or other authority over a bank account, securities account, or other financial account in a foreign country (see instruction V)?		X
P Were you the grantor of, or transferor to, a foreign trust which existed during the current tax year, whether or not you have any beneficial interest in it?		X

If "Yes" you may have to file Forms 3520, 3520-A or 926.

	Yes	No
Q During this taxable year, did you pay dividends (other than stock dividends and distributions in exchange for stock) in excess of your current and accumulated earnings and profits? (See sections 301 and 316.)		X

If "Yes," file Form 5452. If this is a consolidated return, answer here for parent corporation and on Form 851, Affiliations Schedule, for each subsidiary.

	Yes	No
R During this tax year was any part of your tax accounting records maintained on a computerized system?		X
S (1) Did you elect to claim amortization (under section 191) or depreciation (under section 167(o)) for a rehabilitated certified historic structure (see instructions for line 20)? . . .		X

(2) Amortizable basis (see instructions for line 20):

Form 1120 (1979)　　　　　　　　　　　　　　　　　　　　　　　　　　　　　　　**Page 4**

Schedule L — Balance Sheets	Beginning of taxable year		End of taxable year	
ASSETS	(A) Amount	(B) Total	(C) Amount	(D) Total
1 Cash		3,074		5,112
2 Trade notes and accounts receivable	12,429		15,241	
(a) Less allowance for bad debts		12,429		15,241
3 Inventories		168,060		218,374
4 Gov't obligations: (a) U.S. and instrumentalities				
(b) State, subdivisions thereof, etc.		10,000		10,000
5 Other current assets (attach schedule) Prepaid rent		700		600
6 Loans to stockholders				
7 Mortgage and real estate loans				
8 Other investments (attach schedule) 1000 SH ABC		30,000		30,000
9 Buildings and other fixed depreciable assets	359,360		408,483	
(a) Less accumulated depreciation	71,063	288,297	90,248	318,235
10 Depletable assets	86,000		86,000	
(a) Less accumulated depletion	12,420	73,580	21,020	64,980
11 Land (net of any amortization)		29,500		29,500
12 Intangible assets (amortizable only)	200,000		200,000	
(a) Less accumulated amortization	36,800	163,200	55,200	144,800
13 Other assets (attach schedule)				
14 Total assets		978,840		836,842
LIABILITIES AND STOCKHOLDERS' EQUITY				
15 Accounts payable		131,063		149,842
16 Mtges., notes, bonds payable in less than 1 yr.		25,000		25,000
17 Other current liabilities (attach schedule) Taxes		12,425		14,860
18 Loans from stockholders		45,000		30,000
19 Mtges., notes, bonds payable in 1 yr. or more		355,000		330,000
20 Other liabilities (attach schedule)				
21 Capital stock: (a) Preferred stock				
(b) Common stock		100,000		100,000
22 Paid-in or capital surplus				
23 Retained earnings—Appropriated (attach sch.)				
24 Retained earnings—Unappropriated		110,352		187,140
25 Less cost of treasury stock		( )		( )
26 Total liabilities and stockholders' equity		778,840		836,842

Schedule M-1 — Reconciliation of Income Per Books With Income Per Return			
1 Net income per books	76,788	7 Income recorded on books this year not included in this return (itemize)	
2 Federal income tax	13,625		
3 Excess of capital losses over capital gains		(a) Tax-exempt interest $ 675	
4 Income subject to tax not recorded on books this year (itemize) Rental Income Collected in Advance	600	Inc. In Cash Surrender Value of Life Ins. 3456	4,131
5 Expenses recorded on books this year not deducted in this return (itemize)		8 Deductions in this tax return not charged against book income this year (itemize)	
(a) Depreciation . . . . $		(a) Depreciation . . $ 8,340	
(b) Depletion . . . . $		(b) Depletion. . . $ 14,610	
Life Ins. Prem. 1741 Amor. of Goodwill 18400	20,141		21,950
6 Total of lines 1 through 5	111,154	9 Total of lines 7 and 8	26,081
		10 Income (line 28, page 1)—line 6 less 9	85,073

Schedule M-2 — Analysis of Unappropriated Retained Earnings Per Books (line 24 above)			
1 Balance at beginning of year	110,352	5 Distributions: (a) Cash	
2 Net income per books	76,788	(b) Stock	
3 Other increases (itemize)		(c) Property	
		6 Other decreases (itemize)	
4 Total of lines 1, 2, and 3	187,140	7 Total of lines 5 and 6	
		8 Balance at end of year (line 4 less 7)	187,140

APPENDIX B: CHRONOLOGY OF UNITED STATES
CORPORATE INCOME TAX RATES

	Rates on Taxable Income (%)				
Year(s)	First $25,000	Over $25,000	Over $50,000	Over $75,000	Over $100,000
1914	1	1			
1924	12-½[a]	12-½			
1929	11[a]	11			
1939	19[a]	19			
1950	23	42			
1951	28-¾	50-¾			
1952/1963	30	52			
1964	22	50			
1965/1967	22	48			
1968	24.2[b]	52.8[b]			
1969	24.2	52.8			
1970	22.5	49.2			
1971/1974	22	48			
1975/1976	20	22	48		
1979	17	20	30	40	46

1. In 1924, 1929, and 1939:
   a. Corporations with more than $25,000 net income taxable at rates.
   b. Corporations with less than $25,000 net income taxable at lesser rates.
2. In 1968 and 1969, 10% surcharge applied to rates of 22% and 48% resulted in effective rates of 24.2% and 52.8% respectively.

From 1955 through 1967, provision was made for corporations to file *estimated* tax returns during the current year and to make installment payments in the current year against estimated tax in excess of $100,000. It should be noted at this point that there was a gradual acceleration of these payments against estimated tax in excess of $100,000, until in 1967 100% was required to be paid in the current year—25% April 15, 25% June 15, 25% September 15, and 25% December 15. In the years from 1955 through 1967, corporations with over $100,000 estimated tax filed their actual return for the current calendar year on or before March 15 of the following year, and paid the amount of tax shown by this return (reduced by the amounts paid against estimated tax in excess of $100,000) in two installments in the following year—½ on March 15, and ½ on June 15. For the years 1955 through 1967, corporations with less than

$100,000 tax were not required to file estimated tax returns; these corporations filed their actual return for the calendar year on or before March 15 of the following year and paid their tax in two installments—½ on March 15 and ½ on June 15 in the following year.

The 1968 Revenue and Expenditure Act repealed the requirement that only companies with estimated tax in excess of $100,000 file estimated tax returns. This act provided for gradual acceleration of current year installments against the $100,000 so that by 1977 corporations would pay 100% of estimated taxes during the current year.

The date on which a corporation first meets the $40 expected liability determines the number of installments to be made, the due dates of the installments, and the minimum percentage of estimated tax to be paid with each installment. The following table shows the determination and payment dates and the percentages of tax to be paid.

	Percentages of the estimated tax to be paid by the 15th day of the:			
Determination dates	4th Month	6th Month	9th Month	12th Month
Requirements met prior to 4th month of the taxable year	25	25	25	25
Requirements met prior to 6th month of the taxable year (but after 3rd month)		33-1/3	33-1/3	33-1/3
Requirements met prior to 9th month of the taxable year (but after 5th month)			50	50
Requirements met prior to 12th month of the taxable year (but after 8th month)				100

Any tax shown to be owing when the corporation's income tax return is filed is payable on the 15th day of the third and sixth months following the taxable year—March 15 and June 15 for calendar year corporations.

In 1980, the penalty for underpayment of estimated taxes amounted to 12 percent of the underpayment, beginning with the due date of the installment. As penalties are nondeductible for tax purposes, underpayment of estimated tax can be expensive. However, due to the difficulty in ascertaining the correct tax liability on a quarterly basis, there are certain exceptions available which will avoid any underpayment penalty. For companies undergoing growth or involved in a seasonal business, the exceptions can allow a substantial deferral of tax payments if properly utilized.

In any situation, no penalty will be assessed if a corporation's estimated payments equal or exceed 80 percent of the final income tax liability for the year, although the payments must be made in equal amounts. Consistent with this leniency, the penalty is only assessed on a maximum of 80 percent of the final income tax liability. If the 80 percent test is not met, no penalty will be assessed if the corporation has met one of the following exceptions:

1. Amount paid in equal quarterly installments equals or exceeds prior year's income tax liability (beneficial in periods of growth).
2. Amount paid in equal quarterly installments equals or exceeds hypothetical tax on prior year's income using current year rates (beneficial in years in which rates decline).
3. Amount paid equals 80 percent of tax liability using annualized income computed quarterly. (This exception results in estimated payments of 80 percent of final tax liability, but allows deferral if bulk of income is generated in the latter part of the year.)

Corporations must deposit their estimated income taxes in authorized commercial bank depositories or Federal Reserve banks on or before the payment dates.

QUESTIONS AND PROBLEMS

1. Why would the owners of a corporation elect to be taxed as a Subchapter S Corporation?
2. How does an Investment Tax Credit affect a corporation's taxable income? Income tax liability? Net Income?
3. Obtain a copy of IBM's most recent SEC Form 10K. Did IBM pay more in property taxes or Social Security taxes? This information was contained in Schedule XVI of the 1979 Form 10K.
4. The following information was taken from the records of Lin Corporation for the fiscal year ended December 31, 1980.

(1)	Dividends from domestic corporations	100,000
(2)	Interest from municipal bonds	50,000
(3)	Capital Gains	40,000
(4)	Capital Losses	20,000
(5)	Amortization of Goodwill	10,000
(6)	Provision for warranty expense	30,000
(7)	Actual expenditures under warranty provision	10,000
(8)	Investment tax credit	10,000
(9)	Insurance expense on officer lines	2,000

   Explain how each of the above items will affect Lin Corporation's 1980 *taxable* income.
5. Virginia, Inc. had the following income and expense items for the fiscal year ending December 31, 1979.

Sales	$2,500,000
Cost of Sales (excluding depreciation)	1,200,000
Other expenses	800,000
Interest income on Treasury bills	20,000
Depreciation—straight line	200,000
Depreciation—Double declining balance	300,000
Proceeds from life insurance policy on officer	50,000
Investment tax credit	10,000
Capital Gains	20,000
Capital Losses	20,000
Unearned rent (Rent received in advance)	5,000

   Virginia, Inc. used straight line depreciation for reporting purposes and double declining balance for tax purposes.

   Compute Virginia, Inc.'s income tax liability for 1979. (Refer to Appendix B for applicable tax rates).

6. The following information regarding income taxes was taken from the 1980 Annual Report of Jostens, Inc.

	Amount	%
U.S. Statutory Rate	$18,901	46.0
State Taxes on Income	1,128	2.8
Investment Tax Credit	(574)	(1.4)
All other, net	(20)	(.1)
	$19,435	47.3

   A. Explain why a company would include this type of information in a footnote to its financial statements.
   B. What types of items could possibly be included in the line item "all other, net"?

8

Inventories and Cost of Goods Sold for Trading Companies

Accounting for inventories and cost of goods sold for trading companies is considered in Chapter 8, for manufacturing companies in Chapter 9. Chapter 9 will include also, applicable to both trading and manufacturing companies, a discussion of product and period costs, financial statement disclosure, factors affecting investment in inventories, inventory turnover ratio, and inventory characteristics and management decisions.

For a trading company, one which purchases the goods it sells, there is a need to measure:

- Investment in inventories at the end of the accounting period.
- Cost of goods sold during the period.

There are two major problems:

- Determining the cost of goods available for sale during the accounting period, the sum of cost of goods on hand at the beginning of the period, and the cost of goods purchased during the period.

⟨• Allocating the cost of goods available for sale between cost of
   goods sold, and cost of goods on hand at the end of the period.

A diagram of the elements involved is shown in Illustration 8-1.

Cost of goods in beginning inventory					Cost of goods disposed of
plus	*equals*	Total cost of goods available for sale	*to be allocated between*		*and*
Cost incurred in buying or manufacturing goods					Cost of goods in ending inventory

← **Accounting for Acquisition**   **Accounting for Disposition** →

Illustration 8-1   Schematic Diagram of Inventory Accounting

DETERMINING AND ALLOCATING THE COST OF GOODS AVAILABLE FOR SALE

The merchandise inventory account of Corner Drugstore, Inc., was
(see Chapter 3, Illustration 3-4):

Merchandise Inventory (Asset)

4/1/78 Balance	$ -0-	R–Cost of Goods Sold		
C–Purchases in		in 1979	$44,700	
fiscal 1979	57,400	3/31/79 Balance	12,700	
	$57,400		$57,400	

Note that the cost of goods available for sale in fiscal 1979, $57,400,
was determined by adding:

Cost assigned to inventory on hand at the beginning
  of the fiscal year . . . . $ -0-

And the cost of merchandise bought during the year   57,400

Making cost of goods available for sale. $57,400

Note also that the cost of goods available for sale was allocated
between:

Cost of merchandise sold in fiscal 1979 . . . . $44,700

And cost assigned to merchandise remaining in
  inventory at the end of fiscal 1979   12,700

                                                              $57,400

The $12,700 cost assigned to merchandise remaining in inventory at the end of fiscal 1979 becomes the cost assigned to inventory at the beginning of fiscal 1980. This figure is used in determining the cost of goods available for sale in fiscal 1980.

ACCOUNTING FOR ACQUISITION: COST OF MERCHANDISE BOUGHT DURING THE PERIOD

Cost of merchandise bought during the accounting period ideally should represent invoice cost of merchandise purchased and received into stock during the period:

LESS: Available cash discounts for payment of invoices within the stated discount period whether the cash discounts are taken or not.

PLUS: Cost of inbound transportation on merchandise purchased, when the terms provide that the purchaser stand this cost.

The Corner Drugstore determined its cost of merchandise purchased during fiscal year 1979:

Gross amount of purchase invoices		$58,000
Less: Available cash discounts		600
Net amount of purchase invoices		$57,400
Plus: Inbound transporation (See Note)		-0-
Cost assigned to merchandise purchased.		$57,400

Note: The store purchased its merchandise under terms providing for the suppliers to pay transportation costs to the store.

Two other methods of accounting for cash discounts on purchases are discussed in Chapter 12.

PERPETUAL AND PERIODIC INVENTORIES

A trading company may use either a perpetual or a periodic inventory system to allocate cost of goods available for sale between (1) cost of goods sold and (2) cost of goods remaining in inventory.

Under a *perpetual* inventory system, a company maintains a continuous record of the physical quantities and dollar costs of inventory on hand. For each item stocked, the company has to keep a record of the units acquired, disposed of, and remaining on hand—expressed in both physical quantities and dollar costs. Thus, in addition to the entry made for the sale at the selling price of the goods:

Trade Receivables (A)   Incr 100
    Retained Earnings (OE)–(Sales Revenue)   Incr 100

an entry has to be made, at the time each sale is made, for the cost of the goods sold:

Retained Earnings (OE)–(Cost of Goods Sold)   Decr 70
    Inventory (A)   Decr 70

Under such a system, the cost of goods is determined daily, and it is not necessary to wait until a physical inventory is taken at the end of the accounting period to determine cost of goods sold. When a perpetual system is used, physical inventories are taken from time to time to check the perpetual inventory record.

For trading companies, a perpetual inventory system can ordinarily be justified only for high value items, such as automobiles and pianos. Many merchandising companies do use the *retail method of inventory*, which gives them many of the benefits of a perpetual inventory system at less cost. Under the retail method of inventory, records are maintained for:

1. Merchandise in inventory at the beginning of the accounting period:
    a. At cost.
    b. At marked selling prices.

2. Purchases during the period:
    a. At cost.
    b. At marked selling prices.

3. The total dollar amount of markups or markdowns in selling prices during the accounting period.

4. Sales during the period—at selling prices.

With this information, the allocation between cost of goods sold and ending inventory is determined as indicated in Illustration 8-2.

Illustration 8-2

**Example of Retail Method of Inventory for One Department of a
Trading Company for One Month
(In Thousands of Dollars)**

	At Selling Price		At Cost
Beginning inventory	$252		$180
Purchases during period	96		65
Additional markups.	2		—
Total inventory, purchases and markup	$350		$245
% Cost to Selling Price (245 ÷ 350).		70%	
Deduct markdowns.	4		
	$346		
Deduct sales (at selling prices).	106		
Ending inventory–at retail.	$240		
Ending inventory–at cost			
(Calculated: 70% of $240M).			168
Cost of Goods Sold			
(Calculated: $245 less $168)			$ 77

[handwritten annotations:]
Beg. INV + PURCH − End Inv.
(Beginning + 1. INV + PURCH) − less Ending INV'y.

When the retail method is used, it is possible to determine a department's cost of goods sold without taking a physical inventory. Physical inventories, however, are taken from time to time to check the department's retail inventory records and to indicate the inventory shortages arising from shoplifting, employee theft, or other causes.

When a *periodic* inventory system is used, the cost of the beginning inventory and the cost of merchandise bought during the period are maintained in the inventory ledger account. No entries are made in the inventory account to show the cost of the goods sold during the period. At the end of the accounting period, a physical inventory is taken.

1. The merchandise in the store is listed by stock item on inventory sheets.
2. The quantity of each stock item is counted and recorded on the inventory sheets.
3. The unit cost to be used for each stock item is then recorded on the inventory sheets.
4. The dollar cost for each stock item is then determined by multiplying its quantity by its unit cost.

5. The dollar costs are then added to give the total cost of the inventory.

In the case of the Corner Drugstore, Inc., Illustration 3-4, the dollar cost of the inventory at March 31, 1979, determined by a physical inventory, was $12,700. Only after the physical inventory had been taken could the store determine the cost of goods sold during the year:

Cost of goods available for sale in fiscal 1979 (Illustration 3-4)	$57,400
Deduct cost assigned to merchandise on hand, 3/31/79.	12,700
Remainder: Cost assigned to goods sold in fiscal 1979.	$44,700

Note that the $44,700 designated as "cost assigned to goods sold" could have been more precisely stated as "cost assigned to goods sold, lost, or stolen."

Two defects of the periodic inventory system, as compared with the perpetual system or the retail method, are (1) the periodic inventory system requires that a complete physical inventory be taken in order that an income statement and balance sheet may be prepared, and (2) the periodic inventory system offers no record control that will reveal the existence or extent of customer or employee pilferage.

METHODS OF ALLOCATING COSTS OF GOODS AVAILABLE FOR SALE

Various methods are used to allocate costs between units sold and units remaining in inventory. These include:

1. Specific identification.
2. First-in, first-out (FIFO).
3. Last-in, first-out (LIFO).
4. Average unit costs.

The *specific identification* method is used only in those cases when the cost of an article of merchandise or of a lot of merchandise can be clearly identified from the time of its purchase to the time of its sale. If the value of the article is sufficient to justify the specific identification method, its specific cost is identified with the article when it is acquired; and when the article is sold, the inventory account is reduced by the specific cost of the article.

Usually, a company buys many units of a stock item of merchandise at different times and at different unit costs. The problem then becomes which unit costs for the stock item should apply to units sold during the period, and which costs to units remaining in inventory. The answer depends upon whether the company assumes that the costs *assigned to units sold* shall be:

1. The first unit costs into inventory, the first out (FIFO).
2. The last unit costs into inventory, the first out (LIFO).
3. An average of the unit costs into inventory.

The application of these "flow-of-cost" assumptions to a specific example is shown in Illustration 8-3.

Note in Illustration 8-3 that the unit cost of the first lot purchased, $1.05, was higher than the unit cost of the beginning inventory, $1.00, and that the unit cost rose for each succeeding lot purchased. This situation is similar to that experienced by American business in recent years. Note also that under these conditions of rising costs, the cost allocated to the 300 units sold was

Lowest under FIFO.	$315.00
Highest under LIFO.	$330.00
In between under Average costs	$322.50

and that the cost allocated to the 100 units remaining in inventory

Highest under FIFO.	$115.00
Lowest under LIFO	$100.00
In between under Average costs	$107.50

These differences, in this relatively simple example, help explain the varying effects that FIFO and LIFO have had upon (1) the figures shown for cost of goods sold, provision for income taxes, and net income in income statements, and (2) the figures for inventory shown on balance sheets in corporate annual reports during recent years of generally rising prices.

Caterpillar Tractor Company adopted LIFO in 1950. In its Annual

Illustration 8-3

A Comparison of FIFO, LIFO, and Average Methods of Allocating Costs of Goods Available for Sale

A company starts the year with 100 units of a stock item in inventory and purchases three lots of 100 units each during the year. The costs of the 400 units available for sale are:

Beginning inventory	100 units @ $1.00	$100
Purchases - March	100 units @ $1.05	105
- August	100 units @ $1.10	110
- November	100 units @ $1.15	115
Goods Available for Sale	400 units	$430

The company sells *300* units and has 100 left in inventory at year-end.

Allocation of $430 Cost of 400 Units Available for Sale

	Cost Allocated To	
	300 Units Sold	100 Units Remaining
A. *Under First-In, First-Out (FIFO):* For *300 units sold* 100 @ $1.00, 100 @ $1.05, and 100 @ $1.10 ($315) – For *100 units remaining* 100 @ $1.15 ($115)	315.00	115.00
B. *Under Last-In, First-Out (LIFO):* for *300 units sold* 100 @ $1.15, 100 @ $1.10, and 100 @ $1.05 ($330) – For 100 units remaining 100 @ $1.00 ($100)	330.00	100.00
C. *Under Average Cost ($430 ÷ 400 = $1.075):* For *300 units sold*, 300 @ $1.075 (322.50) – For 100 units remaining, 100 @ $1.075 ($107.50)	322.50	107.50

Report for the year 1979, the company noted that had it been using FIFO, it would have shown its inventories $1,655.3 million higher than the $1,670.2 million it showed on its 12/31/79 balance sheet. Had the company used FIFO instead of LIFO, its net income *before* income taxes for the 30-year period, 1950-1979, inclusive, would have been $1,655.3 million higher. If we assume a 50 percent corporate income tax rate, its income taxes for the 30 years would have been $828 million higher. Accordingly, it would have shown net income *after* taxes $828 million higher under FIFO than under LIFO.

In summary, Caterpillar's use of LIFO during the period 1950 to 1979 has meant that:

1. The inventory figures on its balance sheets have been increasingly out of phase with current values.
2. The cost of goods sold figures on its income statements have been substantially in line with current values.
3. The company paid $800 million less income taxes than it would have paid had it used FIFO.

For a number of years, Caterpillar described its "basis of stating inventories" as follows:

> A major portion of the inventories is stated on the basis of the "last-in, first-out" method of inventory accounting adopted January 1, 1950. This is a generally accepted accounting method designed to allocate incurred costs in such a manner as to relate them to revenues on the same cost-price level than would the "first-in, first-out" method used prior to 1950. The general effect is to exclude from reported profits a major portion of the increases in inventory costs which result from rising cost levels.

LOWER OF COST OR MARKET

At year-end, inventories are stated at whichever is lower—cost or market. The lower-of-cost-or-market basis may be applied to each item in the inventory, to various categories of the inventory, or to the inventory as a whole.

Cost may be determined by consistent application of LIFO, FIFO, average, or specific identification methods. The method of cost determination should be disclosed. One cost method may be used for part of the inventory, a different method for another part, if done so consistently from year to year.

Market refers to the market in which the company buys. Thus, market means the current replacement cost at year-end. This is subject to two restrictions: (1) "market" cannot be higher than "net realizable value" (estimated selling price less than cost to sell), and (2) "market" cannot be lower than "net realizable value" less normal profit margin.

Let's see how this concept applies to the 100 units left in year-end inventory in Exhibit 8-3. Suppose the current replacement unit cost at year-end is $1.12, the "net realizable value" $1.20 (estimated selling price $1.50 less $.30 cost to sell), and the net realizable value less normal profit margin $1.05 ($1.20 less $.15 normal profit). The allocation of costs would then be:

	100 Units Remaining in Year-End Inventory			
	Unit Cost	Unit Market	Inventory Figure	Cost Allocated to 300 Units Sold
Lower of FIFO cost or market	$1.15	$1.12	$112.00	$318.00
Lower of LIFO cost or market	1.00	1.12	100.00	330.00
Lower of average cost or market	1.075	1.12	107.50	322.50

In its fiscal 1979 Annual Report, Marshall Field & Company noted:

> Inventory Pricing—Substantially all merchandise inventories are valued by use of the retail method and are stated at last-in, first-out (LIFO) cost, which is not in excess of market, except for the merchandise inventories of the John Breuner Company which are stated at the lower of cost or market using the first-in, first-out (FIFO) method. If the FIFO method had been used instead of LIFO, inventories would have been $25,443,000 and $19,892,000 higher than reported at February 2, 1980 and February 3, 1979, respectively.

QUESTIONS AND PROBLEMS

1. Explain the difference between cost of goods available for sale and cost of goods sold.
2. What are the advantages to a company in using a perpetual inventory system?
3. What effect would you expect the decrease in the cost of computers to have on a company's decision as to whether it should use a perpetual inventory system.
4. Explain to your sister-in-law, the new owner of McDowell's Department Store, why she might want to use the retail method of inventory.
5. What is the logic supporting the valuation of ending inventory at the lower of cost or market? How is cost determined? How is market determined? Can companies use lower of cost or market valuation for income tax purposes?

6. When periodic inventories are used, how would you determine the unit costs to be used on the year-end inventory sheets when the flow-of-cost assumption is (a) FIFO, (b) LIFO, (c) AVERAGE cost?
7. Should the terms FIFO and LIFO be used to refer to methods of *cost-of-goods* accounting rather than to methods of *inventory* accounting? If so, would you refer to the inventory methods as LILO and FILO, respectively?
8. (A)   How would the management of the Corner Drugstore, Inc., know of the existence, and extent, of employee or customer pilferage of merchandise?
   (B)   Would the store's management be better informed concerning this if the store had a perpetual inventory system? The retail method of accounting?
   (C)   Would you recommend the adoption of either a perpetual inventory system or the retail method of accounting for the Corner Drugstore, Inc.? For other trading companies?
9. Refer to Illustration 8-3 and assume that in the following year 300 units were purchased:

March.	100 units at $1.15	$115
August	100 units at $1.10	110
November	100 units at $1.05	105
		$330

If 300 units were sold, how would costs be allocated under *FIFO, LIFO,* and *AVERAGE* (for period) flow-of-cost assumptions? How do your results for this year compare with those for the previous year (Illustration 8-3)? How do the results for the three flow-of-cost assumptions compare for the two years taken together?

10. Listed below are three methods of inventory costing, each of which is identified by a letter. Indicate the method which is referred to in the following descriptive statements. If none of the methods listed below apply to a statement, then so indicate.

A.   LIFO
B.   FIFO
C.   Weighted Average
X.   None of the above

_____ 1. Cost of goods sold is highest in a period of steadily rising prices.
_____ 2. The ending inventory is priced at cost of most recently acquired goods.
_____ 3. Requires that records be maintained at both cost and selling price for goods placed in stock.
_____ 4. Most appropriately matches current costs with current revenues.

_____ 5. Would yield greatest tax savings in a period of inflation.

_____ 6. Produces highest ending inventory figure after a period of steadily falling prices.

11.

Beginning Inventory	800 units at $100 each	$800

Purchases:

Nov. 12	400 units at $.90 each	$360
Nov. 21	1200 units at $.70 each	$840
Nov. 30	400 units at $.60 each	$240

Sales:

Nov. 6	400 units
Nov. 15	600 units
Nov. 25	800 units

Assuming the use of periodic inventory, compute the total cost of ending inventory using the following inventory methods:

A. FIFO   _____
B. LIFO   _____
C. Weighted Average _____

12. The following data was taken from the records of The Bakery for the year 1980:

Beginning Inventory:	100 lbs at $10.00 =	$1,000

Purchases:

	100 lbs at $12.00	1,200
	50 lbs at 10.00	500
	200 lbs at 14.00	2,800
	300 lbs at 13.00	3,900
	50 lbs at 12.00	600
		$9,000

Sales were $8,000 and operating expenses were $1,500.

Determine (1) Cost of Goods Sold, (2) Ending Inventory, and (3) Income Before Tax under LIFO, FIFO, and Lower of FIFO cost or market. Assume the market price is $12 per lb.

13. On the night of May 3 of last year the store of Alfred Welsch burned. Everything except the accounting records, which were in a fireproof vault, was destroyed. Mr. Welsch filed an insurance claim that listed an inventory loss of $25,500. As an insurance adjuster you are called upon to verify this claim. The following information is available from the accounting records:

1. Merchandise inventory on January 1 of last year, $23,400.
2. Sales January 1 through May 3 of last year, $94,830.
3. Sales returns for same period, $2,230.
4. Purchases from January 1 through May 3 of last year, $61,520.
5. Purchases returns for same period, $1,260.
6. Freight-in for same period, $2,660.
7. Average gross profit on sales over the past year was 30 percent of sales.

Required: What is your estimate of the loss?

14. The records of the appliance department for the Bay Discount Store show the following data for the month of March:

Sales	$178,500	Purchases returns (at cost price). . .	2,500
Sales returns.	3,500	Purchases returns (at sales price) . .	3,800
Additional markups.	14,000	Markup cancellations.	4,000
Markdowns	25,000	Beginning inventory (at	
Freight on purchases	2,000	cost price).	105,000
Purchases (at cost price) . .	55,500	Beginning inventory (at	
Purchases (at sales price). .	83,800	sales price)	160,000

Required:

A. Cost to Retail %.
B. Ending Inventory using the Retail Method.

15. The following is data from the income statement of the Shimon Corp.

Sales	$86,000
Beginning inventory	15,000
Purchases.	41,000
Ending inventory	12,000
Operating expenses	35,000
Net income	7,000

(A) What is the amount of the cost of goods sold?
(B) What is the amount of gross profit from sales?

16. The following is data from the income statement of the Hughes Corp.

Beginning inventory	$ 40,000
Ending inventory	32,000
Cost of goods sold	144,000
Gross profit on sales	90,000
Net income	10,000

(A) What is the amount of the sales?
(B) What is the amount of the purchases?
(C) What is the amount of the operating expenses?

17. The following errors were made by Polark Corporation during 1980. Indicate the effect of each of these errors on the financial statements for 1980 and 1981 by completing the answer chart provided below. Use the following codes for your answers: O=Overstated, U=Understated, and N=No Effect. (Polark Corporation uses the periodic inventory system.)

Error 1. The Company failed to record a sale on account of $500 at the end of 1980. The merchandise had been shipped and was not included in the ending inventory. The sale was recorded in 1981 when cash was collected from the customer.

Error 2. The company failed to record a purchase on account of $700 at the end of 1980 and also failed to indicate the goods purchased in the ending inventory. The purchase was recorded in 1981 when payment was made to the creditor.

Error 3. The company failed to make an entry for a purchase on account of $200 at the end of 1980, although it included this merchandise in the inventory count. The purchase was recorded when payment was made to the creditor in 1981.

Error 4. The company failed to count goods costing $400 in the physical count of goods at the end of 1980.

		Total Revenue	Total Expense	Net Income	Total Assets	Total Liabilities	Total O. E.
1980	Error 1						
	Error 2						
	Error 3						
	Error 4						
1981	Error 1						
	Error 2						
	Error 3						
	Error 4						

18. The Westbend Store uses the *retail method* to estimate its inventories for interim income statement purposes, and the following information for the period January 1 through October 31 is available:

	At Cost	At Retail
January 1 inventory	$ 17,210	$ 23,300
Purchases	142,870	204,140
Freight-in	2,110	
Purchases returns	1,050	1,530
Sales		207,780
Sales returns		2,440
Additional markups		4,290
Markdowns		1,240

Required: October 31 inventory $_____

19. The following footnote appeared in the 1977 Annual Report of Josten's, Inc.:

Inventories

Gold and certain diamond inventories aggregating $4,920,000 at June 30, 1977, and $4,147,000 at June 30, 1976, are stated at cost determined by the last-in, first-out method, and are $9,563,000 and $9,310,000 lower in the respective years than such inventories determined under the first-in, first-out cost method.

Question:

If Josten's had used FIFO inventory instead of LIFO inventory during the fiscal year ended June 30, 1977, what effect would this have had on:

(Assume a 50% tax rate and assume that all current taxes owed were paid by the fiscal year-end.)

A. Net income for the fiscal year ended June 30, 1977?
B. "Cash internally generated" for the fiscal year ended June 30, 1977?
C. The amount of deferred income taxes at June 30, 1977?

20. In its 1978 annual report, Dow Jones included the following footnote in reference to Inventories:

Note 3. Inventories

Inventories consist of the following:

	1978	1977
	(in thousands)	
Newsprint	$ 6,951	$6,302
Paper and cloth	1,280	1,005
Work in process and sheet stock.	860	950
Bound books	1,579	1,150
	$10,670	$9,407

At December 31, 1978 and 1977, inventories in the amounts of $8,088,000 and $7,715,000 were determined by the last-in, first-out (LIFO) method. If the average cost method had been used, such inventories would have been approximately $2,987,000 and $2,373,000 higher at December 31, 1978 and 1977, respectively.

If Dow Jones had used the average cost method instead of the LIFO method, what effect would this have had on:

(Assume a 50% tax rate and assume that all current taxes owed were paid by the fiscal year-end.)

A. Net income for the year?
B. The December 31, 1978 Balance Sheet?

9

Inventories and Cost of Goods Sold for Manufacturing Companies

Manufacturing companies are concerned with inventories in three stages of production—raw materials, goods-in-process, and finished goods. The accounting task is essentially one of keeping track of all costs incurred "under the factory roof" from the time raw materials are purchased until the finished goods are shipped to customers. The accounting process is dependent upon the physical manufacturing process, as indicated in Illustration 9-1.

RAW MATERIALS

Accounting for *raw materials* purchased is similar to the accounting for merchandise purchased by trading companies. The raw materials inventory account of the XYZ Manufacturing Company, Inc., for 1980 is shown in Illustration 9-2.

Note that the cost of raw materials available for issue to the factory in 1980, $380,000, consisted of:

Illustration 9-1 Relationship Between Physical Manufacturing Process and the Accounting Process of Manufacturing Companies.

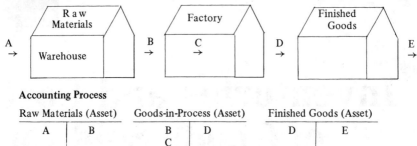

Legend: A = Raw materials purchased and stored in raw material warehouse; B = Raw materials issued to and used in factory; C = Factory labor and all other factory costs in converting raw materials into finished goods; D = Finished goods transferred from factory to warehouse; E = Finished goods shipped to customers.

Cost assigned to raw materials in warehouse at beginning of 1980	$ 80,000
And cost of raw materials purchased in 1980	300,000
Making cost of raw materials available for issue to factory	$380,000

Note also in Illustration 9-2 that the company allocated the $380,000 cost of raw materials available for issue to the factory to:

Cost of raw materials issued to the factory	$280,000
Cost of raw materials remaining in the raw materials warehouse at the end of 1980	100,000
	$380,000

Illustration 9-2

XYZ Manufacturing Co., Inc.
Ledger Account for Raw Materials Inventory for the Year 1980

Raw Materials (Asset)

1/1/80 Balance	$ 80,000	B - Issued to factory	$280,000
A - Purchases in 1980	300,000	12/31/80 Balance	100,000
	$380,000		$380,000
1/1/81 Balance	$100,000		

In assigning costs of raw materials issued to the factory, the company may use FIFO, LIFO, average cost, specific identification, or standard cost (when a standard costing system is used).

GOODS-IN-PROCESS

The *goods-in-process* inventory account of the XYZ Manufacturing Co., Inc., for 1980 is shown in Illustration 9-3.

Illustration 9-3

XYZ Manufacturing Co., Inc.
Ledger Account for Goods-in-Process Inventory

Goods in Process (Asset)

1/1/80	$ 150,000	D - Cost of finished goods transferred to ware-		
B - Raw Material Used	280,000	house in 1980	$1,400,000	
C(1) - Factory Direct Labor Cost incurred in 1980	500,000			
C(2) - Other factory costs (Factory Overhead) incurred in 1980	770,000	12/31/80 Balance	300,000	
	$1,700,000		$1,700,000	
1/1/81 Balance	$ 300,000			

Note that the cost of goods available for transfer as cost of goods finished in 1980, $1,700,000, consisted of:

Cost assigned to goods-in-process in the factory
at the beginning of 1980. . . . . $ 150,000

Cost incurred "under the factory roof" in 1980:
Cost of raw materials issued to factory $280,000
Cost of labor directly used in products   500,000

All other factory costs incurred (Factory Overhead)—supervisory salaries, indirect labor, heat, light power, maintenance of machinery and building, depreciation of

machinery and buildings, property taxes,
insurance, manufacturing supplies used,
etc..   770,000

Total costs incurred "under the factory roof" in 1980   1,550,000

Cost of goods available for transfer as cost of
goods finished in 1980 . . . . $1,700,000

Note also in Illustration 9-3 that the company allocated the
$1,700,000 to:

Cost of finished goods transferred to warehouse $1,400,000

And cost of goods-in-process remaining in the factory
at the end of 1980.   300,000

                                                                          $1,700,000

FINISHED GOODS

The *finished goods* inventory account of the XYZ Manufacturing
Co., Inc., for 1980 is shown in Illustration 9-4.

Illustration 9-4

XYZ Manufacturing Co., Inc.
Ledger Account for Finished Goods Inventory for the Year 1980

Finished Goods (Asset)

1/1/80 Balance	$ 400,000	E - Cost of finished goods shipped to customers in 1980	$1,300,000
D - Cost of finished goods transferred from factory in 1980	1,400,000	12/31/80 Balance	500,000
	$1,800,000		$1,800,000
1/1/81 Balance	$ 500,000		

Note that the accounting for finished goods acquired from the factory is similar to the accounting for merchandise purchased from
suppliers by trading companies.

STATEMENT OF COST OF GOODS MANUFACTURED AND SOLD

The entries in the goods-in-process and finished goods accounts furnish the information needed to prepare the Statement of Cost of Goods Manufactured and Sold. This statement, presented in Illustration 9-5, has been prepared from information in Illustrations 9-3 and 9-4.

Illustration 9-5

XYZ Manufacturing Co., Inc.
Statement of Cost of Goods Manufactured and Sold for the Year 1980

Cost of goods in process at the beginning of the year.		$ 150,000
Add: Costs incurred in factory in 1980:		
Raw material issued to factory	$280,000	
Direct labor	500,000	
Other factory costs	770,000	
Total		$1,550,000
Cost allocable to finished goods manufactured during year and to goods in process at year end		1,700,000
Deduct: Cost assigned to goods in process at year end.		300,000
Cost of finished goods manufactured during year.		1,400,000
Add: Cost of finished goods on hand at beginning of year		400,000
Cost of finished goods available for sale		1,800,000
Deduct: Cost of finished goods on hand at end of year		500,000
Cost of finished goods sold during year		$1,300,000

PRODUCT AND PERIOD COSTS

Product costs are those costs, incurred in buying or manufacturing products, that a company allocates in part to units sold during the period, and in part to units remaining in inventory at the end of the period.

For example, the XYZ Manufacturing Company, Inc., considered as product costs the costs of raw materials, direct labor, and factory overhead (supervisory salaries, indirect labor, depreciation on the factory building and equipment, factory occupancy costs, etc.).

Period costs are costs that are treated as expenses of doing business in the period they are incurred. No part of such costs is assigned to units remaining in inventory at the end of the period. For example, selling expenses are treated as a cost of doing business in the period in which they are incurred. Thus, depreciation on a sales office owned by the company is considered an expense when incurred. By contrast, depreciation of factory buildings and equipment first becomes a part of the cost of finished goods and is considered an expense only when the finished goods of which the depreciation is a part are sold.

For many management decisions, it is useful to consider what costs are relevant in a particular situation. Thus, in periods of under-capacity utilization of a factory, it may be useful to consider only "incremental costs" in determining the costs of manufacturing additional units of finished goods. In such a situation, the only relevant costs may be the costs of raw material, direct labor, and variable factory overhead. By contrast, for purposes of external reporting, and for federal income tax returns, inventory costs should include not only raw material, direct labor, and variable factory overhead, but also a fair allocation of fixed factory overhead. AICPA Accounting Research Bulletin No. 43, Chapter 4, notes that:

> Although principles for the determination of inventory costs may be easily stated, their application, particularly to such inventory items as work in process and finished goods, is difficult because of the variety of problems encountered in the allocation of costs and charges. For example, under some circumstances, items such as idle facility expense, excessive spoilage, double freight, and rehandling costs may be so abnormal as to require treatment as current period charges rather than as a portion of the inventory cost. Also, general and administrative expenses should be included as period charges, except for the portion of such expenses that may be clearly related to production and thus constitute a part of inventory costs (product charges). Selling expenses constitute no part of inventory costs. *It should also be recognized that the exclusion of all overheads from inventory costs does not constitute an accepted accounting procedure.* The exercise of judgment in an individual situation involves a consideration of the adequacy of the procedures of the cost accounting system in use, the soundness of the principles thereof, and their consistent application. (Italics supplied)

In its 1979 Annual Report, FMC Corporation noted:

Inventory costs include manufacturing overhead, less, for most inventories, depreciation, factory administration, property taxes and certain other fixed expenses.

FINANCIAL STATEMENT DISCLOSURE

Inventories are shown on the balance sheet in the current assets section. The basis of stating cost—FIFO, LIFO, average, or other—should be disclosed on the face of the balance sheet or in the notes thereto. The basis for stating inventories should be consistently followed from year to year. AICPA *ARB* No. 43, Chapter 4, provides:

> The basis of stating inventories must be consistently applied and should be disclosed in the financial statements; whenever a significant change is made therein, there should be a disclosure of the nature of the change and, if material, the effect on income.

Easco Corporation's 1979 Annual Report showed:

	1979	1978
Inventories at December 31	70,537,000	80,185,000
Cost of products sold, exclusive depreciation for the year	288,207,000	254,199,000

In its "Notes to Consolidated Financial Statements", the company stated concerning Inventories:

> Inventories are valued at the lower of cost or market value. Costs for 41% in 1979 and 36% in 1978 of the consolidated inventory balance is determined on the last-in, first-out (LIFO) method. The remainder, which comprise 76% in 1979 and 83% in 1978 of Hand Tools segment inventories, are valued on the average cost method.
>
> It is impractical to separate inventory values as among raw material, work in process and finished goods since LIFO inventories are valued using a single dollar value pool.
>
> If the inventories valued using the LIFO method were valued using the first-in, first-out (FIFO) method, such inventories would have been greater by $16,884,000 and $10,076,000 at December 31, 1979 and 1978, respectively.

Easco included supplemental data on cost of goods sold and inventories in a section titled "Financial Reporting and Changing Prices (Unaudited)." The company introduced this section:

> The inflationary trend of the past 10 years is having a significant impact on the business community—an impact which cannot be adequately reflected in financial statements prepared using historical costs. Accordingly, in September 1979, the Financial Accounting Standards Board (FASB) issued a statement establishing standards on an experimental basis for reporting the effects of price changes on accounting data. FASB Statement No. 33, Financial Reporting and Changing Prices, provides guidelines for two variations to historical financial statements which provide information based on past transactions about the effects that general inflation (constant dollar) and other specific price changes (current costs) have on a company's financial statements.

A comprehensive look at FASB Statement No. 33 is to be found in Chapter 17, Accounting for Changing Prices.

Easco's supplemental presentation shows the following information concerning cost of goods sold and inventories (in thousands of dollars):

	As Reported in the Primary Statements	Adjusted for General Inflation (Constant Dollars)	Adjusted for Changes in Specific Prices (Current Costs)
1979 Cost of products sold, exclusive of depreciation	288,207	292,553	294,980
December 31, 1979 Inventories	70,537	Not given	86,723

FACTORS AFFECTING INVESTMENT IN INVENTORIES

The inventory method used—LIFO, FIFO, average cost—affects the dollar amount at which a company shows its investment in inventories. When costs rise from year to year, companies using FIFO will show the same physical inventory at a higher dollar amount each year. When costs rise from year to year, companies using LIFO will show the same physical inventory at the same dollar amount from year to year. One criticism leveled at the LIFO method is that the farther we get from the costs prevailing at the date LIFO was adopted, the more "unrealistic," as compared with current costs, LIFO inventory becomes. Those advocating LIFO point out that this discrepancy may be a small price to pay for stating cost of goods sold at the cost prevailing in the year of sale (which FIFO does not do). However, one may assess the validity of these arguments, the controversy highlights the need to consider the effect of the inventory method that a company uses in evaluating its investment in inventories.

Seasonal, cyclical, and growth fluctuations in sales affect inventory investment. However, the effect of these fluctuations upon inventory is not as direct as their effect upon receivables. If credit and collection policies are not changed, the relationship between sales volume and receivables investment generally stays the same. But the relationship between dollar sales and inventory investment varies from time to time, because:

1. The dollar amount of sales and the dollar amount of inventory may be expressed in dollars of different vintage.
2. A portion of inventory investment is relatively fixed and will not vary proportionally with changes in sales volume.
3. Inventory, under some circumstances, tends to lag behind changes in sales, especially in periods of unforeseen rapidly declining sales.
4. A company may deliberately plan "out-of-phase" inventories in order to schedule level production despite seasonal fluctuations in sales.

The company's purchasing and production methods, the market served, and the way in which the company serves its market affect the company's investment in inventories. The manner in which a company seeks to balance its desire for level production with seasonal sales will affect its investment in inventories, particularly in months of lower-than-average sales. Other features which affect a company's investment in inventory include:

- How the company strikes the balance between inventory sufficiently adequate for good service to customers and sufficiently low to justify carrying costs.
- How much the company produces for stock and how much in response to specific order.
- How long the company's production runs are.

- How many component parts the company makes and how many it buys.
- How much the company sells directly and how much through jobbers, wholesalers, and dealers.
- At how many locations the company maintains inventories.

INVENTORY TURNOVER RATIO

Inventory turnover ratio is calculated by dividing the cost of goods sold figure by the average inventory. When only year-end statements are available, the average inventory is determined by averaging the inventory for the end of the previous year and that for the end of the current year. If monthly or quarterly inventory figures are available, these, of course, should be used in determining the average.

The inventory turnover ratio for Caterpillar Tractor Co. for 1979, as determined from figures in its published financial statements, is calculated as follows:

$$\frac{\text{Cost of goods sold}}{\text{Average inventory}} = \frac{\$6{,}172.3\text{MM}}{(1{,}670.2 + 1{,}522.3) \div 2} = \frac{6{,}172.3}{1{,}596.3} = 3.9 \text{ Times}$$

Inventory turnover ratio measures the number of times the inventory turns over, "on the average." The usefulness of the measure is affected by the validity of the "average" inventory. For example, if there are wide seasonal swings in inventory, use of year-end inventory figure is not likely to produce a valid "average."

The usefulness of the ratio is affected also by the comparability of the basis of costing inventory with the basis of costing cost of goods sold. For example, in the case of Caterpillar Tractor Company, which adopted LIFO in 1950, the basis (past costs) in stating 1979 inventories differs from the basis (1979 costs) used in stating cost of goods sold for 1979. Ideally, we should use current-cost inventories (FIFO) and current-cost cost of goods sold (LIFO). In its "Notes to Financial Statements," Caterpillar indicates that adjustments of $1,655.3MM at 12/31/79 and $1,388.0MM at 12/31/78 are needed to convert its LIFO inventory figures to FIFO. Using adjusted figures, the calculation of Caterpillar's inventory turnover becomes:

$$\frac{\text{Cost of goods sold}}{\text{Average inventory}} = \frac{\$6{,}172.3\text{MM}}{(3{,}325.5 + 2{,}910.3) \div 2} = \frac{6{,}172.3}{3{,}117.9} = 2.0 \text{ Times}$$

This figure of 2.0 for Caterpillar's inventory turnover is a more valid figure than the 3.9 figure initially calculated above.

Another variant of the inventory turnover ratio compares 4th quarter cost of goods sold with year-end inventory. For Caterpillar Tractor:

	1979	1978
(1) 4th Quarter cost of goods sold	1,207.5	1,520.2
(2) Year-end inventories (FIFO)	3,325.5	2,910.3
(3) Ratio of (2) to (1)	0.363	0.522
(4) Annual basis: 4 × (3)	1.452	2.088

Note: Caterpillar's ratio for 1979 was affected by the 4th quarter strike of the United Auto Workers which reduced the company's 4th quarter sales by a third.

INVENTORY CHARACTERISTICS AND MANAGEMENT DECISIONS

Most companies must maintain a minimum investment in inventories in order to carry on their operations. For businesses which are in continuous operation, the investment in inventories is never completely liquidated. Although all the items of stock on hand as of one date may eventually be sold, other items take their place, and so the investment continues. Sometimes companies may completely "sell out" as, for example, companies engaged in seasonal canning operations, companies being liquidated, and companies shut down by long strikes, floods, wars, etc. But a company which produces or sells throughout the year has a continuing investment in inventory similar to its continuing investment in plant. Thus, even though such a company considers its inventory as a current asset, it cannot sell its entire inventory to pay off loans, unless the company goes out of business.

The job of controlling the physical quantities of stock items is essentially one of coordinating purchases and production with sales. For companies which buy or manufacture for stock rather than in response to specific orders, stock on hand serves as a buffer between (a) purchases and production (which are controllable) and (b) sales (which are not). The job of controlling inventory then becomes one of controlling purchases and production to meet forecasted and actual sales demand. When products sold are subject to seasonal demand, control may be directed either toward keeping inventory quantities at a minimum throughout the year by gearing production to sales, or toward scheduling production at a level rate throughout the year by planning for and carrying larger than normal quantities in inventories in certain months.

The dollar amount of investment in inventory is affected both by the physical quantities of the items stocked and by the unit costs used in pricing them. Since dollars invested in inventories are the product of quantities times unit prices, the change in dollar investment in inventories between two dates may be due to changes in both physical quantities and unit costs. One should not, therefore, assume that a change in the dollar amount of inventory between two year-ends represent a corresponding change in physical volume.

The method chosen for stating inventories can have a marked effect upon the net income reported in the income statement and upon the inventory figure on the balance sheet. See Illustration 8-3 and related discussion.

Tax considerations play an important part in management's choice of inventory method because of its effect upon net income reported for taxes and therefore upon income tax incurred. During years of rising prices, inventories are most advantageously stated on a last-in, first-out basis for tax purposes, since this method maximizes the amount that can be written off as cost of goods sold. Under the Revenue Act of 1939, LIFO was authorized for general use in the determination of federal income taxes, but statutory and administrative restrictions have kept many company managements from adopting LIFO. Two factors which give corporate managements concern in deciding whether to adopt LIFO for tax purposes are first, the fear that LIFO will be adopted at the top of a price rise, thereby "locking in" high unit costs (since no recognition is given to lower-of-cost-or-market under the tax regulations); and second, the lack of a relief provision in tax regulations providing against imposition of taxes when physical quantities are drastically and involuntarily reduced because of abnormal shortages resulting from war, threat of war, strikes, or other catastrophes. Despite these concerns, many companies adopted LIFO or extended its coverage when double-digit inflation occurred in 1973 and 1974.

Whatever inventory method a company selects, consistency in application from year to year is required.

A JOINT SUMMARY OF CHAPTERS 8 AND 9

The two major problems in accounting for inventories and cost of goods sold are (1) determining the cost of goods available for sale (or production) during an accounting period, and (2) allocating that cost between goods sold (or transferred) and goods remaining at the end of the period.

The cost of goods available for sale (or production) is determined:

1. For trading companies, by adding to the cost of beginning inventory the cost of merchandise purchased during the period.
2. For manufacturing companies, by adding to the cost of beginning inventory:
   a. of raw materials—the cost of raw materials purchased during the period.
   b. of goods-in-process—the costs incurred "under the factory roof" during the period.
   c. of finished goods—the cost of goods manufactured during the period.

Manufacturers have the problem of deciding which costs incurred "under the factory roof" they will treat as product costs and which as period costs. For many internal purposes, it may be useful to limit product costs to variable costs only and to treat all nonvariable factory costs as period costs. For external financial reporting and for federal income tax purposes, however, complete "direct costing" (under which inventories are shown at variable factory costs only) is not acceptable.

The cost of goods available for sale (or production) is allocated between goods sold (or transferred) and goods remaining at the end of the period. In determining the costs to be allocated to goods sold (or transferred), a company may assume the "flow-of-costs" to be first-in, first-out (FIFO), last-in, first-out (LIFO), or average cost. Thus, what is left over becomes the cost of the inventory at the end of the period. This cost may be further reduced if the company applies a lower market price under the lower-of-cost-or-market inventory basis. Trading companies may use either a perpetual or a periodic inventory system to allocate between cost of goods sold and cost of goods remaining, or they may use the retail method of inventory (which may be considered as a form of perpetual inventory system). Manufacturing companies generally use a perpetual inventory system for raw materials, goods-in-process, and finished goods.

Inventories are shown in the current asset section of the balance sheet at the lower of cost (LIFO, FIFO, average) or market. FASB Statement No. 33 requires disclosure of inventories and cost of goods sold, based in part upon historical costs, after adjustment (1) for general inflation (constant dollars) and (2) for change in specific prices (current costs). (See Chapter 17.)

The factors affecting a company's investment in inventories are (1) the inventory method used, (2) the seasonal, cyclical, and growth fluctuations in sales, and (3) the company's purchasing and production methods, and the market it serves. Inventory turnover ratio, calculated by dividing cost of goods sold by average inventory, indicates the number of times inventory turns over "on the average." Six characteristics of inventories that are important for management and for accounting are:

1. Most companies must maintain a minimum investment in inventories.
2. The job of controlling physical quantities is essentially one of coordinating purchasing and production with sales.
3. Dollar investment in inventories is affected by both physical volume and unit prices.
4. The method chosen for stating inventories can have a marked effect upon the net income reported in the income statement and upon the inventory figure on the balance sheet.
5. Tax considerations play an important part in management's choice of inventory method because of its effect upon net income reported for taxes and therefore upon income tax incurred.
6. Whatever inventory method a company selects, consistency in application from year to year is required.

QUESTIONS AND PROBLEMS

1. Why does a manufacturing company have more than one type of inventory?
2. For each of the companies listed, state whether you think the company would have more dollar value in raw material, work-in-process, or finished goods inventory? Why?

    A. Printing Plant
    B. Paper Manufacturing Company
    C. Speciality Machine Shop
    D. Toy Company
    E. Tire Manufacturer

3. Is any part of a company's investment in inventories a noncurrent asset?
4. Which of the companies listed would you expect to have the highest inventory turn? The lowest inventory turn? Why?

    A. Supermarket
    B. Department Store
    C. Automobile Manufacturer
    D. Jewelry Store

5. Using the following information, prepare a Statement of Costs of Goods Manufactured:

Goods in process inventory, beginning of year.	$ 70,000
Goods in process inventory, end of year.	60,000
Beginning raw materials inventory	50,000
Ending raw materials inventory	42,000
Purchases of raw materials.	100,000
Direct Labor.	230,000
Factory overhead	250,000
Purchase returns and allowances.	3,000
Transportation-in	5,000
Total manufacturing costs.	590,000

6. Use the following information to answer questions (A) through (E).

Raw materials inventory-June 1	$ 75
Raw materials purchased during June	650
Raw materials inventory-June 30	40
Other manufacturing costs-variable	150
Other manufacturing costs-non-variable	220
Direct labor	400
Work in process-June 1.	60
Work in process-June 30	25
Finished goods inventory-June 1	90
Finished goods inventory-June 30.	150
Gross margin	125
Selling & administrative expenses-variable	10
Selling & administrative expenses-non-variable	25

Required: Calculate the following:

(A) The cost of materials used for June.
(B) Without influencing your answer to (A), assume the cost of materials used to be $660 during June, and use this figure for the remainder of this question. This will eliminate carry-through errors.
    What was the cost of goods manufactured for June?
(C) Without influencing your answer to (B), assume that the cost of goods manufactured for June was $1,500.
    What was the cost of goods sold for June?

(D)   Without influencing your answer to (C), assume that the cost of goods sold for June was $1,400.
What was the sales revenue for June?

(E)   What were the earnings for June?

7. The following information is available concerning the Miller Manufacturing Corporation:

Beginning Inventories:

Raw materials	$ 10,000
Goods in Process	4,500

Ending Inventories:

Raw materials	15,000
Goods in Process	6,000
Raw Materials Used	70,000
Direct Labor.	50,000
Total Mfg. Costs	152,000
Cost of Goods Available for Sale	155,000
Cost of Goods Sold	148,000
Gross Profit	127,000
Income	102,000

Required: Compute the following:

Raw Materials Purchased
Raw Materials Available for use
Manufacturing Overhead
Cost of Goods Manufactured
Sales Revenue
Finished Goods Inventory, Beginning
Finished Goods Inventory, Ending
Operating Expenses

8. The following information is available to you concerning the Easy Manufacturing Company:

Raw Materials inventory-Jan. 1, 1980	$ 10,000
Goods in process inventory-Jan. 1, 1980	18,000
Finished goods inventory-Jan. 1, 1980.	30,000
Raw materials inventory-Dec. 31, 1980	12,000
Goods in process inventory-Dec. 31, 1980	20,000
Finished goods inventory-Dec. 31, 1980	50,000
Raw materials purchased.	100,000
Transportation in	5,000
Direct labor	170,000
Factory overhead	120,000
Selling expenses	50,000
General expenses.	15,000
Administrative expenses	49,000

Required: Prepare a Statement of Cost of Goods Manufactured for the Easy Manufacturing Company for 1980.

9. Kilroy Manufacturing Co. started the year's manufacturing operations with the following balances in the inventory accounts:

Raw material	$100,000
Work in process.	70,000
Finished goods	180,000

An analysis of its accounts showed that it had incurred the following:

Purchases of raw materials.	$600,000
Direct labor costs	250,000
Indirect labor	80,000
Factory power	30,000
Depreciation-Plant & Equipment	20,000
Other factory expenses.	50,000
Selling and distribution expenses	80,000
General and administration expenses.	65,000
Interest on bank loan	25,000
Federal and State taxes.	99,000

Kilroy's net sales for 1980 were $1,400,000. According to a physical count at 12/31/80, the ending inventories were:

Raw materials.	$110,000
Work in process.	80,000
Finished goods	190,000

Required: Prepare a Statement of Cost of Goods Manufactured and an income statement for 1980.

10. Selected data from Easco Corporation's 1979 published financial statements are shown below:

Sales, Gross Profit, and Earnings by Quarter
(000's ommitted except per share data)

							Net Income Per Share			
	Net Sales		Gross Profit		Net Income		Primary		Fully Diluted	
Quarter	1979	1978	1979	1978	1979	1978	1979	1978	1979	1978
First	$ 79,539	$ 76,648	$15,961	$15,162	$2,430	$2,332	$ .70	$ .75	$ .66	$ .70
Second	84,476	74,206	15,921	15,062	2,135	2,276	.60	.68	.58	.61
Third	90,132	84,957	16,881	16,439	2,437	2,770	.69	.83	.66	.75
Fourth*	97,574	81,637	14,751	16,586	1,181	3,059	.31	.92	.31	.82
Year	$351,721	$317,448	$63,514	$63,249	$8,183	$10,437	$2.30	$3.18	$2.21	$2.88

*Fourth quarter 1979 operations were adversely affected by manufacturing disruption and related inefficiencies associated with the company's realignment of a major portion of its hand tool manufacturing facilities along with higher overhead and start-up costs at a new plant. These unanticipated high levels of production costs necessitated revisions to previous estimates of average annual inventory costs which were made in connection with closing the earlier quarters of 1979. The effect of such revisions was to reduce 1979 fourth quarter net income by approximately $800,000 or 24 cents per share.

	1979	1978
Cost of products sold, exclusive		
of depreciation	$288,207,000	$254,199,000
Inventories at Dec 31	70,537,000	80,185,000
Inventories at Jan 1	80,185,000	66,155,000

If the inventories valued using the LIFO method were valued using the first-in, first-out (FIFO) method, such inventories would have been greater by $16,884,000; $10,076,000; and $8,152,000 at December 31, 1979, 1978, and 1977, respectively.

Required: Calculate inventory turnover ratios. What do these measures tell you?

11. Let's suppose a corporation began business on January 1, 1975 by issuing capital stock for 100 units of inventory valued at $1,000. Later, in 1975, the corporation purchased for cash 100 units at $11.00, an increase of 10% over the January 1, 1975 inventory cost. Thereafter for the next four years, it purchased for cash 100 units each year at a 10% increase in unit cost each year. Its cash operating expenses were $100 in 1975, and also increased 10% each year. Fortunately, its selling price per unit, $13.50 in 1975, also rose 10% each year. It sold 100 units for cash each year.

In summary, purchase costs, operating expenses, and sales all rounded to nearest dollar were as follows:

	No. Units	Total Purchase Cost	Operating Expenses	Sales Units	Sales Total $'s
On hand, 1/1/75	100	$1,000			
1975	100	1,100	$100	100	$1,350
1976	100	1,210	110	100	1,485
1977	100	1,331	121	100	1,634
1978	100	1,464	133	100	1,797
1979	100	1,610	146	100	1,977
	600	$7,715	$610	500	$8,243

The company paid income tax at a rate of 50% each year. Cash dividends of $30 were declared and paid each year.

In the two sets of accounts as shown below, enter transactions for the 5-year period as a whole: B = Purchases for cash, $6,715; C = Expenses for cash, $610; D = Dividends (cash), $150; E = Cost of goods sold; F = Income tax (cash). How would you summarize your results?

Under FIFO Method

Cash

A	8,243	____	____
		____	____
		____	____
		____	____

Inventory

1/1/75	1,000	____	____
____	____		

Capital Stock

		1/1/75	1,000

Retained Earnings

____	____	A-Sales	8,243
____	____		

Under LIFO Method

Cash

A	8,243	____	____
		____	____
		____	____
		____	____

Inventory

1/1/75	1,000	____	____
____	____		

Capital Stock

		1/1/75	1,000

Retained Earnings

____	____	A-Sales	8,243
____	____		

10

Fixed Assets and Depreciation

This chapter will consider determination of original cost of fixed assets, accounting for periodic depreciation, depletion, and amortization, differences between book and tax depreciation, some misconceptions about the nature of depreciation accounting, and current requirements (FASB Statement No. 33) for the disclosure of the effect of inflation upon fixed assets and depreciation.

A company acquires land, buildings, equipment and other fixed assets to be used in the operations of the business. To determine annual net income, a portion of the original cost of these fixed assets (except land) has to be allocated each year as depreciation, depletion, or amortization expense.

FIXED ASSETS DEFINED

Fixed assets are relatively long-lived assets (1) acquired to be *used* in the business and (2) not intended for sale. Fixed assets include:

Land for factory and office locations
Land improvements such as landscaping, parking lots, etc.
Buildings
Productive machinery and equipment
Jigs, dies, molds, small tools, returnable containers, etc.
Office furniture and fixtures
Company automobiles and trucks
Natural resources such as timber lands, mines, oil wells, etc.
Patents, copyrights, trademarks, leaseholds, goodwill purchased,
    and other intangible long-term assets

Fixed assets (net) are fixed assets shown at their original cost less
the portion of that cost previously allocated to operations as depreciation, depletion, or amortization. For each class (or item) of *buildings and equipment* on which separate records are desired, it is
customary for the original cost to be maintained in one account, and
the portion of original cost previously allocated to be accumulated
in an adjacent *contra asset* account, sometimes called Accumulated
Depreciation, Allowance for Depreciation, or Reserve for Depreciation. For *natural resources*, the contra asset account is called Accumulated Depletion, Allowance for Depletion, etc. For *intangible
fixed assets*, a contra asset account may be used, or there may be just
one account in which both the original cost and the accumulated
amortization are recorded. *Amortization* of an intangible asset is the
allocation of the original cost of the asset over its estimated useful
life.

DEPRECIATION, DEPLETION, AND AMORTIZATION
ALLOCATED EACH ACCOUNTING PERIOD

The depreciation, depletion, and amortization allocated each accounting period may be charged in part to Retained Earnings as an
expense, and in part to Goods-in-Process (to the extent that the depreciation, depletion, and amortization are costs incurred "under
the factory roof"). If charged to Goods-in-Process, the depreciation,
depletion, and amortization become an expense only when the finished goods with which they are associated are sold.

DETERMINATION OF ORIGINAL COST

Generally, original cost of acquisition includes all costs of getting the asset in form and in place for its initial use in the business. For example, the legal costs of obtaining title to a tract of land are a part of its acquisition cost. If a particular tract of land has a building upon it that cannot be used by the purchaser, the cost of razing the building is a part of the purchaser's cost of acquiring the land. When a company contracts for the construction of a new building, all costs incurred up to the time the building is turned over to the company are part of its acquisition costs. Such costs may therefore include architect's fees, payments to the contractor, property taxes and insurance on the building during the course of its construction, and interest on the funds needed to complete the construction of the property. (See FASB Statement No. 34.)

The original cost of machinery and equipment includes purchase cost, transportation cost, and cost of initial installation.

When a fixed asset is purchased, its original cost is measured by the outlay of cash or cash equivalent at the date of acquisition. Accordingly, when a cash discount is received on the purchase of equipment, the cost is shown net of the discount. When equipment is bought on the installment basis, the present value of the total installment obligations at the date of purchase is the purchase cost of acquiring the equipment. When fixed assets are acquired by the issuance of a company's capital stock, the cash equivalent value of the stock is used to measure the cost of acquiring the assets. When an old machine is traded in on a new one, the cash equivalent value of the old machine plus the cash paid becomes the acquisition cost of the new machine.[1]

PROPERTY ACQUIRED BY LEASE

A company may obtain long-term use of property by leasing it

---

[1] Note: Under United States income tax provisions, no gain or loss is recognized when property is traded in for like property. Accordingly, *for tax purposes*, the unallocated cost of an old machine traded in becomes a part of the cost of the new machine. Some companies adopt this tax accounting for trade-ins for their general accounting also.

under a long-term noncancellable lease. For example, a company may negotiate with a financial institution for a store or factory building constructed and equipped according to the company's specifications, and then enter into a 15-year noncancellable lease which provides that the company (1) make a monthly rental payment to the financial institution and (2) pay the property taxes, insurance, and repairs as though it were the owner.

If such a lease meets the criteria for being considered a "capital lease" rather than an "operating lease," FASB Statement No. 13, issued in November 1976, provides for recording the leasehold right as an asset and the lease obligation as a liability. For a more detailed description of lease accounting, see Chapter 13.

DEPRECIATION ACCOUNTING

The object of a company's depreciation accounting is to allocate to the operations of the company's accounting periods the *net costs* of fixed assets over their useful lives in a rational and systematic manner. The *net costs* to be allocated are the original costs of the assets less their salvage values at the end of their useful lives.

Thus, if a company owned only one fixed asset,
a machine, the original cost of which was. $3,000
and it used the machine for seven years, at which
time the company sold the machine for.   200
the *net cost* allocable to the company's operations over
the seven-year period would be $2,800

Note, however, that there is a difference between this illustration and the practical problems which confront a company:

1. The company cannot wait seven years to allocate the *net cost*.
2. The company has to allocate costs to each accounting period at the time, and do so in a rational and systematic manner.
3. The company has to allocate the costs of many assets of varying ages, not the cost of a single asset.
4. The company, provided it continues to operate, never gets to the point where it can look back and know for sure the costs it should have previously allocated.

The depreciation that a company allocates to a particular accounting period is not a precise figure but an approximation only, because the period's depreciation must be based upon prospective estimates of useful lives (and salvage values) of the fixed assets that the company used in its operations during the period. In addition, the company has a choice in its selection of "the rational and systematic manner" in which it allocates the costs of fixed assets over their estimated useful lives. The method of allocation may be straight-line, declining-balance, or sum-of-the-year digits.

In estimating the useful life of an asset or group of assets, one assumes that normal repairs and maintenance will be performed to keep the asset(s) in good operating condition throughout the estimated useful life. Such normal repairs and maintenance will, of course, be considered as expenses when made. When, however, a general overhaul or replacement of major components prolongs the useful life of the asset, this overhaul should be treated as a capital expenditure and be allocated over the revised remaining useful life.

For income tax purposes, the Internal Revenue Service has issued many regulations specifying useful lives for various types of assets. However, a company need not adopt for financial accounting the IRS' useful lives. The company should rather consider the particular conditions under which the assets will be used and the technological obsolescence to which they will be subject.

Depreciation Methods

A company has a choice of several methods of allocating the "net cost" of fixed assets over their estimated useful lives.

1. *The straight-line method.*
   When the straight-line method is used, the annual depreciation is determined by dividing the "net cost" of the asset by its estimated life.

   Example: Original cost $10,000 less estimated salvage value $400 gives "net cost" of $9,600. Estimated useful life is 5 years.

   $9,600 divided by 5 gives annual depreciation of $1,920 for each of the five years of estimated useful life.

2. *Double-declining-balance method.*

Straight-line percentage rate is doubled, and this rate is applied each year to original cost less accumulated depreciation until unallocated cost is reduced to estimated salvage value.

Example: Original cost $10,000 less estimated salvage value $400 gives "net cost" of $9,600. Estimated life is 5 years. Thus, straight-line percentage rate is 20%.

Annual depreciation is 40% of $10,000 or $4,000 for first year, 40% of 10,000 less $4,000 or $2,400 for second year, 40% of $10,000 less $6,400 or $1,440 for third year, etc.

3. *Sum-of-the-years'-digits method.*
    Changing fractions are applied to "net costs." The denominator of the fraction is the sum of the digits of the years of useful life. The numerator is, for the first year, the number of years of useful life, and it declines by one for each succeeding year.

    Example: Original cost $10,000 less estimated salvage value $400 gives "net cost" of $9,600. Estimated life is 5 years.

    Sum of the years' digits (1, 2, 3, 4, and 5) is 15. Depreciation for first year is 5/15ths of $9,600 or $3,200, for second year 4/15ths or $2,560, for third year 3/15ths or $1,920, etc.

4. *Machine-hour method.*   ·
    The number of hours a machine is to be used during its useful life is estimated, and depreciation is allocated according to number of hours actually used during an accounting period.

    Example: Original cost $10,000 less estimated salvage value $400 gives "net cost" of $9,600. Estimated hours to be used are 19,200 and the hours actually used during first year are 1,800. Net costs $9,600 divided by total hours 19,200 yields 50¢ allocated to each hour of use. Depreciation first year $900 (1,800 times 50¢ per hour of use).

5. *Unit-of-production method.*
    This is similar to machine-hour method, except that an estimate is made of the number of units to be produced by the machine during its useful life, and depreciation is allocated according to the number of units actually produced during an accounting period.

·

Example: Original cost of a truck $10,000 less estimated salvage value gives "net cost" of $9,600. Estimated miles to be driven is 100,000, and number of miles actually driven during first year is 25,000. Cost allocated to each mile is 9.6¢ ($9,600 net cost divided by 100,000 total miles). Depreciation first year is $2,400 (25,000 times 9.6¢).

The straight-line, double-declining-balance, and sum-of-the-years'-digits methods are more widely used than the other two. A comparison of the three methods is shown in Illustration 10-1.

The double-declining-balance and sum-of-the-years'-digits methods are referred to as accelerated methods of depreciation. Two reasons advanced for using these accelerated methods are (1) the asset is more useful in its earlier years because it is more efficient and less subject to obsolescence, and (2) repairs and maintenance comple-

Illustration 10-1

A Comparison of Straight-Line, Double-Declining Balance (DDB), and Sum-of-the-Years'-Digits (SYD) Methods of Depreciation

A new machine is purchased January 1 for $10,000 with estimated salvage value of $400 at the end of its 5-year useful life.

Year	Straight-line Depreciation	DDB[a] Depreciation	SYD[b] Depreciation
1st	$1,920	$4,000	$3,200
2nd	1,920	2,400	2,560
3rd	1,920	1,440	1,920
4th	1,920	880	1,280
5th	1,920	880	640
	$9,600	$9,600	$9,600

[a] In the double-declining-balance method, double the 5-year rate of 20%, or *40%*, is applied the first year to the $10,000 cost, the second year to the unallocated balance of $6,000, and the third year to the unallocated balance of $3,600; at the end of three years, when unallocated balance is $2,160, it is permissible and advantageous, for tax purposes, to switch to straight-line, and the depreciation for the fourth and fifth years is computed by deducing the salvage value of $400 from the $2,160, and dividing the $1,760 by two.

[b] In the sum-of-the-years'-digits method, the years' digits 1, 2, 3, 4, and 5 are summed to get *15*. The depreciation is then computed on the $9,600 by applying the fractions 5/15, 4/15, 3/15, 2/15, and 1/15.

ment the accelerated depreciation over the useful life of the asset since repair and maintenance expenses are normally less in the earlier years and greater in later years.

BOOK AND TAX DEPRECIATION

The depreciation charge that a company shows on its books and uses for external reporting need not be the same one it uses on its income tax returns. For example, a company may use the straight-line method on its books, but the sum-of-the-years'-digits method for income tax purposes.

For *book depreciation*, a company should adopt depreciation methods which will give a total depreciation charge for the year that is fair in comparison with other years. For *tax depreciation*, a company should use that method permitted by the IRS that gives it the greatest tax benefit.

Thus, many companies use accelerated methods of depreciation and IRS "guideline" lives for income tax purposes, but the straight-line method and longer lives for general accounting purposes. In such cases, the income tax actually incurred, per the tax return, is not consistent with the income tax that would be due on the income reported for general accounting purposes. Under the generally accepted accounting principle of income tax allocation,[2] provision is made for the income tax on the difference by the following entry:

Retained Earnings (OE)–(Deferred Income Taxes)   Decr _____
    Deferred Taxes on Income (L)   Incr _____

The deferred taxes on income account is considered a noncurrent liability. Presumably, the account will be reduced in later years when the depreciation for income tax purposes becomes less than the depreciation reported for general accounting purposes. For further discussion of deferred income taxes, see Chapter 12.

---

[2] AICPA Accounting Principles Board Opinion No. 11, *Accounting for Income Taxes*, December 1967.

SOME MISCONCEPTIONS ABOUT DEPRECIATION

Some common misconceptions concerning depreciation accounting are the notions that:

- Depreciation for external reporting purposes measures, or should measure, the decline in asset market value; in other words, that original cost less accumulated depreciation should approximate realizable value.
- The purpose of depreciation is to provide for replacement of assets at the end of their useful lives.
- Funds are provided by depreciation.

For external reporting (based upon historical costs), the market value of a fixed asset is pertinent only (1) when the asset is acquired and (2) when the asset is sold at the end of its useful life. By definition, fixed assets are assets acquired to be held over their useful lives and are not intended for sale. Depreciation accounting is defined by the AICPA as "a system of accounting which aims to distribute the cost or other basic value of tangible capital assets, less salvage value (if any), over the estimated useful life of the unit (which may be a group of assets) in a systematic and rational manner. It is a process of allocation, not of valuation." Accordingly, depreciation accounting does not intend (1) that the cost allocated to a period equal the change in asset market value, or (2) that the unallocated cost of assets at the end of any period indicate realizable value.

The object of depreciation accounting is to allocate to each accounting period the net cost of assets that are physically in use during that period. The costs allocated are costs already incurred, without reference to the costs to be incurred when, and if, the assets are replaced. Moreover, depreciation accounting does not assume that assets are to be replaced at the end of their useful lives by similar assets.

In the first several decades of this century, accountants developed a statement they called "source and application of funds." During the course of the statement's development, "funds" came to mean net current assets, and analysis showed that net income before deduction of depreciation measured the net inflow of net current assets from customers. Typically, the funds statement, now called the statement of changes in financial position, listed net income first among the sources of "funds." To adjust this figure to net income before deduction of depreciation, the accountants listed the period's depreciation next. Sometimes the sum of net income plus depreciation was shown with the designation "funds provided by operations," as follows:

Sources of Funds
_____

Net income $630M
Depreciation.........................   76M
      Funds provided by operations $706M

As a consequence of such a separate listing of depreciation under sources of funds, many have been led to the fallacious conclusion that "funds are provided by depreciation." Not so! Net current assets are not provided by the accountant's entry for depreciation. Net current assets are provided by the company's customers, as measured by the excess of sales revenue over expenses (exclusive of depreciation).

AMORTIZATION

The costs of intangible assets should be amortized, by the straight-line method, over their estimated useful lives (not to exceed 40 years).[3] Intangible assets include patents, copyrights, trademarks, organization costs, and purchased goodwill. In a business combination deemed a "purchase" (see Chapter 11), *goodwill* is the term applied to "unidentifiable intangible assets" acquired, and the cost of the goodwill "is measured by the difference between the cost of the group of assets or enterprise acquired and the sum of the assigned costs of individual tangible and identifiable intangible assets acquired less liabilities assumed."[4]

"Goodwill" developed in the normal course of operations is not shown as an asset on a company's balance sheet. Goodwill is shown as an asset *only if it is purchased*.

_____

[3] AICPA Accounting Principles Board Opinion No. 17, 1970. This Opinion applies to all intangible assets *acquired after October 31, 1970*.
  [4] *Ibid.*

DEPLETION

Depletion accounting for natural resources is similar to the unit-of-production method of depreciation accounting for machinery and equipment. An estimate is made of the number of units—barrels of oil, tons of coal, board feet of timber—in an oil well, mine, or tract of timberland. This estimate is divided into the original cost of acquiring the oil well, mine, or timber tract (less its estimated residual value at end of operations) to determine the depletion per unit. For example, if the estimated number of tons of coal in a mine was 200,000 and the mine's original cost (less estimated residual value) was $120,000, the depletion per ton would be $0.60. If, during the first year, 25,000 tons were taken out, the depletion charge for the year would be 25,000 times $.60, or $15,000.

The depletion described above is referred to as *cost depletion*. Another method, known as *percentage depletion*, is permitted under United States tax provisions for certain depletable property such as minerals and other natural resources. Under percentage depletion, the amount of the deduction is determined by taking a flat percentage of the *gross income* from the property. However, the deduction may not exceed 50 percent of the *taxable income* from the property, computed without regard to the depletion deduction.

The amount of the depletion percentage varies according to the type of natural resource. For example, certain oil and gas wells owned by independent producers are permitted a depletion rate of 22 percent for 1980.[5] For tax purposes, accumulated percentage depletion can exceed the cost of the resource. For general accounting purposes, the accumulated cost depletion cannot exceed the original cost of the resource less its estimated residual value.

FINANCIAL STATEMENT PRESENTATION
AND DISCLOSURE

In the *balance sheet*, fixed assets are shown in the noncurrent sec-

---

[5] Tax Reform Act of 1976 provides for reductions in percentage depletion rates subsequent to 1980.

tion. Land is shown at original cost. Buildings, machinery, equipment, natural resources, and intangible assets are shown at original cost less the portion of that cost previously allocated as depreciation, depletion, or amortization.

In the *income statement*, the annual charge for depreciation, depletion, and amortization may be shown in the body of the statement or in a footnote. Or the annual charge may be found in the Notes to Financial Statements, or in the Statement of Changes in Financial Position.

Easco Corporation's 1979 Annual Report showed:

	1979	1978
Balance Sheet as of December 31:		
Land, buildings, machinery, and equipment,		
at cost	90,204,000	85,420,000
Less: Accumulated depreciation	41,634,000	38,820,000
Properties (net)	48,570,000	46,600,000
Income Statement for the year:		
Provision for depreciation of properties	4,772,000	4,706,000

In its "Notes to Consolidated Financial Statements," Easco explained concerning "Property and depreciation":

> The Company and its subsidiaries compute depreciation using the straight line method for financial reporting based on rates ranging from 3% to 25% for machinery and equipment, and 2% to 7% for buildings. Accelerated methods are used for income tax purposes.
>
> Major renewals and betterments are capitalized and ordinary repairs and maintenance are charged against operations in the year incurred.

In compliance with FASB Statement No. 33, Financial Reporting and Changing Prices, Easco included supplemental data on property and depreciation:

	As Reported in the Primary Statement	Adjusted for General Inflation (Constant Dollars)	Adjusted for Changes in Specific Prices (Current Costs)
Properties (net)—at			
12/31/79	48,570	Not given	81,008
1979 depreciation expense	4,772	6,949	7,667

For a comprehensive discussion of FASB Statement No. 33, see Chapter 17.

SUMMARY

Fixed assets are relatively long-lived assets acquired to be used in the business and not intended for resale. They are shown in the balance sheet at their acquisition cost less the portion of that cost allocated to operations as depreciation, depletion, and amortization.

The depreciation a company allocates to the operations of a particular period is not a precise figure but an approximation only. The object of depreciation accounting is to allocate the net cost of assets, original cost less salvage value, over their estimated useful lives in a rational and systematic manner. To allocate in a rational and systematic manner, a number of methods of allocation are available, of which the most important ones are straight-line, double-declining-balance, and the sum-of-the-years'-digits methods. When the depreciation charge that a company shows on its books for external reporting is not the same as that it uses on its income tax return, Accounting Principles Board Opinion No. 11 requires income tax on the difference to be reported in the income statement as a part of income tax expense, and in the balance sheet as deferred income taxes.

Three common misconceptions concerning the nature of depreciation accounting are (1) that it reflects changes in market values, (2) that its purpose is to provide for the replacement of assets, and (3) that depreciation provides funds.

Intangible assets should be amortized over their estimated useful lives (not to exceed 40 years) by the straight-line method. Cost depletion allocates the cost of a natural resource, less its residual value, over the estimated units available, according to the number of units extracted each period. Percentage depletion, an income tax concept, computes the periodic charge as a percentage of gross income from the property without reference to the cost of the property.

FASB Statement No. 33 requires disclosure of fixed assets and depreciation based upon historical costs after adjustment (1) for general inflation (constant dollars) and (2) for changes in specific prices (current costs). See Chapter 17.

QUESTIONS AND PROBLEMS

1. How do fixed assets differ from current assets?
2. Is the purpose of depreciation to provide for the replacement of the fixed asset once its useful life is over? If not, then what is the purpose of depreciation?
3. Why do companies use the contra account "accumulated depreciation"?
4. Is depreciation a source of cash? If not, then why is depreciation added to net income in the statement of changes in financial position?
5. Is depreciation incurred "under the factory roof" treated as a period cost or as a product cost? Explain.
6. What items should be included in determining the original cost of a new machine?
7. If someone donates a new machine to a company, can the company record depreciation on the machine (a) for financial accounting and reporting purposes? and (b) for income tax purposes.
8. How should companies treat the cost of interest incurred during the period of construction of a new plant?
9. Anderson Company decides to build its own machine rather than to purchase a similar one from a machine manufacturer. Should the company capitalize the cost of its own laborers that work on building the machine? Explain.
10. Can a company depreciate a fixed asset that it is leasing from a manufacturer? Explain.
11. Once a company has fully depreciated a fixed asset, can the company continue to use the asset? If so, can the company continue to record depreciation? If not, won't net income be overstated?
12. If a company originally estimates that a machine will last 6 years but after 2 years decides that the total useful life is more likely to be 8 years, how should this change in estimate be treated for financial accounting and reporting purposes?
13. When operations are discontinued at one of a company's plants and the property is offered for sale, should the plant be separately shown on the balance sheet while it is being held awaiting sale? Should the plant be shown at unallocated cost or at estimated selling price less cost to sell? Should it be shown as a current asset if the company plans to sell it within a year? Should the company continue recording periodic depreciation?
14. A piece of real estate appraised for property tax purposes at $60,000 (land, $40,000; building, $20,000) was bought by LMN Company for $100,000. LMN Company bought the real estate with the intention of tearing down the building and converting the tract to a parking lot. Legal costs amounted to $500; the cost of tearing the building down, $3,000; and the cost of grading and surfacing, $10,000. LMN Company received $1,200 for the materials from the old building.

Required: At what cost should LMN Company show the parking lot on its balance sheet?

15. A company signs a contract to buy equipment for $30,000, payable $10,000 down, $10,000 one year from date, and $10,000 two years from date. At what cost should the company show the equipment on its balance sheet at the date of purchase? *State any reasonable assumptions you make.*

16. RST Company owns property, plant, and equipment with an original cost of $3,500,000 on which it shows accumulated depreciation of $1,000,000. It sells the property to VWX Company for 25,000 shares of VWX Company stock, the shares having a par value of $100 per share, a "book value" $120 (Retained Earnings per share equalling $20 a share), and a market value of $150 a share. What entry should the RST Company make? VWX Company?

17. How should a company account for normal repairs and maintenance for a building? For replacement of the roof? For a general renovation of the building including air conditioning? Why?

18. The Digital Computer Company recently purchased a special machine which was made to the company's specifications. This machine was to be used in manufacturing a part for a new line of computers produced by the company.

Digital Computer Company engineers had estimated that the machine would have a physical life of 15 years at the proposed rate of production. The Company's tax department reported that, for machines of this type, the Internal Revenue Service normally specified 12 years as the period over which the machines would be written off.

Required: What factors should the company consider in estimating the useful life of this machine?

19. On January 1, 1980, a company buys a new machine costing $22,000 installed, with an estimated useful life of six years and a salvage value of $1,000 at the end of the six years. It proposes using straight-line depreciation for financial accounting purposes and either DDB or SYD depreciation for federal income tax purposes.

(A) Prepare depreciation schedules for each of the three methods.
(B) Which of the accelerated methods, DDB or SYD, would you recommend the company use for tax purposes? *State any reasonable assumptions you make.*
(C) If the company's tax rate is 46%, how much would its Deferred Taxes on Income account include for this machine at the end of three years?

20. A company records depreciation of its factory buildings and equipment for 1980 at $100,000. Its Work-in-Process and Finished Goods accounts for 1980 show as follows:

	Work-in-Process	Finished Goods
Balance, January 1, 1980	500,000	2,500,000
Additions	10,000,000	9,500,000
	10,500,000	12,000,000
Transferred	9,500,000	8,000,000
Balance, December 31, 1980	1,000,000	4,000,000

The additions to Work-in-Process include the $100,000 depreciation, and the company shows the $8,000,000 transferred out of Finished Goods as cost of goods sold. As a rough approximation the proportion that depreciation bears to total factory costs generally is the $100,000 to the $10,000,000.

(A) Was the $100,000 depreciation an expense for 1980? If so, why so? If not, how much depreciation was an expense for 1980? And if not, how would you account for the difference?

(B) If the company had considered factory depreciation as a period cost, what difference would it have made in its 1980 figures?

21. Equipment costing $19,000, with a scrap value of $4,000, was purchased on January 1, 1980. Estimated life was 5 years or 75,000 units of production. Units produced were 12,000 in 1980 and 16,000 in 1981. Complete the following table.

Depreciation Method	Depreciation Expense		Book Value	
	1980	1981	12/31/80	12/31/81
Straight Line				
Sum-of-the-Years' Digits				
Double-declining Balance				
Units of Production				

22. On January 1, 1980, the Busch Company purchased a new machine at a cost of $120,000 with a salvage value of $10,000 and an estimated useful life of 10 years. Under the assumption that the estimated number of units the machine will produce is 500,000 and that 75,000 units are produced in 1980, complete the following:

Depreciation Method	1980 Depreciation Expense	Book Value 12/31/80
Straight-Line		
Sum-of-the-Years' Digits		
Double-Declining Balance		
Units of Production		

23. XYZ Corporation has recently exchanged an obsolete lathe for a new one of higher capacity.

Original cost of old lathe	$10,000
Accumulated Depreciation (straight line)	4,000
Scrap value	-0-
New lathe list price	12,000
Cash paid out for new lathe	7,000
Scrap value/New lathe (6 yrs. life)	-0-

Required: (A) If the *income tax procedure* is followed, what entry would be required to record the trade-in?

(B) If the *list price method* is followed in costing the new asset, what entry would be required to record the trade-in?

24. Equipment costing $60,000 with an estimated salvage of $5,000 was purchased on January 1, 1980. Estimated life was 10 years or 100,000 units of production. Units produced in 1980 were 12,000. Determine the amount of depreciation to be recorded for 1980 under each of the following depreciation methods:

(A) Straight-line
(B) Sum-of-the-Years' Digits
(C) Double-Declining Balance
(D) Units of Production

25. The Western Mining Corp. paid $3,040,000 for a tract of land containing valuable ore, and spent $280,000 in developing the property during 1979, preparatory to beginning mining activities on Jan. 1, 1980. Company geologists estimated that the mineral deposit would produce 6 million tons of ore, and it is assumed that the land will have a residual value of $20,000 after the ore deposit is exhausted. It is expected that it will take 12-14 years to extract all of the ore.

A record of capital investment during the last half of 1979, exclusive of the development costs previously mentioned, is as follows:

Asset	Est. Service Life	Cost
Mine buildings	30 years	$300,000
Railroad & hoisting equipment	20 years	600,000
Miscellaneous mine equipment	10 years	120,000
Tons or ore mined and sold at $4 per ton		500,000
Mining labor and other operating costs (exclusive of depreciation and depletion)		$950,000
Selling and administrative expenses.		$140,000

The buildings, railroad, and hoisting equipment cannot be economically removed from the mine location, but the miscellaneous equipment is readily movable and has alternative uses.

Operations during 1980 are summarized below:

Tons of ore mined and sold at $4 per ton 500,000
Mining labor and other operating costs (exclusive of
    depreciation and depletion) $950,000
Selling and administrative expenses $140,000

Required: Prepare an income statement for 1980. (Ignore income taxes)

26. On July 1, 1979, Blueridge Corporation acquired a new machine which had
a list price of $70,000. The corporation gave in exchange for the new ma-
chine $50,000 cash and an old machine which had been purchased on July
1, 1969. The old machine had cost $60,000 and had been depreciated under
the straight-line method by using an estimated life of 15 years and no salvage value. The fair market value of the old machine at the time of the trade-
in was $15,000.

Required: Give the entry necessary to record the trade-in of the old machine and the acquisition of the new machine assuming that the
company uses the: (a) income tax method, and (b) the theoreti-
cally correct accounting method.

27. In its 1978 Income Statement, International Telephone and Telegraph
showed a depreciation expense of $424,024,000. The following footnote
was included in the annual report:

"Depreciation: The Corporation normally claims the maximum depreciation
deduction allowable for tax purposes, using those accelerated techniques
which are applicable in its various domestic and foreign statutory environments. It thus minimizes the use of corporate funds for tax payments. In general, for financial reporting purposes, depreciation is provided on a straight-line
basis to distribute costs evenly over the useful economic lives of the assets involved. Gains or losses with respect to retirement of assets are included in
income."

In a footnote on Income Taxes, the company stated that "Deferred income
taxes applicable to accelerated depreciation amounted to $40,179,000" in
1978. The statutory federal income tax rate was 48 percent in 1978.

Required: (A) How much depreciation did ITT deduct on its 1978 *Federal
Income Tax Return*?
(B) If ITT had used accelerated depreciation for reporting purposes as well as for tax purposes, would this have doubled
"the amount of funds" saved in tax payments? Explain.

Long-Term Investments and Other Assets

In this chapter, other assets such as long-term pre-paid expenses and deferred charges that occasionally appear on corporate balance sheets are discussed. Most of the chapter, however, is concerned with accounting for long-term investments. Included are such topics as the equity method of accounting and accounting for business combinations. Consolidated balance sheets prepared under both the purchase method and the pooling of interests method are illustrated, and the financial reporting requirements of diversified companies are discussed.

In addition to categorizing assets into current assets and fixed assets (property, plant, and equipment), the balance sheets of many companies contain a third asset classification, "long-term investments and other assets." This third category includes all of a company's long-term investments in both debt and equity securities, land, or any other type of property, as well as all of a company's other assets not shown on the balance sheet as either current or fixed assets. As an almost endless variety of "other assets" appear on corporate balance sheets, we will limit our coverage of this topic to a few that appear with substantial regularity. Most of this chapter will be concerned with complexities involved in accounting for long-term investments, including the preparation of a consolidated balance sheet.

LONG-TERM PREPAID EXPENSES
AND DEFERRED CHARGES

A *prepaid expense* occurs when a company makes a cash disbursement prior to the time that an expense actually is incurred. Examples include prepayment of rent and prepayment of insurance. To illustrate, suppose that at the time Corner Drugstore signed its first three-year lease on the building in which it was located, it paid the owner of the building (the lessor) the entire three years' rent in advance. Because no expense had been incurred for rent as of that time, Corner Drugstore would have recorded such a cash transaction as follows:

Prepaid Rent (A)	Incr 10,800
Cash (A)	Decr 10,800

Prepaid rent was an asset to Corner Drugstore because it represented the cash paid to insure use of the building for three years. Of the $10,800 prepaid rent, $3,600 represented a current asset (prepaid rent-current) and $7,200 represented an "other asset" (prepaid rent-noncurrent). At the end of each year, Corner Drugstore would recognize an expense of $3,600 for rent, reducing the balance in the prepaid rent account by a similar amount. Thus, at the time a future expense is prepaid, the company making the prepayment records an asset equal in amount to the cash payment. Of this amount, the portion representing the expense to be incurred within a year of the prepayment is classified as a "current asset," and the remainder is classified an "other asset." As the noncurrent portion becomes current, the asset classification changes from "other assets" to "current assets."

Deferred charges are certain types of long-term prepaid expenses that for one reason or another have been "set apart" by preparers of external financial statements. Organization costs are often shown on the balance sheet as deferred charges. Practically speaking, the distinction is not particularly meaningful. Prior to the issuance of Statement of Financial Accounting Standards No. 2, *Accounting for*

Research and Development Costs, effective for fiscal periods beginning on or after January 1, 1975, many companies treated new product research and development expenditures as deferred charges, chargeable against future sales of the product being developed. FASB Statement No. 2 terminated such treatment of R&D costs, however, by requiring that "All research and development costs shall be charged to expense when incurred." We believe that this significant change in the generally accepted accounting treatment of R&D costs will diminish the appearance of the deferred charge classification on corporate balance sheets.

CASH SURRENDER VALUE OF LIFE INSURANCE POLICIES

When a company carries life insurance on the lives of its officers and the company is specified as the beneficiary, the amount of each year's premium payment must be analyzed to determine the portion that represents the year's insurance expense and the portion that represents an increase in assets. The asset to which we refer is the *cash surrender value* of the insurance policy, and the portion of the premium payment to be recognized as an asset is the amount of increase in the policy's cash surrender value resulting from the payment. In the early years of a life insurance policy, there may be little or no cash surrender value. Whatever cash surrender value exists at a balance sheet date is listed under the "other assets" classification.

On a policy insuring the lives of a company's officers, a premium payment of $1,200 that increased the policy's cash surrender value by $200 would be recorded as follows:

Cash Surrender Value of Life Insurance Policy (A)	Incr	200
Retained Earnings (OE) – (Insurance expense)	Decr	1,000
Cash (A)	Decr	1,200

LONG-TERM RECEIVABLES

The "other asset" category also includes any receivables held by a company, the collections of which are not reasonably expected to occur for more than a year. Long-term receivables may arise from transactions such as the sale of land, buildings or equipment, or from the conversion of a short-term receivable into a long-term one. Regardless of their origin, long-term receivables are shown on the balance sheet under "other assets" at an amount equal to the present value of their estimated future collections.

LONG-TERM INVESTMENTS IN MARKETABLE SECURITIES

The three types of investment securities purchased by companies intending to hold securities for a period greater than a year are common stocks, preferred stocks, and bonds. *Common stocks* have been discussed in prior chapters. *Preferred stocks* are securities that carry certain preferences over common stock. Usually, these preferences relate to dividend priorities or priorities in case of liquidation of the corporation. Preferred stocks are covered in greater detail in Chapter 14. *Bonds* are long-term obligations to repay the amount of their face value (maturity value) to the bondholder on the date the bonds become due (mature). Bondholders periodically receive interest on the bonds as stipulated in the bond agreement, commonly called the *bond indenture*. Bonds are covered more fully in Chapter 12.

Our concern at this point is the manner in which long-term investments in securities are carried as assets on corporate balance sheets. One of the factors that affects their balance sheet presentation is whether or not the securities are readily marketable through one or more of the securities markets. Securities for which an established market exists are known as marketable securities; those for which no ready market exists are known as nonmarketable securities. As most corporate investments are readily marketable, we shall limit our discussion to accounting for marketable securities only.

Long-term investment in bonds issued by corporations, federal or state governments, or any other organization are initially recorded by the investing corporation at cost. Any difference between a bond's cost and its maturity value must be recognized as an adjustment to the interest income recognized by the investor over the life of the bond. The process by which this adjustment occurs is discussed in detail in Chapter 12. For now, suffice it to say that as this adjustment to interest income occurs, the carrying value of the bond investment on the balance sheet changes by an equal amount. One purpose of the adjustment is to show the bond investment on the balance sheet at the date of the bond's maturity at an amount exactly equal to its maturity value. Thus, if we bought for $900 a $1,000 face value bond that matured in five years, we would show the following balance sheet valuations for the bond investment:

At the end of year	The balance sheet would show
1	$ 920
2	$ 940
3	$ 960
4	$ 980
5 (Maturity)	$1,000

The balance sheet presentation for long-term investments in bonds, then, is their original cost adjusted annually by an amount that will result in the investment's being shown at its face value on the date that it matures. Companies will sometimes also parenthetically disclose on the balance sheet the current market values of their bond investments.

Prior to 1975, long-term investments in common and preferred stocks could be carried on corporate balance sheets at either cost or market value. Largely because of the substantial declines in market values of many stocks that occurred in 1973 and 1974, the Financial Accounting Standards Board issued FASB Statement No. 12, *Accounting for Certain Marketable Securities*, effective for periods ending on or after December 31, 1975, to standardize financial statement presentation of certain marketable securities, including common and preferred stock. FASB Statement No. 12 requires that long-term investments (as determined by management) in common and preferred stocks must be carried at the lower of *aggregate* cost or *aggregate* market value, as determined at each balance sheet date. Disclosure of both aggregate cost and aggregate market value is also required. FASB Statement No. 12 does not apply to not-for-profit organizations, mutual life insurance companies, employee benefit plans, or investments accounted for by the "equity method" as described in the next section of this chapter.

INVESTMENTS IN UNCONSOLIDATED SUBSIDIARIES AND AFFILIATED COMPANIES

Many companies purchase the common stock of other corporations for purposes of influencing their managements or obtaining control over their operations. Both objectives are accomplished through the right to vote for the company's Board of Directors, a right that ownership of shares of common stock provides. Sometimes the management of a company is consulted prior to the purchase by another corporation of a significant amount of its common stock, and sometimes the company's management is not aware of any such intention until the purchase or offer to purchase occurs. In the latter instance, corporations frequently obtain the number of shares desired as a result of an offer made directly to the shareholders of another company to purchase their shares at some amount above the current market price. This type of solicitation of shares is referred to as "making an unfriendly tender offer," and it became a commonly used means of accomplishing a "corporate takeover" during the 1970s. One of the reasons for the popularity of tender offers was the belief of many corporate executives that the common stocks of various corporations were substantially undervalued by the stock market.

In discussing the accounting treatment of one company's investment in the common stock of another company, we can usefully divide such investments into three categories based on the percentage of outstanding common stock acquired. These percentages are:

1. Less than 20 percent.
2. From 20 percent to 50 percent.
3. More than 50 percent.

When less than 20 percent of a company's outstanding common stock is owned by another company, the investor corporation must carry the investment on its balance sheet in accordance with the requirements of FASB Statement No. 12 previously described; that is, at the lower of aggregate cost or aggregate market value.

When a company owns from 20 percent to 50 percent of the outstanding common stock of another company, Accounting Principles Board Opinion No. 18, *The Equity Method of Accounting for Investments in Common Stock*, effective for fiscal periods beginning after December 31, 1971, requires that such investments be accounted for by the *equity method*. Much like the logic supporting the preparation of the statement of changes in financial position presented in

Chapter 4, the logic supporting the equity method of accounting for common stock investments is somewhat elusive at first.

The basic idea of the equity method is to show the long-term investment in common stock on the investor corporation's balance sheet at an amount that represents the amount of the initial investment adjusted for the investor's share of all subsequent changes in the stockholders' equity of the "investee." As the investee corporations' total stockholders' equity changes, so does the investor's carrying value of the investment; thus, the name "equity method."

We know from earlier chapters that, aside from issuance of additional common stock, only income (or loss) and dividends can change a corporations' owners' equity. The accounting procedures comprising the equity method can, therefore, be summarized as follows:

1. Record the investment in common stock at the amount of its acquisition cost.
2. Increase (or decrease) the carrying value of the investment by the amount of the investor company's share of the investee's reported net income (or loss) each year.
3. Decrease the carrying value of the investment by the amount of the investor company's share of the dividends declared by the investee's Board of Directors each year.

To illustrate, assume that: (1) on January 2, 1980 Company A purchased 30 percent of the outstanding common stock of Company B; (2) the total cost of the investment was $150,000; and (3) for its fiscal year ended December 31, 1980, Company B reported net income of $80,000 and declared and paid dividends of $50,000. Under the equity method, Company A would record these transactions in the following manner:

To record the purchase of Company B's common stock.

Investment in Company B (A)	Incr	150,000
Cash (A)	Decr	150,000

To record 30 percent of Company B's net income.

Investment in Company B (A)	Incr	24,000
Retained Earnings (OE) –	Incr	24,000
(Income from Affiliate)		

To record 30 percent of Company B's dividends.

Cash (A)	Incr	15,000
Investment in Company B (A)	Decr	15,000

This same example can be illustrated somewhat differently as follows:

	Company B		Company A	
	Total	Co. A's 30% Share		
Total Stockholders' Equity (January 2, 1980)	$600,000	$180,000	Cost of Investment	$150,000
1980 Net Income	$ 80,000	$ 24,000	Included in 1980 Income	$ 24,000
Dividends paid in 1980	$ 50,000	$ 15,000	Cash Increased and Investment in Co. B Decreased	$ 15,000
Total Stockholders' Equity (December 31, 1980)	$630,000	$189,000	Investment in Co. B (Dec. 31, 1980)	$159,000

The difficult concept to grasp here is that Company A's investment account was increased to recognize Company B's reported net income even though Company A received no cash pursuant to the recognition. Then, when Company A received cash (the $15,000 dividend), its investment account was decreased. It is erroneous to equate "cash flow" with changes in the investment account; the two simply don't necessarily go together. The secret to understanding the equity method is realizing that when the investee's owners' equity increases or decreases as the result of net income, a net loss, or the payment of dividends, the investment account on the investing company's books is changed to reflect these changes in the investee's equity.

Investments of greater than 50 percent of the outstanding common stock of another company generally result in the preparation of consolidated financial statements, as discussed in the following sections pertaining to business combinations. If consolidated statements are not prepared, then the investment is accounted for by the equity method.

TYPES OF BUSINESS COMBINATIONS

A *business combination* occurs when a corporation and one or more incorporated or unincorporated businesses are brought together into one *accounting* entity, but not necessarily into one *legal* entity. This can be accomplished either through the acquisition of the common stock of the business or through the acquisition of its net assets. In other words, a business combination can occur both through the acquisition of another business's stock or its net assets. When stock is acquired, the business combination can take a variety of legal forms. Although we are primarily concerned with the accounting and management aspects of business combinations, some understanding of their major alternative legal structures is also necessary. The three most common legal forms are:

Merger: Co. A + Co. B = Co. A. In a merger, Co. B is actually merged into Co. A and Co. B terminates its existence. Consequently, at the time the merger occurs, Co. A records on its books the actual assets and liabilities of Co. B. No "investment in Co. B" account appears on the books of Co. A (as Co. B no longer exists), and the assets and liabilities of Co. B appear as part of the assets and liabilities of Co. A immediately following completion of the merger.

Consolidation: Co. A + Co. B = Co. C. In a consolidation (be careful not to confuse this with the term "consolidated financial statements"), Co. A and Co. B actually agree to combine their assets and liabilities to form a new company, Co. C. Both Co. A and Co. B terminate their existence. Consequently, at the time the consolidation occurs, the books of Co. C show the assets and liabilities of both Co. A and Co. B. No "investment in Co. A or Co. B" account appears on the books of Co. C (as these two companies no longer exist), and the assets and liabilities of both Co. A and Co. B appear as the assets and liabilities of Co. C immediately following completion of the consolidation.

Parent-Subsidiary Relationship: Co. A + Co. B = Co. A + Co. B. When a business combination takes the form of parent-subsidiary relationship, Co. A acquires controlling interest in voting common stock of Co. B (generally, "controlling interest" means owning more than 50 percent of the common stock). Co. A (the parent) and Co. B (the subsidiary) both continue to exist as separate legal entities. (Keep in mind, however, that both companies are under the control of the same management.) Co. A carries an account on its books called

"Investment in Co. B," and at the end of each fiscal year consolidated financial statements are normally prepared to reflect both the assets and liabilities and the results of operations for the two companies combined. When preparing consolidated financial statements, all inter-company transactions (those between the parent company and its subsidiary) are eliminated.

As a practical matter, the term merger is often used in financial literature in a broad sense to refer to business combinations in general. Also, the financial literature sometimes uses the terms affiliate and subsidiary interchangeably. Technically, however, there is a difference between them. An affiliate is a company in which another company owns from 20 percent to 50 percent of its outstanding common stock. A subsidiary is a company in which another company (the parent) owns more than 50 percent (controlling interest) of its outstanding common stock. A wholly owned subsidiary is one whose parent company owns 100 percent of its common stock.

ACCOUNTING FOR BUSINESS COMBINATIONS

Regardless of a business combination's legal form, accountants must decide how it should be accounted for. The proper means of accounting for business combinations has been a controversial issue for many years, and there are presently two methods that are generally accepted. One is referred to as the *purchase* method; the other as the *pooling of interests* method. It is important at the outset to understand that the specific legal form that a business combination takes does not in itself preclude its treatment as a purchase or as a pooling of interests. That is to say that both a merger and a consolidation can be treated as either a purchase or a pooling, as can the establishment of a parent-subsidiary relationship. There are, therefore, three important questions to be answered relative to a business combination. First, what is its legal form? Second, does it qualify for accounting purposes as a pooling of interests or as a purchase? Third, is it a taxable or nontaxable transaction?

Because substantial differences in the financial statements of the combined entities can occur solely as a result of the method selected to account for the business combination, it is important to understand the major characteristics of the two generally accepted methods.

As income tax considerations also play a major role in structuring most business combinations, a brief discussion of some of the most important tax aspects is included later in this chapter.

The Purchase Method

Under the purchase method, the assets and liabilities of the acquired company are reported by the acquiring company (either immediately in the case of a merger or a consolidation, or at the end of the fiscal year through the preparation of consolidated financial statements in the case of a parent-subsidiary relationship) at their fair market values on the date the business combination occurs. Any excess of the total acquisition cost over the fair market value of net assets (assets less liabilities) acquired is reported as *goodwill*. Goodwill must then be amortized over its estimated life, not to exceed 40 years.

At the date of the business combination, the retained earnings balance of the combined entity is defined as the retained earnings balance of the acquiring company. In other words, the retained earnings balance of the acquired company is eliminated.

Subsequent to the combination, any financial statements presented to external users which pertain to pre-combination periods must show historical data of the *acquiring* company only.

The Pooling of Interests Method

Under the pooling of interests method, the assets and liabilities of the acquired company are reported by the acquiring company (either immediately in the case of a merger or a consolidation, or at the end of the fiscal year through the preparation of consolidated financial statements in the case of a parent-subsidiary relationship) at their book values on the date the business combination occurs. Fair market values are *not* used, and *no goodwill is recorded*.

At the date of the business combination, the retained earnings balance of the combined entity is defined as the *sum* of the retained earnings balances of the combining companies. In other words, the retained earnings balance of the acquired company is not eliminated but is carried forward. Subsequent to the combination, any financial statements presented to external users which pertain to pre-combination periods must be restated to reflect the data that would have been shown had the companies always been combined.

Prior to 1970, considerable flexibility existed in selecting the method to account for business combinations. In August of 1970, the Accounting Principles Board issued Opinion No. 16 entitled *Business Combinations*. One of the major objectives of this Opinion was to establish a set of criteria to determine whether to account for any given business combination (regardless of its legal form) as a purchase or as a pooling of interests. Both methods were found acceptable but not as alternatives for one another. The Accounting Principles Board concluded that if certain conditions are met, then the combination *must* be treated as a pooling of interests. If *all* the specified conditions are not met, then the combination *must* be treated as a purchase. Therefore, while there continue to be two generally accepted methods of accounting for business combinations, for any specific combination only one method is acceptable.

APB Opinion No. 16 established twelve criteria that must all be satisfied in order to use the pooling of interests method. One of the most restrictive of the criteria requires that the acquiring company consummate the business combination by issuing only voting common stock in exchange for *substantially all* of the voting common stock interest of another company. "Substantially all" is defined by the Opinion as 90 percent or more. It can therefore be concluded that if voting common stock is not issued to consummate a business combination, then it must be accounted for as a purchase. It cannot be concluded, however, that all business combinations consummated by issuance of voting common stock must be accounted for as poolings.

Two possible sources of confusion regarding the application of the pooling of interests criteria just discussed need to be clarified at this point. First, the requirement that the acquiring company obtain "substantially all of the voting common stock interest of another company" can also be met through a transfer to the acquiring company of the *net assets* of another company provided all net assets of the company are transferred in exchange for voting common stock of the acquiring company. Second, the requirement that the acquiring corporation issue "only voting common stock" does permit the acquiror to distribute cash or other consideration for fractional shares and for shares held by dissenting stockholders of the other company.

Before illustrating the purchase and pooling of interests methods, it should be mentioned that prior to the issuance of APB Opinion No. 16, business combinations accounted for by the purchase method sometimes gave rise to an account referred to as "negative goodwill." This account was created when the acquisition cost of common stock was less than the fair market value of the acquiring company's interest in the net assets of the acquired company. Negative goodwill was shown on the combined financial statements either as a "deferred credit" or as a "contra asset" to all of the assets acquired. The Accounting Principles Board concluded in Opinion No. 16 that any such excess of the fair market value of net assets acquired over the acquisition cost should be treated as proportionate reductions in the values assigned to all noncurrent assets, except for long-term investments in marketable securities. Therefore, there should no longer be a need for a negative goodwill account unless all of the noncurrent asset values (other than long-term investments in marketable securities) have been reduced to zero. As a practical matter, then, negative goodwill should seldom be seen on external financial statements for business combinations occurring subsequent to 1970. It is possible, however, for negative goodwill to appear on external financial statements for business combinations that occurred prior to the issuance of APB Opinion No. 16.

As an illustration of the type of footnote to the financial statements that frequently appears in corporate annual reports with respect to business combinations, the following remarks contained in the Notes to the Consolidated Financial Statements of Del Monte Corporation are presented:

> Acquisitions are treated as either pooling of interests or purchases. Under the pooling of interests concept, companies acquired with Del Monte stock are considered to have always been a part of the Corporation; therefore, their operating results are included in current financial statements and in the figures restated for prior years. Net assets are recorded at values carried on the books of the acquired companies. When a company is purchased, its earnings are included only from date of acquisition and the investment is recorded at Del Monte's cost. When the purchase price exceeds the value assigned to the net assets acquired, the excess is recorded as an intangible asset; when the purchase price is less than the value of the net assets acquired, the difference is recorded as an adjustment to noncurrent assets.

To illustrate the accounting entries that result from various types of business combinations accounted for by both the purchase and

Illustration 11-1

Individual Statements of Financial Position of Companies A and B
December 31, 1980
(in millions of dollars)

	Company A	Company B	Combined
Assets:			
Cash	$ 720	$ 80	$ 800
Trade Receivables (net)	200	100	300
Inventories	250	140	390
Property, Plant & Equipment (Net)	700	300	1,000
	1,870	620	2,490
Deduct Liabilities	170	120	290
Net Assets	1,700	500	2,200
Owners' Equity:			
Common Stock ($100 par)	1,000	300	1,300
Retained Earnings	700	200	900
	$1,700	$500	$2,200

Memo: Market Value per share, 12/31/80, $300 for Company A's stock, $200 for Company B's stock.

pooling of interests methods, we have developed examples using the data presented in Illustration 11-1. We will assume that 100 percent ownership of a subsidiary is obtained in each case. Therefore, the problems of accounting for "minority interest" in a subsidiary will not be discussed. Illustration 11-1 will also provide the basis for the preparation of consolidated balance sheets in accordance with both the purchase and the pooling of interests methods.

The Purchase Method Illustrated

If Company A, in Illustration 11-1, were to purchase all the assets and assume all the liabilities of Company B, it might agree to pay $600M ($600 million) cash for the net assets shown on B's book at $500 M. Immediately, there arises the question of what to do with the $100M difference.

One method of dealing with this $100M difference is to ascertain the fair market values of the assets acquired. Assuming values of $180M for B's inventories and $360M for B's property, plant, and equipment (net), Company A would make the following entry:

Cash (A)	Incr 80	
Trade Receivables (A)	Incr 100	
Inventories (A)	Incr 180	
Property, Plant & Equipment (A)	Incr 360	
Payables & Accruals (L)		Incr 120
Cash (A)		Decr 600

Instead of paying cash, if the negotiations between the two companies called for Co. A to issue 2,000,000 shares of its authorized but unissued common stock at $300 per share, Company A would make the following entry under the purchase method:

Cash (A)	Incr 80	
Trade Receivables (A)	Incr 100	
Inventories (A)	Incr 180	
Property, Plant & Equipment (A)	Incr 360	
Payables & Accruals (L)		Incr 120
Common Stock (OE)		Incr 200
Capital in Excess of Par Value (OE)		Incr 400

Illustration 11-2

Statement of Financial Position of Company A
After Purchase of B's Net Assets for $600M
(Based on Illustration 11-1 with Values of $180M and $360M,
Respectively, Assigned to B's Inventories and Property, Plant & Equipment)
December 31, 1980
(In millions of dollars)

	Purchase for	
	Cash	Stock
Assets:		
Cash	$ 200	$ 800
Trade Receivables	300	300
Inventories	430	430
Property, Plant & Equipment (Net)	1,060	1,060
	1,990	2,590
Deduct Liabilities	290	290
Net Assets	1,700	2,300
Stockholders' Equity:		
Common Stock	1,000	1,200
Capital in Excess of Par Value	-0-	400
Retained Earnings	700	700
	$1,700	$2,300

After recording the purchase of B's net assets, Company A would prepare a statement of financial position as shown in Illustration 11-2.

If the book value of the net assets acquired were approximately equal to their fair market value, then the $100M difference would represent goodwill and Company A would make the following entry:

Cash (A)	Incr 80	
Trade Receivables (A)	Incr 100	
Inventories (A)	Incr 140	
Property, Plant & Equipment (A)	Incr 300	
Goodwill (A)	Incr 100	
Payables and Accruals (L)		Incr 120
PLUS *either*		
Cash (A)		Decr 600
or		
Common Stock (OE)		Incr 200
Capital in Excess of Par Value (OE)		Incr 400

The goodwill recognized would be amortized over a period of 40 years or less.

After recording the purchase of Company B's net assets, Company A would prepare a balance sheet, as shown in Illustration 11-3.[1]

If Company A, in Illustration 11-1, were to acquire all of the common stock of Company B for $600 M cash, it would make the following entry:

Investment in Company B (A)	Incr 600	
Cash (A)		Decr 600

Instead of paying cash, if the negotiations called for Company A to issue 2 million shares of its unissued stock at $300 per share, then Company A would make the following entry:

---

[1] While we are primarily interested in what happened to Company A, it may be of interest to comment briefly on what would happen to Company B. Company B would be left with either (1) $600M cash or (2) an investment in 2 million shares of stock in Company A carried at $600M. Company B would have outstanding 3 million shares of its own stock, shown at the par value of $300M, and Retained Earnings $300M ($200M plus the $100M gain on its sale of its net assets to Company A). Company B could then be liquidated by distributing the $600M cash or the 2 million shares of Company A stock to B's stockholders, who would turn in their Company B stock to be cancelled. In the unusual case, Company B might continue in business and use the $600M cash it received from Company A or with the cash would get from selling the capital stock received from Company A to purchase other assets.

Illustration 11-3

Statement of Financial Position of Company A
After Purchase of B's Net Assets for $600M
(Based on Illustration 11-1 with $100M Attributed to Goodwill)
December 31, 1980
(In millions of dollars)

	Purchase for	
	Cash	Stock
Assets:		
Cash	$ 200	$ 800
Trade Receivables	300	300
Inventories	390	390
Property, Plant & Equipment (Net)	1,000	1,000
Goodwill	100	100
	1,990	2,590
Deduct Liabilities	290	290
Net Assets	1,700	2,300
Stockholders' Equity:		
Common Stock	1,000	1,200
Capital in Excess of Par Value	-0-	400
Retained Earnings	700	700
	$1,700	$2,300

Investment in Company B (A)	Incr 600	
Common Stock (OE)		Incr 200
Capital in Excess of Par Value (OE)		Incr 400

If Company A (the parent) were to prepare consolidated financial statements at December 31, 1980, the resulting consolidated statement of financial position would be the same as:

Illustration 11-2 - if values of $180 M and $360M were ascribed to company B's inventories and property, plant and equipment.

or

Illustration 11-3 - if the $100M difference was ascribed to goodwill.

Note that the consolidated balance sheet of Company A and its subsidiary Company B at the date of the business combination is identical to that of Company A after it has purchased the net assets of Company B.

In preparing a consolidated balance sheet (consolidated statement of financial position) under the *purchase method*, the following general procedures are followed:

1. The individual assets and liabilities shown on the balance sheet of a subsidiary are substituted for the parent company's investment in the subsidiary.

2. If there is a difference between the recorded net assets (assets less liabilities) of the subsidiary and the parent company's investment at the date of acquisition, the difference must be ascribed to particular assets of the subsidiary or to an intangible labeled Goodwill, or Excess of Purchase Price over Underlying Net Assets of Subsidiary at Acquisition, or some similar title.

3. If an intangible asset results from the business combination, it should be amortized over its estimated useful life, not to exceed 40 years.

4. If the parent company does not acquire 100 percent of the ownership, the interest of the minority shareholders in the stockholders' equity of the subsidiary and in the subsidiary's net income should be shown on the consolidated balance sheet and in the consolidated income statement.

5. The retained earnings shown on the consolidated balance sheet should include the retained earnings of the parent company plus the parent company's proportion of the subsidiary's retained earnings accumulated since acquisition of the subsidiary. To put it negatively, no part of the retained earnings of a subsidiary earned prior to acquisition by the parent should become a part of the consolidated retained earnings.

6. Intercompany asset and liability accounts between the parent and its subsidiaries and between subsidiaries and other subsidiaries, as well as intercompany revenues and expenses, should be eliminated.

The Pooling of Interests Method Illustrated

If Company A, in Illustration 11-1, were to issue 2 million shares of its authorized but unissued stock to the stockholders of Company B in exchange for their Company B stock, and if all of the other criteria of APB Opinion No. 16 for a pooling of interests were met, the consolidated statement of financial position at the date of business combination would be as shown in Illustration 11-4. Note, in Illustration 11-4, that:

1. The book values of the assets and liabilities of Companies A and B have been combined.

2. The retained earnings of the two companies have been combined and have been carried forward to the consolidated statement.

3. The only difference between the consolidated figures shown in Illustration 11-4 and the combined figures shown in Illustration 11-1 is in Common Stock and Capital in Excess of Par Value. Here, the $200M par value of Company A's stock replaced the $300M par value of Company B's stock, and $100M is shown as Capital in Excess of Par Value.

Illustration 11-4

**Consolidated Statement of Financial
Position of Companies A and B Prepared on Basis of
"Pooling of Interests" (Based on Illustration 11-1)
December 31, 1980
(In millions of dollars)**

Assets:	
Cash	$ 800
Trade Receivables	300
Inventories	390
Property, Plant & Equipment (Net)	1,000
	2,490
Deduct Liabilities	290
Net Assets	2,200
Stockholders' Equity:	
Common Stock	1,200
Capital in Excess of Par Value	100
Retained Earnings	900
	$2,200

The differences between Illustrations 11-2 and 11-3 and Illustration 11-4 highlight the differences between a business combination accounted for as a purchase and one accounted for as a pooling of interests:

1. Under a pooling of interests, net assets are combined at previously existing book values. Under a purchase, the difference between the purchase price and the recorded net assets acquired may require adjusting asset values (as in Illustration 11-2), recording goodwill (as in Illustration 11-3), or both, in order to show fair market values.

2. Under a pooling of interests, no goodwill is recorded. Under a purchase, any goodwill recorded must be amortized over a period not to exceed 40 years.

3. Under a pooling of interests, the retained earnings balances of the combining companies are added together and carried forward on subsequent balance sheets of the combined entity. (Although the total stockholders' equity of the combined entity on the date of the combination under a pooling of interests is always equal to the sum of the stockholders' equities of the combining companies, occasionally it is not possible for the retained earnings of the combined entity to equal the sum of the combining companies' retained earnings. This occurs when the acquiring company issues common stock having a par value and the total par value of the stock issued pursuant to the business combination exceeds the total paid-in capital of the acquired company. The resulting difference is subtracted from the sum of the combining companies' retained earnings.) Under a purchase, the retained earnings balance of the combined entity at the date of the combination is defined as the retained earnings balance of the acquiring company. The retained earnings balance of the acquired company is eliminated.

4. Under a pooling of interests, any financial statements presented to external users subsequent to the combination which pertain to pre-combination periods must be restated to reflect the data that would have been shown had the companies always been combined. Under a purchase, external financial statements prepared subsequent to the combination that pertain to pre-combination periods must reflect the historical data of the acquiring company only.

INCOME TAX CONSEQUENCES OF
BUSINESS COMBINATIONS

In structuring negotiated (friendly) business combinations, considerable attention is usually given by all entities involved to the income tax consequences of proposed combinations. The determination of the probable tax consequences associated with alternative forms of business combinations is a problem for tax experts and is well beyond the province of this text. There are, however, some fundamentally important tax concepts related to business combinations that we believe should be discussed herein.

For income tax purposes, business combinations are classified into two categories: (1) taxable combinations; and (2) nontaxable combinations. Nontaxable (tax-free) combinations are frequently referred to as reorganizations. In accordance with U.S. tax laws, both the mode of business combination and the medium and terms of payment determine whether or not a combination is taxable. Actually, the use of the term nontaxable is somewhat misleading on two counts. First, nontaxable combinations are those for which the tax consequences to the seller are deferred, not nonexistent. Second, nontaxable transactions can be completely tax-free or partially tax-free. The tax basis to the acquiring corporation of the assets or stock received in a completely nontaxable combination is the same as the selling corporation's basis in the assets or the selling shareholders' basis in the stock. In other words, the buyer inherits the seller's tax basis in the stock or assets acquired. In contrast, taxable business combinations have immediate income tax consequences to the seller, and the acquiring company's tax basis in the stock or assets received is equal to the fair market value of the consideration paid to the seller.

In taxable combinations, there are generally no restrictions on the mode of acquisition or on the medium or terms of payment. In nontaxable combinations, U.S. tax laws impose certain limitations on the mode of acquisition and on the medium and terms of payment. Generally, a completely tax-free combination requires that the consideration paid to the seller consist solely of stock, either common or preferred, voting or nonvoting. Partially tax-free combinations are also possible as long as more than half of the total purchase price paid to the seller is in the form of stock of the acquiring corporation. Any cash or property other than stock received by the seller is taxed at that time to the extent of any gain realized.

There are three major methods for accomplishing a nontaxable business combination (reorganization). These are: (1) a statutory merger or consolidation; (2) a stock-for-stock acquisition; and (3) a stock-for-assets acquisition. Of these three methods, the statutory merger or consolidation is generally considered to be the most flexible means of structuring a tax-free business combination, as several types of consideration are permitted by the tax laws under this type of reorganization.

Earlier in this chapter we mentioned that for any business combination an understanding of both its legal form and the accounting method used to account for it was important. We have now added a third dimension: the income tax consequences associated with the combination. Although there is some risk associated with generalizing about the relationship among these three dimensions, we feel that three general observations can be made. First, the legal form of a business combination is of considerably greater importance for tax purposes than for accounting purposes. Second, a business combination accounted for as a pooling of interests will typically be a nontaxable combination regardless of the legal form used. Third, a business combination accounted for as a purchase accomplished *solely* through the payment of cash will be a taxable combination regardless of the legal form used. Business combinations accounted for as purchases where the consideration includes stock, cash, and other property may either be totally taxable or partially taxable depending on the circumstances. No useful generalizations can therefore be made regarding the tax consequences of combinations accounted for as purchases.

Several additional comments regarding the relationship between the tax and accounting aspects of business combinations need to be made before concluding our discussion of this complex topic. They are as follows:

1. The cost basis of assets acquired in a business combination may be different for financial accounting purposes than for tax purposes.

2. The amount of goodwill recognized for accounting purposes as the result of a business combination may not be the same as the amount of goodwill recognized for tax purposes. The reason for this is that the tax laws do not necessarily conform to generally accepted accounting principles with respect to the calculation of goodwill.

3. Goodwill recognized for accounting purposes must be amortized over a period not to exceed 40 years. Goodwill recognized for tax purposes is *not* tax deductible.

There is no doubt that the income tax consequences of a business combination to all parties involved play an important part in determining the specific details associated with its structure and, consequently, indirectly affect the manner in which the combination must be accounted for.

MANAGEMENT CONSIDERATIONS REGARDING BUSINESS COMBINATIONS

Consummating a business combination requires considerable effort by an acquiring company's management. The many business, personal, tax, and accounting issues involved present management with a most challenging task. Certainly many more business combinations are contemplated than are actually consummated.

As a means of accomplishing corporate growth and diversification, business combinations are an integral element of a company's long-term strategic planning process. Any evaluation of a proposed combination would require an in-depth analysis of how it would enhance a company's long-term goals and objectives. Included in any such analysis would be a thorough evaluation of the selling corporation's operations, personnel, physical facilities, and financial position. An assessment would also be made regarding possible violations of government regulations, particularly those pertaining to federal antitrust laws. Some companies use their own staff personnel to identify and evaluate possible acquisition candidates, and other companies rely heavily on consultants and other specialists in the field of business combinations to perform these tasks.

Once a decision has been made to pursue a particular business combination, management must then decide on the mode of acquisition (e.g., unfriendly tender offer or negotiation, purchase of stock or net assets), medium and terms of payment, total acquisition price, and the most desirable legal form, tax consequences, and financial accounting treatment. The two most common areas of disagreement between the buyer and the seller, and those that generally require the greatest amount of negotiation, pertain to the purchase price and the income tax consequences of the proposed combination. As a general rule, the seller wishes to minimize the immediate tax consequences of the transaction, either through the deferral of tax or the recognition of a capital gain. The buyer, on the other hand, usually wishes to maximize the tax basis in the stock or assets acquired.

As the combined or consolidated financial statements prepared subsequent to the consummation of the business combination can differ rather dramatically depending on which of the two generally accepted accounting methods are used to account for the combination, its financial accounting implications usually receive careful consideration by the acquiring company's management. Because several of the conditions that must be met for use of the pooling of interests method cover the two-year period prior to the initiation of the plan of combination, a company contemplating using the pooling method must be careful not to violate any of those conditions during that two-year period. This danger serves to illustrate the need for long-range planning in connection with business combinations.

Both the quantity and the characteristics of business combinations are affected by business, economic, and stock market conditions. As a result, so is the accounting method to be used affected by these factors. There are times when current conditions essentially dictate the medium and terms of payment that must be used, and there are times when management has considerable flexibility in structuring these two aspects. It is in the latter situation that management pays particular attention to the financial accounting considerations related to the proposed combination. Some of the accounting issues of greatest importance to corporate management are summarized below:

1. Whereas the purchase method permits the subsequent combined or consolidated financial statements to include only the results of operations of the acquired company achieved after the date of the business combination, the timing of the combination is frequently more important for those to be treated as purchases.

2. Whereas the pooling method requires the issuance of common stock and also requires that the combined or consolidated financial statements for the year the combination occurs be prepared as if the companies had always been together, the potential impact on the current year's earnings per share is usually greater under a pooling of interests.

3. Whenever the price paid for the stock or net assets of another

company substantially exceeds their book value, treatment of the business combination as a pooling of interests may be particularly appealing to management. The reasons for this preference are twofold. First, the use of the purchase method would result in placing larger values on the assets acquired. Most likely, some of the increased valuations would pertain to depreciable assets, causing future income statements to show larger depreciation expenses and lower incomes. The lower reported income and the higher asset values will have an unfavorable effect on some key financial ratios; e.g., asset turnover and return on assets. Second, the use of the purchase method could result in the recognition of goodwill. The subsequent required amortization of the goodwill would decrease reported net income yet, because goodwill is not tax deductible, would not provide any tax savings.

These three accounting issues of importance to management also illustrate why so much controversy has surrounded the accounting for business combinations through the years. Critics of APB Opinion No. 16 argue that corporate managements should not be able to influence the content of subsequent combined or consolidated financial statements by the way in which they structure the combination. Many of them also argue that the economic substance of a business combination cannot possibly be portrayed by two methods that give such different results as do the purchase and pooling methods. They remain unconvinced that the twelve criteria for use of the pooling of interests method provide a rational basis on which to make a decision about the content of financial statements prepared subsequent to a business combination for purposes of portraying its economic consequences. Because we expect business combinations to continue to play an important role in corporate growth and diversification throughout the 1980s, we feel that the Financial Accounting Standards Board is likely to issue an official pronouncement on this complex and controversial topic sometime during the decade.

EXTERNAL FINANCIAL REPORTING BY DIVERSIFIED COMPANIES

During the 1960s and the 1970s the United States experienced a merger and acquisition movement, one phase of which was the acquisition by publicly held companies of companies in a variety of industries. The highly diversified companies that resulted became known as conglomerates. A parallel movement was the diversification into different industries through internal growth and development rather than by acquisition. For purposes of the following discussion, we will refer to both types of companies as "diversified companies."

During the 1970s, many U.S. companies broadened their activities by establishing operations in one or more foreign countries. The extensive increase in international activities coupled with the industry diversification previously mentioned brought about the need for established guidelines regarding the financial reporting requirements of diversified companies. The Financial Accounting Standards Board responded to this need by issuing FASB Statement No. 14, *Financial Reporting for Segments of a Business Enterprise*, effective for fiscal periods beginning after December 5, 1976.

FASB Statement No. 14 requires diversified companies to group all of their revenue-producing projects and services into "significant industry segments." A "significant segment" is defined as one whose sales, identifiable assets (as defined in Statement No. 14), or operating income or loss is ten percent or more of their respective totals for the company as a whole. For each significant segment, the amount of its revenues, operating income or loss, and identifiable assets must be disclosed in the financial statements. To insure comprehensive disclosure, enough segments must be reported as comprise at least 75 percent of the revenue of all the company's industry segments earned from sales to unaffiliated customers.

Regardless of whether a company has to report financial data by industry segments, it must report separately the revenues, some measure of profitability, and the identifiable assets of its domestic and foreign operations if either foreign sales or foreign identifiable assets represent ten percent or more of their respective totals for the company.

The Financial Accounting Standards Board did not prescribe any specific rules for determining industry segments. Instead, the Board expressed the belief that determining a company's industry segments should depend on management's judgment.

SUMMARY

That portion of prepaid expenses attributable to benefits to be realized within one year are classified as current assets; the remainder are shown as other assets. Long-term investments in another company's common stock of less than 20 percent are presented on the balance sheet at the lower of aggregate cost or aggregate market value. Investments of between 20 and 50 percent of another company's outstanding common stock must be accounted for by the equity method. When more than 50 percent of the outstanding common stock of another company is acquired, consolidated financial statements are usually prepared. Two different methods of accounting for business combinations are generally accepted. When certain conditions are met, a business combination must be accounted for as a pooling of interests. Otherwise, a business combination must be treated as a purchase. The resulting financial statements will be considerably different under these two generally accepted methods.

In structuring a business combination, careful consideration must be given to the income tax consequences to both the buyer and the seller. For tax purposes, a business combination may either be fully taxable, fully nontaxable, or partially nontaxable. The specific legal form of a combination has much greater significance for tax purposes than for accounting purposes. When discussing business combinations, care should be taken to differentiate between their legal form, the accounting method used to record them, and their income tax consequences.

Since 1976, the Financial Accounting Standards Board has required disclosures in corporate annual reports of sales, profitability, and assets of both major U.S. industry segments and foreign operations in response to the needs of investors, creditors, and others to understand the activities of diversified companies.

QUESTIONS AND PROBLEMS

1. Distinguish between prepaid expenses and deferred charges. List two examples of each. How are deferred charges shown on the balance sheet?
2. Is there any difference between the cash surrender value and the loan value of a life insurance policy? Discuss. Do either affect the amount of insurance expense to be recognized during an accounting period? If so, how?
3. Why do companies carry life insurance on their executives? Do you think the premiums paid on executives' life insurance policies are tax deductible to the corporation? Would you expect corporations to pay tax on the insurance proceeds?

4. What type of transaction might give rise to a long-term receivable? Where and at what value are long-term receivables shown on corporate balance sheets?

5. Are a company's long-term investments in marketable common and preferred stocks of other companies shown on its balance sheet at cost, market value, or some other value? As the current market value of the long-term investment fluctuates, does the investing company show any gain or losses in its income statement relative thereto? Are long-term investments in marketable bonds of other companies valued in the same manner as are long-term investments in marketable equity securities (common and preferred stocks)?

6. Explain the equity method of accounting for investments in common stock. Why is it called the equity method? When should it be used?

7. Explain the cost method of accounting for investments in common stock. When should it be used?

8. The equity method is frequently referred to as a "one-line" consolidation. Do you agree? Explain.

9. In applying the guidelines for the percent of common stock owned in another company before use of the equity method is required, is there any need to exercise judgment? Explain.

10. SIVA Company was tired of being number two, and so it acquired 90% of the outstanding common stock of ZTREH Company. The next weekend, three promising young managers employed by SIVA Company were discussing the recent acquisition while playing a not so quick round of golf. Bill stated that he thought the acquisition should be treated as a purchase, but Jack disagreed and stated that he thought it should be treated as a pooling of interests. At this point, Harvey spoke up and reminded his two companions that they were having enough trouble with their golf game without worrying about less important matters such as business combinations. Harvey then stated that their argument was senseless anyway because there was practically no difference between these two accounting methods. Comment on Harvey's statement. Include both balance sheet and income statement considerations in your discussion.

11. Why do generally accepted accounting principles usually require companies that own more than 50% of the outstanding common stock of other companies to prepare consolidated financial statements?

12. What is a conglomerate? How does it differ from a diversified company? Are diversified companies required to provide any breakdown of their activities according to industry segments in their published financial statements? Explain. What is the purpose of any such disclosures? Doesn't the idea of business segment reporting run counter to the logic underlying the preparation of consolidated financial statements?

13. The books of Alpha Corporation contain an account titled "Investment in Beta Company". Each year this account is increased by an amount equal to Alpha Company's share of the annual net income of Beta Company. How

should a cash dividend paid by Beta Company be recorded on the books of Alpha Corporation?

14. A company carries life insurance on the lives of its officers. The cash surrender value of the insurance policies at the beginning of the year was $132,400 and at the end of the year was $141,000. The company paid premiums of $15,700 during the year. Ignoring income taxes, how should the company account for the yearly premium paid? If the company's tax department informed you that life insurance premiums paid are not deductible for tax purposes, would this affect the way the company accounted for the yearly life insurance premiums?

15. As of December 31, 1980, the Atwood Corporation held the following long-term investments in marketable securities, all of which represent less than 10% of the outstanding stock of the individual companies:

Investment	Cost	Market	Lower of Cost or Market
Common Stock of Co. A	$ 50,000	$ 75,000	$ 50,000
Preferred Stock of Co. A	30,000	25,000	25,000
Common Stock of Co. B	80,000	60,000	60,000
Common Stock of Co. C	100,000	95,000	95,000
	$260,000	$255,000	$230,000

Required: At what amount should Atwood Corporation's long-term investments be shown on its December 31, 1980 balance sheet?

16. The balance sheet of Dodge Corporation at December 31, 1980 shows a long-term investment in the common stock of Simms Corporation of $350,000. The investment was purchased by Dodge in January, 1977. The following information pertaining to Simms Corporation is available:

Year	Income or (Loss)	Dividends Paid
1977	($ 30,000)	-0-
1978	120,000	$50,000
1979	150,000	60,000
1980	200,000	80,000

Required: (1) Assuming that Dodge Corporation's investment represents a 10% interest in Simms Corporation, how much did Dodge pay for Simms' stock in January 1977?

(2) Assuming that Dodge Corporation's investment represents a 25% interest in Simms Corporation, how much did Dodge pay for Simms' stock in January 1977?

17. On January 5, 1980, Cole Corporation purchased 30% of the outstanding common stock of Zeller Corporation at a total cost of $600,000. During 1980, Zeller Corporation declared and paid quarterly dividends totaling $120,000. For its fiscal year ended December 31, 1980, Zeller Corporation

reported net income of $290,000. On December 31, 1980, the market value of Cole Corporation's investment in the common stock of Zeller Corporation was $675,000.

Required: (1) Perform an analysis of transactions for Cole Corporation with respect to its investment in Zeller Corporation for the 1980 fiscal year.

(2) At what amount should Cole Corporation's investment in Zeller Corporation be shown on Cole's December 31, 1980 balance sheet?

(3) Answer parts (1) and (2) above assuming that: (a) only 10% of Zeller Corporation's outstanding common stock was purchased on January 5, 1980; (b) the cost was $200,000; and (c) the December 31, 1980 market value of the investment was $225,000.

18. On June 30, 1979, Marta Corporation purchased all of the outstanding common stock of Walden Corporation at a total cost of $520 million. Payment consisted of 13 million shares of $1 par value common stock of Marta Corporation having a market value of $40 per share. As of June 30, 1979, the book value and fair market value of Walden Corporation's net assets are shown below:

Walden Corporation
(in millions)

	Book Values June 30, 1979	Fair Market Values June 30, 1979
Assets:		
Inventory	$ 31.7	$ 34.1
Other current assets	72.9	72.9
Land	6.3	17.1
Property, plant & equipment (net)	39.6	63.6
Trademarks and patents	7.9	96.7
Total Assets	158.4	284.4
Liabilities & Stockholders' Equity:		
Current liabilities	31.6	31.6
Long-term debt	4.8	4.8
	36.4	36.4

Common Stock ($1 par)	10.9	
Additional paid-in capital	12.3	
Retained earnings	98.8	
		122.0
		$158.4

Required: Assuming that Walden Corporation is to become a wholly-owned subsidiary of Marta Corporation, identify the accounts on the consolidated balance sheet of Marta Corporation that will be affected by the acquisition on June 30, 1979, and specify the amounts by which each of these accounts will be affected assuming:

(1) The Purchase method is used.

(2) The Pooling of Interests method is used.

19. The following financial information was presented by Metropolitan Department Stores in its 1980 annual report:

Metropolitan Department Stores
Consolidated Balance Sheet
January 31, 1981
($ millions)

Assets

Current Assets:	
Cash and cash equivalent	$ 30.5
Receivables (net)	154.6
Merchandise inventory, at the lower of cost or market	400.2
Prepaid expenses	42.0
Total current assets	627.3
Properties and equipment (net)	313.8
Net equity in, and advances to, subsidiaries not consolidated	121.1
	1,062.2

Liabilities & Equity

Current Liabilities:	
Payables and accruals	160.8
Federal taxes on income	17.8
Notes payable	64.0
Total current liabilities	242.6
Deferred federal taxes on income	12.9
Long-term debt	150.0
Class A stock	13.9
Common stock	197.3
Earnings reinvested in business	445.5
	$1,062.2

Metropolitan Department Stores
Consolidated Statement of Income and Retained Earnings
For the Fiscal Year Ended January 31, 1981
($ millions)

Net Sales	$1,748.4
Cost of merchandise sold and other expenses	
(excl. depreciation and income taxes)	1,701.7
Pre-tax net income before depreciation	46.7
Depreciation ($17.6M)–and Federal taxes on	
income ($11.7M)	29.3
Net earnings from operations	17.4
Net earnings (after income taxes) of	
subsidiaries not consolidated	6.6
Net earnings	24.0
Earnings reinvested, beginning of year	435.1
	459.1
Deduct cash dividends	13.6
Earnings reinvested, end of year	$ 445.5

The company's Notes to Financial Statements included the following items:

RECEIVABLES	January 31, 1981
Total Receivables (Principally	
customer installment accounts	$913,406,710
Less–Reserves for doubtful accounts	
and unearned carrying carges	20,346,636
	$893,060,074
Less–Accounts sold to credit subsidiary	
(net of amount withheld pending	
collections)	738,487,436
	$154,572,638

PRINCIPLES OF CONSOLIDATION

"The consolidated statements include all subsidiaries except Metropolitan Credit Corporation, (USA) and Metropolitan Credit Corporation (Japan), wholly-owned subsidiaries for which separate or combined balance sheets are presented in this report. The net equity of subsidiaries not consolidated is stated in the Consolidated Balance Sheet at the amount of the Company's investments in such subsidiaries plus accumulated earnings in the net amount of $24,116,815 as of January 31, 1981, which amount is included in Earnings Reinvested."

The balance sheets for the two credit subsidiaries at January 31, 1981 were as follows (in $ millions):

	Credit Corp. (USA)	Credit Corp. (Japan)	Combined Total
Assets			
Current Assets:			
Cash and cash equivalent	$ 2.3	$ .5	$ 2.8
Trade receivables (net)	661.6	76.9	738.5
Receivable from MDS, Inc.	–	.3	.3
Prepaid expenses	1.2	–	1.2
Total current assets	665.1	77.7	742.8
Liabilities & Equity			
Current Liabilities:			
Payables and accruals	1.1	1.5	2.6
Federal taxes on income	3.5	–	3.5
Payable to MDS, Inc.	39.0	1.0	40.0
Notes payable	373.8	.9	374.7
Total current liab.	417.4	3.4	420,8
Deferred federal taxes on income	–	1.5	1.5
Long-term debt	150.0	49.4	199.4
Investment of MDS, Inc.			
Long-term debt	–	19.8	19.8
Capital stock	75.0	2.2	77.2
Earnings reinvested	22.7	1.4	24.1
	$665.1	$77.7	$742.8

Required: 1. Prepare a consolidated balance sheet as of January 31, 1981 for Metropolitan Department Stores, Inc., including the Credit Corporation subsidiaries in the consolidation.

     2. What does this balance sheet show that the consolidated balance sheet presented by the company does not show? Why do you suppose the company did not include the Credit Corporation subsidiaries in its consolidated balance sheet?

     3. If a consolidated statement of income including the two credit companies was prepared, what differences would there be between it and the one presented by the company?

     4. If 20% of the capital stock of Metropolitan Credit Corporation (USA) were owned by outsiders, what difference would it make in the consolidated balance sheet you prepared?

20. On November 9, 1965, Caterpillar Tractor Company merged with Towmotor Corporation by an exchange of one share of Caterpillar for one share of Towmotor. Caterpillar issued 1,891,678 of its shares and accounted for the transaction as a "pooling of interests" rather than as a purchase. In account-

ing for the issue of the 1,891,678 shares, Caterpillar increased its no-par common stock account $3,311,746. Towmotor's retained earnings at 12/31/64 were $25.5 million; Towmotor earned $6.2 million in 1965 and paid dividends of $2.1 million in 1965 up to the time of the merger with Caterpillar on November 9. For the purpose of the questions to follow, assume that the market value of Caterpillar's stock at November 9, 1965 was $50 a share, or a total of $94.6 million for the 1,891,678 shares.

(a) The net assets Caterpillar acquired from Towmotor on November 9, 1965, can be approximated:

Capital stock of Towmotor at 11/9/65— 1,891,678 shares carried to Caterpillar books at $3,311,746.		$ 3.3 million
Towmotor's retained earnings at 12/31/64		$25.5
Net income 1/1/65 to 11/9/65 (313 days)		
313/365 of $6.2	$5.3	
Less Dividends	2.1	3.2
		$28.7 million
Towmotor's estimated owners' equity (net assets) =		$32.0 million

(b) If Caterpillar had treated the transaction as a Purchase rather than a Pooling of Interests, what difference(s) would it have made?

(c) If you had been a Towmotor stockholder, are there any reasons you would have preferred receiving for each Towmotor share you owned one share of Caterpillar stock rather than $50 in cash?

(d) If you were a part of Caterpillar's management, are there any reasons you would have preferred treating the share-for-share exchange as a Pooling of Interests rather than as a Purchase?

21. The statements of financial position of Company X and Company Y at December 31, 1980 were as follows (in thousands of dollars):

	Company X	Company Y	Combined
Assets:			
Cash	$1,100	$ 50	$1,150
Trade Receivables	500	225	725
Inventories	1,000	125	1,125
Property, Plant & Equipment (net)	2,500	250	2,750
	5,100	650	5,750
Deduct Liabilities	750	100	850
Net Assets	4,350	550	4,900
Stockholders' Equity:			
Capital Stock ($100 par)	3,000	200	3,200
Retained Earnings	1,350	350	1,700
	$4,350	$550	$4,900

Memo: Market value per share at 12/31/80 was $200 for Company X's stock and
$400 for Company Y's.

The management of Company X was considering several methods by which to acquire Company Y.

Method 1. If, as of December 31, 1980, Company X negotiated to purchase the assets and assume the liabilities of Company Y for $800,000 cash, ascribing values of $175,000 and $450,000 to Company Y's Inventories and Property, Plant and Equipment (net), respectively.

a. What entry(s) would Company X make? Company Y?
b. How would the statements of financial position look for Company X and Company Y after these entries had been made?
c. What entry(s) would Company X and Company Y make and how would the financial statements look afterwards if the purchase price were paid to Company Y by the issuance of 4,000 shares of Company X's stock?
d. What entry(s) would Company X and Company Y make and how would the financial statements look afterwards if the $800,000 were paid in cash but nothing was said about ascribing specific values to Company Y's assets?
e. What entry(s) would Company X and Company Y make and how would the financial statements look afterwards if the purchase price were paid to Company Y by issuance of 4,000 shares of Company X's stock but nothing was said about ascribing specific values to Company Y's assets?

Method 2. If, as of December 31, 1980, Company X negotiated to purchase from the stockholders of Company Y, their shares for $400 cash per share. Company Y was to become a subsidiary of Company X.

a. What entry(s) would Company X make?
b. What entry(s) would Company Y make?
c. How would the consolidated statement of financial position for Companies X and Y look at December 31, 1980?

Method 3. If, as of December 31, 1980, Company X negotiated with the stockholders of Company Y to issue 4,000 shares of its voting common stock in exchange for 2,000 shares of Company Y's stock. Company Y was to become a subsidiary of Company X.

a. What entry(s) would Company X make?
b. What entry(s) would Company Y make?
c. How would the consolidated statement of financial position of Company X and Company Y look at December 31, 1980?
22. Pre-acquisition balance sheets of Alpha Corporation and Beta Corporation are shown below:

Pre-Acquisition
Balance Sheets
(in thousands)

	Alpha Corp.	Beta Corp.
Assets:		
Cash	$ 8,000	$ 2,500
Marketable Securities	5,000	3,500
Accounts Receivable (net)	7,500	5,000
Inventories (LIFO)	19,000	9,500
Fixed Assets (net)	38,000	23,000
Other Assets	4,500	1,500
Total	82,000	45,000
Liabilities & Stockholders' Equity:		
Accounts Payable	9,500	7,500
Other Current Liabilities	4,000	3,000
Bonds Payable	11,000	
Other Long-term Debt	7,500	12,500
Common Stock ($10 Par)	12,000	
Common Stock ($5 Par)		6,000
Capital in Excess of Par	7,000	2,000
Retained Earnings	31,000	14,000
Total	$82,000	$45,000

Subsequent to a six-month period of intense negotiating, Alpha Corporation agreed to purchase all of the outstanding common stock of Beta Corporation at a price of $29.4 million. In arriving at this price, Alpha Corporation placed the following fair market values on Beta Corporation's assets:

Asset	Fair Market Value (thousands)
Cash	$ 2,500
Marketable Securities	4,500
Accounts Receivable (net)	3,500
Inventories	13,000
Fixed Assets (net)	28,000
Other Assets	-0-
Total	$51,500

According to the terms of the agreement, Alpha Corporation was to issue one share of its common stock in exchange for each share of Beta Corporation's outstanding common stock. Subsequent to the exchange of common stock, Beta Corporation was to become a wholly-owned subsidiary of Alpha Corporation. The current market price of Alpha Corporation's common stock was $24.50 per share.

Required: Alpha Corporation expects to be able to account for its acquisition of Beta Corporation as a Pooling of Interests. There is, however, some question about a possible violation of one of the twelve Pooling criteria. You have been asked by Alpha Corporation's management to prepare a consolidated balance sheet to reflect the acquisition of Beta Corporation under both the Pooling of Interests and the Purchase accounting methods.

23. Pre-acquisition balance sheets of Corporation A and Corporation B are shown below:

Pre-Acquisition
Balance Sheets
($1,000)

	Corp. A	Corp. B
Assets		
Cash and marketable securities	$ 6,000	$1,000
Accounts receivable	5,000	1,400
Inventories	6,400	1,800
Total Current Assets	17,400	4,200
Plant and equipment (net)	10,600	2,800
Total Assets	28,000	7,000
Liabilities and Owners' Equity		
Accounts payable	6,000	1,700
Other current liabilities	1,500	300
Total Current Liabilities	7,500	2,000
Long-term debt	8,200	1,600
Total Liabilities	15,700	3,600
Common stock (No par)*	2,500	700
Retained earnings	9,800	2,700
Total Owners' Equity	12,300	3,400
Total Liabilities and Owners' Equity	$28,000	$7,000
*Number of shares outstanding	1,000,000	100,000

Required: Prepare a consolidated balance sheet to reflect the acquisition of Corporation B by Corporation A assuming that:

a. Corporation A issues 100,000 shares of stock in exchange for 100,000 shares of Corporation B's stock. Current market value of Corporation A's stock is $60 per share. Corporation B is to become a wholly-owned subsidiary of Corporation A.

b. The same facts as in (a) above, but for some technical reason the acquisition is to be accounted for as a Purchase. In connection therewith, Corporation A revalues Corporation B's plant, and equipment (net) at $3,900.

12

Liabilities and Deferred Taxes

In Chapter 2, we discussed the nature of liabilities —debts or obligations of the business. In this chapter we discuss liabilities in the order in which they appear on the balance sheet. Liabilities are normally classified in a balance sheet as either current or noncurrent. Current liabilities are those that have a maturity of less than one year. Noncurrent liabilities have a maturity beyond one year.

Other items appear on the liability side of the balance sheet that are not definite obligations in the same sense that accounts payable to suppliers are obligations. These items are shown as liabilities to maintain the integrity of the A=L+OE equation.

PAYABLES AND ACCRUALS

Accrued liabilities are liabilities that have been recognized. Payables and accruals include payables to trade creditors and others, liabilities for wages, interest, taxes (other than income taxes), and the liability for dividends declared but not paid.

Accounting for accounts payable to trade creditors may be summarized as follows:

Trade Accounts Payable (L)

Payments on Account/Purchase Returns and Allowances	Purchases on Account: At either net invoice amount or gross invoice amount.

The treatment of purchases on account at either the net invoice or gross invoice amount refers to the way in which cash discounts are handled. Since the Corner Drugstore planned to pay all invoices within the discount period, it recorded the *net* invoice amounts in Merchandise Inventory and Accounts Payable. Companies that do not plan to pay all invoices within the discount period may record the *gross* amount of the invoices in their Merchandise Inventory and Accounts Payable accounts. If the Corner Drugstore had used this method of recording, and the gross amount of the invoices for Transaction C, Illustration 3-3, had been $58,000, its entries would have been:

Merchandise Inventory (A)	Incr 58,000	
Accounts Payable (L)		Incr 58,000
Accounts Payable (L)	Decr 58,000	
Merchandise Inventory (A)		Decr 600
Cash (A)		Decr 57,400

Some companies further modify their accounting by recording the $58,000 gross amount of invoices in the Merchandise Inventory account and the $600 discounts in the Retained Earnings account with the description "Discounts Earned on Purchases." They then show this $600 cash discount earned on purchases as *Other Income* in the income statement.

Accounting for other payables and accrued expenses was illustrated in the transactions for Corner Drugstore in Chapter 3. Accounting recognition is granted at the time that the expense is incurred or the liability arises. The liability for a cash dividend is recognized when the Board of Directors declares the dividend. The transaction is recorded as follows:

Retained Earnings (OE)–(Dividends)	Decr xxx	
Dividends Payable (L)		Incr xxx

Payables and accruals are usually payable within twelve months and thus are normally classified as current liabilities.

CURRENT INCOME TAX LIABILITY

A company's period-end liability for income taxes includes federal, state, and foreign taxes accrued but unpaid on taxable income earned to date. The following discussion deals with federal income taxes only since these are greater in amount and more complex in accounting procedure than state and foreign income taxes.

Accounting for federal income taxes is relatively simple if a company

1. has no operating loss carry-back or carry-forwards;
2. has no material and non-recurring adjustments of prior years' taxes;
3. has no extraordinary items affecting net income for the year, and no prior-period adjustments; or
4. has no investment tax credit, no difference between the depreciation it deducts on its income statement and the depreciation it deducts on its tax return, and no other timing differences between the income it reports for external purposes and the income it reports for income taxes.

When a company has none of these complicating factors, it recognizes its federal income tax liability at the period-end by estimating the tax on the period's taxable income and making the following entry on its books:

Retained Earnings (OE)–(federal income tax expense)   Decr xxx
    Liability for federal income taxes (L)   Incr xxx

When the company makes a payment against the liability, it records the payment as follows:

Liability for federal income taxes (L)   Decr xxx
    Cash (A)   Decr xxx

INTERPERIOD TAX ALLOCATION

When a company reports income or deducts expenses on its tax return during a period different from that when income is reported or expenses deducted on its external financial reports, *timing differences* arise, requiring *interperiod tax allocation.* The objective of interperiod tax allocation is to match the income tax expense reported on an income statement for a specific period with the revenues and expenses reported for that period.

Timing differences originate in one period and reverse in subsequent periods. For example, when a company uses the installment method of reporting revenues for tax purposes, revenue may be recognized for reporting purposes during the current period but not be taxable until a future period or periods. A revenue timing difference is illustrated here:

	Tax Return (thousands)	Reported Income (thousands)
Revenues	$100	$1000
Expenses	60	600
Income before taxes	40	400
Income tax at 46%	18	184
Net Income	$ 22	$ 216

Thus, only $18,000 income tax is payable for this period, but the income tax expense shown in the external income statement is $184,000. The entry to recognize this expense is as follows:

Retained Earnings (OE)–(income tax expense)	Decr 184	
Liability for federal income taxes (L)		Incr 18
Deferred income taxes (L)		Incr 166

If the timing difference in revenue reverses in total during the next period, taxable income and reported income will be as follows:

	Tax Return (thousands)	Reported Income (thousands)
Revenue	$900	-0-
Expenses	540	-0-
Income before taxes	360	-0-
Income taxes at 46%	166	-0-
Net Income	$194	-0-

The entry to recognize the taxes will be as follows:

Deferred Income Taxes (L)	Decr 166	
Liability for federal income taxes (L)		Incr 166

The most common item giving rise to timing differences, and consequently to deferred income taxes, is depreciation. Many companies use accelerated methods and guideline lives in determining the depreciation they deduct on their tax returns, while they use the straight-line method and longer lives in determining the depreciation they deduct on their income statement to stockholders.

For purposes of illustration, assume that a company buys a piece of equipment that it depreciates, using the double-declining balance method for income tax purposes and the straight-line depreciation method for reporting purposes. The equipment costs $100,000 and has no assumed salvage value. The company has no other depreciable assets. Presented below are the figures shown in the tax return and in the report to stockholders.

Tax Return (dollar amounts in thousands) Year	1	2	3	4	5	Total
Income before depreciation	$800	$800	$800	$800	$800	
Depreciation	40	24	14	11	11	100
Income before taxes	760	776	786	789	789	
Income taxes at 48%	365	372	377	379	379	1,872
Net Income	$395	$404	$409	$410	$410	$2,028

Reported Income (thousands) Year	1	2	3	4	5	Total
Income before depreciation	$800	$800	$800	$800	$800	
Depreciation	20	20	20	20	20	100
Income before taxes	780	780	780	780	780	
Income taxes at 48%	374	374	374	375	375	1,872
Net Income	$406	$406	$406	$405	$405	$2,028

The total depreciation, the total income tax, and the total net income for the five-year period are the same, the difference is in their timing. In year 1, the entry to record taxes is as follows:

Retained Earnings (OE)–(income tax expense)	Decr 374	
Liability for federal income taxes (L)		Incr 365
Deferred income taxes		Incr 9

In year 2, deferred income taxes increase by another $2,000. In year 3, the timing difference starts to reverse and deferred income taxes decrease by $3,000. They decrease by $4,000 in years 4 and 5.

PERMANENT DIFFERENCES: NO TAX ALLOCATION

For *permanent* as distinct from *timing* differences between taxable income and pretax accounting income, no tax allocation is required. Permanent differences are prescribed by the Internal Revenue Code and involve such items as:

1. The interest on state and municipal bonds that is excluded from taxable income.
2. The premiums, paid on life insurance on lives of officers, excluded from taxable income.
3. The excess of percentage depletion for oil and gas wells, used in determining taxable income, over cost depletion, used in determining pre-tax accounting income.

INCOME TAX LIABILITY AND INCOME TAX EXPENSE ON EXTERNAL FINANCIAL STATEMENTS

The liability for current income taxes is classified as a current liability.

The balance sheet classification for deferred income taxes should be consistent with the assets and liabilities from which the deferred taxes arise. For example, deferred income taxes arising from accelerated depreciation would normally be classified as noncurrent, since the assets being depreciated are noncurrent.

Deferred income taxes are not a liability in the same sense that accounts payable are definite obligations. Deferred income taxes are not actually owed until the timing differences reverse. If a company continues to add property, plant and equipment that are depreciated on an accelerated basis, the deferred tax "liability" arising from depreciation timing differences will never disappear.

Where expenses are deducted for external financial reporting before they are deducted for tax purposes, the deferred tax is carried on the asset side of the balance sheet. For example, if a company sells products under warranty, a warranty provision is established, but the expense cannot be deducted for tax purposes until the warranty service is provided. Thus, the company would show less income tax expense on its external income statement than it shows on its tax return. Accounting for warranty expenses is illustrated below.

	Tax Return (thousands)	Reported Income (thousands)
Income before warranty expense	$1,000	$1,000
Warranty expense	-0-	10
Income before taxes	$1,000	$ 990
Income tax at 48%	480	475
Net Income	$ 520	$ 515

The entry for deferred taxes would be as follows:

Retained Earnings (OE)–(income tax expense)	Decr	475	
Deferred income taxes (A)	Incr	5	
Liability for federal income taxes (L)			Incr 480

In July, 1980 the FASB issued Statement No. 37, *Balance Sheet Classification of Deferred Income Taxes*, which requires deferred income taxes related to an asset or liability to be classified the same as the related asset or liability. Deferred income taxes that are not related to an asset or liability would be classified according to the expected reversal date of the timing difference.

INCOME TAX EXPENSE IN STATEMENTS OF INCOME

Income tax expense for a reporting period consists of:

1. Current taxes on taxable income.
2. Tax effects of timing differences.

3. Tax effects of operating losses.
4. Tax effects of investment credits.

The components of income tax expense for a period should be disclosed separately. APB Opinion No. 11 provides that disclosure may be in either the income statement or a related footnote.

An example of income statement presentation of income tax expense excerpted from the Brockway Glass Company 1979 annual report is shown in Illustration 12-1.

Illustration 12-1

Excerpts from Brockway Glass 1979 Annual Report

	1979	1978
Income from continuing operations before income taxes	$20,191,383	$47,863,318
Income taxes (Note 8)	7,316,000	21,965,000
Income from continuing operations	12,875,383	25,898,318
Discontinued operations (Note 3)	3,517,000	(9,873,906)
Net Income	$16,392,383	$16,024,412
Earnings per common share	$2.22	$2.18

8. INCOME TAXES

Income taxes are summarized as follows:

	1979	1978
Allocation of provision (benefit) for the year		
Continuing operations	$ 7,316,000	$21,965,000
Discontinued operations	–	(1,381,000)
Income (loss) on disposal of discontinued operations	3,733,000	(8,265,000)
	$11,049,000	$12,319,000
Components of the provision		
Current		
U.S. Federal	$ 6,388,500	$15,252,000
State and local	1,417,200	2,698,700
	7,805,700	17,950,700
Deferred		
U.S. Federal	2,787,500	(4,842,400)
State and local	455,800	(789,300)
	3,243,300	(5,631,700)
	$11,049,000	$12,319,000

Illustration 12-1 (continued)

The effective tax rate on income from continuing operations differs from the statutory United States Federal tax rate for the following reasons and by the following percentages:

	1979	1978
Statutory U.S. federal tax rate	46.0%	48.0%
Increases (reductions) in taxes resulting from		
Investment tax credit accruing to the		
benefit of the Company	(13.5)	(5.6)
State and local taxes, net of Federal		
income tax benefit	3.7	3.5
Effective tax rate	36.2%	45.9%

Deferred tax expense (benefit) results from timing differences in the recognition of certain revenue and expense for income tax and financial statement purposes. The sources of these differences and the tax effect of each are as follows:

	1979	1978
Tax over book depreciation	$2,635,900	$ 1,811,900
Inventory reserves	513,700	(126,800)
Repairs charged to expense for		
book purposes	(625,900)	–
Provision for plant closings		
(Not deductible in 1979)	(3,488,000)	–
Replacement furnaces and rebuilt		
machines expensed for tax purposes		
but will be charged as depreciation		
on the books in subsequent years	1,496,800	1,515,400
Loss on disposal of discontinued		
operations (portion not deductible in 1978)	–	(8,831,600)
Portion deductible in 1979	2,390,800	–
Miscellaneous timing differences	320,000	(600)
	$3,243,300	$ (5,631,700)

3. The results of operations and estimated (loss) income on disposition are included in the caption "Discontinued operations" as follows:

	1979	1978
Net sales	$ –	$29,961,534
Costs and expenses	–	32,642,634
(Loss) before taxes	–	(2,681,100)
Income tax (benefit)	–	(1,381,100)
(Loss) from operations	–	(1,300,100)
Estimated (loss) income, net of		
applicable tax (benefit) of		
$3,733,000 and ($8,265,000)	3,517,000	(8,573,806)
	$3,517,000	$ (9,873,906)

SHORT-TERM LOANS AND INTEREST EXPENSE

Short-term loans include short-term bank loans and other short-term borrowings. Loans may be obtained on an interest-from-date basis or on a discount basis. If the principal amount of a loan is $10,000, the loan is for six months, and the interest rate is 10 percent.

1. On an *interest-from-date* basis, the company signs a $10,000 10 percent note due six months from date and receives $10,000 from the lender.
2. On a *discount* basis, the company signs a noninterest-bearing note due six months from date and receives $9,500 from the bank.

In both cases, prevailing practice is to show the note obligation at its face amount, $10,000. For the discounted note, the $500 discount is shown as prepaid interest. In both cases, the interest expense for the six months is $500.

FASB Statement No. 6 requires that short-term loans that the company intends to replace with long-term debt be classified as long-term liabilities, if the company is financially able to consummate the replacement.

LONG-TERM DEBT AND INTEREST EXPENSE

Corporate long-term debt is usually in the form of bonds payable. Let us suppose, for example, that a company on January 1, 1980, sold to a group of underwriters $1,000,000 principal amount of 10 percent bonds, the principal due ten years from date and the interest due July 1 and January 1 each year. If the bonds were in $1,000 denominations, each bond would carry twenty semiannual interest coupons for $50 each. If on January 1, 1980, the group of underwriters were to give the company $960,000 for the bonds (the $40,000 less than the face amount was a "discount" because similar bonds were selling in the market at a rate higher than 10 percent), the company's entry would be

Cash (A)	Incr	960,000
Discount on Bonds Payable (CL)*	Incr	40,000
Bonds Payable (L)		Incr 1,000,000

*Contra liability

Thereafter, at the end of each six months, the company would show its liability for the semi-annual interest and would amortize a portion of the bond discount. APB Opinion No. 21 requires the compound interest method of amortization if the result of using a different method would produce materially different results. The compound interest method reduces the discount or premium by the amount needed to make the nominal interest expense equal the effective rate of interest.

The entry each six months would be as follows, using straight-line amortization:

Retained Earnings (OE) (Interest expense)	Decr	50,000
Accrued Bond Interest (L)		Incr 50,000
Retained Earnings (OE) (Amortization of Bond Discount)	Decr	2,000
Discount on Bonds Payable (CL)		Decr 2,000

Actual payment of the $50,000 semi-annual interest on January 1 and July 1 would decrease Accrued Bond Interest and Cash, and payment of the $1,000,000 principal on January 1, 1990, would decrease Bonds Payable and Cash in Bank.

The net effect on cash over the ten-year period would be an outgo of $1,000,000 for interest, plus $40,000 for the difference between the $960,000 received January 1, 1980 and the $1,000,000 principal amount paid January 1, 1980. The $1,040,000 would be charged to Retained Earnings at the rate of $52,000 for each of the twenty semi-annual intervals, if straight-line amortization is used.

Long-term debt issued at face value is shown on the balance sheet at face value. If the debt is issued at a discount or premium, the discount or premium is shown in the balance sheet as a deduction from or addition to the face amount. In the preceding example, the bonds payable would be shown on the balance sheet at $960,000 at the time of issue.

When the principal matures serially instead of in total at one maturity date, the principal portion maturing at any balance sheet date within the next twelve months is shown in the current liability section as long-term debt due within one year. Long-term debt due after one year is shown in the noncurrent liability section. Footnotes to the balance sheet should give additional information on long-term debt, particularly a maturity schedule and a summary of significant restrictive covenants in bond debentures or loan agreements.

Issue costs of debt should be reported in the balance sheet as a deferred charge and amortized over the life of the issue. A deferred charge is, in effect, a prepaid expense.

EXTINGUISHMENT OF DEBT BEFORE MATURITY

If a company reacquired its debt by exercising call provisions or purchasing its debt securities in the open market, the accounting for this early extinguishment is somewhat more complicated than the normal retirement of debt. APB Opinion No. 26 and FASB Statement No. 4 basically require that any gains or losses from the early extinguishment of debt, that is, retirement at more or less than the amount of obligation carried on the books, should be recognized in the current income statement as an extraordinary item (see Chapter 14).

SUMMARY

Liabilities are debts or obligations of the business. Current liabilities are distinguished from other liabilities by their maturity—one year or less.

Accounting for liability for income taxes, and the related expenses for the year, is complicated when there are operating loss carry-backs or carry-forwards, adjustments for prior years' taxes, extraordinary items affecting net income for the year, prior period adjustments, and tax allocation arising from timing difference of investment tax credits and depreciation.

When a company uses accelerated methods and guidelines lives in determining the depreciation it deducts on its tax return, and this is in excess of the depreciation it deducts on its income statement, the income tax on the excess should be shown as an expense for the year with a credit to deferred taxes on income (a noncurrent liability). Similar treatment should be accorded other timing differences under the concept of comprehensive interperiod tax allocation adopted by APB Opinion No. 11. No tax allocation is required for permanent differences such as those occurring with respect to interest on state and municipal bonds, life insurance premiums on lives of officers, and percentage versus cost depletion.

In presenting income tax liability and income tax expense in external financial reports:

1. The balance sheet should show taxes payable as a current liability and deferred taxes as a noncurrent liability (unless the deferred taxes are related to current assets).

2. The income statement should show
   (a) taxes estimated to be payable,
   (b) tax effects of timing differences, and
   (c) tax effects of operating losses, allocated to income before extraordinary items, and extraordinary items.

3. Disclosure should be made of the reasons for significant variations in accounting income.

QUESTIONS AND PROBLEMS

1. In parallel columns, one for the *net* invoice method and the other for the *gross* invoice method, set up T-accounts for Cash in Bank (A), Merchandise Inventory (A), Accounts Payable (L), and Retained Earnings (OE), and enter the following transactions:

   A—Purchased $300 merchandise on account on terms of 2/10, n/30
   B—Paid discounted amount of invoice, $294, within ten days
   C—Purchased $200 merchandise on account on terms of 2/10, n/30
   D—Paid gross amount of invoice, $200, thirty days after purchase

   Compare, contrast, and evaluate the two methods.

2. At December 31, 1979, the GHI Corporation, which used the calendar year for stockholder reports and Federal income tax returns, showed a balance of $30,000 in its Liability for Federal Income Tax account and a balance of $853,000 in its Deferred Taxes on Income account. In 1980, the following transactions affecting Federal income taxes occurred:

March 15	Paid $30,000 to the Internal Revenue Service on 1979 tax
April 15	Paid $125,000 on estimated 1980 tax
June 15	Paid $125,000 on estimated 1980 tax
July 12	Paid $25,000 to the Internal Revenue Service as an additional assessment for 1978

September 15   Paid $125,000 on estimated 1980 tax
December 15   Paid $125,000 on 1980 estimated tax

On March 10, 1981, GHI Corporation prepared and filed a corporate tax return for 1980 showing income tax for the year of $583,000 before an investment tax credit of $50,000. The return showed 1980 depreciation of $280,000 computed on an accelerated basis and using guideline lives compared to straight-line depreciation of $190,000 to be used on the income statement to stockholders. Note: Use a tax rate of 46% and give effect to the 1980 tax and related items as of December 31, 1980.

Do transaction analysis for above transactions, enter in T-accounts affected, and indicate the figures concerning Federal Income Taxes that will be shown on the company's 1980 Combined Statement of Income and Retained Earnings and on its December 31, 1980 Balance Sheet.

3. On April 1, 1971, the BSG Company sold to a group of underwriters $5,000,000 principal amount of its 8% bonds, the principal due 20 years from date and interest due semi-annually October 1st and April 1st, and received $5,200,000.

    A. Why should the underwriters pay the company more than the face amount of the bonds?

    B. What items concerning the bonds would appear on the company's balance sheet at December 31, 1980, and on its 1980 income statement, and at what amounts?

    C. If the bonds are outstanding for the 20 years, as scheduled, what will be the net interest cost to the company for the 20 years? How much per year?

4. Let us assume that comparative balance sheets at 12/31/50, 12/31/51, and 12/31/52 of GSB Company were as follows (in thousands of dollars):

	12/31/50	12/31/51	12/31/52
Regular Property, Plant, and Equip. (Net)	450	450	450
Emergency Facilities (Net)	-0-	500	450
Cash and Other Assets (Less Current Liabilities)	600	150	300
	1,050	1,100	1,200
Deferred Taxes	-0-	-0-	25
NET ASSETS (EQUITY)	1,050	1,100	1,175

	1951	1952
Income statements for 1951 and 1952 were:		
Sales	1,000	1,500
Costs and Expenses (exclusive of depreciation)	800	1,200
Net Income before Depreciation and Tax	200	300
Depreciation (Straight-line)	100	150
	100	150
Income Tax–Current	50	50
	50	100
Income Tax–Deferred	-0-	25
Net Income	50	75

It is assumed:
(1) The original cost of the regular plant was $1,000,000, its estimated life is 10 years, and it is replaced $100,000 at the beginning of each year, so its unallocated cost remains at $450,000 at each year-end.
(2) The company's income tax rate is 50%; it has no long-term debt, and it declares no dividends.
(3) On December 31, 1951, the company invested $500M in "Emergency Facilities" ("Emergency Facilities" qualified for special tax provisions during the Korean War) which for tax purposes it depreciates over 5 years, but which for general accounting purposes it depreciates over 10 years on a straight-line basis. (The company plans to make no additions to its "Emergency Facilities.")

REQUIRED: On the basis that the above assumptions will hold for the years 1953/1961, together with the assumption that (a) annual sales and (b) costs and expenses (exclusive of depreciation) will be *$1,500,000* and $1,200,000 for the year 1953/1961, prepare income statements and year-end balance sheets for 1953/1961. Evaluate the accounting for income taxes under the conditions assumed.

5. Let us assume that comparative balance sheets at 12/31/73, 12/31/74, and 12/31/75 of the CCD Company were as follows (in thousands of dollars):

	12/31/73	12/31/74	12/31/75
Plant and Buildings (LEASED)	-0-	-0-	-0-
Machinery (Net)	525.0	525.0	525.0
Cash and Other Assets (Less Current Liabilities	300.0	340.0	392.5
	825.0	865.0	917.0
Deferred Taxes	-0-	-0-	12.5
NET ASSETS (EQUITY)	825.0	865.0	905.0

Income statements for 1974 and 1975 were:	1974	1975
Sales	900.0	900.0
Costs and Expenses (exclusive of depreciation)	610.0	610.0
Net Income before Depreciation and Tax	290.0	290.0
Depreciation (Straight-line)	210.0	210.0
Net Income before Income Taxes	80.0	80.0
Income Tax—Current	40.0	27.5
	40.0	52.5
Income Tax—Deferred	-0-	12.5
Net Income	40.0	40.0

It is assumed:
(1) The original cost of machinery used during each year is $1,260,000, representing six successive annual purchases of $210,000 each January 1st. The equipment has an estimated life of 6 years, so each year-end

the accumulated depreciation on $210,000 purchased six years earlier becomes $210,000 and the equipment is written off as of December 31st. On December 31, 1974, the machinery account before the write-off of equipment 6 years old showed:

Date of Purchase	Cost	Accumulated Depreciation	Unallocated Cost
1/1/69	210	210	-0-
1/1/70	210	175	35
1/1/71	210	140	70
1/1/72	210	105	105
1/1/73	210	70	140
1/1/74	210	35	175
	1,260	735	525

The unallocated cost each year-end, on a straight-line basis, is therefore $525,000.

(2) The company's income tax rate is 50%; it has no long-term debt, and it declares no dividends.

(3) In 1975 and in subsequent years, the company adopted S-Y-D depreciation for income tax purposes on its additions subsequent to 12/31/74, but continued to use straight-line depreciation in reporting to stockholders:

ANNUAL DEPRECIATION FOR

	Income Tax Purposes	Stockholder Reporting	Difference
1974	210M	210M	-0-
1975	235	210	25
1976	250	210	40
1977	255	210	45
1978	250	210	40
1979	235	210	25
1980	210	210	-0-

In accordance with prevailing practice, the company accounted for the difference in income taxes attributable to depreciation as deferred taxes in its income statements and as Deferred Taxes liability on its balance sheets.

REQUIRED:

A. Check the company's calculation of annual depreciation for income tax purposes the years 1975/1980. Do you agree that there would be no difference in 1980 between depreciation for income tax purposes and depreciation for stockholder reporting? If so, why so? If not, why not?

B. The company's figures and accounting for depreciation and income taxes being used (assuming sales of $900,000 and Costs and Expenses of $610,000):

    (a) What annual net income would the company report for 1975/1980?

    (b) How would the company's year-end balance sheets be affected?

    (c) What differences are there between the situations of the CCD Company and the GSB Company (No. 4)?

    (d) When will the company get rid of the balance as of December 31, 1980, in its Deferred Taxes account?

C. Suppose the company, instead of maintaining its dollar amount in fixed assets on an even keel, had sought to maintain its physical facilities on an even keel, yet had experienced a rising price level—or, again, suppose the company had been a "growth" company—what difference(s) would this have made?

D. Suppose the company had adopted:

    (a) S-Y-D depreciation for income tax purposes and straight-line depreciation for stockholder reporting, without recognizing deferred taxes on the difference, or

    (b) S-Y-D depreciation for both income tax purposes and stockholder reporting.

What difference would these alternatives make in annual net income 1975-1980 and the year-end balance sheet for 1980, compared to Question No. B above? Which of the three approaches gives the fairest presentation of net income 1975/1980 and of year-end financial position at December 31, 1980?

6. On January 1, 1981, Jody, Inc. issued 10,000,000 principal amount of its 14% bonds. The bonds were to be repaid at the end of 10 years and interest was payable June 30 and December 31 of each year. Jody, Inc. received $9,600,000 for the bonds.

A. Prepare a transaction for the bonds at their issue date, January 1, 1981.

B. Prepare the transactions relating to the bond for June 30 and December 31, 1981.

C. Prepare a transaction for the repayment of the bonds on December 31, 1990.

7. Hamilton, Inc. uses accelerated depreciation for tax purposes and straight-line depreciation for reporting to stockholders. Shown below is accounting and tax information (before taxes) for five years:

	Taxable Income	Reported Income
1981	$400,000	380,000
1980	340,000	340,000
1979	300,000	320,000
1978	280,000	310,000
1977	260,000	300,000

Assume that the corporate tax rate for each of the five years was 48%.

A. Compute the income tax and net income to be reported to stockholders for each of the five years.

B.   What would be the effect on the Deferred Tax Account for the five year period in total?

8.   On November 1, 1980, XYZ Transfer Corporation issued $10,000,000 of 14% Subordinated Debentures due November 1, 1980. Interest is payable quarterly. Proceeds to the Company were $9,760,000.

A.   What entry or entries would XYZ Transfer make on its books on November 1, 1980 to record the issuance of the bonds?

B.   How much cash will XYZ Transfer pay the bondholders for interest during 1980?

C.   How much bond interest expense will XYZ Transfer show on its income statement for the fiscal year ended December 31, 1980?

D.   How much bond interest payable will XYZ Transfer show in its balance sheet as of December 31, 1980?

E.   How much cash will XYZ Transfer pay the bondholders on February 1, 1981?

F.   What is the total amount of bond interest expense that XYZ Transfer will report on its income statement over the life of the bonds?

13

Leases, Pensions,
and Other Liabilities

*This chapter will cover several controversial areas
where accounting standards have been changing in
recent years. We discuss the various classifications
of leases from the viewpoint of the lessor and lessee, their accounting of these different categories
of leases, and show how leases are presented and
disclosed in the lessee's external financial reports.
We next discuss accounting for the cost of pension
plans, explain terms used in pension cost accounting, and discuss the disclosure of pension information in external financial reports. We conclude the
chapter by looking at other liabilities.*

LEASES CLASSIFIED

FASB Statement No. 13,[1] issued in November 1976, classifies
leases from the viewpoint of the lessee into two categories—capital
leases and operating leases. A capital lease is so long-lived and its

[1] As amended by FASB Statements No. 17, 22, 23, 27, 28 & 29. In May 1980, the FASB
issued *Accounting for Leases* incorporating all amendments and interpretations through May
1980.

[handwritten: Lease = Asset; vs. Oper. Lease rec'd. as an Expense.]
[handwritten: → CAPITAL Lease → OPER. Lease]

rental obligation so close to purchase value that the lessee records the rental property as an asset and the obligatory payments as a liability. An operating lease, by contrast, is not recorded as an asset; rental payments are recorded as expenses.

According to FASB Statement No. 13, if a lease meets *one* or more of the following criteria, it is classified as a capital lease:

[handwritten: Lease to Buy = CAPITAL LEASE]

1. The lease transfers ownership of the property to the lessee by the end of the lease term.
2. The lease contains a bargain purchase option.
3. The lease term equals 75 percent or more of the estimated economic life of the leased property.
4. At the beginning of the lease term, the present value of the *minimum lease payments*, excluding that portion of the payments representing executory costs such as insurance, maintenance, and taxes to be paid by the lessor, and including *any profit thereon*, equals or exceeds 90 percent of the fair value of the leased property to the lessor. A lessor shall compute the present value of the minimum lease payments using the interest rate implicit in the lease. The lessee shall compute the present value of the minimum lease payments using his incremental borrowing rate unless (1) is is practicable for him to learn the implicit rate computed by the lessor and (2) the implicit rate computed by the lessor is less than the lessee's incremental borrowing rate. If both of those conditions are met, the lessee shall use the implicit rate.

From the standpoint of the lessor, leases are classified as follows:

1. Sales-type leases.
2. Direct financing leases.
3. Leveraged leases.
4. Operating leases.

From the standpoint of the lessor, a lease is classified as either a sales or direct financing lease if at its inception it meets any one of the preceding four criteria for capital leases and in addition meets *both* of the following criteria: (1) collectibility of the minimum lease payments is reasonably assured and (2) no important uncertainties surround the amount of unreimbursable costs yet to be incurred by the lessor under the lease.

Leases that result in a manufacturer's or dealer's profit or loss to the lessor, in addition to meeting one or more of the four criteria listed above for capital leases and the two additional criteria for lessors are classified as *sales-type* leases.

If the leases do not give rise to a manufacturer's or dealer's profit or loss, but do meet the criteria referred to in the preceding paragraph and are not leveraged leases, they are classified as *direct financing* leases.

Leveraged leases are a specialized category of lease and are defined in paragraph 42 of FASB Statement No. 13.

All other leases are classified as operating leases from the standpoint of the lessor.

ACCOUNTING FOR LEASES

Lessees

A capital lease is recorded as an asset and a liability at an amount equal to the present value (at the beginning of the lease term) of the minimum lease payments, excluding executing costs. In effect, the lease obligation is treated as a liability similar to a bond. Leasing is treated as a means of financing.

The leased asset is amortized according to the lessee's normal depreciation policy for owned assets, if the lease transfers ownership at the end of the lease term or if it contains a bargain purchase option. If not, the asset is amortized over the life of the lease.

Each minimum lease payment is allocated between reduction of the liability and reduction of interest expense. This process is illustrated in the following example:

Ten year lease, $100,000 present value, 10% interest rate. Annual lease payment is $16,287. The asset is to be amortized on a straight-line basis over the term of the lease.

In the first year, the entries to record interest and amortization are as follows:

Retained Earnings (OE)–(Interest Expense)	Decr	10,000
Lease Liability (L)	Decr	6,287
Cash in (A)		Decr 16,287
Retained Earnings (OE)–(Amortization of Lease)	Decr	10,000
Lease Asset (A)		Decr 10,000

Rental on an operating lease is charged as an expense over the lease term as rent accrues. Operating leases are not recorded as assets and liabilities.

Lessors

For sales-type leases, the total of minimum lease payments is recorded as the *gross* investment in the lease. The present value of the total minimum lease payments is recorded as the *net* investment or sales price of the asset. The difference between the gross investment and the net investment is recorded as unearned income and is amortized over the lease term.

The net investment is shown on the balance sheet as either a current or noncurrent asset. The difference between gross investment and net investment (unearned income) is explained in a footnote to the balance sheet. The difference between the net investment (sales price) and the cost of the asset is shown as income in the period in which the lease is executed.

For example:

Assets

Net Investment in sales-type leases (See Note 1)	$10,000

Note 1. Net Investment in Sales-Type Leases. The following lists the components of the net investment in sales-type leases:

Total minimum lease payments to be received	$15,000
Less: Unearned Income (CA)	5,000
Net Investment in Sales-Type Leases	$10,000

If the property being leased cost the lessor $8,000 and there is no anticipated residual value, the transaction would be as follows:

Minimum Lease Payments to be received (A)	Incr	15,000
Retained Earnings (OE) (Cost of Sales-Type Lease)	Decr	8,000
Unearned Income (CA)	Incr	5,000
Retained Earnings (OE) (Sale of Equip.)	Incr	10,000
Inventory of Equipment to be Leased (A)	Decr	8,000

This results in a $2,000 profit on the "sale" of the asset and $5,000 financing income to be earned.

The accounting for direct financing leases is similar to that for sales-type leases, except that the lessor will not normally have a profit or loss on the asset being leased. For example, suppose that a leasing company buys the asset to be leased from a manufacturer and leases it to the lessee. The leasing company makes its profit on the financing charge—not on the sale of the asset.

For operating leases, the lessor records the asset on the balance sheet as it does other types of property. Rent is reported as income as it becomes receivable.

The controversy over accounting for leases has centered on the issue of when a lease is considered an obligation (or an asset). Until FASB No. 13 was issued, many long-term noncancellable leases were not required to be reported on the balance sheet. Lease financing was often referred to as "off-the-balance-sheet" financing.

FINANCIAL STATEMENT PRESENTATION AND DISCLOSURE BY LESSEE

The following information shall be disclosed in the lessee's financial statements or the footnotes thereto:

1. For Capital Leases
   (a) The gross investment presented by major fixed asset classes. This information may be combined with comparable information for owned assets.
   (b) Future minimum lease payments in the aggregate and for each of the 5 succeeding fiscal years, as of the date of the latest balance sheet presented.
   (c) The total minimum sublease rentals to be received in the future under noncancellable subleases.
   (d) Total contingent rentals actually incurred for each period for which an income statement is prepared.
2. For Operating Leases having initial or remaining noncancellable lease terms of more than 1 year.
   (a) Future minimum rental payments in the aggregate and for each of the 5 succeeding fiscal years as of the date of the latest balance sheet presented.

(b) The total minimum rentals to be received in the future under noncancellable subleases.
3. For all operating leases, rental expense for each period for which an income statement is presented.
4. A general description of the lessee's leasing arrangements.

An example of the lessee's presentation and disclosure of leases excerpted from American Airlines, Inc., is shown in Illustration 13-1.

PENSIONS

APB Opinion No. 8, *Accounting for the Cost of Pension Plans*, defines a pension plan as "an arrangement whereby a company undertakes to provide its retired employees with benefits that can be determined or estimated in advance from a document or documents or from the company's practice. Ordinarily, such benefits are monthly pension payments."

Several terms should be defined to provide a basic explanation of pension cost accounting.

1. *Normal cost.* The annual cost assigned, under the actuarial cost method in use, to the years subsequent to the plan's inception. This amount represents the current annual cost of providing future pension benefits to the current employee pool. In determining normal cost, the actuary has to consider such questions as:
   (a) How many of the current employees will continue to work until retirement.
   (b) How long the employees will live after retirement.
   (c) How much interest will be earned on the money paid into the pension fund.
2. *Past service cost.* Pension cost assigned to the years prior to the inception of a plan. *Prior service costs*, often used interchangeably, include past service costs plus the costs of any changes made to the plan since its inception. Past service cost is computed in a manner similar to computation of normal cost, except that past service cost covers benefits earned for the years prior to adoption of or changes in the plan.

3. *To fund.* To pay over to a funding agency. *Funded* refers to that portion of pension cost that has been paid to a funding agency.
4. *Vested benefits.* Benefits that are not contingent on the employee's continuing in the service of the employer.

For fiscal periods beginning after December 31, 1966, APB Opinion No. 8 provides that annual provision for pension cost should be recorded on an accrual basis. The resulting pension cost should be between the *Minimum* and *Maximum* stated below:

1. *Minimum*: (a) Normal cost plus (b) an amount equivalent to interest on unfunded past service plus, where appropriate, (c) a provision for vested benefits.
2. *Maximum*: (a) Normal cost plus (b) 10 percent of the past service cost (until it is fully amortized) plus (c) 10 percent of the amounts of any increases or decreases in prior service cost arising from amendments of the plan (until fully amortized) plus (d) interest on the difference between the provision and the amount actually funded.

The annual provision for pension cost should be based upon an acceptable actuarial cost method consistently applied.

Let us suppose that a company adopted a pension plan as of January 1 of the current year, that the company's actuaries estimated normal cost (sometimes called *current service cost*) for the year at $25,000, and that the principal of past service cost is at $100,000. The company uses an assumed interest rate of 5 percent.

	Minimum	Maximum
Normal cost	$25,000	$25,000
Interest on past service cost*	5,000	
Amortization of past service cost		10,000
	$30,000	$35,000

*At an interest rate of 5 percent, $10,000-level amortization payments would extinguish the $100,000 past service cost in a little over 14 years.

Most pension funds are *trusteed*. That is, the funds are paid to and managed by a trustee. The assets and liabilities of the pension fund do not appear on the balance sheet of the company sponsoring the pension fund. They belong to the pension fund trust.

AMERICAN AIRLINES. INC. AND CONSOLIDATED SUBSIDIARIES

CONSOLIDATED BALANCE SHEET

	December 31.	
ASSETS (in thousands)	**1979**	1978
Current Assets		
Cash and short-term investments (Note 2)	$ 452,143	$ 537,230
Receivables, less allowances for uncollectible accounts		
(1979—$16,639; 1978—$11,927)	495,077	395,471
Inventories, less allowances for obsolescence		
(1979—$26,708; 1978—$21,697)	142,335	95,987
Prepayments and other current assets	14,405	8,834
Total current assets	1,103,960	1,037,522
Equipment and Property (Notes 3 and 5)		
Flight equipment, at cost	1,967,776	1,742,594
Less: accumulated depreciation	953,072	860,531
	1,014,704	882,063
Purchase deposits with manufacturers of flight equipment	111,179	99,529
	1,125,883	981,592
Land, buildings and other equipment, at cost	545,571	459,063
Less: accumulated depreciation	258,430	216,403
	287,141	242,660
Total equipment and property — net	1,413,024	1,224,252
Equipment and Property Under Capital Leases (Note 4)		
Flight equipment	656,803	675,689
Land, buildings and other equipment	152,002	34,014
	808,805	709,703
Less: accumulated amortization	365,857	344,669
Total equipment and property under capital leases — net	442,948	365,034
Investments and Other Assets		
Investment in and advances to unconsolidated subsidiaries (Note 11)	83,528	83,573
Non-current receivables, less allowances and deferred income		
(1979—$4,309; 1978—$6,006)	28,617	6,097
Route acquisition costs — net	42,608	43,700
Other	67,810	7,540
Total investments and other assets	222,563	140,910
Total Assets	**$3,182,495**	$2,767,718

LIABILITIES, REDEEMABLE PREFERRED STOCK AND COMMON	December 31.	
STOCKHOLDERS' EQUITY (in thousands)	**1979**	1978
Current Liabilities		
Accounts payable	$ 362,763	$ 268,197
Accrued salaries and wages	134,924	106,319
Other accrued liabilities	135,032	133,794
Air traffic liability and customers' deposits	260,531	202,600
Current maturities of long-term debt	48,818	35,174
Current obligations under capital leases	41,074	40,303
Total current liabilities	983,142	786,387
Long-Term Debt, less current maturities (Note 5)		
Senior debt	530,260	419,358
Subordinated convertible debentures	138,398	158,628
Total long-term debt	668,658	577,986

Obligations Under Capital Leases, less current maturities (Note 4)	**501,689**	410,272
Other Liabilities		
Deferred federal income tax (Note 6)	**124,018**	155,988
Other liabilities and deferred credits	**11,928**	9,188
Total other liabilities	**135,946**	165,176
Commitments, Leases and Contingencies (Notes 3 and 4)		
Redeemable Preferred Stock (Note 8)		
Cumulative — without par value, aggregate redemption value — $125,000,000; 10,000,000 shares authorized; 5,000,000 shares issued and outstanding	**107,314**	106,218
Common Stockholders' Equity (Notes 5, 7 and 9)		
Common stock — $1 par value; 60,000,000 shares authorized; shares issued and outstanding: 1979—28,696,000; 1978—28,681,000	**28,696**	28,681
Additional paid-in capital	**332,511**	332,395
Retained earnings	**424,539**	360,603
Total common stockholders' equity	**785,746**	721,679
Total Liabilities, Redeemable Preferred Stock and Common Stockholders' Equity	**$3,182,495**	$2,767,718

NOTES TO FINANCIAL STATEMENTS

4. LEASES

American leases various types of property, including aircraft, passenger terminals, ground equipment and various other supporting facilities.

Rental expense, net of sublease income, was $57,900,000 in 1979 and $52,700,000 in 1978. In addition, American incurred airport landing fees of approximately $54,700,000 in 1979 and $49,500,000 in 1978. Airport landing fees are considered a component of American's airport lease obligations.

The future minimum lease payments under capital leases, (together with the present value of net minimum lease payments) as of December 31, 1979, are as follows (in thousands):

Year ending December 31.	
1980	$ 79,000
1981	79,000
1982	77,000
1983	72,000
1984	67,000
1985 and subsequent	579,000
	953,000
Less: Amount representing interest	410,000
Present value of net minimum lease payments	$543,000*

*Includes $240,300,000 guaranteed by American of which $93,300,000 relates to lessors' long-term loan certificates in connection with the leases of seven Boeing 747 aircraft and five Boeing 727 aircraft and $147,000,000 of 1979 Revenue Bonds issued by the cities of Dallas and Fort Worth.

Future minimum lease payments required under operating leases that have initial or remaining noncancellable lease terms in excess of one year as of December 31, 1979 are as follows (in thousands):

Year ending December 31.	
1980	$ 23,000
1981	21,000
1982	21,000
1983	20,000
1984	18,000
1985 and subsequent	327,000
Total minimum payments	$430,000

Minimum payments have been reduced by sublease rentals of $84,100,000 due in the future under non-cancellable subleases.

American has guaranteed payments under capital leases for hotels and other properties operated by Flagship having a present value of approximately $54,200,000 at December 31, 1979. American has also guaranteed other obligations of Flagship aggregating approximately $11,300,000.

In March 1980, the Financial Accounting Standards Board issued a statement of *Accounting and Reporting by Defined Benefit Pension Plans* (FASB Statement No. 35) which concerns accounting and reporting in the financial statements of the plans themselves. The primary objective of a plan's financial statements is to provide financial information that is useful in assessing the plan's present and future ability to pay benefits when due. To accomplish that objective, the financial statements will include information regarding:

1. The net assets available for benefits as of the end of the plan year.
2. The changes in net assets during the plan year.
3. The actuarial present value of accumulated plan benefits as of either the beginning or end of the plan year.
4. The effects, if significant, of certain factors affecting the year-to-year change in the actuarial present value of accumulated plan benefits.

If the date as of which the benefit information (3 above) is presented is the beginning of the year, additional information is required regarding both the net assets available for benefit as of the date and the changes in net assets during the preceding year.

The statement is effective for plan years beginning after December 15, 1980. FASB Statement No. 35 addresses financial reporting by the plan themselves, not the issues relating to disclosures in employers' financial statements about the costs of plans they sponsor.

APB Opinion No. 8 establishes procedures for determining pension cost to be charged as an expense of the period. This amount is not necessarily the amount to be funded. However, paragraph 18 of this Opinion provides that "the difference between the amount which has been charged against income and the amount which has been paid should be shown in the balance sheet as either accrued or prepaid pension cost." Examples of these two methods are:

Retained Earnings (OE) – (Pension Expense)	Decr 100	
Cash (A)		Decr 80
Accrued pension liability (L)		Incr 20
Retained Earnings (OE) – (Pension Expense)	Decr 100	
Prepaid Pension Expense (A)	Incr 20	
Cash (A)		Decr 120

If the company has a legal obligation for pension cost in excess of amount paid or accrued, the excess should be shown in the balance sheet as both a liability and a deferred charge. For example, the balance sheet might record:

Deferred Pension Expense (A)   Incr   20
   Accrued Pension Liability (L)   Incr   20

The opinion also provides that actuarial gains and losses, including unrealized appreciation and depreciation in the value of pension fund investments, should ordinarily be spread over current and future years. They should not be used to substantially reduce or eliminate pension costs of a single period.

FINANCIAL STATEMENT DISCLOSURE

In May 1980, the Financial Accounting Standards Board issued a statement of *Disclosure of Pension Information* (FASB Statement No. 36) which was designed to improve pension disclosure by employers, requires the use of consistent methods for measuring accumulated pension benefits, both vested and nonvested, and the assets available for those benefits. FASB Statement No. 36 requires the following disclosures in the company's financial statements or notes thereto:

1. A statement that pension plans exist, identifying or describing the employee groups covered.
2. A statement of the company's accounting and funding policies.
3. The provision for pension costs for the period.
4. The nature and effects of significant matters affecting comparability for all periods presented.

For its defined benefit pension plans, an employer shall disclose the following data determined in accordance with FASB Statement No. 35 of the most recent benefit information data for which the data are available:

5. The actuarial present value of vested accumulated plan benefits.

6. The actuarial present value of nonvested accumulated plan benefits.
7. The plans' net assets available for benefits.
8. The assumed rate of return used in determining 5 and 6.
9. The date as of which the benefit information was determined.

For plans for which the above data are not available (expected to be only those plans that do not report such information with certain governmental agencies pursuant to ERISA of 1974), the employer shall continue to comply with the disclosure requirements originally contained in Opinion No. 8, namely, the excess, if any, of the actuarially computed value of vested benefits over the total of the pension fund and any balance sheet pension accruals, less any pension prepayments or deferred charges. The reasons why the information required in items 5 through 9 above is not provided for those plans shall be disclosed.

FASB Statement No. 36 is effective for annual financial statements for fiscal years beginning after December 15, 1979. The FASB has embarked on a third phase approach to the overall problems of accounting for pensions. This third phase is a comprehensive project to consider all aspects of accounting by employers for the cost of pensions and related benefits.

Illustration 13-2 presents an example of pension plan disclosure as given in FASB Statement No. 3.

ERISA

The Employee Retirement Income Security Act of 1974 (ERISA) contained major revisions of the United States' private retirement system that affected virtually every private retirement plan in the United States. Not covered by the act are governmental retirement plans, certain church plans, non-United States plans for non-resident aliens, and those non-funded plans, established primarily for highly-paid employees, that provide benefits in excess of Internal Revenue Service limitations.

ERISA does not require any company to establish a pension plan. Rather, it sets federal standards for established and future plans. The major objective of the act is to assure that pension plans are operated and financed in such a manner that employees ultimately receive the benefits to which they are entitled. To accomplish this objective, the

---

Illustration 13-2

Example of Pension Plan Disclosure

The company and its subsidiaries have several pension plans covering substantially all of their employees, including certain employees in foreign countries. The total pension expense for 19X1 and 19X2 was $XXX and $XXX respectively, which includes, as to certain defined benefit plans, amortization of past service cost over XX years. The company makes annual contributions to the plans equal to the amounts accrued for pension expense. A change during 19X2 in the actuarial cost method used in computing pension cost had the effect of reducing net income for the year by approximately $XXX. A comparison of accumulated plan benefits and plan net assets for the company's domestic defined benefit plans is presented below:

| | January 1, | |
	19X1	19X2
Actuarial present value of accumulated plan benefits:		
Vested	$XXX	$XXX
Nonvested	XXX	XXX
	$XXX	$XXX
Net assets available for benefits	$XXX	$XXX

The weighted average assumed rate of return used in determining the actuarial present value of accumulated plan benefits was X percent for both 19X1 and 19X2. The company's foreign pension plans are not required to report to certain governmental agencies pursuant to ERISA and do not otherwise determine the actuarial value of accumulated benefits or net assets available for benefits as calculated and disclosed above. For those plans, the actuarially computed value of vested benefits as of December 31, 19X1 and December 31, 19X2 exceeded the total of those plans' pension funds and balance sheet accruals less pension prepayments and deferred charges by approximately $XXX and $XXX respectively.

---

act provided for stricter minimum funding requirements and stricter vesting provisions, established new eligibility rules and new, more extensive eligibility requirements, and created the Pension Benefit Guarantee Corporation (PBGC), a tax-free entity within the Department of Labor.

ERISA does not affect the accounting for pension costs.

MISCELLANEOUS LIABILITIES

Deferred Income. Deferred income is income received in advance of the time it is earned. It is often called *unearned revenue.* Deferred income includes items such as rent income, interest income, and magazine subscriptions collected in advance. These amounts are carried as liabilities, either current or noncurrent, until the income is earned. As the income is earned, the liability decreases and retained earnings increase.

WARRANTIES AND GUARANTEES

Many companies sell their products with a warranty against defect or a guarantee to replace or repair the product. FASB Statement No. 5, *Accounting for Contingencies*, requires that, if the future warranty costs can be reasonably estimated, they must be accounted for at the time a sale is made. The transaction is recorded as follows:

Retained Earnings (OE)–(Provision for Warranty Expense)	Decr	xxx
Provision for Warranty Expense (L)	Incr	xxx

Then, as the service is performed under the guarantee, the cost of this service is recorded:

Provision for Warranty Expense (L)	Decr	xxx
Cash (A)	Decr	xxx

OTHER CONTINGENT LIABILITIES

The term *contingent liabilities*, as used in this text, refers to conditions existing at the balance sheet date that may result in future definite liabilities. If a loss is probable and the amount can be reasonably estimated, this loss must be provided for by a charge to income. If the loss is not probable and/or cannot be reasonably estimated, FASB No. 5 requires that "disclosure of the contingency shall be made when there is at least a reasonable possibility that a loss . . . may have been incurred. The disclosure shall indicate the nature of the contingency and shall give an estimate of the possible loss or range of loss or state that such an estimate cannot be made."

SUMMARY

From the viewpoint of the lessee, leases are classified into capital leases or operating leases. If a lease meets one or more of the 4 criteria listed under FASB Statement No. 13, it is classified as a capital lease. A capital lease is recorded as an asset and is amortized according to the depreciation policy of owned assets or over the life of the lease, depending on the terms of the lease agreement. Capital leases are distinguished from other properties in the financial statements or notes thereto, and future lease payments and sublease rentals to be received are also presented. Rental on an operating lease is expensed over the lease term as rent accrues. Future lease payments and sublease rentals to be received must be disclosed for operating leases in the notes to the financial statements.

From the viewpoint of the lessor, leases are classified into sales-type, direct financing, leveraged or operating leases. A sales-type lease will normally result in a manufacturer's or dealer's profit or loss to the lessor. The net investment is shown on the balance sheet as either a current or noncurrent asset and the unearned income is explained in the footnotes. Direct financing leases are accounted for in the same way as sales-type leases except that the lessor will not normally have a profit or loss on the asset being leased. For operating leases, rent is reported as income as it becomes receivable and the lessor records the assets on the balance sheet as it does other types of property.

The largest fringe benefit a company provides its employees is normally the pension, that is, payments that employees will receive after they retire. The Employee Retirement Income Security Act of 1974 (ERISA) regulates pension plans. The company's contribution for benefits is a cost to the company and the contribution is a payment of cash to a bank, insurance company, or other agency that acts as trustee for the pension funds. The pension fund thus created is a separate entity with its own set of accounts governed by FASB Statement No. 35.

The annual provision for pension cost should be based on an accounting method that uses an acceptable actuarial cost method and results in a provision between the minimum and maximum amount, as required by APB Opinion No. 8. If the amount charged as an expense for the period exceeds or is less than the amount funded, the difference is shown in the balance sheet as accrued or prepaid pen-

sion cost, respectively. FASB Statement No. 36 requires certain details on pension costs to be disclosed in the notes to the financial
statements for fiscal year beginning December 15, 1979.

Contingent liabilities are disclosed in the notes to the financial
statements, in the president's letter, or as a memo item on the balance sheet itself.

QUESTIONS AND PROBLEMS

1. DSC Company leases an asset-market value $200,000—under conditions
    whereby they agree to pay $47,479.28 for 5 years (single payments at year
    end). The agreement is non-cancellable and five years is the expected eco-
    nomic life of the asset; there is no expected residual value to the asset.
    (Thus, the lease is to be capitalized). The lease is executed on January 1,
    1981.

    A. What entry does the lessee make on January 1, 1981?
    B. What entry does it make at the end of 1981 to record the cash payment
        of $47,479.28?
    C. For the year 1981 what expenses will be reflected on the income state-
        ment with respect to the lease?
    D. How will the lease asset and liability items appear on the books as of
        January 1, 1981? 1982? 1983? 1984? 1985? 1986?
    E. How much of the lease liability will appear as a current item in the
        balance sheet as of December 31, 1981? How much of the leased asset
        will appear as a current item on that date?

    Assume that the company's depreciation of owned assets is always done on
    a straight-line basis.
2. DSC Company leased the asset referred to in Question No. 1 from MSC
    Company. The cost of the asset that MSC Manufacturing Company leases
    to DSC Company is $150,000. (This is a sales-type lease).

    A. What entry does the lessor make on January 1, 1981?
    B. What entry does it make at the end of 1981 to record the cash received
        of $47,479.28? What other entry is required?
    C. For the year ended 1981, what will be reflected on the income state-
        ment with respect to the lease?
    D. What items will appear on the lessor's balance sheet as of December 31,
        1981? 1982? 1983? 1984? 1985?

3. Dardie, Inc., was incorporated on January 1, 1970. On January 1, 1980, it
    adopted a company pension plan for most of its employees. The pension

plan is to be funded by the company and is noncontributory. Dardie used an acceptable actuarial cost method to determine its normal annual pension cost for 1980 and 1981, which was $80,000 and $90,000, respectively. The amounts were funded as incurred.

Dardie funded its actuarially determined past service costs of $600,000 on December 31, 1980. Dardie's policy is to amortize the past service costs at the maximum amount permitted. The actuary assumed an interest factor of 8%.

Prepare transactions to record:

A. The funding of past service cost on December 31, 1980.
B. The pension expenses for 1980 and 1981.

4. At the time of adopting its pension plan on January 1, 1980, GMJ Company's past service pension liability was $842,830. The actuary considers 7% as a reasonable earnings rate on pension fund investments.

A. The company plans to expense the past service costs over 10 years and fund the past service costs over a period of 15 years.
   REQUIRED: What entry must be made on 12/31/80 to record pension expense for past service cost? On 12/31/94?
B. The company plans to expense the past service costs over 15 years and fund the past service costs over a period of 10 years.
   REQUIRED: What entry must be made on 12/31/80 to record pension expense for past service cost? On 12/31/94?

5. Jervis Auto Company owns land on which it can build a new showroom at a cost of $60,000. As an alternative, Jervis can have Ajax Leasing Company build the showroom and Jervis can lease it for $7,010 a year for 15 years, which is the estimated useful life of the building. Jervis would pay all maintenance and insurance costs. The $7,010 a year will give Ajax an 8% return on its investment of $60,000. Lease payments would be made at the *end* of each year.

If Jervis decides to lease the property, the following accounts will be used:

Leasehold Rights (A)
Lease Obligations (L)
Retained Earnings (OE) (Interest Expense)
Retained Earnings (OC) (Amortization of Leasehold Rights)

Questions:
A. According to present GAAP, how should a lease of this type be classified and why?
   (a) By the lessee
   (b) By the lessor
B. If Jervis decides to lease the showroom from Ajax, what entry or entries will Jervis make on its books on January 2, 1982, the date the lease would begin?

C. If Jervis decides to lease the showroom from Ajax, what entry or entries will Jervis make on its books on December 31, 1982, the end of the lease year and the company's fiscal year?

6. Huffy Corporation's Notes to Financial Statements in its 1979 Annual Report included the following:

Sales Returns and Warranty

Charges are made to current operations for sales returns and allowances under product warranties. In addition, charges are made to current operations to provide a reserve against losses which may be incurred as a result of a product recall, correction or similar events related to legislated or industry safety standards and other safety related considerations. The amount of such charges is based on the Company's experience and consideration of the environment in the markets it serves. No such charge to current operations was considered necessary in 1978 and 1979. In 1979, approximately $94,000 was charged against the reserve for a voluntary recall to replace the crank on certain models of bicycles.

A. Using XXX to indicate the amount, please show what accounting entry was originally made to "provide a reserve against losses which may be incurred as a result of a product recall. . ."
B. Where would you expect to find this so-called "reserve" in the Financial Statements?
C. It seems that Huffy either *did not* ("No such charge to current operations was considered necessary in 1978 and 1979.") *or did,* ("In 1979, approximately $94,000 was charged against the reserve for a voluntary recall to replace the crank or certain models of bicycles.") charge this reserve. Explain please.
D. If money has been set aside in this manner as a reserve, where is it kept?

7. Dover Corporation's 1979 Annual Report contained the following footnote with respect to pensions:

> The company has several noncontributory pension plans covering substantially all employees of the Company and its subsidiaries. The Company's policy is generally to fund pension costs as accrued. Pension costs charged to earnings in 1979 were $4,025,000 compared with $3,999,000 in 1978. As of the latest valuation dates, unfunded prior service liabilities under the plans aggregated approximately $18,700,000. The actuarially computed value of vested benefits under certain of the plans exceeded the total of the respective pension funds by approximately $7,309,000; pension fund assets exceeded vested benefits under the remaining plans by $1,058,000.

A. Does this mean that during 1979 the company had to pay $4,025,000 in pension benefits to its retirees? If not, what does the $4,025,000 represent?

B. It appears that less than half of the pension benefits are vested. True? What does vested mean?

C. How much are the total pension fund assets? Where do they appear on Dover's balance sheet? Why?

8. In its 1980 Annual Report, West Point-Pepperell showed the following items pertaining to capital leases.

1. Asset on balance sheet—Leased Property under Capital Leases (Net) $16,390,667.

2. Liabilities on balance sheet—short and long-term obligations under Capital Leases, $12,720,000.

3. In a footnote—Total minimum lease payments, $15,707,000.

Should these three amounts ($16,390,667, $12,720,000, $15,707,000) be the same? Explain how the company would arrive at the amounts for each of the three items.

14

Stockholders' Equity

The purpose of this chapter is to discuss the two main parts of stockholders' equity: (1) that part paid into the company by the stockholder consisting of common stock, preferred stock, and capital in excess of par value and (2) retained earnings. We will examine the presentation of stockholders' equity in external financial statements and discuss briefly extraordinary items affecting the retained earnings account. We will conclude the chapter with a discussion of stock dividends and stock splits.

The difference between the total assets and total liabilities of a corporate entity is known as stockholders' equity. Stockholders' equity is also referred to as owners' equity, capital, net worth, and net assets.

CAPITAL STOCK

Stockholders invest in a company directly when they purchase common or preferred stock or indirectly when the company retains profits that could have been paid out in dividends.

When a company issues common stock, it records the transaction as follows:

Cash (A)	Incr XXX	
Capital Stock (OE)		Incr XXX
Capital in Excess of par value (OE)		Incr XXX

Capital stock is recorded at par or stated value, and the excess of the selling price over par or stated value is entered in the capital in excess of par value account. The par or stated value of a stock has no relationship to market value; it merely satisfies state legal requirements. If a stock has no par or stated value, it may be carried in the capital stock account at the amount for which it was sold.

Preferred stock is a class of stock which has "preference" as to items such as dividends and assets in case of liquidation. Dividends are normally at a fixed rate per share. The sale of preferred stock is recorded in a manner similar to that of common stock. Disclosure of liquidation values, redemption values, conversion privileges, and other features of preferred stock should be made in the financial statements.

Donated Capital

If property is given to a corporation, the fair value is recorded as an asset and, usually, as an increase in capital in excess of par value. If the amount is material, a separate equity account, Donated Capital, may be used.

Capital in Excess of Par Value

As indicated in the preceding section, this account records the excess of issue price over par or stated value. The account also records profits and losses on sales of treasury stock, donated capital, stock dividends, and stock splits. Capital in excess of par value is sometimes capital surplus or paid in capital.

Treasury Stock

When a company reacquires its own previously issued stock, this stock is referred to as *treasury stock*. It differs, therefore, from unissued stock. Unless it is to be retired, treasury stock normally is carried at cost and is deducted on the balance sheet from the total stockholders' equity. If treasury stock is resold, any gains or losses are made as adjustments to Capital in Excess of Par Value or, if this account is not sufficient, to Retained Earnings.

Retained Earnings

Accounting for retained earnings is relatively simple when a company has no prior period adjustments, has no stock dividends, and has no *appropriation* of retained earnings. In such a simple case, retained earnings are increased by net income for the period and decreased by dividends declared.

Some companies classify a portion of retained earnings as *appropriated* to indicate that this portion of retained earnings is not available for dividends. Appropriation does not affect cash. Costs or losses cannot be charged to an appropriation of retained earnings and it cannot be transferred to income, thus, the classification is rarely used.

STOCKHOLDERS' EQUITY ON THE BALANCE SHEET

A company's balance sheet normally classifies stockholders' equity as follows:

1. Preferred stock—by class.
2. Common stock.
3. Capital in excess of par value (sometimes called "capital surplus").
4. Retained earnings.

For each class of stock, the balance sheet or a statement of changes in capital accounts gives the following information:

1. The par or stated value per share.
2. The maximum number of shares authorized by the corporation's charter.

3. The number of shares issued.
4. The dollar amount of issued shares at par or stated value.
5. The number of shares and the cost of treasury stock.

Amstar Corporation showed its "shareholders' investment" in its June 30, 1979, balance sheet as shown in Illustration 14-1.

EXTRAORDINARY ITEMS AND PRIOR PERIOD ADJUSTMENTS

There has been considerable controversy for many years over what items should be included in a current periodic income statement and what items should be charged directly to the retained earnings account. In addition, there has been controversy over how items should be classified within the income statement.

Illustration 14-1

Excerpt from Amstar Corp. Annual Report

	1979	1978
SHAREHOLDERS' INVESTMENT		
Capital Stock		
Preferred Stock, 5.44% cumulative, $12.50 par		
value, authorized and issued 1,800,000 shares	22,500,000	22,500,000
Junior Preferred Stock, without par value,		
authorized 2,500,000 shares; $2.65 Cumulative		
Convertible Series A, authorized, issued and		
outstanding 35,560 shares in 1979 and 47,217		
shares in 1978 at stated value	622,000	826,000
Common Stock, $1.00 par value, authorized		
25,000,000 shares; issued 9,293,641 shares		
in 1979 and 9,253,602 shares in 1978	9,294,000	9,254,000
Capital Surplus	51,471,000	51,214,000
Retained Earnings (Note 4)	208,523,000	199,377,000
	292,410,000	283,171,000
Less cost of treasury stock		
Shares 6/30/79 6/30/78		
Preferred 204,504 204,504	1,962,000	1,962,200
Common 363,224 364,019	4,150,000	4,160,000
Total shareholders' investment	286,298,000	277,049,000

Prior to the 1973 issuance of APB Opinion No. 30, *Reporting the Results of Operations*, considerable differences existed among companies' definitions of various events as *extraordinary items*, to be excluded from Income from Operations on the income statement. Opinion No. 30 established much more specific criteria for classifying events as extraordinary. The generally accepted practices pertaining to such items are summarized below:

1. Extraordinary items (less applicable income tax effects) should be shown separately on the income statement after Income Before Extraordinary Items.
2. Extraordinary items are events and transactions distinguished by their unusual nature and infrequent occurrence. Thus, both of the following criteria should be met to classify an event or transaction as an extraordinary item:
    a. Unusual nature—Should possess a high degree of abnormality and be clearly unrelated to, or only incidentally related to, the ordinary and typical activities of the business.
    b. Infrequency of occurrence—Should not reasonably be expected to recur in the foreseeable future.

Certain gains and losses should not be reported as extraordinary items because they are usual or may be expected to recur as a consequence of customary and continuing business activities. Examples include:

1. Write-down or write-off of receivables, inventories, equipment leased to others, deferred research and development costs, or other intangible assets.
2. Gains or losses from exchange or translation of foreign currencies, including those from major revaluations.
3. Gains or losses on disposal of a segment of a business.
4. Other gains or losses from sale or abandonment of property, plant, or equipment used in the business.
5. Effects of a strike, including those against competitors and major suppliers.
6. Adjustments of accruals on long-term contracts.

Subsequent to the issuance of Opinion No. 30, the FASB Issued Statement of Financial Accounting Standard No. 4, *Reporting Gains and Losses from Extinguishment of Debt*, which requires that gains and losses from early debt extinguishment be treated as extraordinary even though they fail to meet the established criteria.

FASB Statement No. 16, *Prior Period Adjustments*, issued in July, 1977, requires that all items of profit and loss recognized during a period, except for the two items listed next, shall be included in the determination of net income for that period. The two exceptions are (1) correction of an error in the financial statements of a prior period discovered subsequent to their issuance or (2) adjustments that result from realization of income tax benefits of pre-acquisition operating loss carry forwards of purchased subsidiaries.

Thus, for all practical purposes, items recognized during a period which affect net income are shown on the income statement for the period.

STOCK DIVIDENDS AND SPLITS

When the board of directors declares a *stock dividend* payable in the company's own capital stock rather than in cash, there is no change in the assets or liabilities of the company. There is merely a shift of the "fair value" of the stock from Retained Earnings to Capital Stock and Capital in Excess of Par Value. For example, if the directors declare a 5 percent stock dividend on the company's 10,000 shares of $100 par value common stock, and the market value per share after the dividend is issued will be about $130 a share, the "fair value" of the stock dividend will be $65,000. The entry for the transaction is:

Retained Earnings (OE) – (Stock Dividend)	Decr	65,000
Capital Stock (OE)	Incr	50,000
Capital in Excess of Par Value (OE)	Incr	15,000

Accounting Research Bulletin 43 describes a stock dividend as being "prompted mainly by a desire to give the recipient shareholders some ostensibly separate evidence of a part of their respective interest in accumulated corporate earnings without a distribution of cash . . . ."

Stock Split-Ups: ARB 43 distinguishes a *stock split-up* from a stock dividend by referring to a stock split-up as "an issuance by a corporation of its own common shares to its common shareholders without consideration and under conditions indicating that such action is prompted mainly by a desire to increase the number of outstanding shares for the purpose of effecting a reduction in their unit market price and, thereby, of obtaining wider distribution and improved marketability of the shares."

If more than 20-25 percent of the previously outstanding shares are issued, the issuance will normally be accounted for as a stock split-up. If less than 20-25 percent, the issuance will be treated as a stock dividend.

In accounting for stock split-ups, there is no transfer from Retained Earnings to Capital Stock and Capital in Excess of Par Value, other than to the extent required by law. If there are no legal requirements, there is no accounting transaction, because no accounts are affected. Footnotes to the financial statements will disclose the new number of common shares issued and outstanding, and any changes in par value.

STOCK OPTIONS

Many companies, to attract and keep competent managers, issue options to purchase the company's stock at a stated price during some specified time period. The stated price is usually very close to the market price at the time the option is granted so that purchasers' personal income tax is minimized.

If the market value of the stock is the same as the option price at the *measurement date*, which is usually the date the option is granted, no accounting entry is required at that date. When the employee exercises the option, the accounting is the same as if the company sold common stock to the public.

If the option price is less than the market price at the measurement date, the difference is accounted for as additional compensation. The entry is:

Retained Earnings (OE) – (Additional Compensation Expense)	Decr	XXX
Accrued Stock Option Credit (L)	Incr	XXX

When the option is exercised, the entry is:

Cash (A)	Incr	XXX	
Accrued Stock Option Credit (L)	Decr	XXX	
Capital Stock (OE)			Incr XXX
Capital in Excess Par Value (OE)			Incr XXX

Footnotes to the financial statements should disclose the status of option plans, i.e., the number of shares under option, the option price, and the number of shares on which options are exercisable. For options exercised, disclosure should be made of the number of shares involved and the option price.

Accounting for stock options is covered in ARB 43 and APB Opinion 25.

SUMMARY

A company's balance sheet should show, for each class of capital stock the amount of par or stated value and the amount in excess of par or stated value. Capital in excess of par or stated value includes the excess received upon original issues of stock, amounts transferred from retained earnings for stock dividends, and net gains from sale of treasury stock. The cost of treasury stock is usually shown as a deduction in the stockholders' equity section.

Retained earnings represent the accumulated earnings of a corporation which have not been distributed in the form of cash or stock dividends. Retained earnings are increased by net income for each year and decreased by net losses and dividends.

Extraordinary items are events and transactions that are distinguished by their unusual nature and by the infrequency of their occurrence. Extraordinary items should be segregated from the results of ordinary operations and shown separately in the income statement, with disclosure of the nature and amounts thereof.

A stock dividend will cause a transfer from the retained earnings account to the capital stock account equal to the par or stated value of the dividend shares whereas a stock split does not change the dollar balance of any account. Stock options, warrants, and similar arrangements usually have no cash yield and derive their value from their right to obtain common stock at specified prices for an extended period.

QUESTIONS AND PROBLEMS

1. The following information (Note J) was taken from the 1980 Annual Report of West Point-Pepperell, Inc.

Note J: Stockholders' Equity

Changes in stockholders' equity for the two years ended August 30, 1980 are as follows:

	Common Stock		Capital Surplus	Retained Earnings
	Shares	Amount		
		(000 omitted)		
Balance at August 26, 1978	4,833	$ 24,164	$ 10,966	$253,332
Stock options exercised	8	40	156	
Restricted stock issued	14	70	445	
Purchase of treasury stock ... (	303)	(1,515)	(708)	(10,093)
Adjustment due to repurchase of restricted stock			(100)	
Income tax benefits resulting from stock option and stock compensation plans			222	
Net income				27,388
Dividends				(13,585)
Balance at August 25, 1979 : :..	4,552	22,759	10,981	257,042
Conversion of Debentures ...	89	446	2,980	
Restricted stock issued		1	9	
Purchase of treasury stock ... (	2)	(11)		
Adjustment due to repurchase of restricted stock			(74)	
Income tax benefits resulting from stock option and stock compensation plans ..			24	
Net income				42,505
Dividends				(13,256)
Balance at August 30, 1980	4,639	$ 23,195	$ 13,920	$286,291

	August 30, 1980	August 25, 1979
Common Stock:		
Shares authorized	15,000,000	15,000,000
Shares issued	4,948,446	4,858,911
Shares held in treasury	309,392	307,142
Shares outstanding	4,639,054	4,551,769
Reserved for issuance upon conversion of Convertible Debentures (Note G)	562,205	651,465
Reserved for issuance under Restricted Stock and Performance Share Plan (Note H)	199,253	224,575

A. Why is there a surplus of capital?

B. Is there any significance to the fact that the capital surplus is less than the amount in the common stock account even though the par value is only $5.00 and the market price of the common stock during 1980 ranged between $27 and $42?

C. At some date between August 26, 1978 and August 25, 1979 West Point purchased 303,000 shares of its own stock. How much did West Point pay for this stock? What was the accounting transaction for the stock? Why do you think West Point accounted for the purchase the way it was done?

2. Josten's Inc. 1979 Annual Report contained the following Statement of Consolidated Changes in Shareholder's Investment: *" EXCESS OVER PAR "*

	Common Shares		Capital Surplus	Retained Earnings
	Number	Amount		
Balance June 30, 1977 . . .	5,037,691	$1,679,230	$ 8,075,103	$50,591,554
Employee stock options exercised	35,426	11,809	452,596	
Conversion of 4¾% sub-ordinated debentures	84,418	28,139	1,916,861	
Shares issued for stock split–Note G	2,571,251	857,084	(857,084)	
Cash paid in lieu of fractional shares for stock split.	(1,049)	(350)	(20,400)	
Net income				15,386,046
Cash dividends of $.75 1/3 per share				(5,777,227)
Balance June 30, 1978 . . .	7,727,737	2,575,912	9,567,076	60,200,373
Employee stock options exercised	20,947	6,982	179,249	
Conversion of 4¾% sub-ordinated debentures	237,670	79,224	3,762,776	
Net income				18,549,662
Cash dividends of $.92 per share				(7,341,486)
Balance June 30, 1979	7,986,354	$2,662,118	$13,509,101	$71,408,549

Note G contained the following statement:

> "On April 27, 1978, the board of directors declared a three-for-two stock split on the Company's common shares, which was effected in the form of a 50% stock dividend. The par value of the shares issued was transferred from capital surplus to the common shares account."

A. Is Josten's common stock no par or par? Explain. If par, at what value? Explain.
B. Is a stock dividend the same thing as a stock split?
C. Explain to a stockholder owning 100 shares of stock just what happened in the events described in Note G above and how the stockholder will benefit from these events.

3. GSK Company was incorporated on January 1, 1980 and issued the following stock:

100,000 shares of $10 par value common stock at $24 per share (authorized 1,000,000 shares).

50,000 shares of $10 par value 10% cumulative preferred stock at $12 per share (authorized 200,000 shares).

The net income for 1980 was $525,000 and cash dividends of $175,000 were declared and paid in 1980.

REQUIRED: Prepare transactions to record the issue of shares and dividends.

4. On November 21, 1963, the Board of Directors of Eastman Kodak Company declared a stock dividend of one share of Common Stock for each twenty shares outstanding, payable February 10, 1964, to holders of shares of Common Stock of record on January 3, 1964. In a message to stockholders, the Company explained:

> 'The purpose of this stock dividend is to place in the hands of each shareholder tangible evidence of his share in the portion of the earnings of the Company which have been retained for use in the business and which are being capitalized by the stock dividend. . . The receipt by you of this stock dividend does not increase your proportionate equity in the Company. However, a disposal of such dividend will reduce your equity in the Company by $4.7619%. . .

> ". . . $106 per share . . . is an approximation of the market value of the Company's Common Stock prior to the stock dividend declaration, after taking into consideration the dilution resulting from the 5% stock dividend."

The par value per share of the Company's Common was $10, and there were 38,382,246 shares outstanding prior to the declaration of the stock dividend. The Company's retained earnings at September 8, 1963 (the end of the Company's third quarter) was $397,727,028.

A. What entry should the Company make for the stock dividend? When?

B. What was the approximate market value of the Common Stock, prior to the declaration of the stock dividend?

5. Reproduced on the next page is Statement 4 from the 1979 Annual Report of Caterpillar Tractor.

A. Explain the purpose and significance of Statement 4, *Source of Consolidated Net Assets.*

B. What entry(s) was made in 1928 concerning Russell Grader Manufacturing Company? (Make whatever assumptions you feel necessary.)

C. What entry(s) was made in 1949 for the stock split? What is accomplished by such a split?

D. what *summary* entry(s) describes the 1953-54 4% stock dividends?

E. What entry(s) was made for the 1956 stock sale?

F. What entry(s) was made in 1959 for that stock split?

G. What entry(s) was made in 1964 for that stock split? Why was this entry different than for the 1949 Stock Split?

Statement 4

Source of Consolidated Net Assets
(Dollars in millions)

Year	CAPITAL STOCK, COMMON	Number of shares	Amount paid in for stock	Profit employed in the business incorporated in capital accounts	Total in capital accounts	
1925-26	Issued for net assets of predecessor companies	1,625,000(1)	$ 12.3	$ —	$ 12.3	
1928	Issued for net assets of Russell Grader Manufacturing Company	86,127	2.5	—	2.5	
1929	Sold for cash	171,113	8.3	—	8.3	
	Balance	1,882,240	23.1	—	23.1	
1949	Exchange of two shares of $10 par value common for each share of no par common	1,882,240	—	14.5(2)	14.5	
	Balance after stock split	3,764,480	23.1	14.5	37.6	
1951	Issued for entire capital stock of Trackson Company	54,000	2.2	—	2.2	
1952-55	Sold for cash under stock options	38,372	1.7	—	1.7	
1953-54	Issued as 4% stock dividends	311,785	—	16.9(3)	16.9	
	Balance	4,168,637	27.0	31.4	58.4	
1955	Issued one additional share for each share outstanding	4,168,637	—	24.9(2)	24.9	
	Balance after stock split	8,337,274	27.0	56.3	83.3	
1955-59	Sold for cash under stock options	192,038	7.4	—	7.4	
1956	Sold for cash	500,000	33.2	—	33.2	
1956	Issued for entire capital stock of Englehart Manufacturing Company	20,000	1.0	—	1.0	
	Balance	9,049,312	68.6	56.3	124.9	
1959	Exchange of three shares of no par value common for each share of $10 par value common	18,098,624	—	—	—	
	Balance after stock split	27,147,936	68.6	56.3	124.9	
1959-64	Sold for cash under stock options	174,287	3.9	—	3.9	
	Balance	27,322,223	72.5	56.3	128.8	
1964	Issued one additional share for each share outstanding	27,322,223	—	—	—	
	Balance after stock split	54,644,446	72.5	56.3	128.8	
1964-76	Sold for cash under stock options	863,572	29.4	—	29.4	
1965	Issued for net assets of Towmotor Corporation	1,891,678	2.3	1.0	3.3(4)	
	Balance	57,399,696	104.2	57.3	161.5	
1976	Issued one additional share for each two shares outstanding	28,699,848	—	—	—	
	Balance after stock split	86,099,544	104.2	57.3	161.5	
1976-79	Sold for cash under stock options	329,009	15.3	—	15.3	
1978-79	Issued upon conversion of convertible debentures	5,148	.3	—	.3	
		86,433,701	$119.8	$57.3		$ 177.1

Year	PROFIT EMPLOYED IN THE BUSINESS	Profit	Appropriations		Amount at end of period	
			Cash dividends	Incorporated in capital accounts		
1925-77		$3,770.6	$1,539.7	$57.3	$2,173.6	
1978		566.3	161.8	—	2,578.1	
1979		491.6	181.5	—	2,888.2	
		$4,828.5	$1,883.0	$57.3		2,888.2

Source of consolidated net assets (statement 2) $3,065.3

(1) At incorporation, 260,000 shares of common stock were issued for net assets of predecessor companies. In February 1926, those shares were increased to 325,000 shares by a 5-for-4 stock split effected in the form of a 25% stock dividend. In December 1926, a conversion of five shares for one share increased the issued shares to 1,625,000.
(2) Excess of par value of shares outstanding after stock split over amount carried in capital accounts prior to the stock split.
(3) Market value of stock at date issued as 4% stock dividends.
(4) Total of common stock and capital surplus accounts of Towmotor Corporation at the date of the merger.

15

Annual Reports to Stockholders

This chapter has two purposes: to illustrate and explain published financial statements, and to discuss a few of the contemporary controversies in external reporting.

The three major financial statements we will discuss are the statement of income and retained earnings (sometimes referred to as the statement of operations), the balance sheet or statement of financial position, and the statement of changes in financial position.

To illustrate the three types of statements, we present selected financial statements and related footnotes from the 1979 Annual Report of Caterpillar Tractor Company. The general nature of each statement will be described with particular attention given to the effects that the basic concepts discussed in Chapter 1 have on the way the statement is presented. Caterpillar Tractor is used because its annual report is more comprehensive than many. The format of some of the statements and the nomenclature used are somewhat different from those used thus far but will give us an opportunity to see a "real world" report.

STATEMENT OF INCOME AND RETAINED EARNINGS

The statement of income shows for one accounting period, the change in owners' equity arising from the sale of products and service to customers, less the cost of products and services sold and less other expenses of the period. Accordingly, the statement of income shows sales, expenses, and net income *for a period of time*.

1. *Sales.* Sales represents the collectible total, in dollars, for which customers were billed for sales of products and services during the period (without regard to whether the company has yet collected for the sales).
2. *Expenses.* Expenses are the total costs, in dollars, that are incurred in connection with and are properly matched against the sales made during the period. Expenses include:
   a. cost of goods sold;
   b. selling, general, and administrative expenses;
   c. interest on money borrowed; and
   d. income taxes.
3. *Net Income for the Period.* Net income is determined by deducting expenses from sales, and then adding Other Revenue (if any). Net income is the amount, in dollars, which has been earned for the corporation's stockholders during the period, according to generally accepted accounting principles.

The statement of retained earnings shows for a period of time:

Retained Earnings at the beginning of the period.
Plus: Net Income for the period.
Less: Dividends declared this period.
Retained Earnings at the end of the period.

The statement of retained earnings may be combined into one statement with the statement of income, the combined statement called *the statement of income and retained earnings*. Caterpillar Tractor Company presents a combined statement of income and retained earnings to which it gives the title "Consolidated Results of Operations," reproduced as Statement 1.

Let us look at Statement 1, Caterpillar's comparative statements of income and retained earnings for the years 1979 and 1978. Note the following characteristics:

1. The word "consolidated" in the statement title, "Consolidated Results of Operations," is explained by the company in Note 1A as follows:

> Caterpillar Tractor Company has investments in subsidiaries, all of which are wholly owned, and in two affiliated companies, which are 50% owned. The accompanying financial statements include the accounts of Caterpillar Tractor Company and all of its subsidiaries except its two credit subsidiaries.

Business entity was the first basic concept listed in Chapter 1, and it was there noted that when ". . . one corporation owns all or most of the capital stock of other corporations, and this group of corporations is operated as a single economic unit, the external financial reports may be 'consolidated' for the group and the business entity is then identified as the *consolidated group of corporations.*"

2. The statement is expressed "in millions of dollars," shown to one decimal place. Caterpillar is unique in rounding to this extent, though an increasing number of companies are showing their statements in thousands of dollars. Caterpillar's rounding of figures to tenths of millions indicates that the figures are approximations. Thus, the company has recognized the basic concepts of *materiality* and *use of estimates and exercise of judgment.*

3. Statement 1 shows for the year 1979:

Sales	$7,613.2 million
Costs allocated to year	7,155.3 million
	457.9 million
Equity in affiliated companies and subsidiary credit companies	33.7 million
Profit for year—consolidated	$ 491.6 million

Profit per share of common stock (1979):
    assuming no dilution $5.69
    assuming full dilution $5.50

The $5.69 figure of profit per share for 1979 was obtained by dividing the $491.6 million profit for the year by the weighted average number of the company's stock outstanding. Profit per share assuming full dilution gives effect to the potential conversion of the 5.5% Convertible Subordinated Debenture and unexercised stock options. (See Note 6; on page 000.) To a stockholder, *earnings per share* is the

Statement 1

Consolidated Results of Operations for the Years Ended December 31
(Dollar amounts in millions except those stated on a per share basis)

	1979	1978
Sales	**$7,613.2**	**$7,219.2**
Costs:		
Inventories brought forward from previous year	1,522.3	1,288.6
Materials, supplies, services purchased, etc.	4,360.9	3,968.5
Wages, salaries, and contributions for employee benefits	2,262.6	2,158.6
Depreciation (portion of original cost of buildings, machinery, and equipment allocated to operations)	311.8	257.1
Interest on borrowed funds	134.0	105.8
Taxes based on income (note 5)	233.9	396.9
	8,825.5	8,175.5
Deduct: Inventories carried forward to following year	1,670.2	1,522.3
Costs allocated to year (1)	7,155.3	6,653.2
Profit of consolidated companies	457.9	566.0
Equity in profit of affiliated companies (note 9)	30.2	(.8)
Profit of subsidiary credit companies	3.5	1.1
Profit for year — consolidated	**491.6**	**566.3**
Profit employed in the business at beginning of year	2,578.1	2,173.6
	3,069.7	2,739.9
Dividends paid	181.5	161.8
Profit employed in the business at end of year	$2,888.2	$2,578.1
Profit per share of common stock (note 6):		
Assuming no dilution	$ 5.69	$ 6.56
Assuming full dilution	$ 5.50	$ 6.33
Dividends per share of common stock	$2.100	$1.875

(1) Includes cost of goods sold: 1979 — $6,172.3; 1978 — $5,583.7

Report of Independent Accountants

Peoria, Illinois
January 18, 1980

TO THE SHAREHOLDERS OF CATERPILLAR TRACTOR CO.:

In our opinion, the accompanying statements 1 through 5 present fairly (a) the financial position of Caterpillar Tractor Co. and consolidated subsidiaries at December 31, 1979 and 1978, the results of their operations and the changes in financial position for the years then ended, in conformity with generally accepted accounting principles consistently applied and (b) the historical financial data included therein. Our examinations of the statements for the years 1979 and 1978 were made in accordance with generally accepted auditing standards and accordingly included such tests of the accounting records and such other auditing procedures as we considered necessary in the circumstances. We have made similar annual examinations since incorporation of the company.

Price Waterhouse & Co.

single most important figure in the annual report, for it is one response to his question: "What has the company's management done for me this past year?"

4. The sales figure of $7,613.2 million represents the total billings made to customers of Caterpillar and its wholly owned subsidiary companies for sales of products and services in 1979. That these billings were not all collected in 1979 is indicated by the balance of $692.7 million "Receivable from customers and others" at December 31, 1979, shown on Statement 2.

5. The "costs allocated to year" of $7,155.3 million were determined in Statement 1 by:

Adding:	Costs incurred during 1979 for	
	Materials, supplies, services purchased, etc.........	$4,360.9
	Wages, salaries and contributions to employees	2,262.6
	Depreciation (portion of original cost of buildings, machinery, and equipment allocated to operations)...................	311.8
	Interest on borrowed funds.................	134.0
	Taxes based on income...................	233.9
		$7,303.2
To:	Inventories brought forward from previous year ...	1,522.3
		$8,825.5
Less:	Inventories carried forward to following year	1,670.2
Giving:	Costs allocated to year...................	$7,155.3

This presentation of "costs allocated to year" is unique with Caterpillar. In its Form 10-K filed with the Securities and Exchange Commission, Caterpillar uses a more conventional presentation. A condensed "Consolidated Statement of Income," taken from the 10-K form, is shown next.

	1976
Net Sales...............................	$7,613.2
Cost of goods sold.........................	6,172.3
	1,440.9
Deduct:	
Selling, general, and administrative expense	689.8
Other expenses (net)	59.3
	$ 749.1

	691.8
Taxes based on income......................	233.9
Profit of consolidated companies.................	457.9
Equity in profit of affiliated companies and	
profit of subsidiary credit companies............	33.7
Net Profit for Year	$ 491.6

Depreciation for the year, shown at $311.8 for 1979 in Statement 1, is included in cost of goods sold ($283.8) and in selling, general, and administrative expense (28.0) in the 10-K statement of income. Caterpillar explains "Depreciation" in Note 1C, reproduced on page 000.

6. In Statement 1, the company combines the statement of retained earnings with its statement of income by:

Adding:	Profit for year—consolidated	$ 491.6 million
To:	Profit employed in the business at	
	the beginning of the year	2,578.1 million
		3,069.7 million
Less:	Dividends paid	181.5 million
Giving:	Profit employed in the business at	
	end of year	$2,888.2 million

The $2,888.2 million figure for "profit employed in the business at end of year" appears also, of course, on the statement of financial position for December 31, 1979 (Statement 2); and the beginning-of-the year figure, $2,578.1 appears on the statement of financial position for December 31, 1978.

7. Although Statement 1 is a statement for the year 1979, it does not show all that happened in the operation of Caterpillar during the year. It doesn't show how much cash was taken in, how much cash was spent, or the change in cash during the year. It doesn't show how much the company spent for new buildings and equipment. It doesn't show how much money the company borrowed during the year. It doesn't show that the company issued additional capital stock during the year. In short, it *shows only what happened to the stockholders' interest in the corporation as a result of (1) sales to customers less related costs and expenses and (2) dividends to the stockholders.*

8. The comparative statements of income for 1979 and 1978 showed:

Sales increased . . . . $394.0 million
from $7,219.2 in 1978 to $7,613.2 in 1979 or 5.5%

While costs allocated to year increased. . . . .   502.1 million
from $6,653.2 in 1978 to $7,155.3 in 1979 or 7.5%

So that net income (exclusive of equity in profit
of affiliated companies and credit companies)
decreased. . . . .   108.1 million

from $566.0 in 1978 to $457.9 in 1979 or 19.1%

In its 1979 Annual Report (page 38) the company's management analyzed "1979 vs. 1978" as follows:

> Net sales in 1979 were $7,613.2 million, a 5.5% increase over the $7,219.2 million in 1978. The increase was due to higher selling prices directly attributable to inflationary cost increases, partially offset by a decrease in physical volume of approximately 5%. This decrease resulted from a fourth-quarter 1979 strike by the United Auto Workers union. As a result of the strike, the company incurred a loss from operations in the fourth quarter of 1979.
>
> The decrease in physical volume for the year was a significant factor contributing to the reduction in gross margin (from 22.7% to 18.9%.) Gross margin was also adversely affected by the continued weakening of the U.S. dollar and by higher depreciation, start-up, and other costs associated with the company's capital expenditure program.
>
> Higher operating costs were incurred at some subsidiaries outside the United States, as costs in local currencies translated into more U.S. dollars due to higher rates of exchange. This weakening of the U.S. dollar adversely affected profit when selling prices could not be increased proportionately. While the effect cannot be precisely measured, the amount is estimated to be in excess of $20 million after tax.
>
> Interest expense increased from $111.9 million to $139.1 million due principally to increased short-term borrowings that were needed primarily to finance higher receivables, inventories and capital expenditures. Depreciation expense increased 21.3 percent due to significant capital expenditures during 1978 and 1979. Payroll taxes increased from $128.1 million to $153.1 million primarily because of higher employment and wage rates, and social security tax increases.

STATEMENT OF FINANCIAL POSITION

The statement of financial position shows what the corporation owned (assets), what it owed (liabilities), and the remainder (stockholders' equity) as of midnight of the stated date of the statement. It is a still picture of how the corporation stood at that point in time according to the generally accepted accounting principles for such a statement.

Let us look at Statement 2, Caterpillar's comparative statements of financial position as of December 31, 1979 and December 31, 1978. Observe that:

1. Caterpillar presents its consolidated financial position at December 31, 1979, by showing the following items.

Current Assets totaling		$2,606.9 million
Less:	Current Liabilities totaling	1,386.1 million
Giving:	Net Current Assets of.	1,220.8 million
Plus:	Noncurrent Assets totaling	2,796.4 million
		4,017.2 million
Less:	Noncurrent Liabilities of.	951.9 million
Giving:	Net Assets of	$3,065.3 million
Equal to:	Ownership consisting of:	
Common stock of		$ 177.1 million
Profit employed in the business		2,888.2 million
Total stockholders' equity.		$3,065.3 million

2. This same information is presented by most companies in a statement called the balance sheet, in which the assets of the corporation are shown to equal liabilities plus owners' equity. Here is a balance sheet presentation of these figures.

CATERPILLAR TRACTOR COMPANY
Balance Sheet (using summary figures)
December 31, 1979

ASSETS		LIABILITIES AND OWNERS' EQUITY	
Current Assets.	$2,606.9	Current Liabilities.	$1,386.1
Noncurrent Assets . .	2,796.4	Noncurrent Liabilities	951.9
		Total Liabilities.	$2,338.0
		Owners Equity	3,065.3
	$5,403.3		$5,403.3

Statement 2

Consolidated Financial Position at December 31
(Millions of dollars)

	1979	1978
Current assets:		
Stated on basis of realizable values:		
Cash	$ 58.4	$ 51.0
Short-term investments	88.8	193.5
Receivable from customers and others (note 7)	692.7	767.8
Prepaid expenses and income taxes allocable to the following year	96.8	93.7
	936.7	1,106.0
Stated on basis of cost using principally "last-in, first-out" method:		
Inventories (note 1B)	1,670.2	1,522.3
	2,606.9	2,628.3
Deduct: Current liabilities:		
Notes payable (note 10)	404.2	112.6
Payable to material suppliers and others	789.5	853.5
Taxes based on income	133.4	236.7
Long-term debt due within one year	59.0	34.3
	1,386.1	1,237.1
Net current assets (statement 3)	1,220.8	1,391.2
Buildings, machinery, and equipment — net (notes 1C and 8)	2,571.7	2,218.5
Land — at original cost	66.1	62.9
Investments in affiliated companies (notes 1A and 9)	71.3	47.3
Investments in and advances to subsidiary credit companies (notes 1A and 9)	14.0	11.5
Deferred taxes based on income	23.5	(23.9)
Other assets	49.8	62.6
Total assets less current liabilities	4,017.2	3,770.1
Deduct: Long-term debt due after one year (note 11)	951.9	1,018.0
Net assets	$3,065.3	$2,752.1
Ownership (statement 4):		
Preferred stock of no par value (note 12):		
Authorized shares: 5,000,000		
Outstanding shares: none		
Common stock of no par value (note 13):		
Authorized shares: 105,000,000		
Outstanding shares: 1979 — 86,433,701; 1978 — 86,364,757	$ 177.1	$ 174.0
Profit employed in the business	2,888.2	2,578.1
	$3,065.3	$2,752.1

See notes

Notes to Financial Statements

1. Summary of significant accounting policies
A. Basis of consolidation
Caterpillar Tractor Co. has investments in subsidiaries, all of which are wholly owned, and in two affiliated companies, which are 50% owned. The accompanying financial statements include the accounts of Caterpillar Tractor Co. and all of its subsidiaries except its two credit subsidiaries. These credit subsidiaries are accounted for by the equity method; accordingly, their profit is included in the consolidated results of operations as a separate item and the consolidated financial position reflects the cost of the company's investments in and advances to these subsidiaries plus the profit retained

by them. The affiliated companies are also accounted for by the equity method.
Note 9 contains combined financial information of the affiliated companies and the credit subsidiaries.
B. Inventories
With minor exceptions, inventories are stated on the basis of the "last-in, first-out" method of inventory valuation. This method was first adopted for the major portion of inventories in 1950.
If the "first-in, first-out" method had been in use, inventories would have been $1,655.3 million and $1,388.0 million higher than reported at December 31, 1979 and 1978, respectively.

Notes continued

C. Depreciation

Depreciation is computed principally using accelerated methods ("sum-of-the-years-digits" and "declining-balance") for both income tax and financial reporting purposes. These methods result in a larger allocation of the cost of buildings, machinery, and equipment to operations in the early years of the lives of assets than does the straight-line method. If the straight-line method had always been in use, "Buildings, machinery, and equipment — net" would have been $428.9 million and $370.1 million higher than reported at December 31, 1979 and 1978, respectively, and depreciation expense for 1979 and 1978 would have been, respectively, $59.8 million and $47.1 million less.

For financial reporting purposes the depreciation rates used worldwide are principally based on the "guideline" lives established by the U.S. Internal Revenue Service. For income tax purposes the depreciation rates used are principally based on the "guideline" lives for assets acquired prior to 1971 and on the Class Life ADR System for additions after 1970.

When an asset becomes fully depreciated, its cost is eliminated from both the asset and the accumulated depreciation accounts.

D. Interest on borrowed funds

All interest costs are charged against operations as incurred.

E. Investment tax credits

Investment tax credits are accounted for on the "flow-through" method for both income tax and financial reporting purposes. This method recognizes the benefit in the year in which the assets giving rise to the credits are placed in service.

2. Foreign exchange

Exchange gains or losses result from translating certain foreign currency assets and liabilities to U.S. dollars when the relationship between the foreign currency and dollar changes. Exchange gains or losses also result from the conversion of one currency for another or the settlement of a receivable or payable at a rate different from that at which the item was recorded.

Profit for 1979 included net exchange gains of $5.2 million ($1.7 million after tax) and profit for 1978 included net exchange losses of $19.9 million ($10.9 million after tax).

3. Research and engineering costs

Research and engineering costs related to the company's products are charged against operations as incurred. Such costs totaled $283.0 million and $256.1 million in 1979 and 1978, respectively. Of these amounts, $190.5 million in 1979 and $163.0 million in 1978 were attributable to new product development and major improvements to present products. The remainder was attributable to engineering costs incurred during the early production phase as well as ongoing efforts to improve present products.

4. Pension plans

The parent company and its subsidiaries have plans covering substantially all employees. Total pension expense for the years 1979 and 1978 was $151.8 million and $133.7 million, respectively. It is the company's policy to fund pension expense as it accrues.

The computed value of vested benefits exceeded the amount of pension funds at December 31, 1979 by approximately $445 million. The value of vested benefits is an actuarially determined amount representing the present value of the benefits expected to be paid to employees to the extent of their vested rights at the determination date. The excess of the value of the vested benefits over the amount of pension funds results primarily from increases in pension costs related to prior service, which are amortized and funded over periods not to exceed 30 years.

5. Taxes based on income

Taxes charged against operations comprise the following:

	1979	1978
	(Millions of dollars)	
Taxes currently paid or payable	$271.6	$395.9
Tax effect of timing differences	(37.7)	1.0
Taxes based on income	$233.9	$396.9

The timing differences relate primarily to pension expense, unrealized profit excluded from inventories, asset lives used for determining depreciation, and capitalization policy for certain tooling.

Taxes based on income were less than would result from applying the U.S. statutory rate to profit before tax for the reasons set forth in the following reconciliation:

	1979		1978	
	(Millions of dollars)			
Taxes based on income computed at 46% (1979) and 48% (1978)		$318.2		$462.2
Increases (decreases) in taxes resulting from:				
Subsidiaries subject to tax rates other than 46% (1979) and 48% (1978)	$ (2.3)		$(33.1)	
Investment tax credits (note 1E)	(71.8)		(44.1)	
Benefit of Domestic International Sales Corporations	(32.8)		(12.2)	
State income taxes — net of federal tax	14.0		17.8	
All other — net	8.6	(84.3)	6.3	(65.3)
Taxes based on income		$233.9		$396.9

During 1979, two matters related to examinations of certain prior years' tax returns by the U.S. Internal Revenue Service were resolved. The first resulted in the capitalization, for income tax purposes, of certain tooling items previously charged to expense for both financial reporting and income tax purposes. This increased investment tax credits recorded in 1979 by $17.9 million. The second matter related to the company's successful litigation of a dispute concerning the qualification of a Domestic International Sales Corporation (DISC). This resulted in additional DISC benefits recorded in 1979 of $23.4 million.

U.S. taxes on income, net of foreign taxes paid or payable, have been provided on the undistributed profits of subsidiaries and affiliated companies, except in those instances where such profits have been permanently invested and are not considered to be available for distribution to the parent company. In accordance with this policy, the consolidated "Profit employed in the business" at December 31, 1979 included approximately $700 million of undistributed profits of subsidiaries and affiliated companies on which U.S. taxes on income, net of foreign taxes paid or payable, have not been provided. If for some reason not presently contemplated such profits were to be remitted or otherwise become subject to U.S. income tax, available credits would reduce the amount of tax otherwise due.

6. Profit per share information

Profit per share of common stock (assuming no dilution) is computed using the weighted average number of shares outstanding during the respective periods.

Profit per share of common stock (assuming full dilution) gives effect to the potential conversion of the 5½% Convertible Subordinated Debentures (convertible into common stock at $50.50 per share) and unexercised stock options.

7. Receivable from customers and others

Receivables at December 31, 1979 included $63.7 million evidenced by promissory notes from dealers and customers. Approximately $25.7 million of these notes mature beyond one year but were included in current assets in accordance with the accounting practice followed within the industry.

8. Buildings, machinery, and equipment — net

Buildings, machinery, and equipment — net at December 31, by major classification, were as follows:

	1979	1978
	(Millions of dollars)	
Buildings	$1.472.8	$1.298.7
Machinery and equipment	2.736.9	2.338.3
	4.209.7	3.637.0
Deduct: Accumulated depreciation	1.638.0	1.418.5
Buildings, machinery, and equipment — net	$2.571.7	$2.218.5

The company had commitments for the purchase or construction of fixed assets amounting to approximately $635 million at December 31, 1979. Capital expenditure plans are subject to continuous monitoring and changes in such plans could reduce the amount committed.

9. Investments in unconsolidated companies

Affiliated companies

The company's investments in affiliated companies consist of 50% interests in Caterpillar Mitsubishi Ltd., Japan ($70.0 million), and in Tractor Engineers Limited, India ($1.3 million). The other 50% owners of these companies are, respectively, Mitsubishi Heavy Industries, Ltd., Tokyo, Japan, and Larsen & Toubro Limited, Bombay, India.

Combined financial information of these affiliated companies for their most recent fiscal years, as translated to U.S. dollars, is as follows:

	September 30.	
	1979	1978
Financial Position	(Millions of dollars)	
Assets		
Current assets	$661.9	$670.2
Land, buildings, machinery, and equipment — net	108.4	96.8
Other assets	33.2	39.1
	803.5	806.1
Deduct: Liabilities		
Current liabilities	472.8	530.5
Long-term debt (including subordinated debentures)	142.6	131.0
Other liabilities	43.1	48.0
	658.5	709.5
Ownership	$145.0	$ 96.6
Company share of ownership — 50%	$ 72.5	$ 48.3
Intercompany adjustments	(1.2)	(1.0)
Investments in affiliated companies	$ 71.3	$ 47.3

	Years ended September 30.	
	1979	1978
Results of Operations	(Millions of dollars)	
Sales	$901.3	$721.9
Profit after tax	$ 60.8	$ (1.1)
Company share of profit — 50%	$ 30.4	$ (.6)
Intercompany adjustments	(.2)	(.2)
Equity in profit of affiliated companies	$ 30.2	$ (.8)

Profit after tax for the combined affiliated companies in 1979 and 1978 would have been approximately $43.7 million and $26.2 million, respectively, if exchange gains and losses were excluded. The intercompany adjustments result primarily from the exclusion of unrealized profit from inventory.

Certain products are sold to and purchased from the affiliated companies at intercompany prices. In addition, the company received license fees under a license agreement with Caterpillar Mitsubishi Ltd. The total amount of these transactions with the affiliated companies was not material in relation to consolidated results of operations.

Credit subsidiaries

The two credit subsidiaries, Caterpillar Credit Corporation (U.S.) and Caterpillar Overseas Credit Corporation S.A. (Switzerland), assist dealers in the financing of sales of the company's products. At December 31, 1979, the total assets of these two companies were $63.4 million.

10. Short-term debt

The company has arrangements with several U.S. and non-U.S. banks to provide short-term lines of credit. These credit lines, which averaged $791 million (U.S. $367 million and non-U.S. $424 million) during 1979, are changed as the company's anticipated needs vary and are not indicative of the company's short-term borrowing capacity.

The company maintains compensating balances with U.S. banks which average 10% of the total U.S. lines of credit. Compensating balances maintained for the credit lines outside the U.S. were negligible.

Average month-end short-term borrowings during 1979 were $375 million and the approximate weighted average interest rate, significantly influenced by borrowings in Brazil, was 17.1%. At December 31, 1979, the company had confirmed short-term credit lines totaling $800 million of which $709 million was unused. Of the unused portion, $314 million was considered as support for outstanding commercial paper borrowings.

11. Long-term debt

Debt due after one year at December 31 consisted of the following:

	1979	1978
By parent company:	(Millions of dollars)	
Notes — 8.375% due 1982	$100.0	$ 100.0
Debentures — 5.125% due 1981-1986	14.5	14.5
Debentures — 5.30% due 1981-1992	90.0	97.5
Debentures — 6.875% due 1981-1992	76.0	82.0
Debentures — 8.60% due 1985-1999	150.0	150.0
Debentures — 8.75% due 1985-1999	100.0	100.0
Debentures — 8.0% due 1987-2001	200.0	200.0
Debentures — 5.50% due 1986-2000 — convertible subordinated	199.7	199.7
Other	7.8	7.9
By subsidiaries:		
Equivalent to	13.9	66.4
Long-term debt due after one year	$951.9	$1,018.0

The foregoing long-term debt at December 31, 1979 was payable as follows:

	(Millions of dollars)
1981	$ 27.6
1982	116.7
1983	16.5
1984	16.5
1985-1989	230.4
1990-1994	227.6
1995-1999	185.7
2000-2001	130.9
	$951.9

12. Preferred stock

The Board of Directors is authorized to issue up to 5,000,000 shares of preferred stock in series and to determine the number of shares and the dividend, conversion, voting, redemption, liquidation, and other terms of each series. As of December 31, 1979, none of the shares had been issued.

13. Stock options

In April 1970 and April 1977, shareholders approved plans providing for the granting to officers and other key employees of options to purchase common stock of the company. Options granted under both plans carry prices equal to the market price on the date of grant.

Stock appreciation rights may be granted as part of 1977 Plan options or as separate rights to holders of options previously granted under the 1977 Plan. A stock appreciation right permits an option holder to surrender an exercisable option or portion thereof and receive in exchange shares of common stock, cash, or a combination of both. The aggregate amount to be received will have a value equal to the excess of the fair market value of one share of stock, at the date of surrender, over the

Notes continued

option price multiplied by the number of shares covered by the option or portion thereof surrendered.

Changes during 1979 in shares subject to issuance under options were as follows:

	Shares
Options outstanding at December 31, 1978	1,140,623
Exercised	(69,485)
Lapsed	(4,700)
Options outstanding at December 31, 1979	1,066,438
Comprising:	
At average price of $31.59 per share	86,688
At average price of $44.54 per share	254,350
At average price of $55.48 per share	725,400
	1,066,438

No options were granted during 1979. At December 31, 1979, authority existed to grant future options for 477,350 common shares under the 1977 Plan.

14. Litigation

The company is a party to litigation matters and claims which are normal in the course of its operations, and while the results of litigation and claims cannot be predicted with certainty, based on advice of counsel, management believes that the final outcome of such matters will not have a materially adverse effect on the consolidated financial position.

15. Segment information

Business segments

The company is engaged in the manufacture and sale of earthmoving, construction, and materials handling machinery and equipment (Machinery and Equipment), such as track-type tractors, bulldozers, rippers, track and wheel loaders, lift trucks, pipelayers, motor graders, wheel dozers, compactors, wheel tractor-scrapers, hydraulic excavators, log skidders, off-highway trucks and related parts and equipment. The company also manufactures diesel engines for incorporation in its machines, and diesel and natural gas engines for sale as on-highway truck engines, marine and industrial engines, electric power generation systems, and related parts and equipment (Engines). Data on these business segments are as follows:

	1979	1978	1977
	(Millions of dollars)		
For the years ended December 31			
Sales to unaffiliated customers			
Machinery and equipment	$6,475.5	$6,162.5	$5,077.7
Engines	1,137.7	1,056.7	771.2
Transfers between business segments			
Engines	542.6	576.5	487.7
Eliminations	(542.6)	(576.5)	(487.7)
Consolidated sales	**$7,613.2**	**$7,219.2**	**$5,848.9**
Operating profit			
Machinery and equipment	$ 817.0	$ 956.3	$ 804.3
Engines	124.4	234.0	155.6
Eliminations	8.9	(1.3)	3.9
	950.3	1,189.0	963.8
General corporate expenses	(204.5)	(168.3)	(131.6)
Interest on borrowed funds	(134.0)	(105.8)	(95.4)
Miscellaneous income	80.0	48.0	40.3
Taxes based on income	(233.9)	(396.9)	(334.1)
Equity in profit of unconsolidated companies	33.7	.3	2.1
Profit for year — consolidated	**$ 491.6**	**$ 566.3**	**$ 445.1**
Capital expenditures			
Machinery and equipment	$ 473.8	$ 377.4	$ 329.3
Engines	182.6	145.9	168.4
General corporate	19.5	20.1	18.7
	$ 675.9	$ 543.4	$ 516.4
Depreciation			
Machinery and equipment	$ 205.9	$ 173.7	$ 151.4
Engines	99.1	79.0	57.4
General corporate	6.8	4.4	1.7
	$ 311.8	$ 257.1	$ 210.5

31

At December 31			
Identifiable assets			
Machinery and equipment	$3,778.4	$3,427.9	$2,911.1
Engines	1,332.1	1,200.4	1,012.1
Eliminations	(15.7)	(24.6)	(23.3)
	5,094.8	4,603.7	3,899.9
General corporate assets	223.2	368.6	373.2
Investments in unconsolidated companies	85.3	58.8	72.5
Total assets	$5,403.3	$5,031.1	$4,345.6

The major portion of transfers between business segments occurs within the parent company. Transfer values reflect cost and a proportionate share of total operating profit. The high degree of integration of the company's manufacturing operations necessitates the use of a substantial number of allocations in the preparation of the business segment information.

Geographic segments

Manufacturing activities are carried on in 14 plants in the United States, three in the United Kingdom, two each in Brazil and France, and one each in Australia, Belgium, Canada, and Mexico. Four major parts warehousing and distributing facilities are located in the United States and eight are located abroad.

The product of manufacturing operations located outside the United States in most instances consists of components manufactured or purchased abroad which are assembled with components manufactured in the United States and transferred at intercompany prices. As a result, the profits of these operations do not bear any definite relationship to their assets. The company's intercompany pricing philosophy is that prices between Caterpillar companies are established at levels deemed equivalent to those which would prevail in arm's length transactions. Data on the company's geographic segments, based on the location of the manufacturing operation, are as follows:

	1979	1978	1977
	(Millions of dollars)		
For the years ended December 31			
Sales to unaffiliated customers			
United States	$5,982.1	$5,905.7	$4,740.0
Europe	1,115.7	917.1	773.8
All other	515.4	396.4	335.1
Transfers between geographic areas			
United States	147.6	149.6	161.8
Europe	4.7	5.2	5.9
All other	1.9	1.2	—
Eliminations	(154.2)	(156.0)	(167.7)
Consolidated sales	**$7,613.2**	**$7,219.2**	**$5,848.9**
Operating profit			
United States	$ 871.6	$1,114.0	$ 872.5
Europe	46.9	61.3	77.4
All other	30.8	14.8	15.0
Eliminations	1.0	(1.1)	(1.1)
	950.3	1,189.0	963.8
General corporate expenses	(204.5)	(168.3)	(131.6)
Interest on borrowed funds	(134.0)	(105.8)	(95.4)
Miscellaneous income	80.0	48.0	40.3
Taxes based on income	(233.9)	(396.9)	(334.1)
Equity in profit of unconsolidated companies	33.7	.3	2.1
Profit for year — consolidated	**$ 491.6**	**$ 566.3**	**$ 445.1**
At December 31			
Identifiable assets			
United States	$4,054.5	$3,712.9	$3,150.1
Europe	642.2	538.3	486.4
All other	413.0	378.7	284.3
Eliminations	(14.9)	(26.2)	(20.9)
	5,094.8	4,603.7	3,899.9
General corporate assets	223.2	368.6	373.2
Investments in unconsolidated companies	85.3	58.8	72.5
Total assets	$5,403.3	$5,031.1	$4,345.6

Data on the company's sales outside the United States, based on dealer location, are as follows:

	Europe	Africa, Middle East	Canada	Latin America	Australasia	Sales outside United States
			(Millions of dollars)			
1979						
Export sales of U.S. manufactured product	$ 488.5	$579.6	$427.5	$476.4	$527.9	$2,499.9
Sales of non-U.S. manufactured product	664.8	380.6	77.4	239.7	236.1	1,598.6
Total	$1,153.3	$960.2	$504.9	$716.1	$764.0	$4,098.5
1978						
Export sales of U.S. manufactured product	$ 412.9	$496.6	$370.1	$505.8	$398.7	$2,184.1
Sales of non-U.S. manufactured product	519.0	370.0	61.7	168.1	166.7	1,285.5
Total	$ 931.9	$866.6	$431.8	$673.9	$565.4	$3,469.6
1977						
Export sales of U.S. manufactured product	$ 340.5	$508.9	$279.1	$438.2	$290.9	$1,857.6
Sales of non-U.S. manufactured product	398.3	375.9	53.5	161.8	119.4	1,108.9
Total	$ 738.8	$884.8	$332.6	$600.0	$410.3	$2,966.5

Sales outside the United States were 53.8% of consolidated sales in 1979, 48.1% in 1978, and 50.7% in 1977.

---

16. Changing price levels (required supplementary information — unaudited)

The following information on constant dollar restatement of the company's consolidated profit and other financial data is prepared and presented in accordance with Statement of Financial Accounting Standards No. 33 — *Financial Reporting and Changing Prices*.

Adjustments to profit

Constant average 1979 dollars have been used as the basis to restate consolidated profit to reflect the estimated effects of general inflation. Most revenues and expenses, by occurring relatively uniformly throughout the year, are assumed to be approximately the same in nominal dollars and constant average dollars.

In the company's circumstances, the only profit component requiring restatement is depreciation — that portion of the original cost of buildings, machinery, and equipment allocated to operations. Those original costs, incurred over a number of years, were stated in dollars having various units of purchasing power. Depreciation has been restated in constant average 1979 dollars by using the changes in the Consumer Price Index for all Urban Consumers (CPI-U) to represent the rate of general inflation. The restatement is based upon the same methods, useful lives, and salvage values used for nominal dollar depreciation.

Inventory related expenses included in cost of goods sold are virtually the same in nominal dollars and constant average dollars because of the use of the "last-in, first-out" method of inventory valuation (note 1B).

Taxes based on income have not been restated since current tax laws do not permit adjustments to recognize the effects of general inflation. As a result, the effective income tax rate for 1979 increased from 33.8% on a nominal dollar basis to 38.8% on a constant dollar basis.

The company's financial accounting policies and methods tend to reflect the effects of general inflation in the determination of the results of operations. As a result, the adjustment to restate consolidated profit in constant average 1979 dollars is relatively minor.

Purchasing power gain on monetary items

When prices are increasing, the holding of cash and claims to cash results in a loss of general purchasing power because a given amount of money will buy less at the end of a year than it would have bought at the beginning of the year. Similarly, liabilities are associated with a gain of general purchasing power because the amount of money required to settle the liability represents a decreasing amount of purchasing power. These gains and losses of purchasing power (net) have been computed using the CPI-U and are shown below as "Gain from decline in purchasing power of net monetary liabilities."

Adjustments for changes in the general purchasing power of the U.S. dollar for the year ended December 31, 1979
(Millions of dollars)

Profit for year — consolidated (statement 1)		$491.6
Adjustments to restate costs for the effects of general inflation:		
Depreciation — Cost of goods sold	$(81.6)	
— Other	(8.0)	(89.6)
Profit restated in constant average 1979 dollars		$402.0
Gain from decline in purchasing power of net monetary liabilities, in constant average 1979 dollars		$153.1

Five-year summary

The following five-year information has been adjusted, based on changes in the CPI-U, to restate nominal dollars to constant average 1979 dollars. Adjustments have been made to net assets presented in Statement 2 for inventories, land, buildings, machinery, and equipment. Differences between values for the other components of net assets expressed in terms of nominal dollars and constant dollars are insignificant.

Notes continued

**1975-1979 data adjusted for changes in
the general purchasing power of the U.S. dollar**

	1975	1976	1977	1978	1979
			Years ended December 31.		
Millions of constant average 1979 dollars:					
Sales	$6.694.2	$6.429.3	$7.005.8	$8.032.0	$7.613.2
Profit — consolidated	478.4	427.0	469.4	557.1	402.0
Net assets at year-end	3.889.3	4.195.1	4.557.3	5.019.6	5.368.8
Gain from decline in purchasing power of net monetary liabilities	78.3	57.4	137.5	103.4	153.1
Constant average 1979 dollars:					
Per share of common stock					
Profit assuming no dilution	$ 5.57	$ 4.96	$ 5.44	$ 6.45	$ 4.65
Dividends	$ 1.66	$ 1.86	$ 1.89	$ 2.09	$ 2.10
Market price at year-end	$60.79	$72.34	$64.10	$62.95	$51.09
Average consumer price index	161.2	170.5	181.5	195.4	217.4

17. Replacement cost (unaudited)

The Securities and Exchange Commission requires the computation and disclosure of the replacement cost of inventories and productive capacity (buildings, machinery, and equipment) and the related impact on cost of sales and depreciation.

The company has applied the "last-in, first-out" valuation method to the major portion of its inventories since 1950. Therefore, the replacement cost of inventories would be higher than the inventory value recorded in the accounts. Cost of sales based on replacement cost,

however, would approximate the cost of sales using the "last-in, first-out" method of inventory valuation.

The replacement cost of productive capacity would be higher than the historical cost of such assets and, accordingly, replacement depreciation would be higher.

This generalized statement on replacement cost is furnished pursuant to specific commission guidelines and reference should be made to the more detailed and quantitative replacement cost data included in the company's 1979 Form 10-K to be filed with the commission.

18. Selected quarterly financial data (unaudited)

Financial data for the interim periods of 1979 and 1978 were as follows (dollar amounts in millions except those stated on a per share basis):

	1979 Quarter				1978 Quarter			
	1st	2nd	3rd	4th	1st	2nd	3rd	4th
Net sales	$1.923.7	$2.136.7	$2.232.2	$1.320.6	$1.630.1	$1.843.7	$1.816.8	$1.928.6
Gross profit	394.7	461.5	471.6	113.1	380.7	437.7	408.7	408.4
Profit for period	132.3	165.1	167.8	26.4	119.4	150.2	139.2	157.5
Per share of common stock								
Profit assuming no dilution	$1.53	$1.91	$1.94	$ .31	$1.38	$1.74	$1.62	$1.82
Profit assuming full dilution	$1.48	$1.84	$1.87	$ .31	$1.34	$1.68	$1.55	$1.76
Dividends paid	$.525	$.525	$.525	$.525	$.450	$.450	$.450	$.525

Sales and profit for the fourth quarter of 1979 were adversely affected by an extended strike by the United Auto Workers union. As a result, the company incurred a loss from operations. However, this was more than offset by favorable income tax adjustments and profit from unconsolidated companies, principally Caterpillar Mitsubishi Ltd.

Statement 3

Changes in Consolidated Financial Position
(Millions of dollars)

	1979	1978
Additions to net current assets from:		
Operations:		
Profit for year	$ 491.6	$ 566.3
Items affecting profit for year, but not affecting net current assets:		
Depreciation	311.8	257.1
Deferred taxes based on income	(47.4)	(12.1)
Equity in profit of affiliated companies	(30.2)	.8
Profit of subsidiary credit companies	(3.5)	(1.1)
Net current assets provided from operations	722.3	811.0
Long-term debt	2.8	91.4
Capital assets sold or scrapped	4.2	2.8
Common stock sold for cash under stock options	3.1	4.5
Common stock issued upon conversion of convertible debentures	—	.3
Dividends from affiliated companies	6.0	7.1
Dividends from subsidiary credit companies	1.0	—
Reduction in advances to subsidiary credit companies	—	8.7
Reclassification of other assets	10.8	—
Other	5.7	(4.7)
	755.9	921.1
Reductions of net current assets for:		
Cash dividends	181.5	161.8
Land, buildings, machinery, and equipment	675.9	543.4
Long-term debt	68.9	84.4
Reclassification of receivables	—	36.8
	926.3	826.4
Increase or (decrease) in net current assets during year	(170.4)	94.7
Net current assets at beginning of year	1,391.2	1,296.5
Net current assets at end of year	$1,220.8	$1,391.2
Increase or (decrease) in components of net current assets:		
Cash and short-term investments	$ (97.3)	$ 35.1
Receivable from customers and others	(75.1)	119.7
Prepaid expenses and income taxes allocable to the following year	3.1	(12.5)
Inventories	147.9	233.7
Net change in current assets	(21.4)	376.0
Notes payable	291.6	25.3
Payable to material suppliers and others	(64.0)	175.8
Taxes based on income	(103.3)	58.5
Long-term debt due within one year	24.7	21.7
Net change in current liabilities	149.0	281.3
Increase or (decrease) in net current assets during year	**$ (170.4)**	**$ 94.7**

See notes

This statement says, in effect, that the corporation owns property totaling $5,403.3 million for two classes of people, creditors and stockholders, whose interests in the assets are $2,338.0 million and $3,065.3 million respectively.

3. Caterpillar shows the individual asset items in Statement 2 at a hodgepodge of valuations:

	SHOWN AT
Cash and receivables.	Realizable values
Inventories.	Last-in, first-out cost
Buildings, machinery, and equipment	Balance of original cost allocable to future operations
Land.	Original cost
Investment in affiliated companies and subsidiary credit companies.	Cost plus profit retained by affiliate or subsidiary

In 1947, Mr. W. Blackie, then Caterpillar vice-president, commented on the company's adoption of the *financial position* form:

> While the statement of financial position reflects totals which are, of themselves, useful it should nevertheless be thoroughly understood that these totals are composed of elements which are not homogeneous. Recognition of this accounting fact is, in our opinion, fundamental to any proper interpretation of the statement, and it is particularly important that readers realize the limited extent to which current realization values find a place among the conventional and historical bases for asset accounting.[1]

Note: Compare Mr. Blackie's comments with the basic concepts of *going concern* and *historical dollar accounting*.

4. The company explains its basis of stating inventories in Note 18, duplicated on page 000. While Caterpillar uses the last-in, first-out (LIFO) method of allocating costs against sales revenues, many other companies use other methods, such as first-in, first-out (FIFO), or average.[2] Such differences in cost allocation methods between

---

[1] *Financial Statements for Corporate Annual Reports*, by W. Blackie, *The Journal of Accountancy*, March, 1947.

[2] The various methods of allocating costs between cost of goods sold and costs of inventory at the end of the year—first-in, first-out (FIFO), last-in, first-out (LIFO), and the average—are explained in Chapter 8.

companies illustrate the basic concept of *diversity in accounting among independent entities*. And the further fact that Caterpillar has used last-in, first-out consistently from January 1, 1950, illustrates the basic concept of *consistency between periods for the same entity*.

5. The company shows "Buildings, machinery, and equipment— net" at $2,571.7 million for December 31, 1979. In Note 8, the company gives further details that we can summarize:

	December 31, 1979
Buildings, machinery, & equipment at original cost	$4,209.7 million
Deduct: Accumulated depreciation (portion of original cost allocated to operations to date) . .	1,638.0 million
Balance of original cost not allocated to operations to date	$2,571.7 million

The $4,209.7 million represents the dollar cost of buildings, machinery, and equipment acquired in many different years with dollars of varying purchasing power. The $2,571.7 million residual figure also represents dollars of varying purchasing power; it does not reflect either liquidating value or current replacement cost at December 31, 1979. Note again the effect of the basic concepts of *going concern* and *historical dollar accounting*.

Reproduced below is a note regarding replacement cost included in Caterpillar's 10-K report for 1979 filed with the SEC:

Replacement Cost (unaudited)

The Securities and Exchange Commission requires the computation and disclosure of the replacement cost of inventories and productive capacity (buildings, machinery and equipment) and the related impact on cost of sales and depreciation. The Commission anticipates that the replacement cost data will provide information not otherwise available in historical cost statements by demonstrating the impact of inflation and technological change on inventories and productive capacity. While the rules require the determination of replacement cost, generally accepted accounting principles to be followed in such computations have not been established.

There are inherent imprecisions in and general limitations on the usefulness of the replacement cost data being presented. The computations are based on several major hypothetical assumptions: (1) that the Company would replace its entire inventory and productive capacity at the end of its fiscal year; (2) that the funds were available to do so; (3) that such instantaneous replacements were physically possible; and (4) that such replacement would be accomplished without redesign, relocation or other attendant improvements.

The replacement data presented is not appropriate for use in determining economic income. In this hypothetical situation, the Company would expect substantial changes in other income determinants such as labor costs, maintenance and repairs, and utility costs which cannot reasonably be quantified and, therefore, these operating cost changes, which would result from the replacement of existing assets with assets of improved technology, are not reflected in the basic data provided. Also, because of the subjective judgments and specific circumstances involved, the data will not be fully comparable among companies and will be subject to variations in the methods of estimation employed.

Following is a summary comparison of the historical and replacement cost data for 1979 (in millions of U.S. dollars):

	Historical Cost	Replacement Cost
At December 31, 1979:		
Inventories.	$1,670.2	$3,370.1
Buildings, machinery, and equipment (productive capacity)		
Gross amount	4,209.7	8,348.0
Undepreciated amount	2,571.7	4,320.1
For the Year Ended December 31, 1979:		
Cost of goods sold, including $283.8 of historical cost depreciation and $353.4 of replacement cost depreciation	$6,172.3	$6,231.7
Other depreciation expense	28.0	34.8

The Company follows a policy of eliminating the cost of an asset from both the asset and accumulated depreciation accounts when the asset becomes fully depreciated. The historical cost gross amount of Buildings, machinery and equipment does not include such fully depreciated assets still in service which had an historical cost of $457.7 million; however, those assets are included in the replacement cost gross amount of Buildings, machinery and equipment at an estimated replacement cost of $1,437.7 million. Included in both the gross and undepreciated amounts of Buildings, machinery and equipment for historical and replacement cost is $458.9 million of construction in process.

For historical cost purposes Inventories, with minor exceptions, are stated on the basis of the "last-in, first-out" method of inventory valuation. This method was first adopted for the major portion of inventories in 1950. Depreciation is computed principally using accelerated methods.

The replacement cost of Inventories was computed using December 1979 cost levels. Cost of goods sold (excluding depreciation) was computed based on the cost levels experienced at the time of sale.

The replacement cost of productive capacity (Buildings, machinery and equipment) was calculated by its various components. The replacement cost of buildings was computed by applying related published indices to the total of existing facilities by year of acquisition. The replacement cost of machinery and equipment was determined in two parts. First, machinery and equipment, by year of acquisition, was adjusted for inflation by applying indices to the respective major classes of equipment. Second, a further adjustment was made to the price-adjusted amount to reflect technological improvement. This overall degree of technological change was based on the Company's experience in replacing its productive capacity. Replacement cost depreciation was computed by applying the straight-line method to the average replacement cost. Asset lives used in computing historical cost depreciation were maintained for purposes of determining replacement cost depreciation.

6. Statement 2 shows that stockholders' equity at December 31, 1979, consists of:

Common stock (outstanding shares 86,433,701)	$ 177.1 million
Profit employed in the business	2,888.2 million
	$3,065.3

In a separate and unique statement, "Source of Consolidated Net Assets," Caterpillar shows a chronological summary, from 1925 through 1979, of how common stock and profit-employed-in-the-business (retained earnings) came to be shown at December 31, 1979, at $177.1 million and $2,888.2 million respectively:

Common stock:
Amount paid into the corporation by the stockholders
(a) for shares issued at the formation of the
corporation in 1925, and (b) for the additional
shares issued since . . . . $ 119.8 million
Transfer from "profit employed" on account of
stock dividends, stock split-ups, etc. . . . .   57.3 million

    Total for common stock at 12/31/79 . . . . $ 177.1 million

Profit employed in the business:
Total profit earned in the years 1925-1979. . . . . $4,828.5 million
Less: Cash dividends to stockholders $1,883.0
    Transfers to common stock on account of
    stock dividends, stock split-ups, etc. . . . . . .   57.3   1,940.3 million

Accumulated undistributed profit employed
in the business at 12/31/79 . . . . $2,888.2 million

STATEMENT OF CHANGES IN
FINANCIAL POSITION

The increases and decreases between the comparative statements of financial position as of December 31, 1978, and December 31, 1979, are summarized in the company's Statement of Changes in Financial Position for 1979, Statement 3.

The statement of changes in financial position summarizes significant financial *changes* that have occurred between the beginning and end of a company's accounting period. The statement is based upon comparative statements of financial position (balance sheets) at the current year-end and the previous year-end, and upon selected information taken from the statement of income and retained earnings for the current year and from other sources. The year's increases and decreases in various balance sheet items are rearranged according to the sources and application of funds. The concept of *funds* used in many corporation annual reports is *net current assets* (also called *working capital* or *net working capital*). This concept is used by Caterpillar in Statement 3.

Statement 3 shows that in 1979:

Additions to net current assets came from
Net income before deduction of depreciation and other
items (which did not involve an outlay of net
current assets). . . . . $722.3 million
Increase in long-term debt. . . . .   2.8 million
Miscellaneous sources. . . . .   30.8 million
                                                                          $755.9 million

Reductions of net current assets were required for
Cash dividends $181.5
Additions to land, buildings, machinery and
equipment 675.9
Reduction of long-term debt . . . .   68.9 $926.3 million

So net current assets decreased between
December 31, 1978 and December 31, 1979. . . . . $170.4 million

The information presented in the statement of changes in financial position may be used to prepare a cash flow statement as discussed in Chapter 5.

AUDITOR'S OPINION

At the bottom of Statement 1 is a "Report of Independent Accountants" signed by Price Waterhouse & Co. This report is often referred to as the *auditor's opinion.*

The opinion states that:

1. The statements present "fairly" and "in conformity with generally accepted accounting principles."
2. These accounting principles were applied consistently.
3. The auditor's examination was made "in accordance with generally accepted *auditing* standards."

The opinion as presented for Caterpillar is an unqualified, or *clean,* opinion. If the auditor cannot give an unqualified opinion, he may give a qualified opinion, an adverse opinion, or a disclaimer of an opinion. Adverse opinions and disclaimers of opinions are rarely encountered in published annual reports.

SOME CONTROVERSIES IN CONTEMPORARY ACCOUNTING

Responsibility for Establishing Generally Accepted Accounting Principles

In late 1976, the Senate Subcommittee (Metcalf) on Reports, Accounting, and Management of the Committee on Government Operations issued a staff study that recommended, among other things, that financial accounting standards for publicly owned companies be established by the federal government.

In Chapter 1, we discussed the evolution of the various bodies responsible for establishing generally accepted accounting principles. Some people believe that neither the APB, the FASB, nor the SEC have taken the leadership role necessary to establish accounting standards or principles.

In 1980, the SEC had the authority to establish standards and the FASB, in effect, had the responsibility. The "Metcalf" report is sure to generate discussion and controversy over public and private sector responsibilities for years to come.

Objectives of Financial Statements

Many people have argued that it is difficult to establish accounting standards if the objectives of financial statements are not clearly defined. One of the first considerations of the FASB after its formation was a "Conceptual Framework for Financial Accounting and Reporting." In November 1978, the FASB issued a *Statement of Financial Accounting Concepts No. 1—Objectives of Financial Reporting by Business Enterprises.* The objectives in the Statement pertain to general external financial reporting and are not restricted to information cummunicated by financial statements. Later statements are expected to cover the elements of financial statements and their recognition, measurement, and display as well as other related matters such as unit of measurement.

Uniformity vs. Flexibility

Flexibility has been particularly bothersome to critics of the status of accounting standards. Critics say that there is too much leeway in the application of accounting standards, and that therefore the financial statements of different companies are not comparable. The proponents of flexibility argue that uniformity could lead to less comparability because of differences in the ways in which companies operate. Today, companies must disclose their accounting policies in their annual report, so there is some data available for putting statements of different companies on a comparable basis for analytical purposes.

Historical Cost and the Unit of Measurement

Inflation has been a major concern for businessmen and the accounting profession in recent years. As the inflation rate rose above 5 percent, more people realized that an inflationary environment affects business decisions and the reported results of these decisions.

In 1976, the SEC issued Accounting Series Release No. 190, which required certain companies to show, in a note or separate statement in their annual 10-K report, information pertaining to the replacement cost of inventories and property, plant, and equipment.

In September 1979, the FASB issued a *Statement of Financial Reporting and Changing Prices* (No. 33). This Statement requires public enterprises that have more than $125 million of inventories and gross properties, or more than $1 billion of assets, to disclose the effects of both general inflation and specific price changes as supplementary information in their published annual reports. These public enterprises with fiscal years ended before December 25, 1980, may be presented in the first annual report for a fiscal year ended on or after December 25, 1980.

Caterpillar presented this supplementary information in Note 16. The FASB is now developing plans for evaluating the usefulness of information required by the Statement. Chapter 17 discusses, in greater detail, the requirements of this FASB Statement 33.

There is a common agreement that present financial statements based on historical cost are a mixture of "apples and oranges." However, there is no agreement on the common denominator for measurement. A significant amount of research on accounting for inflation is being done around the world. This research should lead to a better understanding of the implications of measuring economic activity in terms other than historical costs.

Materiality

The concept of materiality was discussed in Chapter 1. There has been no established criteria for what is material, and many have believed that this lack has allowed abuses in financial reporting, particularly in the area of appropriate disclosure. The FASB has issued a discussion memorandum on materiality that should lead to standards establishing criteria for determining materiality.

Interim Reporting

Traditionally, interim financial statements have not been *audited* statements and have not necessarily met the reporting standards of annual reports. The FASB has established a task force to reconsider APB Opinion No. 28, *Interim Financial Reporting*.

Pensions

Accounting for pensions was discussed in Chapter 12. Although APB Opinion No. 8 narrowed considerably the latitude in determining pension costs, many people still think that there is too much difference between the minimum and maximum standards established in APB Opinion No. 8. In March 1980, the FASB issued a *Statement of Accounting and Reporting by Defined Benefit Pension Plans* (No. 35), and in May 1980, issued FASB Statement No. 36 on the disclosure of pension information. The FASB is doing further work in the pension area.

Business Combinations

The distinction between a business combination treated for accounting purposes as a "purchase" and one treated as a "pooling of interests" was discussed in Chapter 11. Suffice it to say that this distinction is also under continuing study by the FASB.

Other Controversies

In the chapters related to financial accounting in this book, we have discussed accounting primarily in terms of prevailing practice. A number of areas that have been covered are still considered unsettled and controversial. Among these are:

1. extraordinary items and prior period adjustments,
2. interperiod Income Tax allocation,
3. reporting for segments of a business,
4. earnings-per-share calculations, and
5. foreign currency translation.

A reader of current business periodicals will be familiar with these controversies. Many of the arguments for and against certain accounting treatments can be found in APB opinions and FASB publications.

SUMMARY

Corporations ordinarily issue to their stockholders and other interested parties annual reports summarizing activities of the past year and significant plans for the future. In addition to the financial statements, the annual report contains the auditor's opinion, which states that the underlying records have been examined and that the financial statements are presented fairly in conformity with generally accepted accounting principles applied on a consistent basis.

The notes to the financial statements are considered an essential part of the statement and are necessary for a complete and accurate interpretation of the information contained in the statements. The accounting policies of the company are disclosed in the footnotes, usually in the first note, and provide a starting point for an analysis of the financial statements.

QUESTIONS AND PROBLEMS

1. What are the major limitations of company's annual reports as a source of information useful to management and investors?
2. Get a copy of a corporation's annual report to stockholders and answer the following questions:
   A. What are the three most significant pieces of information you get from a study of the company's Statement of Income?
   B. What are the three most significant pieces of information you get from a study of the company's Balance Sheet?
   C. How well did the company do in the most recent year?
   D. Was the company better off at the end of the most recent year as compared with the preceding year?
   E. How much was the company worth at the end of the most recent year?
   F. Compare the company's book value, par or stated value (if any) and market value per share. How can the values be different?
   G. How do you explain the difference in the company's profit or loss for the year and its change in cash?
   H. How do the nine "basic concepts" listed in Chapter 1, namely:
      1. Business entity
      2. Growing concern
      3. Historical dollar accounting
      4. Realization
      5. Use of estimates and exercise of judgment
      6. Consistency between periods
      7. Diversity in accounting
      8. Conservatism
      9. Materiality

      affect the financial statements presented in the company's annual report?

3. What are the three major controversial areas in accounting today? State your position in each of these areas.
4. For what audience are company annual reports prepared? Do you think this audience has a good understanding of the information presented in the "typical" annual report?

16

Analysis of
Financial
Statements

*This chapter discusses knowledge of the company
and its environment, analysis of its cash flows, and
calculation and interpretation of return-on-investment and nine other financial ratios.*

Analysis of financial statements involves more than the perfunc-
tory calculation of financial ratios. In this chapter we will stress the
need of the analyst first to acquire a knowledge of the company and
its environment and then to gain familiarity with the company's figure relationships in the preparation of the statements for analysis.
For the statements of income and financial position, preparation requires rearranging, condensing, figure-rounding, and taking notes of
significant figure relationships. For the statement of changes in financial position, a conversion to the cash flow statement form is followed
by an analysis of the cash flows and an attempt to project them for
the future. The balance of the chapter is devoted to the description,
calculation, and interpretation of return-on-investment and nine
other financial ratios. Throughout the chapter Caterpillar Tractor
figures for 1977/1979 are used for illustration.

THE COMPANY AND ITS ENVIRONMENT

A review of the company's annual reports and SEC 10-K forms for several years reveals much about the nature of the company, its industry, and the environment in which it has operated. In the case of Caterpillar for the years 1977/1979, one discovers:

- The company was a multinational company with roughly one-half of its sales outside the United States.

- The company sold to 248 dealers, which in turn sold and serviced Caterpillar equipment to customers throughout the world.

- The company designed, manufactured, and marketed two product lines:

  Earthmoving construction and material handling machinery and equipment, and

  Diesel and natural gas engines for earthmoving and construction machines, on-highway trucks, etc.

- Inflation in the United States and abroad affected the company's operations and its financial statements:

  Sales of $7,219 million in 1978 were 23% higher than in 1977 with 40% of the increase attributable to higher prices and 60% of the increase to greater physical volume.

  Sales of $7,613 million in 1979 were 5.5% higher than in 1978, all of the increase, and more, being attributable to higher prices because physical volume decreased 5%.

  The decrease in physical volume in 1979 resulted from a fourth quarter strike by the United Auto Workers Union.

  The weakening of the United States dollar in both 1978 and 1979 adversely affected profits, in excess (after tax) of $30 million in 1978 and $20 million in 1979.

This brief review of Caterpillar's background and environment in 1977/1979 illustrates the kind of information needed. In order to do an adequate job of statement analysis, the analyst needs to learn as much as possible about the company and the environment that produced the statements being analyzed.

PREPARATION OF INCOME STATEMENT
FOR ANALYSIS

The analyst should rearrange, condense, and figure-round a company's published statement of income and retained earnings to facilitate further analysis and, incidentally, to gain familiarity with the company's figures.

In the case of Caterpillar, we have used figures obtained from the company's 1979 and 1978 Annual Reports to prepare Illustration 16-1.[1]

Note, in Illustration 16-1, the figures have been rounded to millions in such a fashion that the figures within the statement "prove."[2] Note also that dollar figures for each year have been placed on a "percentage of sales" basis, and that supplemental data on the effect of changing prices (inflation) have been added at the bottom of the statement. Certain things stand out in Illustration 16-1:

- Cost of goods sold was a much higher percentage of sales in 1979 (81.1%) than in 1978 (77.4%) and in 1977 (77.0%). As a consequence, profit before taxes was 9.1% of sales in 1979 compared to 13.3% in 1978 and 1977.

The company explains:[3]

The fourth-quarter strike of the United Auto Workers Union was the principal reason for the decrease in profit. Profit for 1979 would have exceeded the 1978 level if the work stoppage had not occurred.

- Interest expense increased from $112 million in 1978 to $139 million in 1979 "due principally to increased short-term borrowings that were needed to finance higher receivables, inventories, and capital expenditures."[4]

- Income taxes were a smaller proportion of profit before taxes in 1979 than in 1978 and 1977. The company attributed the decrease in the effective income tax rate from 41.2% in 1978 to 33.8% in 1979 (1) to higher investment tax credits (arising from $675 million capital expenditures in 1979 compared to $543 million in 1978), and (2) to the decrease in the U.S. statutory rate from 48% to 46%.

[1] Compare Statement 1 reproduced in Chapter 15.
[2] Statistical rounding, with a note that the figures do not "prove", is not appropriate.
[3] Page 8, Caterpillar's 1979 Annual Report.
[4] *Ibid.*, page 38.

Illustration 16-1

Caterpillar Tractor Company
Statement of Income and Retained Earnings For 1979, 1978, and 1977
(In millions of dollars)

	1979	1978	1977	1979	1978	1977
				Percentage of Sales		
Sales	7613	7219	5849	100.0	100.0	100.0
Cost of goods sold	6172	5584	4503	81.1	77.4	77.0
Interest expense	139	112	100	1.8	1.5	1.7
Selling and other expenses (net)	610	560	469	8.0	7.8	8.0
Total	6921	6256	5072	90.9	86.7	86.7
Profit before taxes	692	963	777	9.1	13.3	13.3
Income taxes	234	397	334	3.1	5.5	5.7
Profit of consolidated companies	458	566	443	6.0	7.8	7.6
Equity in profit of subsidiary and affiliated companies	34	-0-	2	0.4	-0-	-0-
Profit for year	492	566	445	6.4	7.8	7.6
Dividends	182	162	136	2.4	2.2	2.3
To retained earnings	310	404	309	4.0	5.6	5.3
Retained earnings:						
Beginning of year	2578	2174	1865			
End of year	2888	2578	2174			
MEMOS:						
Annual depreciation	312	257	210			
Per share figures:						
Profit (no dilution)	$5.69	$6.56	$5.16			
Dividends	2.10	1.875	1.575			
4th quarter figures:						
Sales	1321	1929	1518			
Cost of goods sold	1207	1520	1171			

ADDENDUM—Adjustments for Effects of Changing Prices (Inflation):

Pursuant to FASB Statement No. 33, the company reported its adjustments for changes in general purchasing power of the U.S. dollar for the year ended December 31, 1979 (millions of dollars):

Profit for year—consolidated (statement 1)	$492
Adjustment to restate costs for effects of general inflation	(90)
Profit restated in constant average 1979 dollars	$402
Gain from decline in purchasing power of net monetary liabilities, in constant average 1979 dollars	$153

- Dividends to stockholders were 37% of profit in 1979 compared to about 30% in 1978 and 1977. Over the ten-year period, 1970-79, the average payout percentage has been 34%. Nevertheless, dividends per share have shown a steady increase, from $.80 in 1970 to $2.10 in 1979.

- The company has since 1950 been using the LIFO inventory method so that, except for depreciation, its revenues and expenses have been pretty much on a current dollar basis each year. In 1979, historical cost depreciation of $312 million required an upward adjustment of $90 million to place it on a 1979 cost basis. Profit restated in "constant average 1979 dollars" became $402 million, compared to the $492 million reported. The $90 million adjustment for depreciation was more than offset by the $153 million "gain from decline in purchasing power of net monetary liabilities."

PREPARATION OF STATEMENT OF FINANCIAL POSITION FOR ANALYSIS

Caterpillar's statements of financial position for year-end 1979, 1978, and 1977, rearranged and figure-rounded, are shown in Illustration 16-2.

The rearrangement in Illustration 16-2 has condensed assets, liabilities, and owners' equity according to the following pattern:

Assets	*Liabilities*
Cash and cash equivalent	Payables and accruals
Trade receivables (net)	Liability for income taxes
Inventories	Short-term debt
Property, plant and equipment (net)	Long-term debt (due within a year and after)
Investments in affiliated and subsidiary companies	Deferred income taxes
All other assets	Other liabilities

Owners' Equity

Preferred stock
Common stock
Retained earnings

Since the distinction between current and noncurrent assets and lia-

Illustration 16-2

Caterpillar Tractor Company
Condensed Statements of Financial Position
12/31/79, 12/31/78, and 12/31/77
(In millions of dollars)

	12/31/79	12/31/78	12/31/77	Increase/(Decrease) 1978/79	1977/78
Cash and cash equivalent	147	244	209	(97)	35
Receivables (net)	693	768	648	(75)	120
Inventories	1670	1522	1288	148	234
Property, plant and equipment (net)	2638	2282	1999	356	283
Investments in affiliated & subsidiary companies	85	59	73	26	(14)
Other assets	147	156	129	(9)	27
	5380	5031	4346	349	685
Payables and accruals	790	854	678	(64)	176
Liability for income taxes	133	237	178	(104)	59
Short-term notes payable	404	112	87	292	25
Long-term debt (<&> 1 yr.)	1011	1052	1024	(41)	28
Deferred income taxes	(23)	24	36	(47)	(12)
Total liabilities	2315	2279	2003	36	276
Common stock	177	174	169	3	5
Retained earnings	2888	2578	2174	310	404
Owners' equity	3065	2752	2343	313	409
	5380	5031	4346	349	685

MEMO:

Inventories at FIFO	3326	2910	2390
Replacement cost reported to SEC pursuant to ASR 190: Inventories	3370	2957	2434
Productive capacity (buildings, machinery, and equipment)	4320	3794	3230
Excess of above over reported costs of inventories & buildings, machinery, and equipment (net)	3448	3010	2432

bilities serves no useful statement analysis purpose, the distinction is ignored in Illustration 16-2. The figure rounding in Illustration 16-2 has been done in such a way that the figures within the statement prove. Percentage-of-total-assets figures have not been shown in Illustration 16-2 since inventories and fixed assets, stated on a past cost basis, make the total asset figure nonhomogeneous. Instead of percent-of-total figures, we have shown increase/decrease figures 1979 cf. 1978 and 1978 cf. 1977.

In Note B to its financial statements, Caterpillar shows how much higher its inventories stated at LIFO would be if stated on a first-in, first-out basis. In the "Memo" at the bottom of Illustration 16-2, Caterpillar's inventories calculated at FIFO are shown. Also shown in the "Memo" are the 12/31 replacement cost figures for inventories and "productive capacity" reported by Caterpillar to the Securities and Exchange Commission. The excess of replacement costs over reported figures is derived as follows:

	12/31/79	12/31/78	12/31/77
Inventories:			
Replacement cost	3370	2957	2434
Reported figures	1670	1522	1289
Excess	1700	1435	1145
Buildings, Machinery and Equipment (net):			
Replacement cost	4320	3794	3230
Reported figure	2572	2219	1934
Excess	1748	1575	1287
TOTAL EXCESS	3448	3010	2432

Several matters concerning Illustration 16-2 warrant brief comment:

- The UAW 4th quarter strike distorted 1979 year-end figures for normal comparisons. Because of the strike, there was a decrease of $608 million in 4th quarter sales from $1929 million in 1978 to $1321 million in 1979, and this decrease in sales explains the decreases in year-end receivables, payables and accruals, and income tax liability. The increase in year-end inventories raises a question.

- Many companies have used accelerated depreciation for income tax purposes, straight-line for financial reporting—and, as a consequence, have accumulated sizable amounts in their deferred tax liability account. Caterpillar has used accelerated depreciation for both income tax and financial reporting—so deferred income tax has been a comparatively small amount for Caterpillar.

- The FIFO costs of inventories approximate year-end replacement costs. As one would expect, in an inflationary economy, replacement costs at year-end are slightly higher than FIFO.
- If we substitute the 12/31/79 replacement costs for inventories and "productive capacity" for the historical cost figures, we get:

	As Reported	Replacement Costs	Difference
Inventories	1670	3370	1700
Buildings, machinery & equipment (net)	2572	4320	1748
Cash, receivables, land, etc.	1138	1138	-0-
Total Assets	5380	8828	3448
Liabilities	2315	2315	-0-
Owners' Equity	3065	6513	3448
Total	5380	8820	3448

Note: The figures reported to the SEC are not altogether appropriate for this purpose. Caterpillar has deferred until 1980 disclosure of current cost information required by FASB Statement No. 33. See Chapter 17.

CONVERSION OF STATEMENT OF CHANGES IN FINANCIAL POSITION TO A CASH FLOW STATEMENT

Caterpillar's published statements of changes in financial position have been converted to a cash flow statement form[5] for 1979, 1978, and 1977. Illustration 16-3 shows also totals for the three years. Concerning Illustration 16-3, note:

- A careful analysis will indicate some of Caterpillar's problems of operating in an inflationary economy. Annual sales increased from $5042 million in 1976 to $7613 million in 1979, a 3-year increase of $2571 million—the increase in dollar sales attributable about 2/3rds to price increases, 1/3rd to increases in physical volume. The increase in sales was accompanied by a need to finance higher receivables, inventories, and capital expenditures.

[5] See Chapter 5.

Note the increases in year-end receivables and inventories over the 3-year period, broken only temporarily, for receivables, by the 4th quarter strike in 1979.

- A year-to-year inquiry into the factors accounting for "cash internally generated"—$686 million in 1977, $692 in 1978, $482 in 1979—is instructive. A 16% increase in dollar sales in 1977 brought Caterpillar's sales and profit to the then highest levels in the company's history. Net income before deduction of noncash depreciation, etc., was $678 million in 1977, but the increase in year-end receivables and inventories was only 5% and was offset by increases in payables and accruals, and income tax liability—so "cash internally generated" in 1977 was $686 million. In 1978 sales increased to $7219 million, profit to $566 million, and net income before depreciation to $811 million— all three record highs. Year-end receivables rose $120 million and inventories $234 million, and though offset in part by increases in payables and accruals ($176) and income tax liability ($59), the net sum of the four items was a negative $119 million. So "cash internally generated" in 1978 was $692 million— about the same as for 1977—though profit in 1978 was $121 million higher than in 1977. In 1979 annual sales increased 5% to $7613 million, though sales for the 4th quarter decreased 32% because of the UAW strike—despite the strike, profit for 1979, $492 million, and net income before depreciation, $722 million, were the second highest in Caterpillar's history.

Because of the decrease in 4th quarter sales (and profit), decreases in year-end receivables, inventories, payables and accruals, and income tax liability might have been expected. The strike was abnormal, however, and normal relationships were queered, especially as to inventories. However we may hypothesize, the fact is that the net sum of the four items was a negative $240 million, so "cash internally generated" was $482 million in 1979, $200 million less than in 1977 and 1978.[6]

---

[6] In this discussion of factors affecting "cash internally generated", it was necessary to compare 4th quarter sales only for 1979 because in 1976/78, 4th quarter sales were a stable 25%/27% of annual sales:

	Annual Sales (In Millions)	Fourth Quarter Sales	
		Amount (in millions)	% of Annual
1976	5,042	1,263	25.0
1977	5,849	1,518	26.0
1978	7,219	1,929	26.7
1979	7,613	1,321	17.4

Illustration 16-3

CASH FLOW STATEMENT
(Changes that decrease cash are shown in parentheses.)

Company Caterpillar Tractor Co. Year	1979	1978	1977	Total 3 Years
Millions of Dollars Sales	7,613	7,219	5,849	–
Net Income	492	566	445	1503
Add: Depreciation	312	257	210	779
Add: Other noncash expenses–Deferred income taxes	(48)	(12)	25	(35)
Subtract: Noncash revenues–Equity in profit– affiliated and subsidiary companies	(34)	-0-	(2)	(36)
Net income before depreciation and other noncash expenses and revenues	722	811	678	2211
And this might have represented cash inflow but it did not happen this way because the company:				
a. Collected (less than) more than it billed customers, as shown in *Receivables* (increase) decrease	75	(120)	(43)	(88)
b. Bought and manufactured (more than) less than the cost of goods shipped, as shown in *Inventories* (increase) decrease	(148)	(234)	(44)	(426)
c. Paid out (more than) less than the costs it incurred, as shown in *Payables & Accruals* (decrease) increase	(64)	176	55	167

- For the 3-year period 1977-79 as a whole, the most striking thing about Caterpillar's cash flow statement was that the company was able to finance discretionary outgoes for dividends ($480) and net additions to property, plant and equipment ($1724), a total of $2204 million in large part from "cash internally generated," $1860 million. Resort to outside financing was in the form of short-term debt ($373). The company's use of "cash internally generated" to finance its large capital expenditures during the 1970s explains why dividend payout for the ten years has averaged only 34% of reported profit, as noted earlier.

- The cash flow statement model may be used for forecasting. In its 1979 Annual Report, Caterpillar forecasted "1980 sales expected to increase" and result in a physical sales volume "approximately equal to the 1978 level." Suppose we use forecasts

Illustration 16-3 continued.

d. Paid out (more than) less than income tax
incurred, as shown in *Income Tax Liabilities*

(decrease) increase	(103)	59	40	(4)
Total−Four Items	(240)	(119)	8	(351)
so that "cash internally generated" was	482	692	686	1860

There were "discretionary" outgoes of cash for:
Acquisitions of property, plant and equipment

(in excess of dispositions)	(671)	(540)	(513)	(1724)
Dividends to stockholders	(182)	(162)	(136)	(480)
Total Discretionary Outgoes	(853)	(702)	(649)	(2204)
Cash internally generated less discretionary outgoes	(371)	(10)	37	(344)

Financing and other cash inflows and outgoes were:

Increase (decrease) in long-term debt (due <&> 1 yr.)	(41)	29	(39)	(51)
Increase (decrease) in notes payable	292	25	56	373
Issuance of common stock	3	4	6	13
Dividends from, and reduction in advances to, affiliated & subsidiary companies	7	16	9	32
Other	13	(29)	52	36
Total Financing and Other Flows	274	45	84	403

With the effect on the company's cash (and cash
equivalent) being an increase (decrease) of

(97)	35	121	59

(in millions) for 1980: Sales $8500 (4th quarter $2000), profit
$600, depreciation $360, dividends $180, capital expenditures
(net) $650. Our forecast might then be brought together:

Net income (600) before depreciation (360)		960
Receivables increase (40% of 2,000 less 693)	(107)	
Inventories increase to 1,770 (guess)	(100)	
Payables and accruals increase (guess)	75	
Income tax liability increase (guess)	50	
Sum of four items.		(82)
Cash internally generated		878
Discretionary outgoes:		
Capital expenditures (net)	(650)	
Dividends	(180)	
		(830)
Cash internally generated less discretionary outgoes.		48

For statement analysis purposes, a number of cash flow statement forecasts may be made as forecasts of individual items are varied.

- It needs to be observed that the cash flow statements prepared from Caterpillar's traditional statements of income and financial position are valid without making the adjustments of profit, inventories, and fixed assets called for by FASB Statement No. 33. If, for 1979, we used the adjusted statements of income and financial position, we would show (in millions):

Reported profit of $492 less additional
   depreciation of $90 . . . . $402
Add: Depreciation–$312 plus 90 402
Deferred income taxes and equity in profit
   of affiliated and subsidiary companies . . . . (82)

Net income before depreciation and other
   noncash expenses and revenues $722

So there is no change from the $722 figure in Illustration 16-3. The adjustments to the 12/31/79 balance sheet represented an entry:

Inventories (A)	Incr	1700	
Buildings, machinery and equipment			
(net) – (A)	Incr	1748	
Owners' equity (OE)			Incr 3448

Since this entry does not affect cash, it would be reversed for the purpose of our cash flow statement.

RATIO ANALYSIS OF FINANCIAL STATEMENTS

Illustration 16-4 shows the calculation of a number of ratios for Caterpillar Tractor Company for 1979 and 1978, based upon figures taken from Illustrations 16-1 and 16-2.

Return-On-Investment Ratio

Return-on-investment (ROI), as used in this chapter, refers to the relationship between the *net income* of a company (or one of its divisions) and the *total assets* of the company (or its divisions) made available to management to produce the net income. The relationship may also be expressed as return-on-total-capital (ROTC) or as return-on-assets (ROA). The return-on-investment ratio is used to measure management performance at both the division and company levels. The reasoning is that management, either at the division or at the company level, is supplied with a total investment in assets—cash, receivables, inventories, plant and equipment, and other assets—and is expected to manage this total investment so as to earn a satisfactory return on it.

The ratio may be computed directly and simply by dividing net income by total assets. E.I. DuPont de Nemours Company pioneered the use of the two-step calculation which relates both net income and assets to sales as follows:

$$\frac{\text{Net Income}}{\text{Sales}} \quad \text{times} \quad \frac{\text{Sales}}{\text{Total Assets}}$$

DuPont's practice has been adopted by many other companies. The two-step approach is used in Illustration 16-4.

Item 1-A-3 of Illustration 16-4 shows return-on-investment, calculated from Caterpillar's reported figures, declined from 12.0 percent in 1978 to 9.5 percent in 1979. The major cause was the decline in profit on sales (1-A-1), from 7.8 percent in 1978 to 6.5 percent in 1979—attributable for the most part to the 4th quarter strike in 1979. There was also a slight decline in the utilization of assets to produce sales, from 1.54 in 1978 to 1.46 in 1979.

The return-on-investment ratio should be used with care and judgment, for the ratio is usually derived from conventional accounting statements which have many limitations. Because of these limitations and because of the varying purposes for which the ratio may be used, variations in the computation of the ratio are encountered in practice.

When "investment" is defined as average total assets, the average may be computed by averaging total assets shown on the statements of financial position as of the beginning and end of the accounting period, as in Illustration 16-4. For seasonal businesses, average total assets may be more appropriately determined by averaging total assets shown in monthly or quarterly statements. In some cases, "investment" is taken to mean total assets shown on the balance sheet reduced:

1. By the amount of idle assets, or

Illustration 16-4

Caterpillar Tractor Company

Financial Ratios for 1979 and 1978 (Source: Illustrations 16-1 and 16-2)

	COMPUTATIONS		RATIOS	
	1979	1978	1979	1978
1. *Return-On-Investment*				
A-1. "Margin" (Profit ÷ Sales)	492/7613	566/7219	6.5%	7.8%
A-2. "Turnover" (Sales ÷ Avg. Total Assets)	7613 / (5380 + 5031)/2	7219 / (5031 + 4346)/2	1.46 Times	1.54 Times
A-3. R.O.I. (Margin × Turnover)	.065 × 1.46	.078 × 1.54	9.5%	12.0%
Based on Repl. Costs				
B-1. "Margin" (Adj. Profit ÷ Sales)	402/7613	Data Not	5.3%	N.A.
B-2. "Turnover" (Sales ÷ Adj. Total Assets)	7613 / (8828 + 8041)/2	Available in	0.9 Times	N.A.
B-3. Adj. R. O. I. (Margin × Turnover)	.053 × 0.9	Ill. 16-1	4.8%	N.A.
2. *Receivable Collection Period*				
A. Avg. Daily Sales in 4th Quarter	1321 ÷ 92 Days	1929 ÷ 92 Days		
B. Year-End Receivables ÷ Avg. Daily Sales	693 ÷ 14.36	768 ÷ 20.97	48 Days	37 Days

3. Inventory Turnover				
A-1. Average Inventory – At LIFO	(1670 + 1522)/2	(1522 + 1288)/2		
A-2. Cost Goods Sold ÷ Avg. LIFO Inventory	6172 ÷ 1596	5584 ÷ 1405	3.9 Times	4.0 Times
Based on LIFO CGS and FIFO Inventory				
B-1. Average Inventory – At FIFO	(3326 + 2910)/2	(2910 + 2390)/2		
B-2. Cost Goods Sold ÷ Avg. FIFO Inventory	6172 ÷ 3118	5584 ÷ 2650	2.0 Times	2.1 Times
4. Current Ratio At Year-End				
Current Assets ÷ Current Liabilities	2607 ÷ 1386	2628 ÷ 1237	1.88 to 1	2.12 to 1
5. L-T Debt to L-T Debt and Equity at Year-End				
A. Based on Conventional Statement	1011 ÷ 4076	1052 ÷ 3804	25%	28%
B. Based on Repl.-Costs Adj. Statement	1011 ÷ 7524	1052 ÷ 6814	13%	15%
6. Total Debt to Total Assets at Year-End				
A. Based on Conventional Statement	2315 ÷ 5380	2279 ÷ 5031	43%	45%
B. Based on Repl.-Cost Adj. Statement	2315 ÷ 8828	2279 ÷ 8041	26%	28%
7. Earnings on Common Equity				
A. Based on Conventional Statement	$\dfrac{492}{(3065 + 2752)/2}$	$\dfrac{566}{(2752 + 2174)/2}$	16.9%	23.0%
B. Based on Repl.-Cost Adj. Statement	$\dfrac{402}{(6513 + 5762)/2}$	N.A.	6.5%	N.A.
8. Earnings Per Share				
Profit for Common ÷ Weighted Avg. No. of Shares	492 ÷ 86.4	566 ÷ 86.3	$5.69	$6.56
9. Book Value Per Share at Year-End	3065 ÷ 86.43	2752 ÷ 86.36	$35	$32
10. Price/Earnings Ratio				
Market Price (4th Qtr.) ÷ Earnings Per Share	52 ÷ 5.69	57 ÷ 6.56	9 Times	9 Times

2. By the amount of nonoperating assets, or
3. By the amount of assets financed by current liabilities.

Many companies define "investment" to include property, plant, and equipment at original cost rather than at original cost less accumulated depreciation. If we were to adopt this definition for Caterpillar Tractor Company, property, plant, and equipment at 12/31/79 would be figured at $4276 million instead of at $2638 million. DuPont's practice of including fixed assets at their undepreciated cost has no doubt influenced other companies to do so. One argument advanced for the practice is that it is a way of compensating for price level changes (inflation). A more direct way of adjusting for inflation is to use current replacement costs, as we have done in item 1-B, Illustration 16-4. Item 1-B-3 shows 1979 return on investment at 4.8 percent compared to 9.5 percent using conventional figures, primarily because "turnover" is 0.9 times using replacement costs compared to 1.46 using conventional figures.

The "return" numerator to be used in the return-on-investment calculation should be consistent with the "investment" denominator used. In the case of Caterpillar Tractor Company, an adjustment of reported net income by adding back the after-tax cost of interest on borrowed money may be in order. In the case of Caterpillar Tractor for 1979, we might add back $75 million after-tax interest[7] to the reported net income of $492 million; then, if we divided the $567 million adjusted income figure by the $5206 million investment, we would obtain an ROI of 10.9 percent, compared to the 9.5 percent without the adjustment for the after-tax cost of interest. Many of the questions concerning adjustment of the net income figure relate to (1) unusual and nonrecurring income, and income on nonoperating assets, and (2) interest expense income taxes, and unusual and nonrecurring expenses.

In financial literature, the phrase "return-on-investment" is an expression used in many different contexts. Whenever a reader encounters "return-on-investment," he should determine:

1. What is meant by "return" and what is meant by "investment," as witness the various definitions discussed heretofore in this chapter.
2. Whether the return-on-investment is:

---

[7] The company's incremental tax rate in 1979 was 46%. The after-tax cost of $139 million interest at 54%, 100%-46%, is $75 million.

a. Retrospective, as used for performance appraisal in this chapter, or

b. Prospective, as used for project evaluation in capital budgeting decisions.

RECEIVABLE COLLECTION PERIOD, INVENTORY TURNOVER, AND CURRENT RATIO

The receivable collection period was discussed in some detail in Chapter 6. Two conclusions reached there bear repeating: (1) 4th quarter sales when available are more reliable than annual sales for calculating this ratio, and (2) the number of days determined for this ratio can be compared with the company's credit terms, the company's previous experience, and with the collection period for similar companies. In Illustration 16-4, Item 2, we used 4th quarter sales to determine Caterpillar's period to be 48 days for 1979 compared to 37 days for 1978. Because of the 4th quarter strike in 1979, the 48-day period appears to be abnormal. The 37-day figure for 1978 is more typical.

The inventory turnover ratio was considered at some length in Chapter 9. Ideally, both the numerator, cost of goods sold, and the denominator, average inventory, should be at current costs. Caterpillar, using the LIFO method, shows cost of goods sold at current costs but inventories at past costs. Inventory turnover ratios for Caterpillar calculated on this basis, Item 3-A of Illustration 16-4, a turnover of 3.9 times for 1979, 4.0 times for 1978. Both figures are suspect, as the recalculation in Item 3-B using current cost FIFO inventory figures confirms. The Item 3-B turnover figures—2.0 times for 1979 and 2.1 times for 1978—are the more trustworthy.

The current ratio—current assets to current liabilities—is shown in Item 4, Illustration 16-4, 1.88 to 1 for 12/31/79 and 12/31/78. This ratio is of dubious value. The ratio would be meaningful to the short-term creditor only if the company is to be liquidated and the creditor could be assured of first call upon the liquidation proceeds. The liquidation concept, moreover, is contrary to going-concern basis upon which the balance sheet is prepared. The current ratio is of questionable value to management, for if management performance is being appraised by return-on-investment, the less current assets the company has, the higher the rate of return.

DEBIT RATIOS

The ratio of long-term-debt to long-term-debt-and-equity measures the investment of bondholders relative to the investment of stockholders. The larger the ratio, the more the company is said to "trade on its equity." For Caterpillar, Item 5-A of Illustration 16-4 shows the ratio to be 25 percent at 12/31/79 and 28 percent at 12/31/78. The balance sheet figure for debt is on a current dollar basis but the equity figure is not, for Caterpillar's inventory and fixed assets are stated at past dollars with the result that equity is stated in part on past costs. So we have again the numerator, long-term debt, stated on one basis and the denominator stated on another. To correct this, Item 5-B shows equity reflecting replacement costs of inventories and fixed assets. Item 5-B shows the ratio to be 13 percent at 12/31/79, 15 percent at 12/31/78—both ratios indicating a small proportion of long-term debt in the "invested capital" of Caterpillar.

The ratio of total debt to total assets measures the interest of all creditors, not just bondholders, in the assets of the company. Again, the larger the ratio, the more the company "trades on its equity." For Caterpillar, Item 6-1 of Illustration 16-4 shows the ratio to be 43 percent at 12/31/79 and 45 percent at 12/31/78. The numerator again is stated at current costs, the denominator in part at past costs. To correct, Item 6-B reflects current replacement costs of inventories and fixed assets in stating fixed assets. The ratio then becomes 26 percent at 12/31/79 and 28 percent at 12/31/78. Included in Caterpillar's liabilities at 12/31/78 is Deferred Income Taxes, $24 million, a *de minimis* item, but for companies which have a sizable deferred income tax amount, two questions should be raised: Does deferred income tax represent a liability? Should it be considered a part of equity in computing debt/equity ratios?

STOCKHOLDERS' EQUITY AND EARNINGS RATIOS

The ratio of earnings on common equity is a measure of the return on common stockholders' investment, as stated on the company's balance sheet(s). The ratio is affected not only by the return-on-investment ratio but also by the extent to which the company uses debt and preferred stock as a means of financing its investment in assets. The more lower-cost debt is used, the more a company is said to "trade on its equity." And the more a company successfully "trades on its equity," the higher the return to its common stockholders. In the case of Caterpillar Tractor for 1979, the company used $2297 million funds provided by creditors, at an after-tax cost of $75 million, or about 3¼ percent; this enabled the company to earn 16.9 percent on its common stockholders' investment, when its overall ROI was 10.9 percent (adjusted for after-tax cost of interest). The profit-on-common-equity ratio is subject to many of the limitations noted for the return-on-investment ratio. These will not be repeated here.

Earnings per share is based upon the net income figure reported in the income statement and is subject, therefore, to all of the limitations of that statement. AICPA APB Opinion No. 15 provides, in paragraph 12, that "earnings per share or net loss per share data should be shown on the face of the income statement." APB Opinion No. 15 further provides, in paragraph 47, that "computations of earnings per share should be based on the weighted average number of common shares and common share equivalents outstanding during each period presented." Computation of earnings-per-share is relatively simple when a company has no "potentially dilutive convertible securities, options, warrants or other rights that upon conversion or exercise could in the aggregate dilute earnings per common share." When a company does not have these complicating factors, the computation is made by dividing net income available for common shares by the weighted average number of common shares. When a company has both common and preferred shares outstanding, with the preferred being nonconvertible into common, net income is reduced by the amount of preferred dividends in order to determine "net income available for common shares." The computation of Caterpillar's earnings per share is shown in Item 8 of Illustration 16-4—$5.69 for 1979 and $6.56 for 1978—assuming no dilution from potential conversion of convertible debentures and unexercised stock options.

Book value per share is based upon the figures reported in the balance sheet, and is subject, therefore, to all of the limitations of that statement. Many of these limitations were noted in the discussion of return-on-investment, and will not be repeated here. The extent of these limitations, for a particular company, is indicated by the difference between the book value of the company's stock and its market value, if the stock is publicly traded. Note the difference between the book value of Caterpillar's common shares, $35 at 12/31/79, and the market value $52 (in 4th quarter, 1979). For a closely held company, one whose stock is not publicly traded, care should be taken that book value is not equated with fair market value.

The price/earnings ratio is based upon the net income figure reported in the income statement and is subject, therefore, to all the limitations of that statement. It is difficult to measure net income for a single year with preciseness. Additional difficulties are encountered when there are extraordinary items or "potentially dilutive convertible securities, options, warrants or rights"; in such circumstances, one needs to be careful in selecting the earnings-per-share figure for the purpose of computing the price/earnings ratio. Moreover, when we relate today's market price to earnings-per-share for a past period, we are doing something which is somewhat illogical, for presumably an investor buys stock for its *future*, not its *past*, earnings. As a matter of cash exchange, a buyer of stock puts out cash today for his expectations of future cash dividends and the future market price for the stock.

SUMMARY

To do an adequate job of statement analysis, the analyst needs to review the company's annual reports, 10-K forms, and other sources to learn what he can about the company and the environment that produced the statements being analyzed. Both to facilitate his analysis and to gain familiarity with the company's figures, the analyst should rearrange, condense, and figure-round the company's published statements of income, retained earnings, and financial position. The analyst all the while should make notes of:

- Economic developments affecting the company during the period covered.
- The company's accounting policies and practices,
- Supplementary data provided, and
- Figure relationships of special interest.

The company's statement of changes in financial position should be converted to the cash flow statement form explained in Chapter 5, and then that statement should be carefully analyzed and a forecast (or forecasts) of the cash flow statement attempted.

Ratios such as those included in Illustration 16-4 should be calculated and interpreted. A summary of the ten ratios included in Illustration 16-4 follows:

Return-On-Investment (ROI) may be determined by dividing profit by investment, or by multiplying profit on sales by "turnover" of investment. ROI is used to measure management performance at both the division and company levels. ROI can be improved by increasing the percentage of profit on sales or by improving "turnover." Many companies consider *investment* to be average total assets on their balance sheets. Some companies begin with this figure and add back accumulated depreciation so that, in effect, fixed assets are included at original cost. Other companies consider investment to be total assets less current liabilities. Adjustments may be made for price changes (inflation). The *profit* numerator in the ROI calculation should be consistent with the concept of investment employed. Thus, profit may be net income or net income before income taxes, with possible adjustments for interest expense, gain (or loss) from nonoperating assets, and unusual and nonrecurring items affecting income. The return-on-investment ratio should be used with care and judgment, since it is derived from conventional accounting statements which have many limitations. Whenever a reader encounters the expression "return-on-investment" in financial literature, he should seek to determine from the context (1) what is meant by "return" and what is meant by "investment" and (2) whether the return-on-investment measure is *retrospective* as in performance appraisal, or *prospective* as in project evaluation in capital budgeting.

The relationship between sales and receivables is shown by the *receivable collection period*. If appropriate consideration is given to seasonal and other fluctuations in sales, to elimination of any cash sales, and to the presence of any unusual account balances in the year-end receivable figure, the receivable collection period can be the most trustworthy of all the ratios described in this chapter. The relationship between cost of goods sold and average inventory is shown by the *inventory turnover ratio*. Appropriate consideration needs to be given to any difference between the basis on which cost of goods sold is stated and the basis on which average inventories are stated. When cost of goods sold is stated on a current-cost LIFO basis, then average inventories stated on a current-cost FIFO basis should be used in figuring the inventory turnover ratio. The *current ratio* is a ratio which, though readily calculated and frequently cited, is of no value to management, and of dubious value even to the short-term creditor.

The relationship between debt and equity may be expressed by the *long-term-debt to long-term-debt-and-equity ratio*, and by the *total-debt to total-assets ratio*. The debt figure should be a fairly valid "current-dollar" figure. The equity figure when derived from a conventional balance sheet is subject to the limitations of that statement.

Equity and earnings ratios include earnings on common equity, earnings per share, book value per common share, and price/earnings ratio. These ratios also are subject to the limitations of the conventional accounting statements from which they are derived. Earnings-per-share computations are complicated when there are potentially dilutive convertible securities, options, warrants or similar securities.

QUESTIONS AND PROBLEMS

1. The text suggests that the analyst learn as much as possible about the company and its environment.

    (A) Why?

    (B) To what sources should the analyst go?

    (C) Can you cite any specific instances how knowledge of Caterpillar and its environment contributed to an understanding of Caterpillar's 1978 and 1979 figures?

2. Caterpillar's statements of financial position have been condensed in Illustration 16-2 according to a pattern that shows six specified asset items, six specified liability items, and three owners' equity items.

    (A) Would it be possible, and practicable, to condense the balance sheets of most companies according to this pattern?

    (B) Since the "pattern" does not provide for the showing of current assets and current liabilities, is this a significant disadvantage? If so, why so? If not, why not?

    (C) The "pattern" lists deferred income taxes among the liabilities. Why should this item, when it has a credit balance, be shown as a liability? Does deferred income tax represent a liability? Under what conditions could it be considered a part of equity rather than debt in computing debt/equity ratios?

3. The text states that "The return-on-investment ratio should be used with care and judgment, for the ratio is usually derived from conventional statements which have many limitations."

(A) What limitations?

(B) What can the analyst do about these limitations?

(C) What are the arguments for, and against, showing "investment" as:

Total assets including fixed assets at undepreciated cost

Reported total assets less idle assets

Reported total assets less "nonoperating assets"

Reported total assets less current liabilities

Reported total assets with adjustment of inventories and fixed assets to reflect current replacement costs

(D) What are the arguments for, and against, showing "return" as:

Net income before deduction of interest on debt

Net income exclusive of unusual and nonrecurring income

Net income exclusive of income on nonoperating income

Net income adjusted to show depreciation on replacement cost of fixed assets

Net income before deduction of income taxes

4. Under what conditions, and why, can the receivable collection period be the "most trustworthy of all the ratios described in this chapter"? Why are fourth quarter sales a more reliable basis than annual sales for calculating this ratio?

5. In computing inventory turnover, select the best of the following statements and tell why or why not for each.

(A) Cost of goods sold stated at LIFO should be divided by average inventory stated at LIFO.

(B) Cost of goods sold stated at LIFO should be divided by average inventory stated at FIFO.

(C) Cost of goods sold stated at FIFO should be divided by average inventory stated at FIFO.

(D) Cost of goods sold stated at FIFO should be divided by average inventory stated at LIFO.

6. Caterpillar's current ratio was 1.88 to 1 at 12/31/79 compared to 2.12 to 1 at 12/31/78. What does this mean? Is it good or bad? Compared to what?

7. Caterpillar "conventional" debt/equity ratios were as follows:

	at 12/31/79	at 12/31/78
Long-term Debt to Long-term Debt and Equity	25%	28%
Total Debt to Total Assets	43%	45%

(A) What do these ratios tell us about Caterpillar? Compared to other companies?

(B) If replacement costs are used, the ratios become 13% and 15% for the Long-term Debt to Long-term Debt and equity, and 26% and 28% for

Total Debt to Total Assets. What do these ratios tell us about Caterpillar? Are these ratios more useful than those based upon conventional statements?

8. (A) If the numerator in computing earnings per share is subject to all of the limitations of the income statement, how does one account for "earnings per share" being so widely quoted?

   (B) When earnings per share is coupled with market value per share to get the Price/Earnings Ratio, also widely quoted, is the admonition "Handle with Care" appropriate? If so, how so? If not, why not?

9. What does an analysis of Caterpillar's cash flows tell us that the ratios do not?

10. For a company of your choice, do an analysis similar to that done for Caterpillar Tractor Company in Chapter 16. List the conclusions you draw from your analysis.

11. On 1/2/80 Little Materials Co., Inc. was incorporated as a small business corporation—thus it was not subject to corporate income tax since its income was taxable to its stockholders on their individual returns.

1/3/80: Stockholders paid in $250M cash for capital stock
1/4/80: Company paid $220M cash for property, plant, and equipment
In 1980:

   1. Company made sales of $300M, all for cash.
   2. Company carried no inventory, but had its suppliers ship direct to Little's customers—cost of goods was $210 which Little paid in cash to its suppliers.
   3. Little incurred $50M operating expenses which it paid in cash.
   4. Little estimated its property, plant, and equipment would have a useful life of 10 years, with no salvage value at the end—company used straight-line depreciation.
   5. Little paid all of its net income, $18M, as a cash dividend.

Required:

A. Show above transactions in T-accounts.
B. Prepare income statement for 1980 and balance sheet at 12/31/80.
C. Prepare a statement of changes in financial position beginning with the net income figure as a source.

Questions:

(a) Did showing net income as a source require you to show depreciation as a "source" on your statement of changes in financial position? Is depreciation really a source of funds? If so, why so? If you think not, how do you explain the way you treated it on your statement?

(b) If the company had used the sum-of-the-years digits method of depreciation, and had recognized depreciation in the amount of $40M, would its sources of funds have been greater?

(c) From whom and in what amounts did the company get cash in 1980? To whom and in what amounts did it pay out cash?

(d) Would a cash flow statement enable Little to show its cash flows more clearly?

(e) Suppose the company's 1980 transactions (exclusive of those on 1/3/80 and 1/4/80 were to repeat themselves exactly for the next nine years, how would the 10-year cash flow statement for the company look? Show the company's 10-year income statement, and its balance sheet at 12/31/89.

12. On 12/27/79 Moore Materials Co., Inc. was incorporated as a small business similar to Little Materials Co., Inc.

12/27/79: Stockholders paid in $400M for capital stock.

12/28/79: Company paid $220M cash for property, plant, and equipment (10-year estimated life, no salvage value—straight-line depreciation).

12/29/79: Company bought inventory of merchandise on account at a cost of $100M.

In 1980:

1. Company made sales of $300M on account.
2. Cost of goods shipped customers was $210M.
3. Moore incurred $50M operating expenses which it paid in cash.
4. Moore recognized the year's depreciation, $22M, on property, plant, and equipment.
5. Moore paid all of its net income, $18M, as a cash dividend.
6. Moore collected $225M from customers on account.
7. Moore purchased merchandise costing $230M on account.
8. Moore paid suppliers $290M on account.

Required:

A. Prepare comparative balance sheets at 12/31/79 and 12/31/80, and income statement for 1980.

B. Prepare a cash flow statement for 1980 beginning with the net income figure as a source.

Questions:

(a) The expression "cash flow" is sometimes used to denote net income plus noncash charges for depreciation:

   (1) In what respect is this "cash flow" a useful indicator of the company's earning power?

   (2) In what respect is this "cash flow" a useful indicator of the company's internal generation of cash?

   (3) How would you reconcile the company's so-called "cash flow" for 1980 with the change in its cash between 12/31/79 and 12/31/80?

(b) From whom and in what amounts did the company get cash in 1980? To whom and in what amounts did it pay out cash? How do you reconcile these figures with those you used in your cash flow statement?

(c) Suppose for each of the next four years:

(1) The company were to make sales of $300M on account, and collect $75M on the previous year's sales and $225M on current year's sales,

(2) The company were to purchase $210M of merchandise on account—ship goods costing $210M to customers for the $300M sales made them—and pay $210M to suppliers on account, and

(3) The company were to incur $50M operating expenses, and pay these as well as $18M dividends in cash.

Prepare a cash flow statement for these four years. What does it show?

13. In June, 1980, Barca Corporation had put in a new "management team" to operate its wholly owned subsidiary, Kennan, Inc. For some time prior to the change, the officers of Barca had been aware that Kennan had been operating at a small book loss, but assumed that, consideration being given to "noncash" depreciation, Kennan was operating on a cash gain basis. They were somewhat dismayed, therefore, to be receiving reports "from the trade" in June that Kennan was failing to discount its bills. And this despite bank borrowings which Barca had approved for Kennan for the very purpose of assuring that Kennan would take all available discounts.

Kennan's income statement for the second quarter of 1980, shown in Exhibit 1, may be taken as fairly typical of the results achieved by the old management. Also the trend of Kennan's financial condition prior to the change may be considered as fairly well typified by the balance sheets as of March 31, 1980 and June 30, 1980 shown in Exhibit 1.

After three months under the new management, the September 30, 1980 balance sheet and third quarter income statement shown in Exhibit 1 were prepared. There was no appreciable "seasonality" in Kennan's sales.

Required:

A. Prepare conventional statements of changes in financial position for the second quarter—1980 and third quarter—1980.

B. Convert your statements of changes in financial position to cash flow statements.

C. Calculate return-on-investment ratios, receivable collection periods, inventory turnover, and current ratios for the two quarters.

D. On the basis of the above analyses and any others which seem appropriate to you, list the important changes which the new management team brought about in the third quarter compared to the second.

E. You have been asked to prepare:

Projected income statement for the fourth quarter
Projected cash flow statement for the fourth quarter

Exhibit 1
KENNAN, INC.

Balance Sheets and Income Statements
(In thousands of dollars)

	March 31, 1980	June 30, 1980	Sept. 30, 1980
CURRENT ASSETS:			
Cash	$ 120	$ 89	$ 83
Receivables (Net)	1,075	1,128	1,070
Inventories (LIFO)	930	980	890
Prepaid Expenses	61	63	42
	2,186	2,260	2,085
LESS CURRENT LIABILITIES:			
Notes Payable	690	725	595
Accounts Payable	292	260	165
Due Parent Company	12	20	28
Accrued Wages	25	34	71
Other Accruals	71	107	112
Bonds due within one year	–	–	20
	1,090	1,146	991
NET CURRENT ASSETS	1,096	1,114	1,094
Fixed Assets (Net)	1,374	1,347	1,370
	2,470	2,461	2,464
Less Bonds Payable	320	320	300
NET ASSETS	2,150	2,141	2,164
STOCKHOLDERS' EQUITY:			
Capital Stock	2,000	2,000	2,000
Earnings Reinvested	150	141	164
	$2,150	$2,141	$2,164

	2nd Quarter 1980	3rd Quarter 1980
Sales	$ 912	$1,090
Cost of Sales,[a] & Operating Expenses[a]	897	995
Net Operating Profit	15	95
Other Expenses:		
Interest	16	14
Charge for Parent Company Engineering Services	8	8
	24	22
Net Profit (Loss)	(9)	73
Less Dividend Paid	–	50
Net to Earnings Reinvested	$ (9)	$ 23

[a] Includes depreciation allocated to each quarter $34M.

Projected balance sheets as of 12/31/80 based upon two separate sets of assumptions:

(1) Sales for the fourth quarter will increase to $1,200M

(2) $1,200 regular sales coupled with Kennan securing a government order for $350M, billable only upon completion in 1981, and on which Kennan will incur costs in the fourth quarter $200M, two-thirds of the anticipated total costs of $300M.

14. You are asked to analyze the financial statements of The Quaker Oats Company for its four fiscal years ended June 30, 1976. The following company statements have been condensed, and rounded to millions, for you:

Exhibit A: Annual Income Statements for the four fiscal years ended June 30, 1976

Exhibit B: Condensed Comparative Balance Sheets for five fiscal year-ends, June 30, 1972/1976, inclusive

Exhibit C: Condensed Statements of Changes in Financial Position for Biennia (two years) ended June 30, 1976 and June 30, 1974.

Required: Convert Exhibit C to two cash flow statements that will compare the biennium ended June 30, 1976 with the biennium ended June 30, 1974. Do whatever ratio analysis you deem appropriate. Prepare a list of the significant conclusions you draw from your analysis of the company's financial statements.

Some Background Information on Quaker Oats:

1. Two major lines—(1) Grocery Products and (2) Toys (Fisher-Price brand).

2. In the 1975 Annual Report, the company noted that "Since 1973, unprecedented increases in the costs of commodities and packaging materials used in grocery products adversely affected the Company's results. Also, sharply higher petrochemical prices resulted in increased costs of the plastics we use in toys. . ." (It was in 1973/1974 that the U.S. negotiated the Russian Wheat Deal and that the OPEC Oil Embargo occurred). The company explained in its 1976 Annual Report that principal raw materials were purchased in fiscal 1976 at significantly lower costs than in fiscal 1975.

3. In the 1974 Annual Report, it was stated as "Quaker's objective that the ratio of long-term debt to the total of shareholder's equity and long-term debt be maintained below 35 percent."

4. Concerning the issue of 500,000 shares of nonconvertible preference stock, $9.56 dividend per share, in May 1975, the company observed that the "preference stock was chosen instead of common, or securities convertible into common, because it is expected to result in less dilution of future earnings per share."

5. Earnings per common share, dividends per common share, and stock prices per common share, 1973-1976:

	1976	1975	1974	1973
Earnings per Common Share	2.31	1.45	1.91	2.02
Dividends per Common Share	.84	.80	.76	.81
Price range for Common Share	28 3/8–15	24 3/8–11	31 1/4–11*	47 1/2–24 7/8*

*Calendar Year

6. Basis for stating inventories—Lower of cost (principally FIFO or average quarterly cost) of market.

Exhibit A

The Quaker Oats Co.
Condensed Statement of Income
(In Millions of dollars)

	Fiscal Years Ended			
	6/30/76	6/30/75	6/30/74	< 6/30/73
Net sales	$1,473	$1,389	$1,227	$990
Cost of goods sold	1,016	1,029	915	693
Gross margin	457	360	312	297
Operating expenses (net)	346	293	235	212
Income before taxes	111	67	77	85
Provision for income tax	58	36	37	43
Net Income	$ 53	$ 31	$ 40	$ 42
Memo: (1) Depreciation— Prop., Plant, & equip.	34	30	25	20
(2) Amortization— Intangibles	1	1	1	1
(3) Cash dividends	23	18	16	15

Exhibit B

The Quaker Oats Company
Condensed Comparative Balance Sheets
June 30, 1972/1976
(In millions of dollars)

	6/30/76	6/30/75	6/30/74	6/30/73	6/30/72
Assets					
Cash and Marketable Securities	$ 78	$ 18	$ 12	$ 26	$ 23
Receivables (Net)	139	144	160	111	91
Inventories	198	189	225	170	127
Prepaid Expenses	10	7	9	7	7
Current Assets	425	358	406	314	248
Property, Plant, and Equip. (Net)	374	358	319	272	241
Intangible and Other Assets	56	49	51	44	43
	$855	$765	$776	$630	$532
Liabilities and Stockholders' Equity					
Short-Term Debt	$ 46	$ 29	$115	$ 66	$ 36
Current Maturities–L-T Debt	2	1	4	3	4
Payables and Accruals	128	112	96	82	70
Income Taxes Payable	33	7	7	7	7
Current Liabilities	209	149	222	158	117
Long-Term Debt (> 1 yr.)	149	158	171	124	132
Deferred Income Taxes	50	47	37	29	23
Other Long-Term Liabilities	15	10	8	6	2
Total Liabilities	423	364	438	317	274
Stockholders' Equity					
$3 preferred stock	7	6	7	7	7
9.56% preference stock	50	50	-0-	-0-	-0-
Common Stock	123	123	123	122	94
Retained Earnings	252	222	208	184	157
Stockholder's Equity	432	401	338	313	258
	$855	$765	$776	$630	$532

Exhibit C

The Quaker Oats Company
Condensed Statements of Changes in Financial Position
For Biennia Ended 6/30/76 and 6/30/74
(In Millions of Dollars)

	Each of 2 Yrs. Ended	
	6/30/76	6/30/74
Sources of Working Capital:		
Net Income	84	82
Depreciation–Property, Plant & Equip.	64	45
Amortization–Intangible Assets	2	2
Deferred Income Taxes	14	14
Total from Operations	164	143
Proceeds from Issue of Preferred Stock	49	-0-
Proceeds from Issue of Common Stock	1	29
Proceeds from Issue of New L-T Debt	44	73
Increase in Long-Term Liabilities	7	6
Sale of Properties	16	6
Total Provided	281	257
Uses of Working Capital:		
Additions to Properties	135	129
Cash Dividends	41	31
Decrease in Long-Term Debt	67	34
Other (Net)	6	10
Total Used	249	204
Increase in Working Capital	32	53
Change in Working Capital:		
Cash and Marketable Securities	66	(11)
Receivables	(21)	69
Inventories	(27)	98
Prepaid Expenses	1	2
Short-Term Debt	69	(79)
Current Maturities of Long-Term Debt	2	-0-
Payables and Accruals	(32)	(26)
Income Taxes Payable	(26)	-0-
Net Increase	32	53

Accounting for Changing Prices

The purpose of this chapter is to discuss how certain public enterprises report the effects of changing prices in their external financial reports. We will discuss the features of traditional financial statements and examine the objectives of financial reporting by business enterprises in relation to the changing business environment. We will next discuss the disclosure requirements of FASB Statement No. 33, Financial Reporting and Changing Prices, and show how nominal dollar information is restated into constant dollar and current cost figures. We will then show how two large public enterprises presented this supplementary information and conclude the chapter by discussing the usefulness of financial information adjusted for changing prices.

TRADITIONAL FINANCIAL STATEMENTS

In the years since 1970, the United States has experienced a period of rapidly rising prices. In fact, prices as measured by the Consumer Price Index doubled from the beginning of 1970 to the beginning of 1980. This condition of overall rising prices is referred to as inflation. Before proceeding to accounting for changing prices, we will discuss the features of traditional financial statements.

A dominant feature of traditional financial statements is the measurement of the historical cost of inventories, property, plant and equipment, and intangible assets. These assets normally constitute a high proportion of the total assets of most business enterprises and this is the reason why conventional accounting is commonly referred to as "the historical cost model."

A second feature is the reliance of traditional financial statements on exchange transactions at historical costs. Most exchange transactions are recorded at historical costs, but many of them are not. For example, sales and accounts receivables are measured on the basis of historical exchange costs. However, when these costs are adjusted for estimated uncollectibles, they represent their net realizable values and not their historical costs.

A third feature is the use of a variety of current value measurements, which include replacement cost (under lower-of-cost-or-market rule), net realizable value (trade accounts receivables), and present value of expected cash flows (long-term receivables and long-term liabilities). A departure from the use of historical cost to improve financial reports includes the use of the equity method of accounting for unconsolidated subsidiaries and certain other investments.

The departure from the total use of historical costs for financial statements came about through the efforts of the accounting profession and interested related organizations in their attempts to convey meaningful and useful financial information to various decision makers. In the next section, we examine some objectives of financial statements.

Objectives of Financial Reporting by Business Enterprises

In November 1978, the Financial Accounting Standards Board issued a *Statement of Financial Accounting Concepts No. 1: Objectives of Financial Reporting by Business Enterprises*. In that Statement, it is suggested that financial reporting should provide:

- Information that is useful to present and potential investors and creditors and other users in making rational investment, credit and similar decisions.

- Information to help present and potential investors and creditors and other users in assessing the amounts, timing and uncertainty of prospective cash receipts from dividends or interest and the proceeds from the sale, redemption, or maturity of securities or loans.
- Information about the economic resources of an enterprise, the claims to those resources, and the effects of transactions, events, and circumstances that change its resources and claims to those resources.

The Statement goes on to state that financial reporting is expected to provide information about an enterprise's financial performance, and hence the primary focus of financial reporting is information about earnings and its components. The objectives of financial reporting, however, stem largely from the information needs of external decision makers who have a wide range of interests. Some of these interests are not related to earnings.

Financial accounting is not designed to measure directly the value of a business enterprise, but the information it provides may be helpful to those who wish to estimate its value. This is related to one of the objectives—that financial reporting should provide information about how management of an enterprise has discharged its stewardship responsibility to owners (stockholders) for the use of the enterprise resources entrusted to it. Management is accountable for the efficient and profitable use of these resources and for protecting them to the extent possible from unfavorable economic impacts of factors in the economy such as inflation or deflation. The users of financial reports need to have an understanding of the effects of changing prices on a business enterprise to make decisions regarding investing, lending, and other matters.

FINANCIAL REPORTING AND CHANGING PRICES

Financial Statements in the United States have traditionally been prepared using historical costs. Because the statements reflect dollar amounts which have resulted from transactions taking place over a period of years, the purchasing power of the dollars shown in the statements is not the same. A plant built in 1970 does not show on the balance sheet in dollars that are equivalent in purchasing power to the dollars shown on the same balance sheet for a plant built in 1980.

Because of the rapid inflation since 1970, the accounting profession and interested related organizations have been concerned with methods of accounting for inflation. The Accounting Standards Steering Committee of the United Kingdom and Ireland issued in January 1973, Exposure Draft 8: *Accounting for Changes in the Purchasing Power of Money* and in May 1974, issued a provisional statement of Statement Accounting Practice No. 7 with the same title. In 1975, the British government Committee on Inflation Accounting, named the "Sandilands Committee" after its chairman, recommended an entirely different approach which it called "current cost accounting."

In December 1974, the FASB issued an Exposure Draft also calling for certain supplementary disclosures based on financial reporting in units of general purchasing power, using an overall measure of inflation, the GNP Implicit Price Deflator, to measure purchasing price changes. In 1976, the Securities and Exchange Commission (SEC) issued Accounting Series Release No. 190 that required the disclosure of certain inventory and property replacement costs for large nonfinancial companies, commencing with 1976 financial statements. The FASB proposal was withdrawn after the SEC issued its replacement cost requirement.

In September 1979, the FASB issued *Statement of Financial Accounting Standards No. 33: Financial Reporting and Changing Prices*. Statement No. 33 applies only to large public corporations having:

1. Total Assets of $1 billion or more after deducting depreciation, or
2. Inventory plus gross property, plant and equipment of $125 million or more.

The Statement establishes standards for reporting both general inflation (constant dollar accounting) and changes in specific prices (current cost accounting). The term "general inflation" means a rise in the general level of prices or a decline in the general purchasing power of the monetary unit. Since conventional financial statements are recorded in nominal dollars, there is no direct allowance for the variability of the dollar purchasing power. The presentation of certain financial information in units having the same general purchasing power may be useful to decision makers and the method used to compute that information is called "constant dollar accounting." The method used to compute changes in specific prices is called "current cost accounting." Appendix A is a glossary of selected terms useful in understanding the prescribed reporting standards.[1]

In the introduction to Statement No. 33, the FASB states that it is intended to help users of financial statements in the following ways:

1. Assessment of future cash flows
2. Assessment of enterprise performance
3. Assessment of the erosion of operating capability
4. Assessment of the erosion of general purchasing power

There is general agreement that the effects of changing prices should be taken into consideration in interpreting financial statements. There has not been general agreement on how to measure the change in prices. Thus, Statement No. 33 requires *supplementary disclosure* of certain information intended to show the effects of changing prices. The Statement does not change the standards of financial accounting and reporting used in the preparation of the customary historical cost financial statements. The supplementary disclosures were required to be included in annual reports for years ending on or after December 25, 1979. (Current cost information could be deferred until the 1980 annual report.)

The major provisions of the Statement require the following disclosures for the current year:

1. Adjustments for general inflation using an average for the year (or base year) constant dollar basis. The index to be used in computing information on a constant dollar basis is the Consumer Price Index for all Urban Consumers (CPI-U). Appendix B contains the CPI-U from 1919-1979.
2. Adjustments for current costs that may be based on specific price indices, current costs of comparable assets, or other measurement techniques.
3. A statement of income from continuing operations adjusted

[1] *Financial Reporting and Changing Prices*, Appendix F, Deloitte Haskins & Sells, 1979.

for the effects of changing prices on both a constant dollar and current cost basis.

4. The purchasing power gain or loss on net monetary items.
5. The current cost amounts of inventory and property, plant and equipment at the end of the fiscal year.
6. Holding gains or losses on inventory and property, plant and equipment during the year.

There are also additional requirements for disclosure of selected financial data for the five most recent fiscal years. They include the following:

1. Net sales and other operating revenues at historical cost and adjusted to a constant dollar basis.
2. Income (loss) from continuing operations adjusted for the effects of changing prices on both a constant dollar and current cost basis.
3. Income (loss) per common share from continuing operations on a constant dollar and current cost basis.
4. Net assets at fiscal year end on a constant dollar and current dollar basis.
5. Increase or decrease in current cost amounts of inventory and property, plant and equipment held during the year, net of inflation.
6. Purchasing power gain or loss on net monetary items.
7. Cash dividends per common share adjusted to a constant dollar basis.
8. Market price per common share at fiscal year end adjusted to a constant dollar basis.

Illustration of Presenting Supplementary Information

Statement No. 33 lists seven basic steps to restate nominal dollar information into constant dollars. These steps are:

1. Analyze inventory (at the beginning and end of the year) and cost of goods sold to determine when the costs were incurred.
2. Restate inventory and cost of goods sold into constant dollars and current cost.
3. Analyze property, plant and equipment and related deprecia-

tion, depletion and amortization expense to determine when the related assets were acquired.
4. Restate property, plant and equipment and depreciation, depletion and amortization expense into constant dollars and current cost.
5. Identify amount of net monetary items at the beginning and end of the period and changes during the period.
6. Compute the purchasing power gain or loss on net monetary items.
7. Compute change in current cost of inventory and property, plant and equipment and the related effect of the increase in the general price level.

The following is an illustration of the disclosure requirements of FASB Statement No. 33[2]. (The manner of presentation has been changed to follow the seven steps previously listed. The figures have not been changed.)

Exhibit 1 presents the base data for the Blank Company to be used in illustrating the computations necessary to meet the disclosure requirements of Statement No. 33.

Exhibit 1

BLANK COMPANY

1. Balance Sheet of Blank Company as of December 31, 1978

Assets

Current Assets			
Cash			$ 4,000
Accounts Receivable			6,000
Inventory (FIFO)			8,000
Total Current Assets			18,000
Long-Term Assets			
Equipment	$10,000		
Accumulated Depreciation	3,000	7,000	
Patents		5,500	12,500
Total Assets			$30,500

[2] Adapted from an illustration prepared by Deloitte Haskins & Sells in their publication *Financial Reporting and Changing Prices*, © 1979.

Exhibit 1 (continued)   *Liabilities and Stockholders' Equity*

Current Liabilities

Accounts Payable		$ 5,000

Other Liabilities

Deferred Federal Income Taxes		1,000
Total Liabilities		6,000

Stockholders' Equity

Capital Stock (1000 shares issued and outstanding)	$16,500	
Retained Earnings	8,000	24,500
Total Liabilities and Stockholders' Equity		$30,500

2. Combined Statement of Income and Retained Earnings of Blank Company for the Year Ended December 31, 1979

Sales		$60,000
Cost of Goods Sold (exclusive of depreciation expense)	$40,000	
Operating Expenses	8,000	
Depreciation of Equipment	2,000	
Amortization of Patents	500	50,500
Income Before Taxes		9,500
Federal Income Taxes		4,750
Net Income ($4.75 per share)		4,750
Retained Earnings, 12/31/78		8,000
		12,750
Dividends Paid ($3 per share)		3,000
Retained Earnings, 12/31/79		$ 9,750

3. Balance Sheet of Blank Company as of December 31, 1979

Assets

Current Assets

Cash		$ 8,000
Accounts Receivable		8,000
Inventory (FIFO)		12,000
Total Current Assets		28,000

Long-Term Assets

Equipment	$10,000		
Accumulated Depreciation	5,000	5,000	
Patents		5,000	10,000
Total Assets			$38,000

Liabilities and Stockholders' Equity

Current Liabilities

Accounts Payable		$ 6,000
Taxes Payable		4,750
Total Current Liabilities		10,750

Other Liabilities

Deferred Federal Income Taxes		1,000
Total Liabilities		11,750

Stockholders' Equity

Capital Stock (1000 shares issued and outstanding)	$16,500	
Retained Earnings	9,750	26,250
Total Liabilities and Stockholder's Equity		$38,000

4. Additional Data

a. *Current cost data*

Inventory:

Current cost at 12/31/78	$ 9,000
Current cost at 12/31/79	$12,500
Units in inventory at 12/31/79	10,000
Current cost per unit at 12/31/79	$ 1.25

Equipment (acquired in 1977)

Current cost at 12/31/78	$10,300
Current cost at 12/31/79	$ 6,500

Cost of goods sold:

Units sold	40,000
Weighted average current cost per unit	$ 1.05

Specific price index for machinery:

December 1979 index	546
Average 1977 index	420

Recoverable costs of inventory and property, plant and equipment exceed current costs.

b. *Other data*

- Sales are not seasonal
- Purchases are uniform over the year and total $44,000
- Operating expenses are uniform over the year
- Dividends are paid quarterly
- Depreciation rate is 20%, straight-line
- Patent, acquired 12/31/78, is amortized over 11 years
- Federal income tax rate is 50%

Consumer Price Index for All Urban Consumers (CPI-U):
Average Index:

1967	100 (Base year)
1975	161
1976	171
1977	182
1978	195
1979	217 (Estimated)

Monthly Index:

December 1978	203
December 1979	229 (Estimated)

Quarterly Index:

4th quarter 1978	202
2nd quarter 1979	214
4th quarter 1979	227 (Estimated)

c. *Prior years' data*

Year	Net sales	Cash dividends per common share	Market price per share of common stock at year end
1979	$60,000	$3.00	$60
1978	58,000	3.00	60
1977	57,000	2.50	58
1976	54,000	2.50	50
1975	52,000	2.25	52

Step 1—Analyze Inventory. The Statement recognizes the complexity of aging inventories, and permits alternative methods and shortcut procedures. One of the most useful shortcuts is to group inventories, in some cases without taking into consideration the stage of completion of the goods. The use of turnover indices and similar estimates result in the determination of a range of acquisition data rather than specific dates of acquisitions. From Exhibit 1, it can be determined that the inventory turnover for the Blank Company is four times per year. Because the company uses FIFO, the inventory on hand was purchased during the fourth quarter, 1979.

Step 2—Restate Inventory and Cost of Goods Sold. The constant dollar amount of inventory at the end of the current fiscal year is obtained by multiplying the historical cost amount by the average for the year index and dividing the result by the index for the applicable measurement data. For example:

Inventory, 12/31/79—as stated in the financial statements	$12,000
Average-for-the-year CPI-U	217
Measurement-date (date of purchase, fourth quarter 1979) CPI-U	227
Inventory, 12/31/79—as stated in average 1979 constant dollars ($12,000 × 217 ÷ 227)	$11,471

The current cost of inventory can be obtained by direct pricing or indicing. For the Blank Company, we will use direct pricing using the December 31, 1979 inventory cost of $1.25 per unit.

Inventory, 12/31/79—as stated in the financial statements	$12,000
Physical units of inventory, 12/31/79	10,000
Purchase price per unit, 12/31/79— as stated in suppliers' price lists	$1.25
Inventory, 12/31/79—as stated at current cost ($1.25 × 10,000)	$12,500

In order to compute income from continuing operations in constant dollars, cost of goods sold must also be restated.

| | Average-for-the-year CPI-U | | 217 |

Measurement-date (date of purchase, fourth quarter 1978) CPI-U — 202

Measurement-date (date of purchase, fourth quarter 1979) CPI-U — 227

	As Stated in the Financial Statements	Conversion Factor	As Stated in Average 1979 Dollars
Inventory, 1/1/79	$ 8,000	217 ÷ 202	$ 8,594
Purchases	44,000	217 ÷ 217	44,000
	52,000		52,594
Inventory, 12/31/79	12,000	217 ÷ 227	11,471
Cost of goods sold	$40,000		$41,123

The Statement requires that cost of goods sold be computed at current cost, or lower recoverable amount, at the date of each sale or at the date on which resources are used or committed to a specific contract. Satisfactory estimation of the current cost of goods sold ordinarily cannot be derived solely from the current cost of inventories at the end of the year. When using FIFO inventory, a weighted average cost of items purchased is useable to determine cost of goods sold. If LIFO is used, the LIFO cost of goods sold is a suitable approximation of the current cost.

Cost of goods sold—as stated in the financial statements	$40,000
Number of items sold	40,000
Weighted average purchase price— as shown by supplier's price lists	$1.05
Cost of goods sold—as stated at current cost ($1.05 × 40,000)	$42,000

Note: LIFO cost of goods sold usually may be used as a reasonable approximation of current cost of goods sold, except when LIFO cost layers are invaded or if turnover is slow.

Step 3—Analyze property, plant and equipment and related depre-

ciation. The property owned by the Blank Company was acquired in 1977.

Step 4—Restate property, plant and equipment and depreciation. The applicable measurement date for accumulated depreciation is not the date the depreciation was recorded, but the measurement date of the corresponding asset. Constant dollar accumulated depreciation normally is calculated by applying the method and rates of depreciation used in the primary financial statements restated to constant value of the assets.

Property, plant and equipment, 12/31/79— as stated in the financial statements	$10,000
Accumulated depreciation, as stated in the financial statements	$ 5,000
Average-for-the-year CPI-U	217
Measurement-date (date of purchase, 1977) CPI-U	182
Property, plant and equipment, 12/31/79— as stated in average 1979 constant dollars ($10,000 × 217 ÷ 182)	$11,923
Accumulated depreciation, 12/31/79—as stated in average 1979 constant dollars ($11,923 × 50%)	$ 5,961

For current cost restatement, the following methodology is used:

Property, plant and equipment, 12/31/79— as stated in the financial statements	$10,000
Accumulated depreciation, 12/31/79— as stated in the financial statements	$ 5,000
Specific price index for machinery, 12/31/79	546
Specific price index for machinery (at assumed date of purchase, 1977)	420
Property, plant and equipment, 12/31/79—as stated at current cost ($10,000 × 546 ÷ 420)	$13,000
Accumulated depreciation, 12/31/79—as stated at current cost ($13,000 × 50%)	$ 6,500

Note: This would be the procedure followed for one age group of assets. In a more complex situation, this example might be one line in a schedule of many items in property, plant and equipment.

Depreciation expense for the year stated in average for the year constant dollars should be computed by applying the depreciation rates used in determining the historical cost depreciation to the average for the year constant dollar amount of property, plant and equipment.

Property, plant and equipment—as stated in average 1979 constant dollars	$11,923
Depreciation rate	20%
Depreciation expense—as stated in average 1979 constant dollars ($11,923 × 20%)	$ 2,385

Constant-dollar depreciation expense for the year should be allocated to assets, cost of goods sold, and other components of income from continuing operations in the same manner that historical-cost depreciation expense is allocated to those items.

Current cost depreciation expense must be based on the average of the current cost of property, plant and equipment for the year, or lower appropriate value. In general, it will be necessary to compute current cost (or lower value in use, if applicable) of property, plant and equipment only at the beginning and end of the fiscal year and compute depreciation expense for the year on the resulting average figure.

Net property, plant and equipment:	
At current cost, 12/31/78	$10,300
At current cost, 12/31/79	$ 6,500
Average at current cost—during 1979	$ 8,400
Remaining useful life at 12/31/78	3.5 years
Depreciation expense—as stated at current cost ($8,400 ÷ 3.5)	$ 2,400

Note: This example is based on the assumption that all the property, plant and equipment was purchased at the same time. Where assets were purchased in different years, a similar computation would have to be made for each asset. Statement No. 33 gives a more detailed example working with assets acquired at different times.

Step 5—Identify amount of net monetary items and changes. (See glossary for definition of monetary assets and liabilities and Appendix C for an illustrative classification of these items.)

Step 6—Compute purchasing power gain or loss. After identifying all monetary items, opening and ending balances and net changes should be computed at historical costs. Net changes may be computed on a monthly, quarterly, or annual basis by comparing beginning and ending balances for each period.

The amount of purchasing power gain or loss on net monetary items for the year, stated in average-for-the-year constant dollars, is calculated by adding the year-end balance and any decreases, and deducting the beginning of the year balance and any increases, all as restated in average-for-the-current-year dollars.

Average-for-the-year CPI-U			217
Beginning-of-the-year (12/78) CPI-U			203
End-of-the-year (12/79) CPI-U			229

	As Stated in the Financial Statements	Conversion Factor	As Stated in Average 1979 Dollars
Net monetary assets, 1/1/79	$4,000	217 ÷ 203	$4,276
Annual increase	250	217 ÷ 217	250
			4,526
Net monetary assets, 12/31/79	4,250	217 ÷ 229	(4,027)
Purchasing power loss on net monetary items			$ 499

Note: Increase may be computed monthly or quarterly.

Step 7—Compute change in current cost of inventory and property and the related effect of the increase in the general price level. Increases or decreases in the current costs of inventory and property held during the period are increases or decreases between the start of the period (or date of acquisition, if later) and the end of the period (or date of realization, if earlier). These increases or decreases are commonly known as holding gains or losses. The calculations are illustrated here:

Balances, 1/1/79—at current cost:	
Inventory	$ 9,000
Property, plant and equipment, net	$10,300

Balances, 12/31/79—at current cost:
Inventory	12,500
Property, plant and equipment, net	6,500
Average-for-the-year CPI-U	217
Beginning-of-the-year (12/78) CPI-U	203
End-of-the-year (12/79) CPI-U	229

	As Stated at Current Cost	Conversion Factor	As Stated in Average 1979 Dollars
Balance, 12/31/79	$19,000	217 ÷ 229	$18,004
Cost of goods sold	42,000	217 ÷ 217	42,000
Disposals	—		—
Depreciation expense	2,400	217 ÷ 217	2,400
Acquisitions and production expenses	(44,000)	217 ÷ 217	(44,000)
Balance, 1/1/79	(19,300)	217 ÷ 203	(20,631)
Holding gain	$ 100		
Holding loss, net of general inflation			$ 2,227

A reasonable simplification, if there are no major fluctuations in the level of inflation or the volume of transactions during the year, is to consider that all current amounts of acquisitions and dispositions, as stated, are reasonable approximations of average-for-the-year current-cost amounts. Beginning and end of year balances, however, would have to be determined on a current-cost basis.

For purposes of complying with the provisions of the Statement, holding gains or losses are segregated between those that are realized and those that are unrealized.

After eliminating the effects of general inflation (by restating all historical-cost and current-cost amounts in average-for-the-current-year constant dollars), the holding gain or loss is the effect of the differences between the changes in the current cost of the assets held during the year and the changes in the general level of prices. If during the year the specific prices of the assets held increased more than the general level of prices, the enterprise will show a holding gain, net of inflation. If instead, the general level of prices increased more than

	As Stated in the Financial Statements	As Stated at Current Cost	Difference
Inventory, 1/1/79	$ 8,000	$ 9,000	$1,000
Inventory, 12/31/79	12,000	12,500	500
Cost of goods sold	40,000	42,000	2,000
Purchases	44,000	44,000	—
Property, plant and equipment 1/1/79	7,000	10,300	3,300
Property, plant and equipment, 12/31/79	5,000	6,500	1,500
Depreciation expense	2,000	2,400	400

	Inventory	Property, Plant and Equipment	Total
Unrealized gains:			
At 12/31/79	$ 500	$1,500	$2,000
At 1/1/79	1,000	3,300	4,300
Increase (decrease) in unrealized gains	(500)	(1,800)	(2,300)
Realized gains	2,000	400	2,400
Increase (decrease) in current cost of assets held during the year	$1,500	($1,400)	$ 100

the specific prices of the assets held, the enterprise will show a holding loss, net of inflation.

These net holding gains or losses may also be expressed as:

- The holding gains or losses, net of inflation, realized during the year, and
- The change in unrealized holding gains or losses, net of inflation, between the beginning and end of the year.

Companies are also required to present a five-year summary of selected financial data to aid users in assessing trends. The following discussion and examples are in reference to the five-year summary.

	Historical Costs as Adjusted for General Inflation	Current Costs as Adjusted for General Inflation	Difference
Inventory, 1/1/79	$ 8,594	$ 9,621	$1,027
Inventory, 12/31/79	11,471	11,845	374
Cost of goods sold	41,123	42,000	877
Purchases	44,000	44,000	–
Property, plant and equipment, 1/1/79	8,346	11,010	2,664
Property plant and equipment, 12/31/79	5,961	6,159	198
Depreciation expense	2,385	2,400	15

	Inventory	Property, Plant and Equipment	Total
Unrealized gains, adjusted for general inflation:			
At 12/31/79	$ 374	$ 198	$ 572
At 1/1/79	1,027	2,664	3,691
Increase (decrease) in unrealized gains, adjusted for general inflation	(653)	(2,466)	(3,119)
Realized gains, adjusted for general inflation	877	15	892
Increase (decrease) in current cost of assets held during the year, net of changes in the general price level	$ 224	($2,451)	($2,227)

Basis for Five-Year Summary Amounts

To ensure comparability, all information included in the five-year summary must be expressed in constant dollars having the same purchasing power. The enterprise may choose to report in average-for-the-current-year constant dollars, which is the basis used for the one-year supplementary information, or in base-year (1967 CPI-U = 100) constant dollars.

If average-for-the-current-year constant dollars are used, the information developed for prior years (which had been restated in average-for-the-prior-year constant dollars) must be rolled forward. This is done by multiplying the prior year's amounts by the average-for-the-current-year CPI-U, and dividing the results by the average-for-the-prior-year CPI-U. Furthermore, it will be necessary to roll forward prior-period amounts each year.

Average 1979 CPI-U					217
Average 1978 CPI-U					195
Conversion Factor (217 ÷ 195)					1.1128

	1975	1976	1977	1978	1979
Net sales, in average 1978 dollars	$62,981	$61,579	$61,072	$58,000	—
Conversion factor	1.1128	1.1128	1.1128	1.1128	—
Net sales, in average 1979 dollars	$70,087	$68,526	$67,962	$64,544	$60,000

The advantage of using this method is that the one-year and five-year data are reported in the same constant dollars, and that the purchasing power of the average-for-the-current-year dollar may be more familiar to users of the financial statements.

If base-year constant dollars are used, the information developed for the current year (which has been restated in average-for-the-current-year constant dollars) must be rolled back. This is done by multiplying current-year amounts by the base-year CPI-U (100) and dividing the result by the average-for-the-current-year CPI-U. Current year data only need to be rolled back. Prior period information is already restated in base-year constant dollars, and does not need to be restated again, unless the Bureau of Labor Statistics changes the base-year for the CPI-U.

Average 1979 CPI-U	217
Base-year (average 1967) CPI-U	100
Conversion factor (100 ÷ 217)	4608

	1975	1976	1977	1978	1979
Net sales, in base-year dollars	$32,298	$31,579	$31,319	$29,744	–
Net sales, in average 1979 dollars					$60,000
Conversion factor					.4608
Net sales, in base-year dollars	$32,298	$31,579	$31,319	$29,744	$27,650

The advantage of using this method is that the data reported in the five-year summary are not changed each year. Also, comparisons can be made with prior year's data over time and trends and ratios can be more easily maintained and presented. However, the current year's information will be expressed in different constant dollars in the one-year and five-year summaries. Also, users may not be familiar with or attach as much significance to the purchasing power of the base-year dollar.

It is important to analyze carefully all the data to be included in the five-year summary to ascertain that both current-cost and constant-dollar data are expressed in the same constant dollars (whether average-for-the-year or base-period). The dating of dollars is a new idea for many preparers and users of financial statements, and special efforts must be made to identify clearly the unit of measurement being used in reporting each item in the supplementary disclosures in order to minimize confusion. Care also must be exercised in comparing results derived from using different bases because in most situations they will not be comparable.

Net Assets at Fiscal Year End

The Statement requires the disclosure of net assets at the end of each of the last five fiscal years expressed on both a current-cost basis and a constant-dollar basis. However, to determine the required amounts, only the impact of price changes on inventory and property, plant and equipment needs to be considered. Inflation adjustments for all other nonmonetary items are not required. The resulting constant-dollar or current-cost net assets as of the end of each year must be stated in average-for-the-current-year or base-period constant dollars.

To determine the required amounts for each of the last five years on each basis, the following adjustments must be made:

Constant-dollar basis. Add (deduct) the excess of end-of-the-current-year constant-dollar amounts over historical costs at year-end of inventory and property, plant and equipment to the amount of net assets (stockholders' equity) at year-end as reported in the financial statements. Roll back the resulting amounts to average-for-the-current-year (or base-period, if elected) dollars.

Example of Constant-Dollar Basis:

Average 1979 CPI-U	217
Average 1977 CPI-U	182
End-of-the year (12/79) CPI-U	229
Fourth Quarter 1979 CPI-U	227

	As Stated in the Financial Statements	Conversion Factor	As Stated in Year-End Constant Dollars
Inventory	$12,000	229 ÷ 227	$12,106
Property, plant and equipment	10,000	229 ÷ 182	12,582
Accumulated depreciation	(5,000)	(50% × 12,582)	(6,291)
	$17,000		$18,397

Net assets (stockholders' equity), 12/31/79— as stated in the financial statements		$26,250
Inventory and property, plant and equipment, net:		
Year-end constant dollar amount	$18,397	
Financial statement amount	17,000	1,397
Net assets, 12/31/79—as stated in year-end constant dollars		$27,647

Multiply by conversion factor	$217 \div 229$
Net assets, 12/31/79—as stated in average 1979 constant dollars	$26,198

Current-cost basis. Add (deduct) the excess of current cost over historical cost of inventory and property, plant and equipment at year-end to the amount of net assets (stockholders' equity) at year-end as reported in the primary financial statements. Roll back the resulting amounts to average-for-the-current-year (or base-period, if elected) dollars.

Example of Current-Cost Basis:

Average 1979 CPI-U			217
End-of-the-year (12/79) CPI-U			229

	As Stated in the Financial Statements	As Stated at Current Cost
Inventory	$12,000	$12,500
Property, plant and equipment, net	5,000	6,500
	$17,000	$19,000

Net assets (stockholders' equity), 12/31/79—as stated in the financial statements		$26,250
Inventory and property, plant and equipment, net:		
Current-cost amounts	$19,000	
Financial statement amounts	17,000	2,000
Net assets, 12/31/79— as stated at current cost		$28,250
Conversion factor		$217 \div 229$
Net assets, 12/31/79—as stated at current cost in average-for-the-year dollars		$26,770

Exhibit 2 which follows illustrates the disclosure required by Statement No. 33, based on the computations given in earlier examples.

Exhibit 2
Illustrative Disclosure
Blank Company

In this Exhibit the required disclosures are illustrated and certain additional background data are given, arranged as follows:

- Supplementary Financial Data Adjusted for the Effects of Changing Prices, for the Year Ended December 31, 1979:
- Reconciliation format
- Statement format
- Supplementary Five-Year Comparison of Selected Financial Data Adjusted for the Effects of Changing Prices:
- In average 1979 dollars
- In average 1967 (base-year) dollars
- Notes to the Supplementary Financial Data Adjusted for the Effects of Changing Prices

Reconciliation Format

BLANK COMPANY

**Supplementary Financial Data Adjusted for the Effects of Changing Prices
For the Year Ended December 31, 1979
(In 000s of Dollars)**

Income from continuing operations as reported in the primary statement of income		$ 4,750
Adjustment to restate costs for the effects of general inflation		
Cost of goods sold	($1,123)	
Depreciation	(385)	($ 1,508)
Income from continuing operations adjusted for the effects of general inflation (in average 1979 dollars)		3,242
Adjustment to reflect the difference between general inflation and changes in specific prices (current costs)		
Cost of goods sold	(877)	
Depreciation	(15)	(892)
Income from continuing operations adjusted for changes in specific prices (in average 1979 dollars)		$ 2,350
Purchasing power loss on net monetary assets held during the year		$ 499
Increase in current cost of inventory and equipment held during the year (based on specific price changes)		$ 100
Effect of increase in general price level (*)		2,327
Decrease in current cost of inventory and equipment held during the year (based on specific price changes) net of changes in the general price level (net holding loss) (†)		$ 2,227

Inventory and Property, Plant and Equipment at December 31, 1979 Adjusted for Changes in Specific Prices—Current Costs

Inventory	$12,500
Equipment—net of accumulated depreciation	$ 6,500

(*) Presentation is not required by FASB Statement No. 33.
(†) The total increase in specific prices of inventory and equipment is less than the increase in the general price level during the year. This results in a *decrease* of the current costs in relation to the general price level.

Notes to the Supplementary Financial Data
Adjusted for the Effects of Changing Prices

Note 1. Basis of preparation

The Company's primary financial statements are prepared based mainly on historical prices, that is, the prices that were in effect when the transactions occurred. The supplementary financial information discloses certain effects of inflation and changes in the prices of the Company's inventory and property, plant and equipment as required by Statement of Financial Accounting Standards No. 33, *Financial Reporting and Changing Prices*, issued by the Financial-Accounting Standards Board.

Part of the information relating to years ended on or before December 31, 1978 is omitted, because it has proved impracticable to obtain such information.

The *Consumer Price Index for All Urban Consumers (CPI-U)*, prepared by the Bureau of Labor Statistics of the U.S. Department of Labor, is used to measure the effects of general inflation in the United States.

Note 2. Inventory and cost of goods sold

The current cost of inventory and cost of goods sold represents the cost of purchasing the goods concerned, or of acquiring the resources necessary to produce them, at year-end prices for inventory and at prices in effect at the date of sale for cost of goods sold. The information relating to prices at the different dates is obtained from current invoices, price lists and quotations from the Company's principal suppliers.

Note 3. Equipment and depreciation

To determine the current cost of equipment, the *Specific Price Index For Machinery* prepared by the Blank Industry Association, an independent trade association, is used. The Company believes that the application of this index results in a reasonable approximation of the current cost of acquiring used equipment with the same service potential as the equipment owned.

Current cost depreciation expense is determined on the basis of the average estimated current cost of equipment, using the same method and rates of depreciation as are used to prepare the Company's primary financial statements.

Note 4. Income taxes

As recommended by Statement of Financial Accounting Standards No. 33, no adjustments are made to income tax expense for any deferred income taxes that might be deemed to arise because of the differences between income reported on a current cost basis and income reported for tax purposes.

The income tax expense for the year shown in the primary financial statements is included in income from continuing operations adjusted for changes in specific prices (current costs). No portion of such tax expense is allocated to the increase or decrease in the current cost of inventory and equipment.

Statement Format

BLANK COMPANY

Supplementary Financial Data Adjusted for the Effects of Changing Prices for the Year Ended December 31, 1979
(In 000s of Dollars)

	As Stated in the Financial Statements	Adjusted for General Inflation (in average 1979 dollars)	Adjusted for Changes in Specific Prices (Current Costs)
Net sales	$60,000	$60,000	$60,000
Cost of goods sold (exclusive of depreciation)	40,000	41,123	42,000
Operating expenses	8,000	8,000	8,000
Depreciation of equipment	2,000	2,385	2,400
Amortization of patents	500	500	500
Federal income taxes	4,750	4,750	4,750
Total expenses	55,250	56,758	57,650
Income from continuing operations	$ 4,750	$ 3,242	$ 2,350
Purchasing power loss on net monetary assets held during the year		$ 499	$ 499
Increase in current cost of inventory and equipment held during the year (based on specific price changes)			$ 100
Effect of increase in general price level (*)			2,327
Decrease in current cost of inventory and equipment held during the year (based on specific price changes) net of changes in the general price level (net holding loss) (†)			$ 2,227

Inventory and Property, Plant and Equipment at December 31, 1979

Inventory			$12,500
Equipment—net of accumulated depreciation			$ 6,500

(*) Presentation is not required by FASB Statement No. 33.
(†) The total increase in specific prices of inventory and equipment is less than the increase in the general price level during the year. This results in a *decrease* of the current costs in relation to the general price level.

BLANK COMPANY

Supplementary Five-Year Comparison of Selected Financial Data Adjusted for the Effects of Changing Prices
(Average 1979 Dollars, in 000s Except Per Share Data)

| | Year Ended December 31 | | | | |
	1975	1976	1977	1978	1979
Historical cost information adjusted for general inflation					
Net sales	$70,087	$68,526	$67,962	$65,544	$60,000
Income from continuing operations	*	*	*	*	3,242
Income from continuing operations per common share	*	*	*	*	3.24
Purchasing power gain (loss) on net monetary items held during the year	*	*	*	*	(499)
Net assets at year end	*	*	*	*	26,198
Current cost information†					
Income from continuing operations	*	*	*	*	2,350
Income from continuing operations per common share	*	*	*	*	2.35
Excess of increase (decrease) in current cost of inventory and equipment held during the year (based on specific price changes) over changes in the general price level	*	*	*	*	(2,227)
Net assets at year end	*	*	*	*	26,770
Other information					
Cash dividends declared per common share	3.03	3.17	2.98	3.34	3.00
Market price per common share at year end	67.98	62.36	67.67	64.14	56.86
Average Consumer Price Index	161	171	182	195	217 (Estimated)

*Disclosure is not required for years ended before December 25, 1979
†Presentation of 1979 current-cost data may be deferred until 1980

BLANK COMPANY

Supplementary Five-Year Comparison of Selected Financial Data Adjusted for the Effects of Changing Prices
(Average 1967 Base-Year Dollars, in 000s Except Per Share Data)

	Year Ended December 31				
	1975	1976	1977	1978	1979
Historical cost information adjusted for general inflation					
Net sales	$32,298	$31,579	$31,319	$29,744	$27,650
Income from continuing operations	*	*	*	*	1,494
Income from continuing operations per common share	*	*	*	*	1.49
Purchasing power gain (loss) on net monetary items held during the year	*	*	*	*	(230)
Net assets at year end	*	*	*	*	12,073
Current cost information†					
Income from continuing operations	*	*	*	*	1,083
Income from continuing operations per common share	*	*	*	*	1.08
Excess of increase (decrease) in current cost of inventory and equipment held during the year (based on specific price changes) over changes in the general price level	*	*	*	*	
Net assets at year end	*	*	*	*	(1,026)
					12,336
Other information					
Cash dividends declared per common share	1.40	1.46	1.37	1.54	1.38
Market price per common share at year end	31.33	28.74	31.18	29.56	26.20
Average Consumer Price Index	161	171	182	195	217 (Estimated)

*Disclosure is not required for years ended before December 21, 5979.
†Presentation of 1979 current-cost data may be deferred until 1980.

FINANCIAL STATEMENT PRESENTATION

FASB Statement No. 33 requires no changes in the basic financial statements. The required information is to be presented in supplementary statements, schedules, or supplementary notes in financial reports.

In Exhibit 3, General Electric Co. showed the effects of changing prices in its 1979 annual report as supplementary information. Shell Company has published price level adjusted financial information each year since 1974 and presented the supplementary information as shown in Exhibit 4.

The FASB realized the difficulties of standardizing presentation and has written the Statement to provide more flexibility than is customary in Board Statements. It encourages experimentation within the guidelines of the Statement and the development of new techniques that fit the particular circumstances of the enterprise. This has resulted in some variations in the presentation of the supplementary information on the effects of changing prices, especially for enterprises of different industries.

In December 1979, the FASB published *Illustrations of Financial Reporting and Changing Prices* to help companies apply Statement No. 33 and disclose information on changing prices. The publication portrays the effects of changing prices on various types of enterprises and reflects the views of management in assessing the impact on their business operations.

It should be noted that application to income producing real estate properties and unprocessed natural resources have not yet been resolved adequately at the time of this writing. Such companies are not required to disclose current cost information about such assets (the assets are exempted but not the companies). There are no special exemptions from requirements to disclose information on a historical cost/constant dollar basis.

LIMITATIONS AND USEFULNESS OF FINANCIAL INFORMATION ADJUSTED FOR CHANGING PRICES

The special characteristics of an industry can be important factors in determining the kind of information that is most useful for assess-

EXHIBIT 3

Financial issues:
the impact of inflation

Inflation is commonly defined as a loss in value of money due to an increase in the volume of money and credit relative to available goods and services, resulting in a rise in the level of prices. Inflation in the U.S. is generally recognized to be caused by a combination of factors, including government deficits, sharp increases in energy costs, and low productivity gains including the effect of proliferating government regulations.

Although loss of purchasing power of the dollar impacts all areas of the economy, it is particularly onerous in its effect on savings — of both individuals in forms such as savings accounts, securities and pensions, and of corporations in the form of retained earnings.

For the individual, with inflation of 6% a year, the dollar saved by a person at age 50 will have lost three-fifths of its value by the time the person is age 65. With a 10% inflation rate, almost four-fifths of the dollar's value is lost in 15 years. This problem affects almost everyone, including those presently working and especially those who are on fixed incomes.

The situation is rendered even more difficult by the progressive income tax system. A Congressional staff study reports that a family of four with an income of $8,132 in 1964 would need a 1979 income of $18,918 to have kept pace with the increase in the Consumer Price Index over the years. However, the 1979 income of $18,918 puts the family into a higher tax bracket which, when coupled with increased Social Security taxes, reduces real after-tax income $1,068 below the equivalent 1964 level.

Your Company and all U.S. businesses face a similar problem. Business savings are in the form of retained earnings — the earnings a company keeps after paying employees, suppliers and vendors, and after payment of taxes to government and dividends to share owners. If a company is to continue in business, much less grow, it must be able to save or retain sufficient earnings, after providing a return to its share owners, to fund the cost of replacing — at today's inflated prices — the productive assets used up. Retention of capital in these inflationary times under existing tax laws is a challenge facing all businesses.

U.S. tax regulations permit recognition of the impact of inflation on a company's inventory costs by use of the LIFO (last-in, first-out) inventory method. In general, under the LIFO method, a company charges off to operations the current cost of inventories consumed during the year. With inflation averaging over 11% last year, the negative impact on operations of using current costs with respect to a supply of goods is substantial. Financial results are portrayed more accurately when the LIFO method is used in periods of high inflation, and GE has used LIFO for most of its U.S. manufacturing inventories for a quarter-century. The Statement of Earnings on page 32 is on that basis. As supplementary information to that Statement of Earnings: use of the LIFO method increased 1979 and 1978 operating costs by $430.8 million and $224.1 million (to $20,330.7 million and $17,695.9 million), respectively, with a corresponding reduction of reported pre-tax profits.

Unfortunately, U.S. tax regulations fail to provide an equivalent to LIFO for the impact of inflation on a company's costs of property, plant and equipment. Instead, deductions for wear and tear on these assets are based on original purchase costs rather than today's replacement costs. In general, the resulting shortfall must be funded from after-tax earnings.

The supplementary information shown in Table 1 restates operating results to eliminate the major effects of inflation discussed above. Table 1 compares GE operating results as reported on page 32 with results adjusted in two ways. First, results are restated to show the effects of general inflation — the loss of the dollar's purchasing power — on inventories and fixed assets. The second restatement shows results restated for changes in specific prices — the current costs of replacing those assets. Your management feels that the last column in Table 1 is the more meaningful and has therefore shown, in Table 2 on page 30, five years of results on that basis, also adjusted to equivalent 1979 dollars. While the techniques used are not precise, they do produce reasonable approximations.

In these earnings statements, specific adjustments are made to (1) *cost of goods sold* for the current cost of replacing inventories and (2) *depreciation* for the current costs of plant and equipment. The restatements for inventories are relatively small because GE's extensive use of LIFO accounting already largely reflects current costs in the traditional statements. However, a substantial restatement is made for the impact of inflation on fixed assets, which have relatively long lives. The $624 million of depreciation as traditionally reported, when restated for general inflation, increases to a total of $880 million. But the restatement necessary to reflect replacement of these assets at current costs grows to $980 million. The net effect of these restatements lowers reported income of $6.20 a share to $4.68 on a general inflation-adjusted basis and $4.34 on a specific current cost basis.

It is significant to note that for the five years 1975-1979, even after adjustment for inflation, your Company has shown real growth in earnings and a steady increase in share owners' equity over the entire period. After adjusting earnings for current costs and restating all years to equivalent 1979 dollars, your Company's average annual growth rate in real earnings was 21% since 1975 and 8% since 1976. This means that the growth in GE's earnings has been real, not just the product of inflation.

An important insight from these data is depicted in the pie charts at right. These show that, over the five years 1975-1979, because of inflation 10% more of GE's earnings were taxed away than appeared to have been the case using traditional financial statements. While the traditional earnings statements indicated an effective tax rate of 41% over this period, the "real" tax rate averaged 51% of profits before taxes. Consequently, earnings retained for growth were cut in half to 16% of income before tax, not 32% as reflected in the traditional financial statements. Over the period, share owners received a measure of protection against inflation's impact as about two-thirds of after-tax earnings were distributed — equivalent to an average annual growth rate of about 8% in real dividends.

An area receiving special attention by management is experimentation with the use of inflation-adjusted measurements at the individual business and project level for capital budgeting. Since 1973, your Company has been experimenting with various techniques to measure the impact of inflation, to incorporate the perspectives provided by such measurements into decision-making, and to stimulate awareness by all levels of management of the need to develop constructive business strategies to deal with inflation. The objective is to ensure that investments needed for new business growth, productivity improvements and capacity expansions earn appropriate

Table 1: supplementary information – effect of changing prices (a)

(In millions, except per-share amounts)	As reported in the traditional statements	Adjusted for general inflation	Adjusted for changes in specific prices (current costs) (b)
For the year ended December 31, 1979		The notes on page 30 are an integral part of this statement.	
Sales of products and services to customers	$22,461	$22,461	$22,461
Cost of goods sold	15,991	16,093	16,074
Selling, general and administrative expense	3,716	3,716	3,716
Depreciation, depletion and amortization	624	880	980
Interest and other financial charges	258	258	258
Other income	(519)	(519)	(519)
Earnings before income taxes and minority interest	2,391	2,033	1,952
Provision for income taxes	953	953	953
Minority interest in earnings of consolidated affiliates	29	16	13
Net earnings applicable to common stock	$ 1,409	$ 1,064	$ 986
Earnings per common share	$ 6.20	$ 4.68	$ 4.34
Share owners' equity at year end (net assets) (c)	$ 7,362	$10,436	$11,153

Use of each dollar of earnings
Based on total earnings before taxes 1975-1979

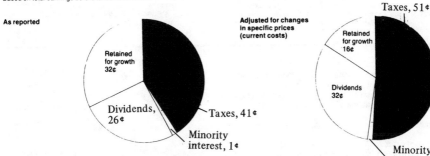

Taxes, 51¢

As reported

Adjusted for changes in specific prices (current costs)

Retained for growth 32¢

Retained for growth 16¢

Dividends, 26 ¢

Dividends 32¢

Taxes, 41 ¢

Minority interest, 1 ¢

Minority interest, 1 ¢

Table 2: supplementary information – effect of changing prices (a)

(In millions, except per-share amounts)

Current cost information in dollars of 1979 purchasing power (b)					
(All amounts expressed in average 1979 dollars)	1979	1978	1977	1976	1975
Sales of products and services to customers	$22.461	$21.867	$20.984	$20.015	$19.022
Cost of goods sold	16.074	15.548	14.793	14.145	13.914
Selling, general and administrative expense	3.716	3.566	3.606	3.360	3.018
Depreciation, depletion and amortization	980	1.000	986	979	1.006
Interest and other financial charges	258	249	238	222	251
Other income	(519)	(466)	(467)	(350)	(235)
Earnings before income taxes and minority interest	1,952	1,970	1,828	1,659	1,068
Provision for income taxes	953	995	926	853	620
Minority interest in earnings of consolidated affiliates	13	13	20	26	26
Net earnings applicable to common stock	$ 986	$ 962	$ 882	$ 780	$ 422
Earnings per common share	$ 4.34	$ 4.22	$ 3.88	$ 3.45	$ 1.88
Share owners' equity at year end (net assets) (c)	$11,153	$11,020	$10,656	$10,526	$10,056
Other inflation information					
Average Consumer Price Index (1967 = 100)	217.4	195.4	181.5	170.5	161.2
(Loss)/gain in general purchasing power of net monetary items	$(209)	$(128)	$ (61)	$ (20)	$ 19
Dividends declared per common share	2.75	2.78	2.52	2.17	2.16
Market price per common share at year end	47⅞	50½	58¼	69⅜	60¼

Notes to supplementary information — Tables 1 and 2

(a) This information has been prepared in accordance with requirements of the Financial Accounting Standards Board (FASB). Proper use of this information requires an understanding of certain basic concepts and definitions.

The heading "As reported in the traditional statements" refers to information drawn directly from the financial statements presented on pages 32 to 44. This information is prepared using the set of generally accepted accounting principles which renders an accounting based on the number of actual dollars involved in transactions, with no recognition given to the fact that the value of the dollar changes over time.

The heading "Adjusted for general inflation" refers to information prepared using a different approach to transactions involving inventory and property, plant and equipment assets. Under this procedure, the number of dollars involved in transactions at different dates are all restated to equivalent amounts in terms of the general purchasing power of the dollar as it is measured by the Consumer Price Index for all Urban Consumers (CPI-U). For example, $1,000 invested in a building asset in 1967 would be restated to its 1979 dollar purchasing power equivalent of $2,174 to value the asset and calculate depreciation charges. Similarly, 1978 purchases of non-LIFO inventory sold in 1979 would be accounted for at their equivalent in terms of 1979 dollars, rather than in terms of the actual number of dollars spent.

The heading "Adjusted for changes in specific prices (current costs)" refers to information prepared using yet another approach to transactions involving inventory and property, plant and equipment assets. In this case, rather than restating to dollars of the same general purchasing power, estimates of current costs of the assets are used.

In presenting results of either of the supplementary accounting methods for more than one year, "real" trends are more evident when results for all years are expressed in terms of the general purchasing power of the dollar for a designated period. Results of such restatements are generally called "constant dollar" presentations. In the five-year presentations shown above, dollar results for earlier periods have been restated to their equivalent number of constant dollars of 1979 general purchasing power (CPI-U basis).

Since none of these restatements is allowable for tax purposes under existing regulations, income tax amounts are the same as in the traditional statements (but expressed in constant dollars in the five-year summary).

There are a number of other terms and concepts which may be of interest in assessing the significance of the supplementary information shown in Tables 1 and 2. However, it is management's opinion that the basic concepts discussed above are the most significant for the reader to have in mind while reviewing this information.

(b) Principal types of information used to adjust for changes in specific prices (current costs) are (1) for inventory costs, GE-generated indices of price changes for specific goods and services, and (2) for property, plant and equipment, externally generated indices of price changes for major classes of assets.

(c) At December 31, 1979, the current cost of inventory was $5,251 million, and of property, plant and equipment was $7,004 million. Estimated current costs applicable to the sum of such amounts held during all or part of 1979 increased by approximately $1,111 million, which was $329 million less than the $1,440-million increase which could be expected because of general inflation.

Exhibit 3 continued.

real rates of return commensurate with the risks involved. Such supplemental measurements can assist in the entire resource allocation process, starting with initial project approval, implementation and subsequent review.

Improving productivity to offset inflationary forces is a primary goal established by top management that is being stressed throughout General Electric. As discussed on the back cover of this Annual Report, the Company has committed significant levels of resources to research and development activities to accelerate innovation and increase productivity. In addition, General Electric's production base continues to be expanded and modernized through increasing investments in plant and equipment. For example, $1,262 million and $1,055 million were spent on strengthening General Electric's production base in 1979 and 1978, respectively. Imaginative and diligent coupling of production techniques and equipment is critical to the maintenance and improvement of your Company's profitability.

EXHIBIT 4
Supplementary Information Regarding Inflation and Changing Prices

For some years there has been growing concern about the impact of inflation on the performance of business enterprises as measured by traditional financial statements. In an effort to assist readers of financial statements in understanding the severity of this impact, Shell has published price-level adjusted financial information each year since 1974.

During 1979, the Financial Accounting Standards Board (FASB) issued Statement No. 33, Financial Reporting and Changing Prices, which provides new rules for the publication of certain inflation related information. The data that follows is presented in accordance with this statement. The FASB has decided, and Shell fully agrees, that traditional financial statements should be retained as the primary record of performance but that these should be supplemented by inflation adjusted information.

Shell's primary financial statements, which appear on pages 30 to 33, are prepared under generally accepted accounting principles and are known as historical cost financial statements. They record actual transactions in terms of the number of dollars received or expended without regard to changes in the purchasing power of the currency or changes in the cost of goods and services consumed. The result is that investments made over extended periods of time are added together as though the dollars involved all have the same value. Moreover, the amortization of these prior period costs is deducted from current period revenues so that net income is the result of matching revenues and costs in dollars with differing amounts of purchasing power.

Another objection to traditional financial statements is that they reflect the historic cost rather than the current cost of assets consumed. Costs change for many reasons in addition to inflation, e.g., technological improvements, changes in productivity, variations in supply and demand, etc. These changes are usually at different rates than that of general inflation. In recognition of the separate problems created by inflation and by changing prices, the FASB has mandated two forms of supplemental disclosure. One is to isolate the impact of general inflation and is called Constant Dollar reporting. The second is an attempt to identify the other components of changing prices on a company's performance as well, and is called Current Cost reporting. Both approaches are reported on page 45.

Constant Dollar Data

Constant dollar data measures the effects of general inflation on the financial results of the Company. Although some minor variations in techniques have been adopted by the FASB, in prior years we have referred to this as price-level adjusted financial information. It is calculated according to a precise mathematical procedure and is, therefore, objective and comparable among companies.

Under this method, historical cost financial information is adjusted only for changes that have occurred in the general purchasing power of the dollar as measured by the Consumer Price Index. Therefore, the result is a restatement of the traditional financial information in a common unit of measurement, which in the attached schedule is the dollar

as valued at the end of 1979. It is appropriate to note that the results of this approach do not purport to represent appraised value, replacement cost, or any other measure of the current value of the underlying assets. Although the constant dollar information in this schedule is presented in summary form, comprehensive restatements were made of all financial statement elements to determine the amounts shown.

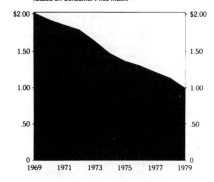

Purchasing Power of the Dollar
(Based on Consumer Price Index)

Current Cost Data

The second form of disclosure prescribed by Statement 33 measures the impact of changes in the specific prices of property, plant and equipment, inventories, depreciation and depletion, and costs and expenses.

Because of the large number of assets owned by Shell, current cost measurement of individual assets was not feasible. Therefore, various indexes were employed that appear to be compatible with the changing costs experienced by Shell. Although the resulting estimates are believed to be reasonable, they do involve a number of subjective judgments. For example, about one-fourth of the balance in the property, plant and equipment categories is for unexpired costs of developing oil and gas reserves. The current cost adjustment was made by applying an index based on the industry's average cost of drilling and equipping wells. Therefore, the results are not projections of future costs but are approximations of the amounts that would result had past drilling and development occurred at today's prices. The adjusted amounts for depreciation, depletion and amortization are based on these same premises. All current costs are expressed in year-end 1979 dollars.

Purchasing Power Gain on Net Monetary Items

In addition to the impacts just described, inflation also affects monetary assets and liabilities. Holders of cash and receivables lose purchasing power during inflationary periods because they will buy less as prices rise. Conversely, those holding liabilities stand to gain because less purchas-

Exhibit 4 continued.

Historical Dollars 1979	Millions of dollars, except per share amounts	Dollars of Current Purchasing Power*			
		Constant Dollar Data		Current Cost Data	
		1979	1978	1979	1978
	Summary Statement of Income				
$14,546	Revenues	$15,374	$13,081	$15,374	$13,081
	Cost and Expenses:				
704	Depreciation, depletion, etc.	1,107	1,015	1,219	1,217
1,090	Income and operating taxes	1,152	917	1,152	917
11,626	Other costs and expenses	12,337	10,545	12,362	10,684
1,126	Income from Continuing Operations	778	604	$ 641	$ 263
	Purchasing power gain on net monetary items	337	236	$ 337	$ 236
$ 1,126	Net Income	$ 1,115	$ 840		
	Increase in current cost valuation of inventory and property, plant & equipment held during year			$ 2,149	$ 1,158
	Effect of increases in general price level			1,754	1,176
	Excess of increase in specific prices over increase in general price level...............			$ 395	$ (18)
	Balance Sheet Data				
$ 520	Inventories of Oils and Chemicals	$ 880	$ 890	$ 2,231	$ 1,557
$12,385	Net Property, Plant & Equipment	$16,043	$11,469	$17,178	$13,051
$ 7,004	Shareholders' Equity	$11,131	$10,257	$13,617	$12,505
	Per Share Data†				
$ 7.32	Income from Continuing Operations	$ 5.06	$ 4.05	$ 4.17	$ 1.76
$ 7.32	Net Income	$ 7.26	$ 5.63	—	—

Five-Year Comparisons *(In December 1979 dollars)*	1979	1978	1977	1976	1975
Revenues	$15,374	$13,081	$12,912	$12,551	$11,732
Constant dollar net income	$ 1,115	$ 840	$ 805	$ 778	$ 593
Cash dividends per share†	$ 2.22	$ 2.04	$ 1.98	$ 1.85	$ 1.80
Closing market price per share	$ 54.25	$ 36.54	$ 41.37	$ 52.02	$ 33.86
Consumer price index — end of year	229.9	202.9	186.1	174.3	166.3
Ratios:					
Net Income to Shareholders' Equity:					
Historical cost basis	18.4%	15.1%	16.2%.	18.2%	14.4%
Constant dollar basis	10.9%	8.8%	9.1%	9.7%	7.7%
Income from Continuing Operations to Shareholders' Equity:					
Historical cost basis	18.4%	15.1%	16.2%	18.2%	14.4%
Constant dollar basis ....:................	7.6%	6.3%	7.4%	8.5%	6.0%
Current cost basis	5.1%	2.2%	—	—	—

*Current cost and constant dollar amounts are expressed in December 1979 dollars. Changes are measured by the consumer price index.

†Per weighted average shares outstanding each year.

ing power will be required to satisfy their obligations. These gains and losses have long been considered to be an integral part of the constant dollar concept of income and are therefore included in constant dollar "Net Income" in the table on page 45.

Income Taxes

In conformance with Statement 33, income taxes included in the supplemental statement of income are the same as reported in the primary financial statements except that the amounts are expressed in year-end dollars. Present tax laws do not allow deductions for higher depreciation or other cost adjustments for the effects of inflation. Consequently, taxes are levied on industry and individuals at effective rates well in excess of statutory rates for many years following periods of high inflation.

Review of Information Presented

As shown on page 46, Shell has reported substantial growth in both sales and net income under traditional accounting measurements. A further perspective of Shell's progress is obtained by expressing all financial statement amounts in constant dollars. On this basis, Income from Continuing Operations was $778 million in 1979, significantly lower than the comparable historic cost measurement. The high rates of inflation also caused large purchasing power gains on Shell's net monetary liabilities. When these gains are added to Income from Continuing Operations the resulting Net

Income is about the same as historic cost Net Income. However, it is important to relate any measure of income to the investment required to generate it. As indicated in the Five-Year Comparisons on page 45, Shell's profitability ratios are significantly lower when both income and Shareholders' Equity are stated in constant dollars. For example, the 1979 ratio of Net Income to Shareholders' Equity is reduced from 18.4 percent to 10.9 percent when viewed on a constant dollar basis.

Although current cost data is of necessity subjective, it provides an approximation of the margin between Shell's current revenues and the current costs of goods consumed and services utilized. During 1979 and 1978, this margin was substantially less than income based on historical costs.

In addition, Statement 33 requires that current cost disclosures include supplemental information on changes in the purchasing power of monetary items and changes in the current cost of inventories and property, plant and equipment. The FASB believes these disclosures may provide information that is useful as an indicator of potential future cash flows.

Shell's 1979 increase in the current cost of inventories and property, plant and equipment was largely attributable to the rising costs of crude oil and increasing costs of productive facilities. Shell believes it is important to recognize that such increases would only be realized in the unlikely event that these assets were totally liquidated.

---

ing the effects of changing prices. This is particularly so for enterprises which own assets subject to high technological changes. There is difficulty in obtaining an accurate current cost of such assets; the greater the degree or rate of technological changes affecting an enterprise's equipment or product, the less accurate will be the current cost computation.

In its first year of introduction, many shortcomings were detected in implementing the Statement that have led to certain confusion and hamper a clear understanding of financial information adjusted for changing prices. A major shortcoming is the failure of Statement No. 33 to require a comprehensive restatement for constant dollar information. This has resulted in the different treatments accorded to nonmonetary assets. Several public enterprises have significant investments in nonmonetary assets such as equity subsidiaries and joint ventures, intangible assets (patents), and marketable securities. These assets are affected by inflation but Statement No. 33 does not require their adjustments. With flexibility accorded to these public enterprises, some have adjusted these assets while others have not, which have led to confusion and incomplete and noncomparable data.

The five-year disclosure of net assets has also been affected by the different treatment accorded to nonmonetary assets, especially when they are material in amount.

Similarly, a comprehensive restatement would require unconsolidated finance subsidiaries to be restated for the impact of inflation (note that Statement No. 33 does not require unconsolidated finance subsidiaries and other equity investments to be restated). Since substantially all the assets and liabilities of a finance subsidiary are monetary, a monetary loss will result to the extent of the parent company's equity investment during a period of inflation. By substituting a nonmonetary investment that is not adjusted for inflation for the subsidiary's monetary assets, the parent company can show different results than if the subsidiaries were consolidated.

Another shortcoming is the requirement to use average-for-the-year dollars rather than the end-of-the-year dollars. The use of the average-for-the-year dollars to simplify calculation and avoid adjustments to revenue and certain other expenses has led to year-end inventories, market price of stocks and dividends being reported at lower absolute amounts than historical cost when they are adjusted to constant dollars using average-for-the-year dollars. It could be difficult to explain to the layman why inventory, market price of stocks and dividends adjusted for the effects of inflation are deflated while property, plant and equipment are inflated.

The option given by Statement No. 33 that allows constant dollar information to be presented in terms of a base year that can either be the current year or the base year of the Consumer Price Index (1967) has led to unnecessary confusion. The use of the current year dollar as the base year would require the five-year summary information to be restated every year. This restatement every year would change the previous four years' information which will add to further confusion. Nevertheless, users of supplementary information who want to make company-to-company comparison should watch for such differences. The conversion of a company's data from one base year to the base year (which is different) of the other company is not difficult since the index for each year is provided. To convert, multiply the data by a fraction, the numerator of which is the index for the base year you want the data in and the denominator of which is the base year the data is in.

The exclusion of the purchasing power gain or loss from the determination of constant-dollar income would seem to raise some doubt as to whether such gains or losses are real. The purchasing power gain or loss is a real reflection of inflation and the requirement that it be

reported separately makes the constant-dollar statements more difficult to explain.

These are some problems that arose from the early application of
the Statement and represent deficiencies which present problems in
quality and comparability of the information. Despite these deficiencies, some trends and patterns are emerging from the information
being reported.

One leading accountant has made the following observations based
on emerging trends and patterns:[3]

1. *Income from operations, excluding purchasing power gain or
   loss, will decrease.* The extent of the decrease will depend on
   the industry, but overall the decrease will probably exceed
   40%. The major cause of the decrease is price-level-adjusted
   depreciation expense. A secondary cause is the effect of holding inventories during a time of inflation. For example, General
   Electric, General Motors and Shell Oil reported decreases from
   historical-cost income to constant-dollar income of 24%, 39%
   and 31%. Their current-cost decreases were similar. These companies are all on LIFO. If they were on FIFO, the declines
   would have been more significant. More capital-intensive companies, such as Inland Steel and American Telephone and Telegraph, had larger decreases—53% and 70%. Historical cost
   captures such inflation gains in inventory leading to the so-
   called inflationary profits. These profits are eliminated from
   constant-dollar disclosures.

2. *Tax rates will skyrocket.* On an average, they may increase by
   as much as 25% to an effective rate of 55% to 65%. This was
   the increase in the effective tax rate in a 1974 survey of 80
   companies on the impact of constant-dollar accounting. In
   1979, General Electric, General Motors and Shell Oil had increases in effective tax rates of 7% (from 40% to 47%), 13%
   (from 45% to 58%) and 7% (from 46% to 53%). Many utilities' tax rates are close to 100% on an adjusted basis. Many
   companies are prominently displaying such tax rates to emphasize the need for legislation.

3. *The purchasing power gain or loss will vary significantly from
   company to company.* By and large, it will be a gain. In fact,

---

[3] *Inflation and Its Impact on Financial Executives* by Duane R. Kullberg, Chairman
and Chief Executive Officer, Arthur Andersen and Company, May 30, 1980.

for the average company the purchasing power gain may just about equal the decrease in operating income resulting from adjusting depreciation and inventory, plant and equipment. Thus, the fact that Statement 33 does not include the purchasing power gain in restated income will tend to exaggerate the negative impact of inflation. Some conservatively capitalized companies such as IBM, however, show a loss from monetary items.

4. *Rates of return on stockholders' equity will decline.* Return on investment decreases dramatically as a result of both the decline in earnings and the increase in equity resulting from price-level adjustments to inventory and property, plant and equipment.

5. *Debt-to-equity ratios will improve.* A potential benefit of constant-dollar adjustments could be a more realistic assessment of debt-to-equity ratios. Such ratios have deteriorated in historical dollars. However, rules of thumb for financial analysis purposes have not changed. If the improvement resulting from inflation adjustments is widely accepted, some of the pressure for off-balance-sheet financing may be mitigated. Ultimately, the importance of Statement 33 will be measured by the reaction of the investment community. Investment analysts are already making some interesting observations on the impact of constant-dollar accounting.

6. *Many companies are reporting deflated or decreasing dividend rates.* Those companies whose dividend increases have fallen below the rate of general price inflation may be encouraged to increase their dividends. However, dividend payout ratios may be used to defend against raising dividends. For example, in constant dollars, General Motors had a dividend payout ratio of 86% (compared to 53% in historical dollars), Inland Steel of 97% compared to 45%, and American Telephone and Telegraph of 204% compared to 62%.

7. *Resistance to LIFO may decrease.* Some companies have resisted the use of LIFO because of its negative impact on nominal dollar earnings. Such resistance may decrease since constant-dollar costs of sales approximate LIFO cost of sales. The tax

advantages of LIFO are more likely to overcome the perceived accounting result disadvantages of LIFO.

8. *New tests for evaluating leverage barriers or debt-equity ratios may emerge.* Some companies with weak debt-equity ratios in nominal terms will be perceived to be stronger than expected in constant terms. Maybe there will be a return to the more traditional forms of financing.

9. *Pricing policies may be reconsidered.* Restated expense information is revealing that on a constant-dollar basis, price increases may not be keeping up with inflation in certain industries. All of this suggests a need for a real sensitivity to the effects of inflation on operating and financing decisions.

Traditional management rules to manage a public enterprise do not change during a period of inflation. Inflation, however, results in additional emphasis being placed on certain rules. The following is a list of positive things a public enterprise (and mostly everyone else) can do to increase return during a time of inflation:[4]

1. *Minimize monetary assets.* Companies' treasurers have grown quite sophisticated in this area, and perhaps there is no room for improvement in such things as cash collections, the use of lock box systems and the timely investment of available cash. However, accounts receivable are also monetary assets. Some companies carry receivables as part of a marketing strategy. This strategy should be evaluated in light of inflation.

2. *Review credit and collection policies.* Credit limits, payment terms, deposit requirements, progress payments, discount availability and collection procedures require special consideration in times of inflation, as do policies regarding delinquent accounts. It may no longer be profitable to carry the customers' receivables for 90 days or more. That kind of marginal business may not be profitable during times of inflation.

3. *Maximize monetary liabilities.* This is the one management rule that differs under inflation from traditional corporate fi-

[4] *Ibid.*

nancial management. Everyone understands the advantages of being in debt during times of inflation. An article in the March 12 edition of *The Wall Street Journal* suggested that inflation has helped reduce bankruptcy because borrowings are paid back in cheaper dollars. The Journal pointed out that the bankruptcy rate in 1961 was 64 out of every 10,000 companies that went under. In 1979, the rate had dropped to 30 out of every 10,000. Price-level information will be helpful when seeking funds to borrow. Restated debt-equity ratios will also be helpful in selling the company's financial strength. Debt provides a hedge during times of inflation. Obviously, the benefits of the hedge must be weighed against the risks of further leveraging.

4. *Manage nonmonetary assets.* Inventory is a particularly important asset to manage during inflationary times. Product pricing is critical. It is essential that companies review inventory systems to make certain that management receives needed information on a timely basis. Inventory systems must provide current-cost information continuously to provide the information necessary for proper product pricing. Decisions to increase prices must be made quickly and accurately. Obviously, escalation clauses should be incorporated into pricing whenever possible. Inventory levels are important in inflation, and inflation itself becomes an important element of inventory carrying costs. Inventory carrying costs should be recalculated because inflation is a negative carrying cost. Inventory may be a better investment than marketable securities if prices in your industry are rising faster than general price changes. But if specific prices in the industry lag general price increases, then inventory should be minimized and the resulting cash flow should be invested in marketable securities. It is obvious that the impact of inflation on inventories is different from that of receivables.

5. *Plan in inflation-adjusted dollars.* Inflation's impact on the business should be more important to internal management than to stockholders. Projections and business plans should utilize inflation-adjusted data, and several assumptions about levels of inflation may be used to achieve flexibility. Computerized financial modeling may be helpful to provide timely adjustments in a period of rapidly changing prices. It will be

necessary for management to face up to the company's actual performance on an inflation-adjusted basis. If management doesn't, the market certainly will. Planning based on inflation is not new to some companies. Shell Oil, for example, uses inflation-adjusted data in internal reports, and General Electric does its planning in current-cost dollars. In its annual report, General Electric points out that its objective "is to ensure that investments needed for new business growth, productivity improvements and capacity expansions earn appropriate real rates of return commensurate with the risks involved."

6. *Reevaluate tax-planning decisions.* Decisions that were rejected in the past because of marginal benefits may now have a positive impact on earnings because of inflation. Because taxes are paid on both real profits and inflation profits, the tax system really confiscates capital. As a result, it may be necessary to reconsider adopting LIFO. Depreciation lives and methods should be reconsidered so maximum amounts are claimed. Receivable reserves should reflect collection slowdowns. Pension payments should be delayed as long as the law permits.

7. *Capital needs must be carefully planned and evaluated in relation to capital availability.* Leasing should be considered as an additional source of funds. Sale and leaseback transactions may free up funds. Factoring receivables may provide a source of cash. Joint-venture arrangements are becoming a more popular vehicle for financing large projects. Dividend policies may also need reconsideration. Each of these possibilities involves good, commonsense management.

SUMMARY

Traditional financial statements have been prepared based mainly on historical costs, with the use of a variety of current value measurements. In order for financial reporting to provide meaningful and useful financial information to internal and external decision makers, financial reporting has to adjust itself to the changing economic, legal, political and social environment. With inflation running above 10 percent, traditional accounting data often presents false comfort.

Inflation adjusted data may provide more meaningful and useful information for management decision making.

FASB Statement No. 33 establishes standards of reporting for both general inflation and changes in specific prices. It applies to public corporations having total assets of $1 billion or more after deducting depreciation or having inventories plus gross property, plant and equipment of $125 million or more. The Statement requires no change in the basic financial statement and the required information is to be presented in supplementary statements, schedules or supplementary notes in the financial reports.

Although several problems have been detected in applying Statement No. 33, trends and patterns have emerged from the information reported that will prove useful to the various decision makers. This information will enable the management of the corporation to emphasize certain management rules in managing the corporation to maximize returns during a period of inflation.

APPENDIX A

Glossary

ASR No. 190 Accounting Series Release No. 190, issued by the Securities and Exchange Commission, requires reports issued by certain companies to include measurement of cost of goods sold, depreciation, inventory and property, plant and equipment on the basis of replacement cost.

Backlog depreciation The Statement defines backlog depreciation at the end of an asset's useful life to be "the gap between the total depreciation expense during the life of an asset and its current cost at the end of its life." The backlog depreciation at any point in the life of an asset may be measured by the gap between depreciation to date (accumulated depreciation) based on the year-end replacement cost ("gross" current cost) and the cumulative amount of current cost depreciation charged to income.

Base-year dollars Dollars having purchasing power equal to that of dollars of the base period used by the particular index. For the CPI-U, 1967 is currently the base year, and 1967 dollars are base-year dollars. (See Appendix E. 1.)

Constant dollar A dollar having a constant general purchasing power.

Constant-dollar accounting Accounting and reporting using a constant-dollar unit of measurement.

Consumer Price Index The Consumer Price Index for All Urban Consumers published by the Bureau of Labor Statistics of the U.S. Department of Labor.

CPI-U The Consumer Price Index for All Urban Consumers

Current cost The cost of replacing the identical asset owned, that is, one of the same age and of the same operating capacity. Measurement of current cost based on a new asset requires adjustment for depreciation to date and for any differences between the operating capacities and operating costs of the new asset and the asset owned.

Current-cost accounting Accounting and reporting based on current costs or lower recoverable amounts measured at the balance sheet date, or date of use or sale, if earlier within the period.

Current-cost/constant-dollar accounting Current-cost accounting using a constant-dollar unit of measure.

Current replacement cost The lowest cost of replacing an asset owned with a new asset of equivalent operating capability (incorporating advanced technology, if available), and adjusted for depreciation to date based on the age or expired life of the asset owned.

Direct pricing Pricing by reference to current prices of comparable assets.

General inflation A rise in the general level of prices or a decline in the general purchasing power of the monetary unit.

Historical-cost/constant-dollar accounting Transaction-based accounting using historical prices measured in constant dollars.

Historical-cost/nominal-dollar accounting Transaction-based accounting using historical prices measured in actual dollars of the period of the transaction.

Holding gain or loss Increase or decrease in the current costs, or lower recoverable amounts, of inventory and property, plant and equipment held during the year. Holding gain or loss may be stated in average dollars or in constant dollars.

Income from continuing operations Income after deducting income taxes, exclusive of the results of discontinued operations, extraordinary items and the cumulative effects of accounting changes.

Inventory Raw materials and supplies, goods finished and in process of manufacture, and merchandise on hand, in transit, in storage, or consigned to others.

Monetary assets Assets whose amounts are fixed in terms of units of currency by contract or otherwise and that are not dependent on future prices. (See also definition appearing in APB Opinion No. 29, *Accounting for Nonmonetary Transactions*.)

Monetary liabilities Indebtedness or obligations whose amounts are fixed in terms of currency by contract or otherwise, and that are not dependent on future prices. (See also definition appearing in APB Opinion No. 29, *Accounting for Nonmonetary Transactions*.)

Net monetary items The net balance of monetary assets less monetary liabilities.

Net realizable value Dollar proceeds from the sale of an asset, net of related or out-of-pocket costs incurred to make the sale.

Nominal dollars Dollars expressed without adjustment for changes in the underlying value of the dollar. The basis of measurement in the primary historical-cost financial statements.

Primary financial statements The annual financial statements presented in reports to stockholders, including the balance sheet, income statement, statement of changes in financial position, and accompanying footnotes.

Public enterprise A business enterprise (a) whose debt or equity securities are traded on a United States stock exchange or the over-the-counter market, including securities quoted only locally or regionally, or (b) an enterprise that is required to file financial statements with the Securities and Exchange Commission. An enterprise is considered to be a public enterprise as soon as its financial statements are issued for the sale of any class of securities in a domestic market. This definition differs slightly from the one included in FASB Statement No. 21, *Suspension of the Reporting of Earnings Per Share and Segment Information by Nonpublic Enterprises*.

Purchasing power The quantity of a particular class of goods and services that may be purchased for a given sum of money at a given time or for a given period.

Purchasing power gain or loss on net monetary items held The gain or loss of purchasing power resulting from the holding of monetary items during a period of changing prices. In inflationary periods, the purchasing power of monetary assets held declines, giving rise to losses, whereas the decline in the purchasing power of the units of money needed to liquidate monetary liabilities results in purchasing power gains.

Recoverable amount An estimate of the net realizable value of an asset subject to near-term sale or the net present value of expected future cash flows derived from an asset that is to be used in business operations.

Roll back To restate in constant dollars of a prior period amounts stated in current-period constant dollars.

Roll forward To restate in current-period constant dollars amounts expressed in prior-period constant dollars.

Supplementary disclosures Information outside of the basic financial statements required to be presented by professional standards or voluntarily presented by the reporting entity. Required supplementary information should be distinct from the basic financial statements and separately identifiable from other information outside the financial statements.

Value in use The net present value of future cash flows, including the proceeds of the ultimate disposal, expected to be derived from the use of an asset in an enterprise.

APPENDIX B

U. S. Department of Labor, Consumer Price Index for All Urban Consumers (CPI-U) (1967=100)

Year	Jan.	Feb.	Mar.	Apr.	May	June	July	Aug.	Sep.	Oct.	Nov.	Dec.	Avg.
1919	49.5	48.4	49.0	49.9	50.6	50.7	52.1	53.0	53.3	54.2	55.5	56.7	51.8
1920	57.8	58.5	59.1	60.8	61.8	62.7	62.3	60.7	60.0	59.7	59.3	58.0	60.0
1921	57.0	55.2	54.8	54.1	53.1	52.8	52.9	53.1	52.5	52.4	52.1	51.8	53.6
1922	50.7	50.6	50.0	50.0	50.0	50.1	50.2	49.7	49.8	50.1	50.3	50.5	50.2
1923	50.3	50.2	50.4	50.6	50.7	51.0	51.5	51.3	51.6	51.7	51.8	51.8	51.1
1924	51.7	51.5	51.2	51.0	51.0	51.0	51.1	51.0	51.2	51.4	51.6	51.7	51.2
1925	51.8	51.6	51.7	51.6	51.8	52.4	53.1	53.1	52.9	53.1	54.0	53.7	52.5
1926	53.7	53.5	53.2	53.7	53.4	53.0	52.5	52.2	52.5	52.7	52.9	52.9	53.0
1927	52.5	52.1	51.8	51.8	52.2	52.7	51.7	51.4	51.7	52.0	51.9	51.8	52.0
1928	51.7	51.2	51.2	51.3	51.6	51.2	51.2	51.3	51.7	51.6	51.5	51.3	51.3
1929	51.2	51.1	50.9	50.7	51.0	51.2	51.7	51.9	51.8	51.8	51.7	51.4	51.3
1930	51.2	51.0	50.7	51.0	50.7	50.4	49.7	49.4	49.7	49.4	49.0	48.3	50.0
1931	47.6	46.9	46.6	46.3	45.8	45.3	45.2	45.1	44.9	44.6	44.1	43.7	45.6
1932	42.8	42.2	42.0	41.7	41.1	40.8	40.8	40.3	40.1	39.8	39.6	39.2	40.9
1933	38.6	38.0	37.7	37.6	37.7	38.1	39.2	39.6	39.6	39.6	39.6	39.4	38.8
1934	39.6	39.9	39.9	39.8	39.9	40.0	40.0	40.1	40.7	40.4	40.3	40.2	40.1
1935	40.8	41.1	41.0	41.4	41.2	41.1	40.9	40.9	41.1	41.1	41.3	41.4	41.1
1936	41.4	41.2	41.0	41.0	41.0	41.4	41.6	41.9	42.0	41.9	41.9	41.9	41.5
1937	42.2	42.3	42.6	42.8	43.0	43.1	43.3	43.4	43.8	43.6	43.3	43.2	43.0
1938	42.6	42.2	42.2	42.4	42.2	42.2	42.3	42.2	42.2	42.0	41.9	42.0	42.2
1939	41.8	41.6	41.5	41.4	41.4	41.4	41.4	41.4	42.2	42.0	42.0	41.8	41.6
1940	41.7	42.0	41.9	41.9	42.0	42.1	42.0	41.9	42.0	42.0	42.0	42.2	42.0
1941	42.2	42.2	42.4	42.8	43.1	43.9	44.1	44.5	45.3	45.8	46.2	46.3	44.1
1942	46.9	47.3	47.9	48.2	48.7	48.8	49.0	49.3	49.4	49.9	50.2	50.6	48.8
1943	50.6	50.7	51.5	52.1	52.5	52.4	52.0	51.8	52.0	52.2	52.1	52.2	51.8
1944	52.1	52.0	52.0	52.3	52.5	52.6	52.9	53.1	53.1	53.1	53.1	53.3	52.7
1945	53.3	53.2	53.2	53.3	53.7	54.2	54.3	54.3	54.1	54.1	54.3	54.5	53.9

Year													
1946	54.5	54.3	54.7	55.0	55.3	55.9	59.2	60.5	61.2	62.4	63.9	64.4	58.5
1947	64.4	64.3	65.7	65.7	65.5	66.0	66.6	67.3	68.9	68.9	69.3	70.2	66.9
1948	71.0	70.4	70.2	71.2	71.7	72.2	73.1	73.4	73.4	73.1	72.6	72.1	72.1
1949	72.0	71.2	71.4	71.5	71.4	71.5	71.0	71.2	71.5	71.1	71.2	70.8	71.4
1950	70.5	70.3	70.6	70.7	71.0	71.4	72.1	72.7	73.2	73.6	73.9	74.9	72.1
1951	76.1	77.0	77.3	77.4	77.7	77.6	77.7	77.7	78.2	78.6	79.0	79.3	77.8
1952	79.3	78.3	78.8	79.1	79.2	79.4	80.0	80.1	80.0	80.1	80.1	80.0	79.5
1953	79.8	79.4	79.6	79.7	79.9	80.2	80.4	80.6	80.7	80.9	80.6	80.5	80.1
1954	80.7	80.6	80.5	80.3	80.6	80.7	80.7	80.6	80.4	80.2	80.3	80.1	80.5
1955	80.1	80.1	80.1	80.1	80.1	80.1	80.4	80.2	80.5	80.5	80.6	80.4	80.2
1956	80.3	80.3	80.4	80.5	80.5	81.4	81.9	82.0	82.0	82.5	82.5	82.7	81.4
1957	82.8	83.1	83.3	83.6	83.8	84.3	84.7	84.7	84.8	84.9	85.2	85.7	84.3
1958	85.7	85.8	86.4	86.6	86.6	86.6	86.8	86.7	86.7	86.7	86.7	86.7	86.6
1959	86.8	86.7	86.7	86.8	86.9	87.3	87.5	87.4	87.7	88.0	88.0	88.0	87.3
1960	87.9	88.0	88.0	88.5	88.5	88.7	88.7	88.7	88.8	88.7	89.3	89.3	88.7
1961	89.3	89.3	89.3	89.3	89.3	89.4	89.8	89.7	89.9	89.9	89.9	89.9	89.6
1962	89.9	90.1	90.3	90.5	90.5	90.5	90.7	90.7	91.1	91.1	91.1	91.0	90.6
1963	91.1	91.2	91.3	91.3	91.3	91.7	92.1	92.1	92.2	92.3	92.3	92.5	91.7
1964	92.6	92.5	92.6	92.7	92.7	92.9	93.1	93.0	93.3	93.5	93.2	93.6	92.9
1965	93.6	93.6	93.7	94.0	94.2	94.7	94.8	94.6	94.9	95.1	94.8	95.4	94.5
1966	95.4	96.0	96.3	96.7	96.8	97.1	97.4	97.9	98.1	98.5	98.5	98.6	97.2
1967	98.6	98.7	98.9	99.1	99.4	99.7	100.2	100.5	100.7	101.0	101.3	101.6	100.0
1968	102.0	102.3	102.8	103.1	103.4	104.0	104.5	104.8	105.1	105.7	106.1	106.4	104.2
1969	106.7	107.1	108.0	108.7	109.0	109.7	110.2	110.7	111.2	111.6	112.2	112.9	109.8
1970	113.3	113.9	114.5	115.2	115.7	116.3	116.7	116.9	117.5	118.1	118.5	119.1	116.3
1971	119.2	119.4	119.8	120.2	120.8	121.5	121.8	122.1	122.2	122.4	122.6	123.1	121.3
1972	123.2	123.8	124.0	124.8	124.7	125.0	125.5	125.7	126.2	126.6	126.9	127.3	125.3
1973	127.7	128.6	129.8	130.7	131.5	132.4	132.7	135.1	135.5	136.6	137.6	138.5	133.1
1974	139.7	141.5	143.1	143.9	145.5	146.9	148.0	149.9	151.7	153.0	154.3	155.4	147.7
1975	156.1	157.2	157.8	158.6	159.3	160.6	162.3	162.8	163.6	164.6	165.6	166.3	161.2
1976	166.7	167.1	167.5	168.2	169.2	170.1	171.1	171.9	172.6	173.3	173.8	174.3	170.5
1977	175.3	177.1	178.2	179.6	180.6	181.8	182.6	183.3	184.0	184.5	185.4	186.1	181.5
1978	187.2	188.4	189.8	191.5	193.3	195.3	196.7	197.8	199.3	200.9	202.0	202.9	195.4
1979	204.7	207.1	209.1	211.5	214.1	216.6	218.9	221.1	223.4	225.4	227.5	229.9	217.4

APPENDIX C

Illustrative Classification of Monetary and Nonmonetary Items

The Statement provides guidance for the classification of certain assets and liabilities as monetary or nonmonetary. The classifications indicated should not be utilized without adequate review of the circumstances involved in each individual application. Illustrated below is the application of the monetary and nonmonetary definitions under typical circumstances.

Monetary Items:

Assets

    Cash on hand and demand bank deposits
    Time deposits
    Foreign Currency (on hand and claims to foreign currency)
    Preferred stock (nonconvertible and nonparticipating)
    Bonds (other than convertible)
    Accounts and notes receivable
    Allowance for doubtful accounts
    Variable rate mortgage loans
    Loans to employees
    Long-term receivables
    Refundable deposits
    Advances to unconsolidated subsidiaries
    Cash surrender value of life insurance
    Advances to suppliers (not on a fixed price contract)
    Deferred income tax charges
    Deferred life insurance policy acquisition costs

Liabilities

    Accounts and notes payable
    Accrued expenses payable
    Cash dividends payable
    Obligations payable in a foreign currency
    Advances from customers (not on a fixed price contract)
    Accrued losses on firm purchase commitments
    Refundable deposits
    Bonds payable and long-term debt
    Unamortized premium or discount and prepaid interest on bonds or notes payable
    Convertible bonds payable
    Deferred income tax credits

Life insurance policy reserves
Property and casualty insurance loss reserves
Deposit liabilities of financial institutions

Nonmonetary Items:

Assets

Common stocks (not accounted for on the equity method)
Inventory (other than inventories used on contracts)
Equity investments in unconsolidated subsidiaries or other investees
Property, plant and equipment
Accumulated depreciation of property, plant and equipment
Purchase commitments (portion paid on fixed price contracts)
Patents, trademarks, licenses and formulas
Goodwill
Deferred property and casualty insurance policy acquisition costs
Other intangible assets and deferred charges

Liabilities

Sales commitments (portion collected on fixed price contracts)
Obligations under warranties
Deferred investment tax credit
Unearned property and casualty insurance premiums

Items Requiring Individual Analysis:

Assets

Preferred stock (convertible or participating) and convertible bonds
If the market values the security primarily as a bond, it is monetary: if it values the security primarily as a stock, it is nonmonetary.

Inventories used on contracts
If the future cash receipts on the contracts will not vary because of future changes in prices, they are monetary. Goods used on contracts to be priced at market upon delivery are nonmonetary.

Prepaid insurance, advertising, rents and other prepayments
Claims to future services are nonmonetary. Prepayments that are deposits, advance payments or receivables are monetary because the prepayment does not obtain a given quantity of future services but rather is a fixed money offset.

Pension, sinking and other funds under enterprise control
The specific assets in the fund should be classified as monetary or nonmonetary.

Liabilities

Accrued vacation pay
    If it is paid at the wage rates as of the vacation dates and if those rates may
    vary, it is nonmonetary. If they do not vary, then it is monetary.

Deferred revenue
    Nonmonetary if an obligation to furnish goods or services is involved.

Accrued pension obligations
    Fixed amounts payable to a fund are monetary; all other amounts are non-
    monetary.

QUESTIONS AND PROBLEMS

1. What is the difference between changes in the general price level and changes
   in specific prices?
2. CWS Company commenced business on 1/1/1975. The following data was
   extracted from CWS's books of accounts and other reliable sources:

    Extract from Income Statement

Sales	$1,500,000
Less: Cost of goods sold (exclusive of depreciation)	900,000
Gross Margin	$ 600,000

    Extract from Balance Sheet

	12/31/80	12/31/81
Inventory (LIFO since 1/1/1975)	$60,000	$90,000

    Current Cost Data

Inventory:	
Current cost at 12/31/80	$ 120,000
Current cost at 12/31/81	165,000
Units in inventory at 12/31/80	12,000
Units in inventory at 12/31/81	15,000

Cost of goods sold:	
Units sold	85,000
Weighted average cost per unit	$10.50

    Other Data
    Sales are not seasonal and purchases of $930,000 were made in 1981. The in-
    crease in inventory was from purchases made in the first quarter of 1981.

    Consumer Price Index for All Urban Consumers (CPI-U):

Average Index:		Monthly Index:		Quarterly Index:	
1975	161	December 1980	246	1st Quarter '75	157
1979	217	December 1981	265	1st Quarter '81	252
1980	238			4th Quarter 1980	244
1981	258			4th Quarter 1981	262

Based on the above information, restate the inventory and cost of goods sold in constant dollar and current cost in accordance with FASB Statement No. 33. What is the gross margin adjusted for general inflation and for changes in specific prices?

3. You have extracted the following information from KKF Corp:

Extract from Income Statement
Depreciation $55,000

Extract from Balance Sheet

	12/31/80	12/31/79
Property, plant, and equipment	$550,000	$450,000
Less: Accumulated depreciation	170,000	130,000
Net property, plant, and equipment	$380,000	$320,000

Details of fixed assets at 12/31/1980 are as follows:

Date Acquired	Percent Depreciated	Historical Cost	Acc. Depn.
1975	60	$100,000	$ 60,000
1977	40	150,000	60,000
1979	20	200,000	40,000
1980	10	100,000	10,000
		$550,000	$170,000

Depreciation is calculated at 10% per annum and all fixed assets were acquired on January 1. There were no assumed salvage values.

Current cost of property, plant, and equipment

An independent appraiser has measured the current cost as follows:

	12/31/80		12/31/79	
Date Acquired	Current Cost	Acc. Depr.	Current Cost	Acc. Depr.
1975	$180,000	$108,000	$165,000	$ 82,500
1977	210,000	84,000	190,000	57,000
1979	220,000	44,000	200,000	20,000
1980	100,000	10,000	–	–
	$720,000	$246,000	$555,000	$159,000
Acc. Depr.	246,000		159,000	
Net Current Cost	$474,000		$395,000	

The net recoverable amount has been determined by management to be in excess of net current cost.

CPI-U

Average Index:
1980   238

Monthly Index:
    January 1975 156
    January 1977 175
    January 1979 205
    January 1980 233

Based on the above information, restate property, plant, and equipment and depreciation in constant dollar and current cost in accordance with FASB Statement No. 33.

4.   The balance sheets of MDW Company are as follows:

	12/31/80	12/31/79
Current Assets		
Cash	$ 2,500	$ 5,000
Accounts receivable	90,000	75,000
Inventories, at FIFO cost	157,500	140,000
Total current assets	250,000	220,000
Property, plant and equipment at cost	250,000	220,500
Less: accumulated depreciation	140,000	115,000
Net property, plant and equipment	110,000	97,500
Total assets	$360,000	$317,500
Current Liabilities		
Bank indebtedness	$ 87,500	$ 55,000
Accounts payable	25,000	21,250
Accrued expenses	5,000	3,750
Income tax payable	15,000	15,000
Current portion of long-term debt	12,500	12,500
Total current liabilities	145,000	107,500
Long-term debt	100,000	110,000
Total liabilities	245,000	217,500
Shareholders' equity	115,000	100,000
Total liabilities and shareholders' equity	$360,000	$317,500

Other data:

Consumer Price Index for All Urban Consumers

    Average   1980   238
    December 1979   230
    December 1980   246

Based on the above information, calculate purchasing power gain or loss on monetary items in accordance with FASB Statement No. 33.

5. Selected data for GMT Company is presented below:

Year	Average CPI-U	Net Sales $'000	Cash Dividends Per Common Share	Market Price Per Share of Common Stock At Year End
1980	238	1,020	$5.00	$70
1979	217	835	4.00	55
1978	195	621	3.00	43
1977	182	415	2.00	31
1976	171	236	1.00	19

Based on the above information, prepare a five-year summary in average-for-the-current-year constant dollars and base year (1967 CPI-U = 100) constant dollars.

6. The Full Blown Company, a wholesaler of sound equipment, commenced business in 1977. Selected data for the company are presented in Exhibit 1.

   Based on the data in Exhibit 1, and the requirements of FASB Statement No. 33, please prepare supplementary financial data as illustrated in Chapter 17, Exhibit 2, *Statement Format*.

   Based on the statements adjusted for changing prices, please explain the difference between these statements and the primary financial statements presented by the company.

Exhibit 1
Full Blown Company
Selected 1980 Information

	12/31/79		12/31/80	
1. Balance Sheets				
Current Assets				
Cash		$ 8,000		$ 12,000
Accounts Receivable		12,000		16,000
Inventory (LIFO)		16,000		16,000
Total Current Assets		36,000		44,000
Non-Current Assets				
Land		17,000		17,000
Plant and Equipment	20,000		22,000	
Accumulated Depreciation	12,000	8,000	16,400	5,600
Marketable Equity Securities (at cost)		3,000		3,000
Total Assets		$64,000		$ 69,600
Current Liabilities				
Notes Payable		8,000		10,800
Accounts Payable		10,000		12,000
Total Current Liabilities		18,000		22,800

Long-Term Debt	5,000	4,000
Stockholders' Equity		
Capital Stock (2,000 shares)	20,000	20,000
Retained Earnings	21,000	22,800
Total Liabilities & Equity	$64,000	$ 69,600

2. Combined Statement of Income and Retained Earnings for the year ended December 31, 1980.

Sales		$120,000
Cost of Goods Sold	94,000	
Operating Expenses (exclusive of depreciation)	16,000	
Depreciation	4,400	114,400
Income Before Taxes		5,600
Federal Income Tax		2,800
Net Income ($1.45 per share)		2,800
Retained Earnings 12/31/79		21,000
		23,800
Dividends Paid (.40 per share)		800
Retained Earnings 12/31/80		$23,000

3. Additional Data

   a. Current Cost Data

Inventory:	
Current Cost at 12/31/79	$ 19,000
Units in inventory at 12/31/80 & 12/31/79	10,000
Current Cost per unit at 12/31/80	$ 2.80
Company first purchased inventory of 10,000 units in January 1977.	
Land and Equipment	
Land (acquired in January 1977)	
Current Cost at 12/31/79	$ 22,000
Current Cost at 12/31/80	$ 26,000
Equipment (acquired in January 1977 and January 1980)	
Current cost at 12/31/79 (Net)	$ 9,520
Cost of goods sold:	
Units Sold	40,000
Weighted average cost per unit	$ 2.35
Specific price index for equipment:	
December 1980 index	1092
January 1980 index	1005
January 1977 index	840
December 1979 index	1000

b. Other data
  - Sales are not seasonal
  - Purchases are uniform over the year
  - Operating expenses are uniform over the year
  - Dividends are paid quarterly
  - Federal Income tax rate is 50%
  - Depreciation is 20% straight line

  CPI-U (average)

1967	100 (Base Year)
1975	161
1976	171
1977	182
1978	195
1979	217
1980	238

  Monthly Index:

December 1979	229	January 1977	175
December 1980	246	January 1980	231

  Quarterly Index:

4th quarter 1979	227
4th quarter 1980	242

Appendix

GLOSSARY

Accelerated Depreciation. A generally accepted depreciation method that results in progressively smaller amounts of depreciation expense each accounting period until the total depreciable cost of a long-lived asset has been expensed. Examples are: sum-of-the-years' digits method and the double-declining-balance method.

Account. A device used for recording increases and decreases in specific asset, liability, and components of owners' equity. In its simplest form, an account resembles the letter "T". Every account consists of an account title, an account number, and a left and right side.

Account Payable. A liability representing an amount due to a creditor, usually in payment for purchases of merchandise, materials, or supplies.

Account Receivable. An asset representing an amount owed to a business by a creditor, usually arising from the sale of merchandise or services.

Accounting. The process of identifying, measuring, and communicating economic information to permit informed judgments and decisions by users of the information. Accounting is a service activity that provides financial information about an entity that is useful in making rational investment, credit, and similar decisions.

421

Accounting Concepts. Broad fundamental concepts that have helped provide a basis for the establishment of generally accepted accounting principles.

Accounting Cycle. Another name for the *accounting process*.

Accounting Equation. Assets equal liabilities plus owners' equity. (A = L + OE)

Accounting Period. A period of time at the end of which the basic financial statements are prepared. Commonly used accounting periods are a month, three months, six months, nine months, and a year.

Accounting Policies. The specific accounting principles and practices adopted by a business.

Accounting Principles. Those concepts, methods, and procedures that have become generally accepted as the basis for recording business transactions and for the preparation of an enterprise's financial statements.

Accrual Basis of Accounting. A method of income determination whereby revenues are recorded at the time they are earned and expenses are recorded at the time they are incurred.

Accumulated Depreciation. A contra-asset account that is subtracted from a long-lived asset for purposes of balance sheet presentation. The balance in the accumulated depreciation account represents the sum of the depreciation expense recorded relative to the long-lived asset to date. The original cost of a long-lived asset minus the accumulated depreciation on that asset results in an amount referred to as the book value of the long-lived asset.

Adjunct Account. An account whose balance is added to the balance of another account for purposes of balance sheet presentation. The account *premium on bonds payable* is an example of an adjunct account.

Allowance for Uncollectible Accounts. A contra-account to accounts receivable that represents the estimated amount of accounts receivable that an enterprise expects not to be able to collect.

Annual Report. The report prepared for a company's stockholders and other interested parties that a company prepares annually following the end of the fiscal year. It frequently includes a letter to the shareholders from the Chairman of the Board, management's discussion of previous financial performance, and a variety of financial highlights in addition to the basic financial statements. The annual report also includes the auditor's report wherein the independent accountants express an opinion as to the fairness of the financial data presented in the financial statements.

Appropriated Retained Earnings. Retained earnings that have been earmarked for a specific purpose and consequently cannot be used as the basis for paying a dividend.

Asset. Something of value owned by a business entity. An asset may be tangible or intangible.

Audit. A comprehensive review and evaluation of an enterprise's accounting records for the purpose of expressing an opinion on the financial statements prepared from those records. Audits are performed by independent certified public accountants.

Auditor's Report. A statement made by an independent certified public accounting firm, wherein the firm expresses its opinion, using somewhat standardized terminology, that: (1) the accounting firm has examined and tested the records upon which a company's financial statements were prepared, and (2) in the accounting firm's opinion, the financial statements fairly present the financial position, changes in the financial position, and results of operations for the company in conformity with generally accepted accounting principles applied on a basis consistent with that of the previous year.

Bad Debt. An account receivable considered to be uncollectible.

Bad Debt Expense. An estimate (if the allowance method is used) of the dollar amount of credit sales made during the accounting period that will eventually prove to be uncollectible. The actual bad debts that are written-off if the direct write-off method is used.

Balance. The difference between the total left hand entries and the total right hand entries made in an account.

Balance Sheet. A financial statement showing that an enterprise's total assets are equal to its total liabilities plus owners' equity. The account form of the balance sheet shows assets on the left hand side and liabilities and owners' equity on the right side. The report form of the balance sheet shows assets listed first then liabilities and owners' equity listed below the assets. The balance sheet is also called the *statement of financial position*.

Bond. A debt certificate. The principal amount to be repaid upon maturity is referred to as the par value or the face value of the bond. The bond coupon rate is the annual rate of interest payable in accordance with the terms of the bond issue. Bonds frequently are issued in $1,000 units and pay interest semi-annually.

Bond Discount. The amount by which the net proceeds of a bond issue are less than the amount of the principal that must be repaid at maturity. The amount of the bond discount must be amortized over the life of the bond issue, the effect of which is to make the bond's effective rate of interest greater than its coupon rate of interest.

Bond Indenture. The written contract between the issuer of bonds and the bond holders, wherein the details associated with the bond issue are specified.

Bond Premium. The amount by which the net proceeds of a bond issue exceed the amount of the bond principal that must be repaid upon maturity. The amount of the bond premium must be amortized over the life of the bond issue, the effect of which is to make the bond's effective rate of interest less than its coupon rate of interest.

Book Value. The amount shown in an organization's books for any asset, liability, or owners' equity account. The book value of a depreciable asset is its original cost less its accumulated depreciation. The book value of an organization is the excess of its total assets over total liabilities. The book value per share of common stock is a company's stockholders' equity divided by the number of shares of common stock outstanding.

Business Combination. When a corporation and one or more incorporated or unincorporated businesses are brought together into one accounting entity, but not necessarily into one legal entity.

Capital. Another name for owners' equity. Also used to mean the total assets of an organization.

Capital Budgeting. The process of selecting from among a variety of investment proposals for the acquisition of long-lived assets. This process frequently considers the present value of projected cash flows for proposed investments. It may also include consideration of the alternative means of financing future capital investments.

Capital Stock. Equity securities of a corporation representing ownership. Capital stock consists of both common stock and preferred stock.

Capital Surplus. Another name for capital in excess of par (or stated) value of common stock. Use of this term has been discouraged in recent years.

Capital in Excess of Par Value. Represents the amount paid into a corporation in exchange for its capital stock in excess of the par value of the capital stock issued.

Cash Basis of Accounting. A method of accounting whereby revenues are recorded at the time the cash is received and expenses are recorded at the time cash disbursements are made. Unlike the accrual basis of accounting, no attempt is made to match revenues with the expenses incurred in generating those revenues.

Cash Discount. A reduction in an item's sale price granted whenever payment is made within a specified period of time.

Cash Flow Statement. A statement of changes in financial position that explains what caused the change in a company's cash balance during a specified period of time. Also, a statement of cash receipts and cash disbursements.

Certified Public Accountant (CPA). An accountant who has passed the Uniform CPA examination prepared by the American Institute of CPAs and who has met the prescribed educational, experience, and other requirements of the state issuing the CPA certificate.

Chart of Accounts. An organized listing of the names and corresponding numbers of the accounts in an organization's ledger.

Collateral. Specific assets pledged by a borrower to a lender as part of a loan agreement. These assets may be claimed by the lender if the borrower is not able to repay the loan.

Common Stock. Capital stock that does not carry any preference with regard to dividends or to distribution of assets in the case of liquidation. Common stock usually carries the right to vote at the annual stockholders' meeting, and common stockholders are the "true" owners of a corporation.

Compensating Balances. The percent of a line of credit or of a loan that a bank requires a borrower to keep on deposit at the bank. The amount of the compensating balance is negotiated between the bank and the borrower, and the effect of the compensating balance is to increase the effective interest rate of any amount borrowed.

Compound Interest. A method of calculating interest whereby interest is figured both on the principal of a loan plus any interest previously earned but not distributed.

Conservatism. An accounting concept that states: provide for all possible losses but do not record any gains or profits until they are actually realized.

Consolidated Financial Statements. Financial statements prepared for a business entity composed of a number of separate legal corporations operated as one business organization. They are prepared based on the financial statements of the individual companies, but all inter-company assets, liabilities, equities, revenues, and expenses must be eliminated.

Contra-Account. An account whose balance is subtracted from the balance of another account. Accumulated depreciation and discount on bonds payable are two examples of contra-accounts.

Contributed Capital. The sum of the capital stock accounts and the capital in excess of par (or stated) value accounts. Also called paid-in capital.

Convertible Bond. A bond whose terms of issuance gives the bond holder the right to convert the bond to a specified number of shares of capital stock during a specified future period of time.

Convertible Preferred Stock. Preferred stock whose terms of issuance give the preferred stockholders the right to convert their stock into a specified number of shares of common stock during a specified future period of time.

Corporation. A legal entity whose charter is granted according to state law.

Cost of Goods Manufactured. The total cost associated with a manufactured product. Included in this cost are materials, labor, and manufacturing overhead.

Cost of Goods Sold. The cost associated with the goods that were sold by an enterprise during a specified period of time.

Current Assets. Cash and other assets that normally will be converted into cash or used within a year or within an operating cycle of a particular business, whichever is longer. Current assets include cash, marketable securities, accounts receivable, inventory, and current prepayments.

Current Cost Accounting. A method of accounting based on current costs rather than on historical costs. Certain current cost data are required to be disclosed as supplementary information by FASB Statement No. 33.

Current Liabilities. A liability whose repayment will require the use of a current asset. As a practical matter, current liabilities may be thought of as those that are due within one year of the balance sheet date. Current liabilities include accounts payable, short-term notes payable, and other types of short-term liabilities.

Debenture. An unsecured bond.

Deferred Charge. An asset that represents an expenditure whose related expense will not be recognized in the financial statements until a future period. At such time, the deferred charge will be written off the books and an expense will be recognized. Prepaid rent is an example of a deferred charge.

Deferred Credit. A seldom used term that represents an unusual type of liability. Customer deposits are frequently thought of as deferred credits.

Deferred Income Tax Liability. A liability that represents the accumulated difference between the income tax expense reported on a company's books and the lesser income tax actually incurred by the company. This difference arises because of significant differences in the way a company reports various revenue and expense items on its books and the way it reports these same items on its tax return. For example, a company may report depreciation on a straight-line basis for external reporting purposes but on an accelerated basis for income tax purposes.

Depletion. A non-cash expense similar to depreciation but incurred by using-up a natural resource.

Depreciation. A non-cash expense representing a portion of a company's investment (cost) in long-lived assets allocated to a particular accounting period. In calculating depreciation, it is necessary to estimate the useful lives of the long-lived assets and to estimate salvage values at the end of their useful lives. Depreciation may be thought of as the process of allocating the cost of a long-lived asset, less any estimated salvage value, over its estimated useful life in a systematic and rational manner. Depreciation is a process of allocation, not a process of valuation.

Dividend. A distribution of earnings to the stockholders of a corporation, usually in the form of cash.

Donated Capital. The increase in owners' equity resulting from a donation of an asset to a company. Generally recorded at fair market value.

Double-Declining-Balance Depreciation. A method of calculating depreciation whereby a percentage equal to twice the straight-line percentage is multiplied by the declining book value to determine the depreciation expense for the period. Salvage value is ignored when calculating double-declining-balance depreciation.

Double-Entry Accounting. A system of accounting that requires the financial consequences of every transaction be recorded by equal amounts placed on the left side of some accounts and on the right side of other accounts.

Thus, every transaction results in the recording of equal left-hand and right-hand amounts.

Double Taxation. When after-tax income is distributed to shareholders in the form of dividends and such dividends are again taxed as income to the stockholders.

Doubtful Account. An account receivable thought to be uncollectible.

Earned Surplus. Another name for retained earnings. Use of this term has been discouraged in recent years.

Earnings. Income or profit.

Effective Interest Rate. The true interest rate incurred by a borrower. The effective interest rate of a bond is frequently referred to as the *yield to maturity* at the time of the bond issue.

Equities. Liabilities plus owners' equity.

Expense. The decrease in owners' equity (net assets) incurred during an accounting period for the purpose of earning revenue.

External Reporting. Financial reporting to stockholders and others outside of an enterprise.

Extraordinary Items. Items affecting net income that are both unusual in nature and infrequent in their occurrence compared with the typical or normal activities of a business entity. When extraordinary items occur, the income statement should show (a) income before extraordinary items, (b) extraordinary items, and (c) net income.

Face Amount of a Bond. The par value, stated value, or maturity value of a bond.

Factory Overhead. Another name for manufacturing overhead.

Federal Income Tax. The income tax levied by the federal government on corporations and individuals.

Financial Accounting. Provides external users with quantitative information regarding an enterprise's economic resources, obligations, and financial performance.

Financial Statement. The four basic financial statements are: the balance sheet, the income statement, the statement of retained earnings, and the statement of changes in financial position.

Finished Goods Inventory. Completed inventory that is ready to be sold.

First-In, First-Out (FIFO). The inventory costing method by which the cost of ending inventory is determined from the cost of the most recent purchases and cost of goods sold is determined from the cost associated with the oldest purchases, including beginning inventory.

Fiscal Year. The twelve-month (or 52-53 week) period selected by a business as its accounting period for financial reporting purposes. It may or may not be a calendar year.

Fixed Assets. Long-lived assets acquired to be used in the business rather than to be sold. Fixed assets may be both tangible and intangible.

FOB. Free-on-Board, some location. Examples are FOB Shipping Point and FOB Destination. The location denotes the point at which title passes from the seller to the buyer.

Footnotes. Informative disclosures appended to and considered to be a part of a company's published financial statements. Footnotes frequently cover such matters as basis of consolidation, depreciation and inventory methods, long-term obligations, taxes, dividend restrictions, and contingent liabilities.

Freight-In. Freight costs associated with purchasing inventory.

Freight-Out. Freight costs associated with the sale of inventory.

Funds Statement. Another name for the statement of changes in financial position.

Generally Accepted Accounting Principles (GAAP). Those accounting principles that provide the basis upon which external financial statements are prepared and upon which the independent accountants base their opinions regarding a company's financial statements. Since 1973, the Financial Accounting Standards Board has had the responsibility for establishing generally accepted accounting principles.

General Price-Level Changes. Changes in the aggregate prices of a wide variety of goods and services. These price changes are measured using a general price-level index such as the Consumer Price Index for all urban consumers (CPI-U).

Goodwill. An imprecise term referring to the excess of the purchase price over the recorded net assets acquired when one company purchases another company. Goodwill is shown as an asset only after it has been purchased from another company. No accounting recognition is given to internally generated goodwill.

Gross Profit. Net sales less cost of goods sold.

Historical Cost. Original cost; acquisition cost.

Income. The excess of revenues over expenses. Earnings or profit.

Income Statement. The basic financial statement that shows the change in owners' equity during an accounting period arising from the sale to customers of goods and services, less cost of goods sold and other expenses. The financial statement showing revenues, expenses, and net income.

Income Tax. An annual tax levied on the income of individuals and organizations by the federal and other governments.

Inflation. A rise in the general level of prices. A general decline in the purchasing power of a currency.

Intangible Assets. A non-current, non-physical asset. Examples are patents, copyrights, trademarks, and goodwill. All intangible assets must be amortized over a period not to exceed 40 years.

Inter-Period Tax Allocation. Income tax allocation between accounting periods brought about because of timing differences between when revenues and expenses are reported on the financial statements and when they are reported on the income tax return.

Investment Tax Credit (ITC). A direct reduction in a company's income tax liability granted by the federal government as an incentive to purchase equipment. The amount of the investment tax credit is calculated by multiplying a specified percentage (e.g., 10%) by the purchase price of the equipment.

Journal. The book of original entry where transactions are first recorded.

Last-In, First-Out (LIFO). The inventory costing method by which the cost of the ending inventory is determined from the cost of the oldest purchases, including beginning inventory, and cost of goods sold is determined from the cost of the most recent purchases.

Ledger. The book containing a company's accounts.

Liability. A debt or obligation.

Line of Credit. An agreement with a bank whereby an organization has obtained previous authorization for short-term borrowings up to a specified amount.

Long-Lived Assets. Fixed assets purchased for use rather than for resale.

Lower of Cost or Market (LCM). A generally accepted accounting principle regarding inventory valuation that requires the inventory amount shown on the balance sheet to be the lower of (1) acquisition cost (however determined) or (2) current replacement cost (market).

Management Accounting. Provides internal users with quantitative information regarding an enterprise's resources, obligations, and financial performance.

Manufacturing Overhead. All manufacturing costs other than direct materials and direct labor.

Marketable Securities. Stocks and bonds that are readily marketable.

Minority Interest. The amount that represents the equity of minority shareholders in a subsidiary company that is shown on consolidated balance sheets either as a liability or as part of stockholders' equity.

Monetary Items. Assets and liabilities whose amounts are fixed in terms of number of dollars regardless of what happens to the general price level. Examples are cash, accounts receivable, accounts payable, and bonds payable.

Net Assets. Total assets minus total liabilities. Owner's Equity.

Net Current Assets. Current assets minus current liabilities. Working capital.

Net Income. The excess of revenues over expenses.

Net Loss. The excess of expenses over revenues.

Net Sales. Gross sales minus sales returns, allowances, and discounts.

Net Worth. Another name for owners' equity. In recent years, the use of this term has been discouraged.

Non-Current. Not due for a period greater than one year or an operating cycle, whichever is longer.

Operating Cycle. Normal time that it takes a company to recover its investment in inventory. That is, the average length of time between the investment in inventory and the subsequent collection of cash from the sale of that inventory.

Operating Expenses. Expenses incurred that pertain to the ordinary activities of the organization.

Owners' Equity. The excess of assets over liabilities. For a corporation, owners' equity is referred to as stockholders' equity.

Paid-in Capital. Represents the total amount paid by the shareholders for capital stock. Also called contributed capital.

Par Value. Face Value. Has no direct relationship to market value.

Past Service Cost. The present value of future amounts owed to employees at the time a pension plan is adopted for services performed prior to the plan's adoption.

Pension Plan. A plan whereby a company agrees to pay retirement benefits to its employees.

Periodic Inventory. A method of recording inventory that requires that a physical inventory be taken before financial statements can be prepared. A continuous record of inventory and cost of goods sold is not maintained.

Perpetual Inventory. A method of recording inventory whereby a continuous record of inventory and cost of goods sold is maintained. Physical inventories must still be taken, however, as a check on the accuracy of the perpetual inventory records.

Pooling of Interests Method. A method for accounting for business combinations whereby the assets and liabilities of the acquired companies are reported by the acquiring company at their previous book values. Fair market values are not used, and no goodwill is recorded.

Pre-emptive Right. The right of stockholders to maintain their proportionate ownership in a corporation by purchasing a proportionate share of any new stock that is issued.

Preferred Stock. Capital stock that is preferred as dividends at a stated amount per share or as to the distribution of assets in the case of liquidation.

Prepaid Expense. An expenditure made prior to the incurring of an expense. Prepaid expenses are shown as assets on the balance sheet.

Prior Period Adjustments. Items shown in the statement of retained earnings that represent material adjustments specifically identified with prior accounting periods.

Profit. Income.

Pro-Forma Financial Statements. Hypothetical, as if, or projected financial statements.

Purchase Method. A method of accounting for business combinations whereby the assets and liabilities of the acquired companies are reported by the acquiring company at their fair market value at the time the business combination occurred. Any excess of the total acquisition cost over the fair market value of the net assets acquired is reported as goodwill.

Raw Materials. Goods purchased for use in the manufacturing process.

Reserve. An overused accounting term with a variety of meanings whose use has been discouraged in recent years. Instead of "Reserve for Doubtful Accounts," a better phrase is "Allowance for Uncollectible Accounts"; instead of "Reserve for Depreciation," a better phrase is "Accumulated Depreciation."

Retained Earnings. Total net income over the life of a corporation minus all distributions of income in the form of dividends.

Revenue. The increase in owners' equity during an accounting period representing the sale of products or services. Revenue is measured by the inflow of net assets to an organization.

Salvage Value. The estimated future selling price of a fixed asset at the end of its useful life.

Short-Term. Due within one year or an operating cycle, whichever is longer.

Stock Dividend. A dividend payable in a company's own capital stock rather than in cash. Payment of a stock dividend has no affect on a company's assets or liabilities.

Stock Split. An increase in the number of common shares outstanding resulting from a corresponding decrease in the par or stated value per share of common stock.

Stockholders' Equity. The owners' equity of a corporation. Stockholders' equity is comprised of paid-in capital and retained earnings.

Straight-Line Depreciation. A depreciation method that results in equal periodic amounts of depreciation expense.

Subchapter S Corporation. A corporation with no more than 15 stockholders that elects to be taxed as if it were a partnership.

Sum-of-the-Years' Digits Depreciation. An accelerated depreciation method.

T-Account. An account shaped like the letter "T". Each T account has a title, a number, and a left side and right side.

Timing Differences. Differences in the timing of the reporting of certain revenues and expenses for tax purposes and for book purposes.

Treasury Stock. Shares of its own capital stock issued by a corporation and subsequently reacquired, usually by purchase. The cost of treasury stock is usually treated as a reduction in total stockholders' equity.

Trial Balance. A listing of a company's accounts and their balances prepared prior to the preparation of the company's financial statements in order to prove that the books are in balance; i.e., that the total of the left side account balances equals the total of the right side account balances.

Uncollectible Account. An account receivable that a company expects not to be able to collect.

Vested Benefits. Pension benefits to which employees are entitled upon retirement regardless of whether they continued to be employed by the company until they reached retirement age.

Weighted-Average Inventory Method. An inventory costing method by which both ending inventory and cost of goods sold are reported at the weighted average cost of inventory.

Working Capital. Current assets minus current liabilities. Also called net current assets and net working capital.

Work in Process. Partially completed inventory of a manufacturer.

Index